"Dianne Elise, in this beautifully written book concept of the erotic in a way that I believe bution to psychoanalytic theory and practice. maternal eroticism is an essential component of the life of the mother and infant, and similarly, the analyst's eroticism is an essential component of the life of the analytic field. In the absence of eroticism, the mother–infant bond and the analyst–patient relationship are flat and lifeless; creativity is stifled or killed. The ideas Elise introduces are now requisite for anyone engaged in the life-long project of learning to become a psychotherapist."

Thomas Ogden, author of *Reclaiming Unlived Life* and *Creative Readings: Essays on Seminal Analytic Works*

"Dianne Elise notices that analytic theory has portrayed a disembodied engagement of minds—Freud's 'victory of intellectuality over sensuality,' paternity over maternity. A generative analytic field, she claims, must include body and analytic eroticism, especially, fantasy transformations of a maternal Eros—the mother's bodily sensuality, for women, a mother-daughter erotic—experienced from infancy. Elise shares palpably alive descriptions of the analytic field she and her patients create, a consulting room where both experience and confront Eros in fantasies, bodily imagery, dreams and verbal exchanges. Readers will gain a transformed sense of the analytic field."

Nancy J. Chodorow, author of *The Reproduction of Mothering* and *Individualizing Gender and Sexuality*

"Dianne Elise's book is a rewarding and fascinating read. Not only does the author deal with one of the most intriguing and conflicted psychoanalytic issues—Eros and libidinal life—she inserts it within the frame of the analytic field, itself a challenging theoretical perspective and new paradigm in psychoanalysis. This conjunction gives Elise the opportunity to develop a discourse that is both original and respectful of our classical tradition while giving back center stage to the somewhat neglected topic of sexuality as an enlivening factor in analysis. Her style of writing shows abundantly this same quality of being vital and 'real.' This book is a great achievement."

Giuseppe Civitarese, author of *Sublime Subjects: Aesthetic Conflict and Intersubjectivity in Psychoanalysis*

Creativity and the Erotic Dimensions of the Analytic Field

Creativity and the Erotic Dimensions of the Analytic Field centers on the mutually reinforcing relationship between erotic and creative energies. Erotic embodiment is given context within a contemporary model of clinical process based in analytic field theory and highlighting Winnicott. Dianne Elise uses clinical material to bring theory alive, giving clinicians an explicit picture of how they might utilize the ideas presented.

In a fascinating return to Freud's emphasis on libido and Eros, a creative mind is seen as located within a libidinal connection to the erotic body. The erotic is underscored as an important ingredient of the clinical situation—a lively spontaneity that partakes of the analyst's as well as the patient's creative self, vitalizing the field of clinical engagement. A full formulation of the analytic field must include awareness of the centrality of the erotic in the maternal matrix, in ongoing development, and in the clinical setting. The erotic-aesthetic dimension of the mind potentiates the creative interplay of the analytic process.

Written in an engaging and accessible style, this original contribution makes complex theory available to psychoanalytic clinicians at all levels, and to a wide range of readers, while offering sophisticated theoretical and clinical innovations. Elise addresses the need to engage multiple aspects of erotic life while maintaining a reliable professional boundary.

Dianne Elise is a Personal and Supervising Analyst of the Psychoanalytic Institute of Northern California, USA. Nationally recognized for her innovative contributions to the psychoanalytic literature on gender and sexuality, she has consistently challenged conventional accounts of development.

The Relational Perspectives Book Series (RPBS) publishes books that grow out of or contribute to the relational tradition in contemporary psychoanalysis. The term *relational psychoanalysis* was first used by Greenberg and Mitchell[1] to bridge the traditions of interpersonal relations, as developed within interpersonal psychoanalysis and object relations, as developed within contemporary British theory. But, under the seminal work of the late Stephen A. Mitchell, the term *relational psychoanalysis* grew and began to accrue to itself many other influences and developments. Various tributaries—interpersonal psychoanalysis, object relations theory, self psychology, empirical infancy research, and elements of contemporary Freudian and Kleinian thought—flow into this tradition, which understands relational configurations between self and others, both real and fantasied, as the primary subject of psychoanalytic investigation.

We refer to the relational tradition, rather than to a relational school, to highlight that we are identifying a trend, a tendency within contemporary psychoanalysis, not a more formally organized or coherent school or system of beliefs. Our use of the term *relational* signifies a dimension of theory and practice that has become salient across the wide spectrum of contemporary psychoanalysis. Now under the editorial supervision of Lewis Aron, Adrienne Harris, Steven Kuchuck and Eyal Rozmarin, the Relational Perspectives Book Series originated in 1990 under the editorial eye of the late Stephen A. Mitchell. Mitchell was the most prolific and influential of the originators of the relational tradition. Committed to dialogue among psychoanalysts, he abhorred the authoritarianism that dictated adherence to a rigid set of beliefs or technical restrictions. He championed open discussion, comparative and integrative approaches, and promoted new voices across the generations.

Included in the Relational Perspectives Book Series are authors and works that come from within the relational tradition, extend and develop that tradition, as well as works that critique relational approaches or compare and contrast it with alternative points of view. The series includes our most distinguished senior psychoanalysts, along with younger contributors who bring fresh vision. A full list of titles in this series is available at https://www.routledge.com/mentalhealth/series/LEARPBS.

---

1 Greenberg, J. & Mitchell, S. (1983). *Object relations in psychoanalytic theory.* Cambridge, MA: Harvard University Press.

Creativity and the Erotic Dimensions of the Analytic Field

Dianne Elise

LONDON AND NEW YORK

First published 2019
by Routledge
2 Park Square, Milton Park, Abingdon, Oxon OX14 4RN

and by Routledge
52 Vanderbilt Avenue, New York, NY 10017

Routledge is an imprint of the Taylor & Francis Group, an informa business

© 2019 Dianne Elise

The right of Dianne Elise to be identified as author of this work has been asserted by her in accordance with sections 77 and 78 of the Copyright, Designs and Patents Act 1988.

All rights reserved. No part of this book may be reprinted or reproduced or utilised in any form or by any electronic, mechanical, or other means, now known or hereafter invented, including photocopying and recording, or in any information storage or retrieval system, without permission in writing from the publishers.

Trademark notice: Product or corporate names may be trademarks or registered trademarks, and are used only for identification and explanation without intent to infringe.

British Library Cataloguing-in-Publication Data
A catalogue record for this book is available from the British Library

Library of Congress Cataloging-in-Publication Data
Names: Elise, Dianne, 1949- author.
Title: Creativity and the erotic dimensions of the analytic field / Dianne Elise.
Description: Abingdon, Oxon ; New York, NY : Routledge, 2019. | Series: The relational perspectives book series | Includes bibliographical references and index.
Identifiers: LCCN 2019004649 (print) | LCCN 2019006841 (ebook) | ISBN 9780429459900 (Master) | ISBN 9780429862113 (Adobe) | ISBN 9780429862090 (Mobipocket) | ISBN 9780429862106 (ePub3) | ISBN 9781138625419 (hardback : alk. paper) | ISBN 9781138625426 (pbk. : alk. paper)
Subjects: LCSH: Psychoanalysis. | Psychotherapy. | Sex (Psychology) | Creative ability.
Classification: LCC RC506 (ebook) | LCC RC506 .E44 2019 (print) | DDC 616.89/17—dc23
LC record available at https://lccn.loc.gov/2019004649

ISBN: 978-1-138-62541-9 (hbk)
ISBN: 978-1-138-62542-6 (pbk)
ISBN: 978-0-429-45990-0 (ebk)

Typeset in Times New Roman
by Swales & Willis Ltd, Exeter, Devon, UK

 Printed in the United Kingdom by Henry Ling Limited

Remembering my mother, whose hands danced animating her speech

Contents

Foreword by Adrienne Harris, Ph.D.   xi
Acknowledgements   xv

Introduction   1

PART I
Erotic vitality in analytic process   23

1 Moving from within the maternal: the choreography of analytic eroticism   25
2 Desire and disruption in the analytic relationship   53
3 Blocked creativity and inhibited erotic transference   75

PART II
Potential space and orientations of the erotic   103

4 Psychic bisexuality and creativity: gender repertoires   105
5 Male fears of psychic penetration   125
6 Reclaiming lost loves: transcending unrequited desires   145

PART III
Women and desire: erotic dysphorias   161

7 Sex and shame: the inhibition of female desires   163

8 Erasure of the female erotic	190
9 Failure to thrive: masochistic submission in women	213

PART IV
Erotic betrayal and poisoned desires   235

10 Infidelity and the betrayal of truth	237
11 Betrayal and the loss of goodness in the analytic relationship	261
12 Narcissistic seductions and the collapse of the creative	284
Index	299

Foreword

Adrienne Harris, Ph.D.

This book is a collection of fascinating and engaging papers by Dianne Elise. This collection covers over 25 years of writing experience and a longer history of practice. Her intense and deeply generative focus on Eros and creativity, on gender and its complexities, and on the living of these matters in analytic practice is visible from start to finish. As a woman analyst, evolving in practice and in writing through feminism and a deep engagement with sexuality and diversity in North American psychoanalysis, Elise is both a leader and a powerful influence on the evolution of theory and practice. She is also a theorist and practitioner who you can see changing and developing throughout this writing and analyzing process. There is always in her work, conviction and development, clarity and movement.

I think it important to see that her early engagement with maternal and analytic erotics was really quite ahead of her time in its beginning. Here is how she introduces her particular attunement to Eros:

> For the purposes of this book, I ask the reader to keep in mind that erotic is the adjective of Eros and can be used to refer to embodied affective energies initially derived from the sexual impulse that include libidinal vitality, tempestuous passions, unruly urges, vigor, ardor, and a stimulating vibrant frame of mind. (p. 1)

In the last half decade, perhaps since Laplanche's death in 2014 and the appearance of so much work in translation, we have a huge influx of material and influence emanating from his model of translation and enigmatic messages and the power of parental sexuality/seduction. Elise's writing here will certainly evoke these ideas and links to Laplanche. But it is important to see that her work has been much more grounded in Kristeva and in feminist work on sexuality which has emerged since the 1970s. Her ideas and ways of working derive from a different tradition even as we might now see overlap and linking.

Throughout this book, looking at many aspects of development, gender differences, the power of the erotic, its dangers and the costs of betrayal and trauma, she holds to a commitment to understanding the power of the maternal erotic in particular. Whether in the unfolding of growth in the context of maternal and analytic erotics, the damage from withheld or damaged libidinal ties to the maternal object, or in the underestimated difficulties in the loss of the maternal object for women in particular, the power of Eros to engage and promote development is held firmly in Elise's mind and work.

Holding, containing and stimulating are poles around which development can flourish or founder, and in these chapters, with ample clinical material, we see both the power and dangers in the erotic, noting that the danger of erotic absence is an ongoing element in her thought and practice. This is a particularly significant intervention for thinking about female development where the homoerotics in the maternal relation can be often quite seriously occluded. Elise examines developmental and clinical implications of the erotic ties between mother and child and the complex griefs around separation for both/all genders.

Entwined in Elise's interest in the erotic is a strong interest in creativity and in the links between Eros and creativity. Erotic inhibitions may reflect, produce, and reproduce other kinds of inhibitions and blocks in agency, thinking and playing. A central focus on creativity is actually one of her deepest theoretical convictions, and creativity and its inhibition is very explicitly tied, for Elise, to the fate of early attachments both oedipal and pre-oedipal. The mutative force of some moment of creativity is a frequent clinical insight in the work she presents in this book. I think this is one of her particular and unique contributions to thinking about intersubjective process as the site of change. Creativity is, in a sense, functioning for Elise as reverie does for Ogden and the aesthetic for Ferro and Civitarese, that is, as a critical site for psychic change and transformation.

This interaction of sexual and creative energies and resistances inspires both the imaginative clinical work Elise reports and her theorizing. One sees her creativity in the evocation of the exciting mother. Psychoanalysis has, for too long, been hostage to a focus on the dangerous or depleting mother. Elise restores to our theory and our clinic the mother of delight, excitement, expansiveness, desire and aliveness. One sees the influence of Kristeva in these projects leading to many areas of innovation and evolution in Elise's clinical work.

Along with offering this enhanced vision of the libidinally engaging pre-oedipal mother, Elise can address and speak to the effect of cultural dystonia and the too frequent eclipse of female sexuality in that context. Betrayal, avoidance and repression have a place in Elise's clinical observation. She is attuned to the difficulties and dysfunction in male and female development, and her clinical insights are astute. Shame and envy can flood both male and female developmental and clinical narratives. This book which displays clinical work and thinking over a wide range of situations shows Elise with such an even hand and such attunement to the suffering of persons of all genders and sexualities. She is adept and deeply sensitive in pointing out the damage we inflict on each other in our fear of our vulnerability and of our excitements. Whether she is addressing problems of betrayal and destructiveness or problems of loss and constriction and inhibition, Elise keeps her deep sense of all of our humanities.

I think that it is important to see how innovative is Elise's work on oedipal and pre-oedipal dynamics. So often these structures have been organized through heterosexuality and heteronormativity. Repudiation of the maternal can become naturalized as an inevitable outcome, as though distance from the mother and the maternal body was simply relief rather than deep loss and reluctant disentangling. The recuperation of homoerotic desires for women and men seems a radical move.

In the final section of the book, Elise takes up difficult and painful experiences of betrayal. She considers the betrayals that occur in intimate relationships in families and couples and those that occur in clinical situations that reverberate in the institutional communities and cultures as well as in the complex mournings and recoveries that must occur for patients. In this section, looking at the destruction that can be an outcome of erotic conflicts of many kinds, Elise is sober and reflective and clinically helpful regarding the demands on analysts and on the analytic field to maintain the safety and psychic health of our work inside the consulting room and outside. We can be grateful for her work and counsel in these matters, matters that impact every psychoanalyst and every patient.

This collection of papers, widely ranging over clinical problems for individuals, for couples and for the therapeutic dyad, reflects a unique career and trajectory, touching on the movements of liberation and social change that defined the late 20th century, and staying in very deep theoretical waters: feminist psychoanalytic and cultural texts, object relations theory, analytic field theory, the particular contemporary West Coast psychoanalytic scene: Ogden, Spezzano, Gerson and others. She integrates and works with these figures and theories in a very particular manner. The Winnicott who emerges in Elise's work is so richly present with all the erotic, creative and emotional force that his work can underwrite and privilege. We can see the aesthetic preoccupations of field theory in her work on creativity and its generative impact on analyst and analysand.

In these chapters, this brilliant psychoanalyst—clinician and thinker—has offered us an education, a guide to working, and a vision.

Acknowledgements

I wish to express my appreciation to the following people who at different points through the years supported my efforts and stirred my thinking: Rose Barry, Lynne Harkless, Jan Stites, Robin Deutsch, Jonathan Palmer, Adrienne Harris, Tom Ogden, Raymond Poggi, Charles Spezzano, Charles Dithrich, Mildred Dubitzky, Diane Ehrensaft, Daphne de Marneffe, Shelley Nathans, Rachael Peltz, Rosemary Balsam, Paul Schwaber, Nancy Kulish, CAPS Group 6, the "Semi-baked" group, and finally, though first, my parents.

A special thanks to my sister Janine Williams for the cover photography.

Chapter 1 is based on "Moving from within the Maternal: The Choreography of Analytic Eroticism", *Journal of the American Psychoanalytic Association*, 65: 33–60. (2017) Used with permission of SAGE Publications, Inc. doi: 10.1177/0003065116688460

Chapter 2 is based on "The Black Man and the Mermaid; Desire and Disruption in the Analytic Relationship", in Aron, L. and Harris, A. (Eds.), *Relational psychoanalysis: Expansion of theory - evolution of process*, Vol. 5. New York: Routledge, pp. 265–286. (2011)

Chapter 3 is based on "Blocked Creativity and Inhibited Erotic Transference", *Studies in Gender and Sexuality*, 3: 161–195. (2002)

Chapter 4 is based on "Gender Repertoire: Body, Mind and Bisexuality", *Psychoanalytic Dialogues*, 8: 379–397. (1998)

Chapter 5 is based on "Unlawful Entry; Male Fears of Psychic Penetration", *Psychoanalytic Dialogues*, 11: 499–531. (2001)

Chapter 6 is based on "Reclaiming Lost Loves: Transcending Unrequited Desires. Discussion of Davies' 'Oedipal Complexity'", *Psychoanalytic Dialogues*, 25: 284–294. (2015) All by permission of Taylor & Francis LLC, http://www.tandfonline.com

Chapter 7 is based on "Sex and Shame: The Inhibition of Female Desires", *Journal of the American Psychoanalytic Association*, 56: 73–98. (2008) Used with permission of SAGE Publications, Inc. doi:10.1177/0003065108315685

Chapter 8 is based on "Woman and Desire: Why Women May Not Want to Want", *Studies in Gender and Sexuality*, 1: 125–145. (2000) By permission of Taylor & Francis Ltd, http://www.tandfonline.com, and on "The Absence of the Paternal Penis" *Journal of the American Psychoanalytic Association*, 46: 413–442. (1998) Used with permission of SAGE Publications, Inc. doi:10.1177/00030651980460020301

Chapter 9 is based on "Failure to Thrive: Shame, Inhibition, and Masochistic Submission in Women", in Holtzman, D. and Kulish, N. (Eds.) *The clinical problem of masochism.* New York: Jason Aronson, pp. 161–185. (2012) Permission granted by Rowman and Littlefield.

Chapter 10 is based on "The Danger in Deception: Oedipal Betrayal and the Assault on Truth", *Journal of the American Psychoanalytic Association*, 60: 679–705. (2012) Used with permission of SAGE Publications, Inc. doi:10.1177/0003065112449187

Chapter 11 is based on "Unraveling: Betrayal and the Loss of Goodness in the Analytic Relationship", *Psychoanalytic Dialogues*, 25: 557–571. (2015)

Chapter 12 is based on "Psychic Riptides: Swimming Sideways: Reply to Dimen, Gabbard, and Harris", *Psychoanalytic Dialogues*, 25: 593–599. (2015) Each by permission of Taylor & Francis LLC, http://www.tandfonline.com

Permission given for Chapter 6 use of excerpts from the 2011 Program notes for John Neumeier's *The little mermaid* © San Francisco Ballet.

Introduction

Might we think of psychoanalysis as an erotic project? I believe that we can, and this premise forms the foundation of this book. I will be writing about erotic dimensions of the psyche and of the psychoanalytic process. I propose that a creative aesthetic can provide a clinical container for the engagement and exploration of erotic life within the analytic field of each treatment.

What is meant by *erotic*? The word *erotic* with its specific connotation of sexuality elicits both excitement and uneasiness. Ironically, given our Freudian beginnings, this uneasiness is especially prevalent within psychoanalysis. As many have noted, sexuality has receded as a focus, the profession de-sexualized in the object relational emphasis on a maternal matrix that is itself presumed to be asexual (Chodorow, 1978; Benjamin, 1988; Balsam, 2012; Kristeva, 2014). Interestingly, analysts seem to be comfortable with the term Eros, understood to mean a generalized life force even though bearing the name of the Greek god of sexual love. For the purposes of this book, I ask the reader to keep in mind that *erotic is the adjective of Eros* and can be used to refer to embodied affective energies initially derived from the sexual impulse that include libidinal vitality, tempestuous passions, unruly urges, vigor, ardor and a stimulating, vibrant frame of mind.

Eroticism within the analytic field also pertains to how the profession as a whole holds, or does not hold, the erotic. The long history of sexual boundary violations within analytic practice does not seem to have improved, suggesting that the erotic is not well contained by the profession (see Alpert & Steinberg, 2017). A central goal of this book is to put forth direct, nuanced attention both clinically and within theory building to many facets of the erotic. Hopefully, a skillful, fluent, and creative inhabiting of what I conceptualize as *analytic eroticism* will expand the clinical container for the erotic as both a subject of analytic theorizing and as an experience within the treatment dyad. As an analytic aesthetic approach, analytic eroticism can provide a stimulus to emotionally engaged thinking—linking—that can lead to transformations in many dimensions including the erotic.

In what has been conceptualized as the ethical *seduction* of an analysis, carried out within a context of care and responsibility toward a patient (Laplanche, 1992, 1997; Scarfone, 2013; Chetrit-Vatine, 2014), eroticism can seem to wane away. I favor an *explicit* retaining of the *erotic* in our developing view of how the analytic relationship works. I emphasize that an invitation is issued to an embodied experience of maternal eroticism (Kristeva, 2014), where an atmosphere of libidinal energy is a crucial aspect in enlivening—"vitalizing" (Alvarez, 2012)—the intersubjective field. When fully articulated as an energy potential in both participants, analytic eroticism can offer libidinal engagement within an ethical frame.

Fortunately, sexuality finds a place within the maternal matrix in the notable theorizing of Laplanche (1992, 1997), taken up by Stein (1998, 2008), Bollas (2000), Celenza (2014), Kristeva, (2014), Saketopoulou (2014), Benjamin & Atlas (2015), Atlas (2016), and other contemporary authors writing on sexuality understood as originating in the mother–infant relation. Laplanche elaborated the manner in which the mother's sexual unconscious permeates her relation with her infant, implanting within the infant's mind enigmatic messages compromised by sexuality. However, my focus is not the normatively or pathologically *traumatic* aspects of the parental sexual unconscious infiltrating or invading the child's psyche through implantation or intromission, respectively. I want to enlarge our scope beyond that of a traumatic overload of parental enigmatic signifiers as compromised or contaminated communications that disrupt (Scarfone, 2013) the mother–infant. Instead, I am concentrating on the stimulus to the development of the child's libidinal self by being enveloped in an embodied, erotic relation with each of the parents. I am bringing attention to the *healthy* contribution of parental eroticism to the child's development, with pathology resulting from *deficiencies* in the parental erotic matrix. As Kristeva (2014) wrote:

> If the lover's libido is lacking in the mother, her maternal eroticism would be merely defensive or operational, and it would result in some deficiencies in the sexualization[1] of the child, *including its ability to think.*
>
> (p. 75, emphasis added).

When Freud (1905) discovered infantile sexuality, he recognized that maternal care-taking stimulated the infant's psychosexual progression, but basically Freud's was a one-person conceptualization of intrapsychic development and was focused on the oedipal father. With object relations theory we have a two-person conceptualization that includes the psyche of the mother and the intersubjective relation of the mother–infant. Kristeva (2014) builds upon both Freud and Laplanche, depicting with much specificity the erotic, bodily relationship of mother and infant in which the infant as a sexual being comes to life. I view Kristeva's concept of *maternal eroticism* as the theoretical and developmental counterpart to Freud's concept of *infantile sexuality*. Joining maternal eroticism and infantile sexuality, we can now theorize the potential space of the mother–infant erotic matrix.

Readers may wonder, "Why *maternal* eroticism? What about fathers?" Certainly a father's libidinal energy is important to a child,[2] and yet, our human inheritance as *mammals* is generally to begin life with the pregnancy and then breast-feeding of the mother (advances in technology notwithstanding) as central to her embodied care of her infant. A quick appeal here to "gender equality" reflects, I suggest, an anxiety regarding maternal *eroticism*—a sense of threat about sexually imbued mothering even though we each, female and male, can in good circumstances benefit from our internalization of maternal eroticism. We are in the realm of sexed bodies: differences exist. Women can bring their sexed body to infant care in ways that men cannot. Let's give to the maternal erotic its due.

I also want to make clear to the reader that while I am focusing on the contributions of maternal eroticism in its positive manifestations to optimal development, this emphasis does not imply an idealized relationship devoid of limits, frustrations, aggressive components, and contentious conflict. Quite the contrary, libido leads to feistiness and sometimes to fury. My elaboration of maternal eroticism should not be construed as positing an idyllic dyad free of areas of difficulty. Although I am highlighting the vitality and creativity stimulated through parent–infant erotic interplay, much regularly can and does go awry in parenting, as the vast psychoanalytic literature attests. My attention is to the advantages of ample maternal eroticism and to the problems stemming from a deficit—a deficit that cannot conceptually be reduced to a uniform expression but that must be understood to take form in an extensive range of manifestations that undermine the vitality of the child.[3] Of course, *over*-stimulation can lead to pathology, as will perverse manifestations of maternal eroticism (each well theorized by Laplanche and many others). Just as we regularly encounter failures in holding and containing, so too can maternal eroticism go awry in a number of directions. Similarly, analytic eroticism can be used productively or, alternatively, fall prey to destructive dynamics.

I consider Kristeva's 2014 publication a landmark paper of profound significance for analytic theorizing. Her concept of maternal eroticism opens to a wider view of the mother's role as a sexual being. Parental libidinal energies are understood to fuel the child's erotic vitality and to facilitate mental development. Throughout my writing, beginning with a 1998 publication to most recently in early 2017, I have described the nursing couple (Winnicott, 1965, 1971) as libidinally engaged, their sensual interaction forming a primal template for developing sexuality as well as for the mind more generally. Thomson-Salo & Paul (2017) recently offered a compelling account of infant sexuality in reciprocal interaction with parents that provides support to my theorizing. Drawing from infant observation, neurophysiology research and infant-parent clinical work, they exquisitely detail parent–infant erotic life. We can recognize that attachment and sexuality are intertwined beginning with earliest object relations (see Widlocher, 2002; Benjamin, 2017) rather than theorizing a pre-oedipal attachment that is then sequentially followed by a sexual development seen entirely as oedipal.

Certainly, providing a calm, secure atmosphere ("holding") and modulating distress ("containing") are crucial parental capacities, but in order to thrive, children also need stimulating engagements. I emphasize that the marked affect of parental response needed for the development of mentalization (Fonagy, 2008) rests upon libidinal energy in care-takers for a certain level of excited response to a child's excitement. "Interest excitement" (Spezzano, 1993), as a key affect, is a central component of childhood where ideally parents join their child in a love affair with the world in its cascade of surprises and adventures. Parental libidinal energy also is needed, as Kristeva (2014) delineated, in order that parents can hold up during the varying demands of caring for a child, maintaining their investment in the face of much that is not gratifying in any immediate sense. All this has a parallel in the analytic situation.

I suggest that Kristeva's concept of maternal eroticism is on a par in heuristic and clinical value with Winnicott's concept of maternal holding and with Bion's concept of maternal containment, both in understanding development in the early mother–infant relation and in the relevance that each of these formulations has for the technical approach of the analyst. Holding and containing are each highly developed metaphors conceptualizing the functioning of the analyst within the clinical process. I believe that similar theoretical work can be done in employing the concept of maternal eroticism to delineate an additional, equally salient capacity in the analyst within the analytic field. The analyst holds, contains, *and stimulates*; each of these capacities is mobilized in the service of the patient's growth.[4]

While infantile sexuality stirred by maternal "seduction" was a core aspect of Freud's developmental theorizing, he had no corresponding agenda for the analyst's position; in fact his recommended (paternal) stance of abstinence, neutrality, often rendered the "non-gratifying" analyst an *anti*-libidinal figure. Winnicott's and Bion's use of a maternal metaphor provided analysts with a very different conceptualization of our technical approach, but with libido drained away rather than subject to restraint. Maternal eroticism, as the libidinal vitality and investment that a mother brings to her fully embodied engagement with her child, offers a metaphor for technique that can incorporate an analytic eroticism. However, clinicians can fear encountering, let alone utilizing, the erotic in the clinical situation, especially when it escapes the bounds of the more familiar oedipal transferences (see Vaughan, 2017; Brady, 2018). Understanding our role in terms of attachment has been much more palatable, allowing for distance from the enormity of passions experienced in undefended vulnerability to the maternal (Elise, 2015, 2017).

The maternal erotic matrix

We each begin with our mother. The fact that we exist is because she is a sexual creature. Her sexuality does not stop with conception. She goes on conceiving (of) us in her (erotic) imagination: She waits for us, like a lover, eagerly anticipating our arrival. There we are: magnificent! If things go well, she adores us, loves us up, erotically consumes us, consummates us. We begin enveloped in an erotic relation *à deux*. Embraced in her arms, sucking at her breasts, we are her lover and she ours—maternal eroticism. It's just we two (we believe). Ignorance is truly bliss.

Yet, who is this fantastic creature we come into the world to meet? She belongs to us, or does she? Doubt creeps in, tainting paradise. One thing is clear: *we want her*, and in the most erotic of ways—body and soul. Our lust is total, all-encompassing. She *must* be ours. Possession is essential. But she is coy, not always available, making us wait, playing "hard to get." Where does she go? (We don't yet know to wonder—too painful—"Who (else) is she with?") We are each a lover naïve to the possibility of infidelity. She is *surely* ours; it is a question of waiting—which is hard enough, almost impossible. But she is worth the wait. When she returns, she is lovely, wonderful, the most beautiful, sensual of creatures on any earth. We are together; this is heaven on earth. What could go wrong? (We have, for the moment, forgotten about the waiting part . . .).

One can easily picture the sensual fascination infants and toddlers have with the mother's bodily presence: the "jewelry" of her face, eyes glistening, surely glass ornaments in their color and shine; teeth gleaming like a string of pearls, sensuous swirls of hair, the aromatic scent of her flesh, her milk. These aspects of color, light, and texture—beauty—must surely stir a pleasure center in the brain and intensify the erotic attachment to the mother, who appears as an aesthetic immanence sparkling like a human mobile over the crib (Elise, 2006). As noted above, this stimulating erotic engagement builds the mind: "The infant-soul's interaction with the body spaces of the world-mother constitutes the formation of Mind . . . the inside emerging outside, the outside sinking in and holding like a dream" (Meltzer and Harris Williams, 1988, p. 186).

In his writing on the aesthetic conflict in the apprehension of maternal beauty, Meltzer's (Meltzer and Harris Williams, 1988) vivid depictions of the impact on the infant of the mother's beauty surely convey the erotic and the tantalizing:

> Her outward beauty, concentrated as it must be in her breast[s] and in her face, complicated in each case by her nipples and her eyes, bombards [the infant] with an emotional experience of a passionate quality, . . . The mother is enigmatic . . . she giveth and she taketh away . . . This is the aesthetic conflict . . . the aesthetic impact of the outside of the 'beautiful' mother, available to the senses, and the enigmatic inside which must be construed by creative imagination. Everything in art and literature, every analysis, testifies to its perseverance throughout life.
>
> (pp. 21–22)

In Meltzer's depiction, the maternal enigmatic is a stimulus to creative imagination. Winnicott (1971), as well, saw in the mother–infant relation a state of being from which a creative reaching out can occur: "It can be looked on as sacred to the individual that it is here that the individual experiences creative living" (p. 103). As envisioned by Winnicott (1968), the maternal message to the infant is: "Come at the world creatively, create the world; it is only what you create that has meaning for you" (p. 23).

Winnicott and creative living

Analysts have for some time had a growing interest in psychoanalysis as a creative project. We are a profession that values creating a space for meaningful personal truths to be put into words, or into some sense of shared communication, in order that the experiencing that accompanies those communications can be accessed and elaborated. Foregoing the original professional aspiration to "scientific" objectivity, analysts recognize the unique unfolding of each treatment. Current conceptualizations of the analyst's role stress that an analyst is a co-participant in the creative unfolding of a dyadic conversation meant to further the development of the patient's capacities of mind toward increasing elaboration of personal meaning: "The patient's experience of *being creative* in the act of communicating is an essential part of the process of his 'dreaming himself more fully into existence' (Ogden 2004b, p. 858), coming into being in a way that is uniquely his own" (Ogden, 2018, p. 401). The analyst as well must engage in these acts of creativity. I believe our ability to do so is greatly served by a connection with our libidinal, embodied energies. This creative unfolding is each dyad's work of art—the aesthetic dimension (de Cortinas, 2009, 2013) of the therapeutic process—taking place within an analytic field. In keeping to "the dream dimension, the virtual, or 'field' element of the analytic encounter," the analyst is engaged "in creating a dream space, a stage set or play area" (Civitarese, 2012, p. 172).

In his uniquely nuanced attention to the importance to an individual of creative vitality in living (see Goldman, 2017; Phillips, 2016), Winnicott has much to offer analytic field theory. This subject is the heart of Winnicott. Being creatively alive is not solely excitement/pleasure, but the soil in which psychic pain can be metabolized. Winnicott (1971) underscored that access to this quality of experiencing is just as crucial for the analyst as it is for the patient. The analyst's emotionally alive presence offers to a patient an object relationship with potential, a potential space where the patient might risk coming to life rather than remaining frozen in psychic stasis. This psychic awakening will likely be painful—like hands, numb with cold, first being warmed—and must be approached carefully by both analyst and patient as they evolve their pairing. A patient's encounter with an analyst as engaged presence and creative co-participant will bring a slow, yet shocking awareness of what has not been. Yet, new potentials emerge.

Winnicott (1971) identified that "the work done by the therapist is directed towards bringing the patient . . . into a state of being able to play" (p. 38): "If the therapist cannot play, then he is not suitable for the work. If the patient cannot play, then something needs to be done to enable the patient to become able to play . . . The reason why playing is essential is that it is in playing that the patient is being creative" (p. 54). Winnicott described psychoanalysis "as a highly specialized form of playing in the service of communication with oneself and others" (1971, p. 41) that "takes place in the overlap of two areas of playing, that of the patient and that of the therapist" (1971, p. 38). Playing "is an experience in the space-time continuum, a basic form of living" (Winnicott, 1971, p. 50).

Winnicott (1971) traced the developmental line in his theorizing that directly connects the concepts of transitional phenomena, dreaming, playing, potential space, creativity, and an intermediate/third area as the location of cultural experience; these concepts articulate a realm of overlapping outer and inner realities, facts and creative fictions—an intersubjective field expanding beyond the encompassed individual personalities. In the infant's early contacts with maternal reverie, transitional experiencing is encountered, created, and lived by the mother–infant pair. This experience is also to be fostered in the analytic situation.

As Winnicott emphasized throughout his work, an analyst's capacity to relate within and through a personally creative modality provides a particular environment that supports the patient's contact with the true self. It is important to recognize that Winnicott's concept of the true self does not refer to a static entity—a fixed representation of self; it is a quality of experiencing, *being*, that involves spontaneity, vitality, imagination, and aliveness in contrast to the compliance of the false self. The primary creativity of the true self needs to be understood as distinct from talent; instead, it is a "talent" for living: "a kind of creative fury that will not let

[one] rest content with a merely compliant adaptation" (Milner, 1969, pp. 384–385). However, Winnicott (1971) noted: "In a tantalizing way many individuals have experienced just enough of creative living to recognize that most of their lives they are living uncreatively" (p. 65). When able to be accessed by both members of the clinical dyad, this intermediate area of experience is "in direct continuity with the play area of the small child who is 'lost' in play" (p. 13) that "throughout life is retained in the intense experiencing that belongs to the arts and to religion and to imaginative living" (Winnicott, 1971, p. 14). This "third area of potential space" (Winnicott,1971, p. 53) is integral to the ability to dream and to play with time in order to create a psychic space with potential.

In his conception of a third area, Winnicott (1971) comes closest to his explicit statement of an analytic field theory: "cultural experience is located in the *potential space* between the individual and the environment" (p. 100). Evident in the "capacity to experience in the cultural field" (p. 101) is "a third area of human living, one neither inside the individual nor outside in the world of shared reality" (Winnicott, 1971, p. 110). Winnicott synthesized his core theme: "We experience life in the area of transitional phenomena, in the exciting interweave of subjectivity and objective observation, and in an area that is intermediate between the inner reality of the individual and the shared reality of the world that is external to individuals" (1971, p. 64).

The clinical relationship as an analytic field

In what might be regarded as a paradigm shift within psychoanalysis, a convergence of theorizing on technique has brought together thinking from multiple directions. We have the intersubjective focus developed within relational theory, the concept of the analytic field as an interactive matrix of psychic forces, and the increasing recognition that many patients struggle with difficulties in symbolic expression, where unrepresented states elude meaning and lead to significant technical challenges. We also see a burgeoning literature on creative expression in the analyst's contribution to the clinical enterprise, as well as renewed attention to sexuality and libidinal life in a fascinating and, to me, welcome return to Freud's emphasis on libido and Eros. Holding and containing are increasingly theorized to be active, (though not yet erotic) complex processes on the part of the analyst.

Clinicians are thus contending with significant changes in contemporary understandings of our analytic stance. Even the word "stance" to describe what we are attempting to do—within a given session and throughout the treatment arc—sounds outdated, rigid, fixed, and immobile, though likely representing an improvement over the inanimate "blank screen." I prefer to think in terms of an analytic *approach*; 'approach' conveys an image of embodied activity—to move toward—that can include recognition of a need to be still or even to step back in the service of promoting greater contact. Clinicians aim to work with each patient in a manner that will be most helpful to *that* patient in ameliorating the difficulties that have brought him or her to seek treatment. In this effort, many analysts see analytic field theory as a particularly sophisticated and felicitous model presenting a fresh approach to clinical process as an intersubjective, co-created journey.

The clinical intricacies of working within the analytic field are richly detailed in the prolific writing of Ogden, Ferro, and Civitarese, as well as by others involved in developing field theory, a model that is gaining increasing momentum (see Stern, 2015, Katz, 2017).[5] De Cortinas (2009) described Bion's (1961) ideas regarding primitive group mental functioning as expanding the area of analytic space: "In the multi-dimensional space of the analytic session," through the process of projective identification, both patient and analyst communicate "across a wider field" (p. 77) than even each of their own individual personalities in intersubjective interaction. This understanding of an analytic field—larger than the sum of the parts—leads to a changed role for the analyst, not as objective observer of the patient's mental contents, but as an implicated subject who must also attempt to register and articulate the unfolding experiences within the field. This approach to technique—now not solely to follow the patient, but also *to initiate*—focuses on the analyst's imaginative agency rather than on an over-reliance on a technical expertise based in theoretical abstractions.

Especially evident in Ogden's (1994a, 1994b, 2004a, 2004b) articulation of the analytic third—itself a field theory—and in the work of Ferro (1992, 2002, 2005, 2006) and Civitarese (2010, 2012, 2016), the field is viewed as encompassing the subjectivities of both patient and analyst, where each is implicated in its formation *and formed by it*. Ogden (2004a) identified that the analytic third "is a subjectivity that seems to take on a life of its own in the interpersonal field" (p. 169). Ogden described the need for the analyst to be able to reflect on the emotional position to which she has become captive as well as a contributor in order to emerge with the patient from psychic subjugation to greater freedom of movement—a repeating pattern that *is* the analytic process. Ferro and Civitarese (2015) see the capacity to develop an evolving narrative (*gestalten* in German) as increasing the containing function *of the field* as well as of the individuals within it. Each of these authors places emphasis on creative use of metaphors (Ogden, 1997; Civitarese and Ferro, 2013) in narrating the experiences of the analytic field.

Finding much to appreciate in Bionian conceptualizations of the analytic field put forth by Ferro and Civitarese, I have also found my thoughts gravitating to parallel concepts in Winnicott's writing that I believe, as suggested above, are themselves formative for a theory of the analytic field—both with regard to the analyst's role and to understanding how the dyad interacts in the service of the analytic goals. These conceptualizations developed by Winnicott—aligning to a large extent with Bionian theorizing—lend themselves to a similar approach yet have generally remained "silent" in the articulation of an analytic field theory that thus far, within an object relations model, has tended to be seen as synonymous with Bionian thinking. Yet, relative neglect of Winnicott at this forward-moving edge of analytic technique can shift as theorizing of the analytic field continues to evolve. I believe it would be fruitful to integrate more fully the richness of Winnicott's contributions into a field theory of analytic process.

As Ogden, Ferro, and Civitarese each compellingly illustrate throughout their work, the creative capacities of the analytic pair to imaginatively co-construct an aesthetic form gives shape and meaning to personal experience. I emphasize that this analytic process is not solely to *contain*, as in the modulation and tolerance of affect, but to *elaborate* the symbolic capacities of the patient's mind that in the analytic setting will most often unfold in a narrative building process. Analytic process can transform painful affect not primarily by naming, but through *the enlivening experience of creating that, in itself, promotes healing* and is thus "an essential element" (Schore, 2012, p. 142) of therapeutic progress.

From within the perspective of an analytic field theory, one way of viewing the relationship of Winnicott's and Bion's respective contributions might be to see Bionian thinking as a complex articulation of the coercive pressures of the field and Winnicottian thinking as giving more voice to the creative potentials of the field. Both perspectives are essential in a field theory approach to technique: the first in order to comprehend the powerful manner in which an analyst will be drawn into dynamics of mutual projective identification that she cannot initially, but must retrospectively, identify; the second in order to understand that areas of relative freedom within the field allow for a creative effort by the dyad that is central to the analytic goals. Winnicott's style of thinking is particularly evocative in envisioning what we might give life to in the analytic conversation. As analyst and patient "play" with and within the metaphoric realm, they create an emotionally meaningful narrative that not only has the potential to contain and transform psychic pain, but to vitalize the creative energy of the personality.

Bringing erotic life to the analytic field

In thinking of my own clinical approach as embodying a Winnicottian field theory (Elise, 2018), I am including in this model my specific emphasis on the erotic dimension of the psyche. Winnicott's account most especially emphasizes the development of a *creative* sense of self. I add that personal creativity is located within a libidinal connection to the erotic body. One might say that I am adding a Freudian element to analytic field theory in my attention to the libidinal aspects of embodied psychic life. As I have been identifying, to recognize that psychoanalysis has an erotic nature—that patient and analyst are libidinally engaged—can be troubling. Passion can destabilize one's sense of self—both in a clinician as well as in a patient—yet, we hope for an opening of the self to aliveness, richness of experience and meaning. Erotic energy is a source of creativity. Creativity is exciting. Can we play with sexuality; can we engage the erotics of play?

Many have noted Winnicott's apparent neglect of sexuality (see Caldwell, 2005; Joyce, 2016), and indeed it is worth noting that sexuality is not a focus in Bionian theory. I believe Winnicott was attempting to counter a Freudian emphasis on genital sexuality that he felt overshadowed other crucial aspects of development. He wrote: "[T]he subject of playing has been too closely linked with masturbation and the various sensuous experiences . . . [It is] *true that when we witness playing we tend to wonder what is the physical excitement that is linked* . . . But playing needs to be studied as a subject on its own . . . It may very well be that we have missed something" (1971, p. 39, emphasis added). Whereas I feel that we are *now* missing something in having so removed our thinking from the libidinal physicality of excitement infusing creative engagement that Winnicott, in his generation, took as *a psychoanalytic given*. In linking his idea of "a True Self with the spontaneous gesture," Winnicott (1965) added: "Fusion of the motility *and erotic elements* is in the process of becoming a fact at this period of development of the individual" (p. 145, emphasis added).

Winnicott (1988) affirmed: "Childhood sexuality is a very real thing" (p. 57); "In the imaginative elaboration of genital functions the continued importance of the pregenital shows itself" (p. 43); "The healthy child becomes capable of the full dream of genital sexuality" (p. 58); and "any theory that bypasses these matters is unhelpful" (p. 36). I add that a corresponding limitation exists in a technical approach that bypasses the imaginative elaboration of erotic life in the dream that is the analytic field. I specifically underscore the erotic as an important ingredient of the clinical situation—a lively spontaneity that partakes of the analyst's as well as the patient's creative self. While forging a connection between Winnicott's theorizing and the erotic challenges the way in which Winnicott's work typically has been held, I see his emphasis on creativity and on embodiment as providing a bridge to the erotic. I suggest that his central focus on creativity combined with his concepts regarding embodied experience—in-dwelling, psychesoma, personalization—lend to linkage with the erotic. Creative vitality is erotically derived, rooted, embedded.

As I highlight throughout this introduction and this book, for Winnicott personal creativity facilitates the ongoing expansion of the personality in the most far-reaching sense. This emphasis, I suggest, can extend our understanding of what is meant by enlarging the containing function of the field toward a clinical aim that encompasses more than developing the patient's capacity to tolerate emotional pain. Furthermore, I put forward that it is the erotic that unites the container and the contained within a libidinal matrix that supports the creative vitality of the dyad. Thus, I propose two expansions of analytic field theory: 1) more explicit attention to the creative potentials of the analytic field, and 2) conceptualization of an erotic dimension as the motive force by which creative potential is vitalized.

Anyone who has felt the sweep of creative expression of self registers the sense of "thrill" that is imbued with the erotic. Erotic vitality is a stimulus to creative expression that is itself further stimulating. This relationship can be understood as mutually reinforcing: *erotic* ←—→ *creativity*.[6] Both the erotic and the creative have a further reinforcing relation to the expansion of the overall personality, expressed as: *erotic* ←—→ *creativity* ←—→ *expansion of the personality*. Each of these three aspects of experience develops in reciprocal relation to one another. Expansion of the entire personality is facilitated by an analytic process that integrates bodily components of experience, rooted in erotic vitality, with creative elaborations of emotional truth. Along with the aim of enlarging the containing function, we might think, with Winnicott in mind, of an increasing "creative function" as leading toward greater psychic health and well-being—not solely through the transformation of psychic pain, but in the expansion of the creative expression of one's unique and, I add, erotic being.

Winnicott and Bion each drew a detailed picture of the mother–infant relationship as central to the development of the personality. Although Winnicott underlined the importance of embodied experience, neither he nor Bion theorized an erotic texturing as foundational to both the development of the psyche and the analytic process. I see primary maternal preoccupation, reverie and containment as *resting within, and only made possible by*, a mother's deeply embodied connection to her libidinal self; her erotic sensibilities provide the "juice" for her complex emotional engagement with her infant. A full formulation of the analytic field must include awareness of the centrality of the erotic in both the maternal matrix and in that of the field. This erotic-aesthetic dimension potentiates the creative interplay of the analytic process. By moving into a potential space of poetic ambiguity, creative imagination, and erotic vitality, we play with, and within, time and space in our relationship with each patient. Each analyst hopefully attempts to embody in a personal analytic style an approach to analytic process that catalyzes the healing potential of shared creation.

Sex and sexuality in psychoanalysis

In the following chapters my intention is to bring sustained attention to erotic dimensions of the analytic field as they manifest on multiple levels: infant sexuality within the matrix of maternal eroticism, oedipal development and sexual object choice, psychic bisexuality and gender identities, adult sexuality, erotic transference and countertransference, and analytic eroticism as a clinical energy. Clinical material will include specific topics such as masturbation, sexual history, adult sex, sexual fantasy, inhibitions, anxieties and conflicts. The goal is to have clinicians thinking developmentally, dynamically and transferentially about sexual matters—that sex matters; "interwoven into the fabric of all our minds, in bold colors, or in indistinct threads . . . [sexuality is] always a force to be reckoned with and understood" (Kulish, 2011, p. 268, 269). Kernberg (1991) underscored "the importance of the analyst's internal freedom in dealing with these basic aspects of human sexuality" (p. 361). Developed in earliest object relations, "libido originates in primitive affect states, including the peak affect state of elation characterizing the early infant-mother relation" (Kernberg, 1991, p. 344). As the core element of libido, "sexual excitement as an affect involves the total field of psychic experience" (Kernberg, 1991, p. 345). In this book I attempt to bring sex and sexuality more fully into the analytic field.

As conceptualized in Chapter 1, analytic eroticism as a vitalization of the clinical situation—a libidinal force field—constitutes an expanded meaning of erotic transference-countertransference, where both patient and analyst engage their erotic energies and where this engagement is not specific to (though it may include) erotic desire for the other. I link the embodied art of dance to the clinician's creative vitality in contributing to the shaping of the movement of a session. Chapter 2 considers the impact of de-sexualization of the maternal on the development of female sexuality. I argue that a girl's oedipal experience is encased within a patriarchal structuring of sexuality where the mother is rendered solely reproductive and nurturing, not erotically sexual. I suggest that a female sense of genital inadequacy and inferiority may have a component of not being able to link the mother's (and in the transference, the analyst's) use of her genitals with her use of her mind/maternal function. In Chapter 3, I pursue the relationship between erotic transference and creativity. Erotic transference is not solely a resistance to treatment; treatment can involve a resistance to erotic transference, the dynamics of which can have parallels in the inhibition of creativity. I underscore the detrimental impact of *resistance to* erotic desire and romantic love for the analyst.

In Part II, I analyze gender-specific experiences in developing psychosexuality that have been an ongoing focus of my work as I have delineated the ways in which psychoanalytic theory historically may have constricted rather than enriched understanding of various dynamics that impact females and males. Psychic bisexuality is discussed in Chapter 4, and beyond, as a creative use of potential identifications that can elaborate an individual's erotic repertoire. Although psychic bisexuality is a contested term with a complicated history (see Perelberg, 2018), I use this concept to denote an array of possible gendered and sexual identifications not limited to one or even two "locations" along a continuum. While some people may feel singularly fixed in such identifications, other individuals may be mobile, even agile, in integrating multiplicity into a sense of self. In what Harris (2005) aptly termed "soft-assembly," it is possible to have a reasonably secure sense of self that encompasses a more expansive experience of gender and desire. In Chapter 5, I describe phallicism as a fortress of emotional self-sufficiency in a subjective sense of masculinity that both shapes and limits men's desire and access to their fullest creative and erotic potential. Continuing my long-standing project to rehabilitate the oedipal concept from heteronormative presumptions, in Chapter 6 I attest to the ongoing centrality of the oedipal constellation both in development and in analytic treatment.

Each of the chapters (7, 8, 9) in Part III focuses on female development and on inhibitions in erotic life that I link to the relinquishment of the maternal figure as erotic object. In order to shed light on female erotic dysphoria, I unfold a developmental narrative that centers on bodily-based narcissistic injury and sense of shame in response to unrequited oedipal longings. Through a subjective sense of oedipal defeat in relation to both mother and father, a female sense of inadequacy and shame can be internalized and accepted as one's identity, in contrast to a male phallic-omnipotent trajectory. The demise of genital narcissism in females is seen to underlie various expressions of pervasive inhibition, masochistic submission and failure to actualize desire.

Part IV takes up the painful topic of the erotic "gone wrong": I approach erotic betrayal through the experiences of infidelity both in adult couples (Chapter 10) and in the analytic couple when a patient experiences her clinician as having been "unfaithful" to the analytic commitment (Chapter 11). The final chapter of the book addresses a concern frequently raised in discussions of my concept of analytic eroticism: sexual boundary violations. Attending to how libidinal energy can be misdirected, I emphasize the role of narcissistic dynamics in clinical breaches of an ethical treatment frame. I consider the broader context in which we train and practice and the pressure on clinicians, especially in training, to perform a role as a knowledgeable and knowing authority—a role that shuts down for both participants the creative vitality of the analytic endeavor.

The material presented in these chapters comprises my theoretical contributions developed over three decades, now significantly re-shaped to reflect the current expression of my thinking. My desire is to stimulate further thinking about how we actually practice and about how analytic eroticism imbues that practice. In my view, psychoanalysis rests on an ability to take nothing at face value, to have a questioning mind, to seek deeper understandings hidden in, and *by*, plain sight. We go against the grain, challenging the ingrained, seeking novel connections between disparate "facts." Psychoanalysis is a continuing practice of extricating ourselves from anything rote, or remote, in order to arrive at a place of spontaneous interchange, surprising truths, and painful realizations, weaving all this into an understanding that can welcome the unwelcome and relish the emotional immediacy of one's experience.

Psychoanalysis is play in the sense that one can let one's mind play with possibilities; we engage metaphor where flexibility of mind forms images that capture emotional truth and that can stir the soul. Although interpretation can be very powerful, psychoanalysis is also about *invitation*—an invitation to a vital exchange and a meaningful narration of the self. Psychoanalysis involves a deep listening to what is being said, what is not being said. It involves flexibility and fluidity of both thought and affect in interaction. Psychoanalysis is more than ameliorating distress; it is an ongoing process of expansion of the personality in many respects toward greater sense of personal vitality. As is true for a patient, a clinician must be a fully embodied participant for this process to unfold.

Psychoanalysis involves perseverance, attention, and intention, a steadiness, steadfastness of purpose, courage, commitment, a passionate investing in the mobility of the self and the capacity for change, a being with, and a bringing together. It is pain, excitement, humility, and hope. Analytic practice requires patience, immense patience, and kindness and respect. The clinician needs to stay alive in the face of much that is deadening, that works toward stasis; this effort takes tremendous libidinal energy, stamina, fortitude, poised readiness, and, in addition to receptivity, the ability to come forward and to initiate when needed.

Psychoanalysis is a relationship that provides a context for a patient to locate an undefended sense of self—and to be more aware of the defensive strategies that hide this self—in a search for, and hopefully a revealing of, an experience of authenticity. We seek through compassionate and passionate curiosity to engage in a deep exploration into the development of the personality, how it has come to be shaped. In what ways does that shape express the unique and valuable individuality of the person? In what ways does it interfere with a rewarding unfolding of life? What is in the way; what other way might be found? We are searching for what is, what has been and also for what can become. Each clinical pair both shapes and is shaped by the analytic space.

Psychoanalysis requires a "hello"—which may take days or years—and a *good* "goodbye," with a long time in between where we do not give up. We work to envision a future seeded in the present that will afford a space to look back. Psychoanalysis is a conversation that lasts well beyond termination and that rests in the capacity to be humble in the face of the sadness of living while not refusing the potentials for joy.

Notes

1 Kristeva's (2014) use here of "sexualization" refers to the healthy facilitation of the infant's development as a sexual being rather than the pathological connotations typically associated with this term.
2 Even without being the biological mother and breast-feeding, any individual parent/infant caregiver plays a crucial role with their unique libidinal contribution. Yet breast-feeding is the evolutionary design of the human species, one that extends female sexuality from conception through to the early care of the infant. This reality—the implications of which are assiduously avoided by both society and psychoanalysis—needs to be reckoned with.
3 Green's concept of the dead mother would describe an extreme deficit in maternal eroticism: "The dead mother . . . is a mother who is [physically] present. She continues to take care of the child, but she has lost the impulse of love . . . she is accomplishing her duty, but it is not what is expected in the relationship" (Meadow & Green, 2006, p. 12).
4 See Brady's (2018) attention to "erotic insufficiency" in clinicians.
5 Civitarese and Ferro (2013) provide a succinct history of the development of Bionian field theory within a Kleinian/Bionian lineage that builds on the seminal theorizing of the analytic field by the Barangers (1961–1962/2008). Stern (2013a, 2013b), in offering a depiction of an *implicit* concept of the field within interpersonal and relational psychoanalysis, compares and contrasts this model with Bionian field theory. Katz (2017) articulates a contemporary comparative approach to psychoanalytic field theory.
6 Used in Bionian thinking, the notation of the double arrow expresses the bi-directional, ongoing development between the terms.

References

Alpert, J. L. and Steinberg, A. (2017). Introduction: Sexual boundary violations: A century of violations and a time to analyze. *Psychoanalytic Psychology*, 34: 144–150.

Alvarez, A. (2012). *The thinking heart: Three levels of psychoanalytic therapy with disturbed children*. London: Routledge.

Atlas, G. (2016). *The enigma of desire: Sex, longing and belonging in psychoanalysis*. London: Routledge.

Balsam, R. (2012). *Women's bodies in psychoanalysis*. London: Routledge.

Baranger, M. and Baranger, W. (1961–1962/2008). The analytic situation as a dynamic field. *International Journal of Psychoanalysis*, 89: 795–826.

Benjamin, J. (1988). *The bonds of love*. New York: Pantheon.

— (2017). *Beyond doer and done to: Recognition theory, intersubjectivity and the third*. London: Routledge.

Benjamin, J. and Atlas, G. (2015). The "too muchness" of excitement: Sexuality in light of excess, attachment and affect regulation. *International Journal of Psychoanalysis*, 96: 39–63.

Bion, W. R. (1961). *Experiences in groups*. London: Tavistock.

Bollas, C. (2000). *Hysteria*. London: Routledge.

Brady, M. (2018). Braving the erotic field in the treatment of adolescents. *Journal of Child Psychotherapy*, 44: 108–123.

Caldwell, L. (Ed.) (2005). *Sex and sexuality: Winnicottian perspectives*. London: Karnac.

Celenza, A. (2014). *Erotic revelations: Clinical applications and perverse scenarios*. New York: Routledge.

Chetrit-Vatine, V. (2014). *The ethical seduction of the analytic situation: The feminine-maternal origins of responsibility for the other*. London: Karnac.

Chodorow, N. (1978). *The reproduction of mothering*. Berkeley: University CA Press.

Civitarese, G. (2010). *The intimate room: Theory and technique of the analytic field*. London: Routledge.

— (2012). *The violence of emotions: Bionian and post-Bionian psychoanalysis*. London: Routledge.

— (2016). *Truth and the unconscious in psychoanalysis*. London: Routledge.

Civitarese, G. and Ferro, A. (2013). The meaning and use of metaphor in analytic field theory. *Psychoanalytic Inquiry*, 33: 190–209.

de Cortinas, L. P. (2009). *The aesthetic dimension of the mind*. London: Karnac.

— (2013). Transformations of emotional experience. *International Journal of Psychoanalysis*, 94(3): 531–544.

Elise, D. (1998). Gender repertoire: Body, mind and bisexuality. *Psychoanalytic Dialogues*, 8: 379–397.

— (2006). Beauty and the aesthetic impact of the bejeweled mother: Discussion of papers by Debra Roth and Elaine Freedgood. *Studies in Gender & Sexuality*, 7: 207–215.

— (2015). Eroticism in the maternal matrix: Infusion through development and the clinical situation. *fort da*, 21(2): 17–32.
— (2017). Moving from within the maternal: The choreography of analytic eroticism. *Journal of the American Psychoanalytic Association*, 65: 33–60.
— (2018). A Winnicottian field theory: Creativity and the erotic dimension of the analytic field. *fort da*, 24(1): 22–38.
Ferro, A. (1992). *The bi-personal field: Experiences in child analysis*. London: Routledge.
— (2002). *In the analyst's consulting room*. London: Routledge.
— (2005). *Seeds of illness, seeds of recovery. The genesis of suffering and the role of psychoanalysis* (P. Slotkin, Trans.) Hove, UK: Brunner-Routledge.
— (2006). *Mind works: Technique and creativity in psychoanalysis*. London: Routledge.
Ferro, A. and Civitarese, G. (2015). *The analytic field and its transformations*. London: Karnac.
Fonagy, P. (2008). A genuinely developmental theory of sexual enjoyment and its implications for psychoanalytic technique. *Journal of the American Psychoanalytic Association*, 56: 11–36.
Freud, S. (1905). Three essays on the theory of sexuality. *The Standard Edition*, 7: 130–243. London, Hogarth Press, 1953.
Goldman, D. (2017). *A beholder's share: Essays on Winnicott and the psychoanalytic imagination*. London: Routledge.
Harris, A. (2005). *Gender as soft assembly*. Hillsdale, New Jersey: Analytic Press.
Joyce, A. (2016). Infantile sexuality: Its place in the conceptual developments of Anna Freud and Donald W. Winnicott. *International Journal of Psychoanalysis*, 97: 915–931.
Katz, S. M. (2017). *Contemporary psychoanalytic field theory: Stories, dreams and metaphor*. New York: Routledge
Kernberg, O. (1991). Sadomasochism, sexual excitement, and perversion. *Journal of the American Psychoanalytic Association*, 39: 333–362.
Kristeva, J. (2014). Reliance, or maternal eroticism. *Journal of the American Psychoanalytic Association*, 62: 69–85.
Kulish, N. (2011). Exploring core concepts: Sexuality, dreams and the unconscious. Response. *International Journal of Psychoanalysis*, 92: 267–269.
Laplanche, J. (1992). *Seduction, translation, drives*. London: Institute of Contemporary Arts.
— (1997). The theory of seduction and the problem of the other. *International Journal of Psychoanalysis*, 78: 653–666.
Meadow, P.W. and Green, A. (2006). "Freud and modern psychoanalysis": A discussion. *Modern Psychoanalysis*, 31: 7–24.
Meltzer D. and Harris Williams, M. (1988). *The apprehension of beauty*. Strath Tay, Scotland: Clunie Press.
Milner, M. (1969). *The hands of the living God*. New York: Routledge.

Ogden, T.H. (1994a). The analytic third: Working with intersubjective clinical facts. *International Journal of Psychoanalysis*, 75: 3–20.
— (1994b). *Subjects of analysis*. Northvale, New Jersey: Aronson/London: Karnac.
— (1997). Reverie and metaphor: How I work as a pyschoanalyst. *International Journal of Psychoanalysis*, 78: 719–732.
— (2004a). The analytic third: Implications for psychoanalytic theory and technique. *The Psychoanalytic Quarterly*, 73: 167–195.
— (2004b). This art of psychoanalysis: Dreaming undreamt dreams and interrupted cries. *International Journal of Psychoanalysis*, 85: 857–877.
— (2018). How I talk with my patients. *The Psychoanalytic Quarterly*, 87: 399–413.
Perelberg, R. J. (Ed.) (2018). *Psychic bisexuality: A British-French dialogue*. New York: Routledge.
Phillips, A . (2016). *Unforbidden pleasures: Rethinking authority, power and vitality*. New York: Farrar, Straus and Giroux.
Saketopoulou, A. (2014). To suffer pleasure: The shattering of the ego as the psychic labor of perverse sexuality. *Studies in Gender and Sexuality*, 15: 254–268.
Scarfone, D. (2013). A brief introduction to the work of Jean Laplanche. *International Journal of psychoanalysis*, 94: 545–566.
Schore, A. (2012). *The science of the art of psychotherapy*. New York: Norton.
Spezzano, C. (1993). *Affect in psychoanalysis: A clinical synthesis*. Hillsdale, NJ: The Analytic Press.
Stein, R. (1998). The poignant, the excessive and the enigmatic in sexuality. *International Journal of Psychoanalysis*, 79: 259–268.
— (2008). The otherness of sexuality: Excess. *Journal of the American Psychoanalytic Association*, 56: 43–71.
Stern, D. (2013a). Field theory in psychoanalysis, Part 1: Harry Stack Sullivan and Madeleine and Willy Baranger. *Psychoanalytic Dialogues*, 23: 487–501.
— (2013b). Field theory in psychoanalysis, Part 2: Bionian field theory and contemporary interpersonal/relational psychoanalysis. *Psychoanalytic Dialogues*, 23: 630–645.
— (2015). *Relational freedom: Emergent properties of the interpersonal field*. New York: Routledge.
Thomson-Salo, F. and Paul, C. (2017). Understanding the sexuality of infants within caregiving relationships in the first year. *Psychoanalytic Dialogues*, 27: 320–337.
Vaughan, S. (2017). In the night kitchen: What are the ingredients of infantile sexuality. *Psychoanalytic Dialogues*, 27: 344–348.
Widlocher, D. (Ed.) (2002). *Infantile sexuality and attachment*. New York: Other Press.
Winnicott, D.W. (1965). *The maturational processes and the facilitating environment: Studies in the theory of emotional development*. The International Psychoanalytical Library, 64: 1–276. London: Hogarth Press.

— (1968). Communication Between Infant and Mother, and Mother and Infant, Compared and Contrasted. In Joffe, W. G. (Ed.), *What is Psychoanalysis?* London: Balliere, Tindall & Cassell Ltd., published for the Institute of Psychoanalysis, 1968, pp 15–25.
— (1971). *Playing and reality*. London: Tavistock Publications.
— (1988). *Human nature*. New York: Schocken Books.

Part I

Erotic vitality in analytic process

Chapter 1

Moving from within the maternal
The choreography of analytic eroticism

In this chapter, I describe the clinician's analytic activity as akin to that found in choreography, where the structuring of a dance or of a session each expresses an inner impulse brought into narrative form. I link the embodied art of dance to the clinician's creative vitality in contributing to the shaping of the movement of a session. In offering my formulation of an *analytic eroticism*, I hope to expand the terrain of what might traditionally be viewed as erotic transference and countertransference.

Just as photography captures and preserves a series of images, choreography creates and preserves a series of images of the human body in motion infused with the vitality of libidinal energies. Clinically, when the creation of a symbolic narrative moves into the verbal while retaining this embodied, affective component, transformation of psychic pain is possible. The aesthetic capacity to keep this embodied vitality alive in the analytic relationship is the quality I refer to as analytic eroticism. Taking up the concept of maternal eroticism presented by Kristeva (2014), I explore the "multiverse" of mother/child erotic sensibilities—the dance of the semiotic *chora*—as well as considering a parallel engagement within the analytic dyad.

Kristeva (2014) offers an evocative pairing: "Reliance, or maternal eroticism" (p. 69). An intimate equivalence is suggested. The relationship between the two intrigues. Yet, *who* is it that relies on maternal eroticism? Kristeva indicates that a mother relies on her eroticism in mothering her child, but also that the child relies on the mother's eroticism in developing a vibrant sense of self. The encounter with the mother as erotic being brings into being the child's erotic self, both in the specifically sexual and in the most general sense: vitality in living, a curious and creative engagement with life—Eros, rather than functional adaptation. We as a species rely on our inheritance of maternal eroticism as crucial to our humanity—a generational transmission of tantalizing tenderness and fierce passions in an embodied relationship with mother, with self, and with the world. This bequest is, I suggest, what we as clinicians—women and men—may hope to help each patient access and elaborate, as well as, necessarily, to contact in ourselves. In Kristeva's conceptualization of maternal eroticism, we find hints of an enlarged understanding of what might be encompassed within the erotic life of the analytic couple.

Kristeva (2014) emphasizes that reliance does not mean maternal omnipresence, but is instead concerned with releasing "another living subject to the world" (p. 76) while "accompanying the living" (p. 78). The mother–infant dyad relies on circulating eroticism within their pairing—a force of life, a rhythmic pulsing that brings them together and sends them apart. A mother relies on her eroticism to *invest* in her baby and in its development *and* to turn her in directions of desire other than her child, setting a limit, a line between the two, allowing for a state of *emergence* from the stasis of a closed unit, and thus supporting the child's unique unfolding *as well as her own*. This dynamic pairing would ideally form the foundation for an experience of a couple relation that breathes—connecting in, releasing out, oscillating, but sustaining over time. Maternal capacity in this regard rests on an internalization of erotic vitality from her own mother (and father)[1] that forwards her own unique trajectories in multiple directions.

As Kristeva states, the mother *holds*; she is not a passive by-stander; she stands by her child; she is committed. Without abandoning, she also needs to release any "hold" that would grip, constrict. Contact with her erotic self supports each of these activities that can seem to be opposing but are each essential to life—hers, the baby's, the couple's, the species's. The parental sexual couple must also be kept in view; maternal eroticism is not solely in relation to the child, for the child, but an aspect of a woman as a sexual being in fullness.

In this chapter, and in this book as a whole, I hold to the *erotic* in maternal eroticism, which is not typically what comes to mind when thinking of an ethic of responsible care and concern. My focus is on the potentiating capacities of eroticism for the analytic dyad. Thus, I will not be addressing directly the ways in which aggressive impulses and the metabolism of hate play an important role in a mother's relationship to her infant. Kristeva's (2014) conceptualization of maternal eroticism is a highly complex formulation regarding the dynamic interplay of conflicting impulses and feeling states. My concern is that, in the very complexity of her theorizing, the erotic is in danger of slipping away from sustained attention. Psychoanalytic theorizing seems to find it easier to stay with themes of tender attachment, violent attack or the abject. We quickly lose any erotic rooting. In thinking about what maternal eroticism might mean for us as clinicians, we need to be able to envision how maternal eroticism materializes—in what ways it matters—between an actual mother and her child, and then between an analyst and patient.

As Kristeva so provocatively elaborates, an *erotic* environment exists between mother and baby. In these developmental beginnings, the relation with the mother provides a sensuous matrix, "a phonic and kinetic envelope" (Widawsky, 2014, p. 62)—an aesthetic birthplace of movement, meaning, and shaping of the self: "For Kristeva, the semiotic is not simply part of the signifying process; it is also a component of the identity and construction of the self" (Widawsky, 2014, p. 62).

I have described the *nursing couple* (Winnicott, 1965) as engaged in the first, primal act of intercourse, with breast-feeding sexually stimulating for infants of both sexes, as well as for the mother (Elise, 1998b, 2001).[2] In my work on maternal desire, I include the *mother's* desire and desire *for* the mother (Elise, 1998a, 1998b, 2000a, 2000b, 2001, 2002a, 2002b, 2007, 2008, 2012, 2015a, 2015b). Encountering the erotic beauty of the mother, the infant experiences an aesthetic world "scintillating with meaning" (Meltzer and Harris Williams, 1988, p. 14) and feels, with excitement, the pulsing vibrations of its own psychesoma. Bodily movement is emotional life now given visible form in a mutual dance of desire.

Maternal eroticism is the affective atmosphere, the embodied vitality of this psychic space that, in Winnicottian (1971) terms, might be thought of as the "environmental mother," but is here conceptualized as alive with the erotic. An impulse to move rhythmically derives from maternal eroticism that libidinally energizes the mother–infant duet.[3] Their sensual dance becomes the infant's first choreography, in the repetition and patterning of these expressive movements. Civitarese (2012) suggests "from the interaction with the mother the child's . . . flow [of] sensations and emotions receives its first cadence . . . the rhythmic repetition of sensory-motor patterns produces configurations and schemas that give shape to experience and a sense of continuity to the body" (p. 143). This "dancing" already partakes of the mother's adult sexuality, albeit enigmatically (Laplanche, 1992) and is, for the infant, a full-bodied, nude embrace with excitation to every part of the mind and body, including genitally (Freud, 1905), that will form the template for the adult dance of sex.

Eroticism in the maternal matrix: the dance of development

As envisioned by Kristeva (2014), maternal eroticism is both a libidinal energy and a creative surround. This semiotic *chora* is a space for mutual creation within the maternal matrix—"womb"—where the sensually embodied mother–infant interaction can be shaped reciprocally and given increasing symbolic form. This "primary maternal preoccupation" (Winnicott, 1956, p. 300)—the mother's preoccupation with the infant, as well as the infant's with the mother (Elise, 2007)—should not be viewed reductively as a "symbiotic" relationship, but as a complex, mutual engagement leading to increasing individuation. Borrowing the term from Plato, "Kristeva emphasizes the *chora's* motility," (McAfee, 2004, p. 20)—a rhythmic space of spontaneous movement by which significance is constituted. Moving from within the maternal, a child eventually takes its first steps into the symbolic, a realm that is most meaningfully expressive when enlivened by semiotic motility.

I propose dance as paradigmatic of the semiotic and choreography as exemplifying a symbolic communication that retains its bodily, affective force. Dance gives shape to affective expression through embodied motion, e-motion. When patterned and available for recollection and reiteration, dance becomes choreography—an embodied narrative of emotional experience. Choreography is uniquely expressive of the transformations of the semiotics of dance into symbolic representation, where the link to affective embodiment remains intact: dance becomes symbolic narration without losing the libidinal energies of bodily motility alive in the *chora*.[4]

Although the term choreography derives from a slightly different Greek root (*choreia*: dance) than *chora* (place), there exists "an element of similarity in that the Greek root for dance was related to a (certain) space" (Ramo, 1999, p. 324; cited in Das, 2012, p. 117). Dance unfolds in the place where maternal eroticism enlivens the space, unleashing libidinal energies and creative imagination, the meaningful patterning of which is choreography: "Signification is like a transfusion of the living body into language" (Oliver, 1997, p. xx)—an aesthetic leap into the symbolic.

I underscore that dance, with its primal beginnings, both pre and postnatal, is the *most fully embodied* form of art, giving shape to affective life through movement. Each human starts out prenatally with mother as dance partner. Held in the embrace of the mother's swaying body, the prenatal infant is waltzed around the womb, set in motion, always accompanied by the rhythmic beat of mother's heart, the song of her voice, even when she is not actually singing. The fetus eventually responds with a solo—a first kick, so exciting to the mother (and to the fetus?). Surely there must be, in this mother–infant duet, continuity from the womb to the rocking embrace of the mother's arms and lap,[5] with nursing returning the baby to proximity with the musical beat of the mother's heart emanating from the depths of her body.[6]

Torsti (2000) describes this "dance":

> At four months, the infant seems to begin a dreamy movement of the hand during breastfeeding, (p. 289) . . . In some children, this movement develops into an extensive plastic motion of the hand, dreamily and with a wide sweep . . . *As the infant grows, this movement may take on a dance-like form* . . . The rhythm of the sweeping movement of the hand is from the very beginning, at the age of four months, quite different from the rhythm of sucking the breast. It seems to express an inner music or a calm breathing. In fact I observed one baby making these movements at the point of falling asleep, when the father began to play the piano. In my view, *in these movements the infant expresses its own, separately experienced kinesthetic image of itself;* . . . *The sweeping, dance-like movement forms a space for self-definition and draws the outline of the self.*
>
> (p. 290, emphasis added)[7]

I am putting forth that this mother–infant dance *is* maternal eroticism, and that when maternal eroticism is foreclosed, the dance is as well: "The dance did not develop in any of those infants whose mothers experienced anxiety during the feeding" (Torsti, 2000, p. 290). Torsti is referring to a deep and pervasive anxiety, not an idealized expectation that a mother be without any anxiety. When a *pas de deux* is able to flourish, these movements of the body-self evolve throughout development into increasingly complex "choreographies" that express personal creativity in the shaping of the self. Such dances unfold and gather form in repeated sequences—choreographies unique to that pairing, available for recall and to give meaning in a symbolic realm that expands beyond the verbal:

> Language is but one manifestation of symbolic functioning. Other manifestations of symbolic functioning include the use of sign language, gesture, pantomime, mimicry, the dance, the use of visual imagery in organizing thought, music, mathematical symbols, and dramatically-organized actions . . . All of these are expressions of the underlying semiotic function. When we speak of the language of the body, we should, to be more accurate, refer to expressions of the bodily self. The artist and the musician express feelings and communicate with others without utilizing language.
> (Call, 1980, p. 260)

In so doing, artists connect us to our mother–child origins and to the aesthetic pleasures of our first communications.

Choreography as artistic expression and as metaphor for clinical process

Dance as a creative art form is a lyrical language that uses the body to speak—a communication uniquely shaped to express deep feeling. In dance, one listens attentively to the music, actual or internal, and to how it moves you to move. A feeling is evoked by the music along with a wish to convey this feeling in bodily movement. Dance is an emotional process—a transference, one might say, to the music. From an internal impulse, one responds with a particular gesture and then another and another, out of the myriad of ways the human body can move, the multitude of possible steps. Finding certain movements that "fit" with an inner feeling in response to a registering of the particular qualities of the music, one develops these steps choreographically into recognizable, but varying, and increasingly complex, patterns.

Going beyond improvisation, in choreography one is conscious of building up a narrative, placing chosen steps in a refrain that can be recalled and revisited. One listens to each musical phrase repeatedly, (as we each listen attentively to the "notes" of our patients), and gradually finds and develops the movements that most express what you want to say with your body. An emotionally expressive communication is being shaped that can be made use of over time, returned to for further reflection; the process is like composing a symphony or crafting a poem, *and* it is like the narrative building process of psychoanalysis.

With writing, one arranges words on paper in order to convey a compelling theme. As with writing, a "topic" suggested in dance by a piece of music engages one in a personal way and you find your theme to express in a structured sequence. Each of these creative expressions differ from improvising in that one will take much time to choreograph an intricate pattern—a creative sequencing of emotionally salient themes—that can be held in mind. A choreographed dance sequence gives creative expression to an emotional truth and is itself beauty. As with any art form, there is a mastered technique underlying the aesthetic expression of dance and choreography.

Psychoanalysis has a richly developing literature on musical or dramatic improvisation as a metaphor for a clinical process (see especially Knoblauch, 2000; Ringstrom, 2001; Markman, 2006; Kindler, 2010). Such clinical exchanges of creative spontaneity in intersubjective engagement might be thought of as various forms of a squiggle game (Winnicott, 1971). Adding to, and extending from this literature, I make use of choreography specifically, rather than improvisation alone, as a metaphor for the psychoanalytic process of *creating symbolic narratives.*

My focus on the transformation of psychic pain through a dyadic capacity for narrative building and creative use of metaphor draws upon the work of Ogden (1997) and Civitarese and Ferro (2013), as well as upon the psychoanalytic theorizing of unrepresented states and deficits in the capacity to symbolize (see de Cortinas, 2009, 2013; Levine, Reed, and Scarfone, 2013). My approach—what I think of as a Winnicottian field theory—I bring to my engagement with Kristeva's (2014) conceptualization of the erotic within the mother–infant relationship.

In my emphasis on meaningful sequencing derived from two-person spontaneous improvising, I most especially want to retain, as is the case in dance, the connection to the erotic vitality that derives from maternal eroticism—embodied, and *moving*—both physically and emotionally. The erotic is an important ingredient of the clinical situation, fueling the creative self of both the analyst and the patient. This perspective has implications for the psychoanalytic process, especially in the qualities of the activity of the analyst, as reflected in the analyst's person, presence, and personal creativity—an area of increasing interest and consideration.

I suggest that a choreographic process takes place in productive clinical work, both in individual sessions and in the overall treatment arc. Our clinical narratives become verbal choreographies that need to retain affective resonance with bodies in motion. We know that this "dance" of psychoanalysis is not the creative product of the patient's mind alone. Clinical work invites, *requires*, a choreographic engagement by the clinician in concert with that of the patient. A clinician cannot do this creative work without embodied responsiveness to the patient's "music"—the patient's verbal and non-verbal communications—and personal repertoire of "steps."

Even more challenging is the situation of working with a patient who is without music or movement—someone for whom maternal eroticism has failed and where the mother–infant dance has not developed. Kristeva (1993) describes "maladies of the soul" where representational failures silence the self. With such patients in whom symbolic representation is restricted or foreclosed, analytic eroticism is a crucial element in awakening both the analyst's and the patient's capacity for narrative meaning-making. De Cortinas (2009) refers to this capacity for creative symbolization as the aesthetic dimension of the mind: "This dimension enlightens the crossroads between psychoanalysis, art and myth" (p. xxiii). Civitarese (2012) writes that, "aesthetic experience continues to help the subject on different occasions throughout his life to find a fuller sense of consonance and contact between mind and body" (p. 145). Such is the clinical aim.

Clinical illustration: a still and arid landscape

When Sue, single and in her mid-thirties, first sat across from me, my immediate reaction was a registering of a profound asexuality. I was quite surprised by this palpable feeling, as I do not tend to consciously assess people on a scale of sexuality. I tried to account for my reaction in her very bland appearance: pale coloring without make-up or jewelry, drab, shapeless clothing with skirts just below the knees; sitting with both feet planted squarely on the floor, Sue seemed neutral to the point of neutered. I had the image of someone a century ago from a farm in a "Great Plain" state. Yet clearly this visual image was the tip of the iceberg; something was wrong at a much deeper level, creating a feeling that something human was missing, frozen out, as if a lizard was coolly regarding me.

Sue reported that her childhood in a small town seemed "normal, uneventful; nothing much happened." Both parents had been accountants, as Sue now was; an older brother, a physicist, remains unmarried. Sue did not date during high school; descriptions of sex with a current boyfriend sounded mechanical, transactional. When exploring what had brought her to see me, she had difficulty getting affective hold of anything meaningful and vaguely offered, "something doesn't seem right . . . I want to get married." She seemed a female Mr. Spock (Star Trek) looking with perplexity at the emotional tribulations of the humans around her. Diagnostically, I thought in terms of schizoid mechanisms and the anti-libidinal self (Fairbairn, 1944).

Sue had recently seen another analyst for a few months, whom she described as "accounting for my childhood with a lot of ideas, but nothing came of it." Her word choice conveyed the absence of reciprocal stimulation, nothing consummated, coming alive. Sue experienced the analytic relationship as an intellectualized exchange between disembodied talking heads, accounting for things in a way that "didn't match up," reminiscent of her accountant parents who tallied numbers, but were not accountable for emotional engagement and bodily relation.

Over the next year or so, Sue reported details of her life as an accountant, describing problems at work, "numbers not lining up" in a deadening delivery that matched the content. Never have I been more challenged clinically to stay alert and engaged, recruiting my own vitality in what felt like a monumental effort on my part to enliven any of the material. I watched the clock inching along in five-minute increments, during what would seem like an infinity of time. Nevertheless, I did manage in most sessions to pull something together from this void of material, linking her recitation to what felt to me to be a more affectively enlivening connection, between thoughts, and between Sue and me. I was feeling both relieved, and a bit amazed, that this could be accomplished and fairly pleased with my ability to make something of her flat, arid presentation.

Then, at one point, things came to a complete dead halt; I asked Sue how she was feeling with me. She responded in a very direct and matter of fact way: "You seem quite depressed." I was quite stunned by this pronouncement and rendered speechless for a few moments until I managed to ask gently what her ideas were about the source of my depression.

Sue: (silent for several moments) . . . "Maybe you lost a child." After another pause, I inquired: "lost?" and Sue replied: "you know, . . . dead." We were both quiet for several minutes taking in this exchange. I then softly commented: "There is a dead baby and a depressed mother; it's not clear which happened first." Sue was quiet for the last few moments of this session. The next day she went back to describing the challenges of accounting.

I palpably feel that I am an analyst, woman, mother who cannot keep her baby alive. I start to have an image of the couch on which Sue is lying as a sterile, metal incubator, almost a cage, where conditions would meet requirements for maintaining life support, but nothing more. Nothing soft or warm is provided that would meet or awaken sensual needs. There is no mother, no nursing couple, no erotic duet that would ever lead to a full-bodied dance of adult sexuality. I too am hard and sterile, inanimate, no flesh, no breasts, no sexuality. I experience myself as the "wire mother monkey" so familiar to those in our field from the Harlow studies (1959). Clinically, I realize that I need to inhabit this transference/ countertransference situation (Carpy, 1989; Mitrani, 2001) of deadness and dehumanization, *while at the same time holding onto my analytic eroticism as a latent capacity in my embodied, feeling self.* I will need to wait for an opportunity where I can call up this aspect of my person and of my analytic presence in order to introduce it to my patient in a manner that she might be able to register and digest.

Feeling that a scientific study might pique her interest, I ask Sue if she has heard of the Harlow monkey study. She reads a science journal and I think that she might have come across a reference to it. She replies: "Maybe, but I don't recall." Proceeding quite slowly, gently, with the cadence and tones of telling a story to a latency age child, I relate the set-up of the study where the baby monkey, in a cage, is presented with both a wire mesh "mother" with a bottle of milk attached and with a cloth "mother" with no milk.

A: What do you imagine the baby monkey did?
P: I don't know; I've never had a pet before . . . Well it would need the milk, but it probably wouldn't know what to do with that other one.

In her phrasing, "I've never had a pet *before*," is an intimation that I have just given Sue her *first* pet and with it the chance to mother and be mothered, to pet and be petted, with such petting as foreplay to adult sexuality. She had never had a pet, or a pat, from her mother; she was not petted; no breast-mother exists. In giving her a pet, I am introducing maternal erotic energies—mine and the potential for hers—in the experience of touching and being touched, emotionally as well as physically. In my feeling tone and rhythm of telling the "story," the poignancy of the baby monkey's plight is brought to life, as in a ballet. I now begin to feel that in the patient I have a human infant—one who needs an IV drip of maternal eroticism, an infusion of vitality into an infant who does not yet know what to do with the flesh and blood mother holding her. Previously I had been either the wire mother with my intellectual "formula," or the cloth mother who did not have any recognizable "food."

In my introducing a "baby" for the two of us—"our pet"—and a symbolic blanket for the couch, the incubator cage and wire mother begin to transform; something starts moving; our bodily selves engage. Ours is not just a story creation *about* (missing) maternal eroticism, but an experience developing from within the analyst's own expression *of* maternal eroticism—"the medium as the message," matching and enlivening the content. Now relational space opens for us to develop our dance of embodied relation to one another, supporting our continuing quest for affective meaning. Although the verbal content of our exchanges is the easier to identify and report, much is taking place kinesthetically in our unfolding relationship.

Time passes and one day Sue is describing a film:

P: It had a lesbian sex scene . . .
A: Your reactions?
P: (Long pause) lots of breasts.

This rather odd statement gives rise in my mind to Picasso-esque images of disjointed female figures. I am not sure if "lots of breasts" represent a positive or negative image for the patient. In exploring her feelings, Sue becomes able to articulate a feeling that she has not previously "encountered" breasts: "I don't think of my mother as having breasts. I don't relate to having breasts myself; what are they there for? They seem in the way, extraneous." Her mother's sexual body is seen in dislocated, confusing images, where human parts are not assembled in any recognizable manner; sexuality does not "come together." There is an acute sense of not being of the human species—not *mammalian*—that conveys the absence of eroticism from the outset in relation to her mother's psychesoma and her own.

Whereas, in the film scene, the sexual engagement of two women allows for the opportunity to both suck and to be suckled, an erotic mouth-nipple contact which is genitally stimulating to each partner, unfolding into a full sexual experience—a coming together. As Sue and I absorb the images of this scene, and attune to them over time in our verbal and non-verbal communication, a space opens for a sexual sense of self. In our dyad, this development was not expressed as conscious erotic desire *for* the other (as in traditional conceptualizations of erotic transference–countertransference), but as two women who can each embody erotic vitality individually and in a more lively engagement with one another. Sue starts to come alive as a woman who has breasts. Her analyst begins to take form as an erotic woman with breasts and a sexuality—a woman whose erotic connection with her baby will not only keep the baby alive, but ensure that she thrives and can mate/matter/mother:

P: You have breasts.
A: Does that seem to offer any possibilities?
P: I think so; I'm not sure about it.

Paradoxically, our dance of maternal deprivation shapes the beginning of our connection, offering an invitation to vitality, an *"invitalization"* of the analytic relationship. This vitalization (Alvarez, 2012) of the clinical situation—a libidinal force field—constitutes the expanded meaning of erotic transference–countertransference that I have in mind, where both patient and analyst engage their erotic energies and where this engagement is not specific to (though it may include) erotic desire for the other. While becoming more erotically alive with one another, Sue and I choreograph, slowly with much repetition, an embodied narrative of missing mothers and deadened babies.

What I had, in the initial months of the analysis, hoped to inject into the analytic atmosphere, had gone unrecognized by Sue: my libidinal energy was accessible to me, but she had no "receptor sites." I begin to name the problem in my introducing the figure of the motherless monkey—a casting of a character within the analytic field (Ferro and Civitarese, 2016): "What matters is that the choice of characters—which we repeat, must be accepted rather than imposed, since it is after all an aesthetic choice—should lead to the weaving of a narration with the potential for favorable development" (p. 138).

My affective telling of the monkey's plight opens up a path forward that eventually leads to the possibility of an intercourse between us as suggested in the lesbian sex scene; breasts make an appearance in the patient's psychic life. We are now warm-blooded mammals who can become hot-blooded sexual beings. Gradually Sue develops the awareness regarding her relational beginnings with her mother that "something was probably left out—skipped." Things are warming up for us on the dance floor.

Over the next many months, small steps are taken by Sue that show up in timid changes in her appearance, with spots of color appearing both in clothing and in make-up, reflective of a brightening of her personality. One day she comes in looking very appealing, pretty even, in a lively print skirt that is now above the knee and swirling with movement, as is her now longer, curlier hair. Viewing this transformation is like watching a withered branch that suddenly springs to life in a profusion of blooms after a long winter: Something is budding. Sue announces that she is going to a salsa class.

Ours is a small choreography—a minuet—carefully danced, and tentative, though not tepid. Although our duet shows no signs of turning into a torrid tango or a passionate *pas de deux*, it is emotionally meaningful to the two of us, full of poignant, painful feeling about missed opportunities, in a way that previously could not be narrated or even known. Ferro (2006a) wrote of a patient who at a pivotal moment, linking both her relationship to her analyst and to her lost mother, dreamt of doing classical dance. Emotions were:

> progressively being released and coming alive inside her ... rewriting in metaphorical form a history that was previously not fully thinkable, and therefore also not fully expressible in words. . . . The story of the trauma makes its entrance into the analytic field in this way
> (pp. 1052–1053)

I certainly do feel more of the energies of my own creative activity in my engagement with other patients and more rewarded by the intricacies of other duets and the opportunities afforded therein. With Sue I do not experience the thrill of a more intricately choreographed sequence possible with other patients who, even with areas of symbolic failure, bring much more of their own liveliness and creativity to our encounter. Yet, it is especially with deadened patients that analytic eroticism is so vital an element, breathing life and dimensionality into a flat landscape.

With Sue, I initially had the experience of approaching a woman who was more wall than wall-flower. Something was in need of being brought into life—to become animate, before animated—in order to even invite her out onto the dance floor. Kristeva (2014) emphasizes that maternal eroticism involves libidinal stamina to stand by one's commitment to another—"a refusal to collapse" (p. 77) in one's concern for and "care of the living" (p. 77): "This specific eroticism, which *maintains the urgency of life* up to the limits of life, I call *reliance*"(p. 79)—"a *herethic*"(p. 82), heretical in its claim of maternal eroticism as ethical care.[8] I propose a parallel heresy within the clinical situation.

Analytic ardor: the heretical ethics of the analyst's eroticism

The Harlow (1959) studies on attachment demonstrated that, in a choice between provisions of food or softness, sensuality wins out. The long-term import of being without the erotic presence of a live mother is not apparent until it is noted that none of these monkeys at maturity could mate. I underscore that the babies could not "mate," matter, with their actual mothers as a nursing couple in a full-bodied, skin to skin, "dance." We note the shared root of the words mater, matter, and mate yet can lose that maternal erotic connection in a desexualized understanding of attachment and early object relations, when sexuality is sequestered in the province of the oedipal (Elise, 1998b, 2007, 2015a). In the actuality of the mother–infant bond, the infant's erotic body is "mapped"[9] (Laplanche, 1992) by the sensuous care of the mother, derived from her own embodied eroticism and sexuality (Freud, 1905).

For Sue, instead of *enigmatic* signifiers (Laplanche, 1992), the signifiers were *absent* and there was no encounter with the enigma of human sexuality as presented in the maternal matrix. As an adult, Sue, like her brother, was having trouble mating. Psychoanalytic theorizing itself has been having trouble mating sexuality with early object relations (Elise, 1998b); clinicians may themselves be walled off from the enigmatic variations of the erotic that encompass the evolutions of both the semiotic and the symbolic, the pre-oedipal and the oedipal. I believe that Kristeva's

(2014) perspective, building on Freud and Laplanche, illuminates the infusion of the erotic throughout development and into what is seemingly other than sexual: "It falls to us to create new metapsychological concepts in order to develop—by paying attention to the sexuality of the lover—the elucidation and support of maternal eroticism, in all its specificity" (p. 82).

In working with Sue, I could not rely solely on my intellectual knowledge of child development gone awry, using analytic theory to form interpretations; we would have remained at a *stale*-mate where intellects cannot create anything alive to break up the deadness of the non-interchange. Lombardi (2011) described this dynamic as one where "you can wind up with *two* surrogates in the office" in the effort to conduct a "scientifically correct" analysis (p. 4). The situation was not one of *re*vitalizing, but of newly vitalizing. An absence of the analyst's erotically embodied vitality as the core, *chora*, of analytic activity would undermine the potential to create together a symbolic narrative with emotional salience. I needed to actively contribute my own creative sensibilities to the effort to symbolize a narrative choreography with the patient that could speak to her unnamed, and as yet, unnamable, problem.

I believe that this type of energy with its erotic substrate is what analysts frequently call upon in clinical work; otherwise, less progress would be made. My intent is to *make this erotic, energic component explicit in theorizing a clinical technique*, rather than left as tabooed, neglected, or cordoned off into a narrow conceptualization: "erotic countertransference." Maternal eroticism is introduced clinically through the aesthetic overture of analytic eroticism. I underscore the *aesthetic* component in my conceptualization of analytic eroticism; the analyst's erotic vitality is made use of creatively, just as an artist can paint or photograph an erotic nude without it being pornography. This sensory/semiotic dance evolves into a choreographic capacity for symbolic expression, not as dry abstraction, but as genuine emotional experience embedded in embodied eroticism. If it seems heretical to claim an erotic component in ethical analytic presence, *why* is this the case? Can we speak of an analytic ardor?

Kristeva's (2014) conceptualization of maternal eroticism leads her to posit a heretical ethics of maternal care: "To live and to think the maternal as *erotic*, wouldn't that be as provocative as infantile sexuality" (p. 69). Yet, I believe that Kristeva's culminating choice of descriptors for herethics—such as "care," "concern," "love," and "tenderness"—will likely be settled upon by readers who wish to comfortably retreat from the provocation of the erotic. As each of the articles contextualizing Kristeva's text highlight, analysts, even while acknowledging infantile sexuality, still balk at the idea of maternal eroticism—a topic "too hot to handle" (Litowitz, 2014, p. 58)—resulting in a disappearance of the mother's sexual body. Balsam (2014) argues that: "We have strayed far from the centrality of libido" (p. 87): In contrast to Kristeva's work where "the mutuality of erotics springs to life" (p. 89), we see "the massive resistance we are up against with this topic" (p. 94). This is what Wilson (2014) describes as "a shrinking of psychoanalytic theory building in the face of the . . . flesh, the feminine, the maternal" (p. 105). I emphasize that psychoanalytic theorizing exhibits possibly an even more profound recoiling from analytic eroticism. Paraphrasing Kristeva, I propose in parallel formation: To live and to think the *analytic* as erotic, wouldn't *that* be provocative.

If we could overcome obstacles to analytic eroticism, we might then consider the ways in which psychoanalysis is indeed an erotic project. We are besieged with lamentable examples of the destructive aspects of erotic desire in the treatment relationship—sexual boundary violations—leading, I believe, to a heightened sense of fear in clinicians about engaging the erotic, their patients' and their own (Elise, 2002a, 2015a). Keeping Kristeva's sensibilities near, how might we think of eroticism as constructive to a treatment; can analytic eroticism actually "hold" the clinical couple?

Analysts tend to focus predominantly on the patient's libidinal attachment to the analyst in the transference. Yet what of the analyst's excitement, not altruism or duty, in contributing to the development of a person—the clinician's libidinal investment in that unique patient, in that analysis? An analysis cannot rest on the patient's libidinal energies alone. We might, instead, think of erotic energy as circulating in multiple directions in the intersubjective field of an analysis—a libidinally alive matrix. Often viewed *solely* as problematic countertransference, which it certainly can be, *the analyst's erotic energy has the potential be a healing ingredient necessary for the analytic process*. A clinical situation of vibrancy can foster patients' increased libidinal investments in *themselves*, not just in the analyst. If our creative self, imbued with our libidinal being, is not actively contributing to the unfolding of the clinical process and narrative, the analysis is deprived of the life force of the erotic.

How might an ongoing reflection on, and self-inquiry into, our erotic selves effect a subtle shift in the self we each bring to the consulting room?

Can we allow for more of the full palette of *our* psyches within the clinical venture rather than being restricted to a pale version of ourselves (Elise, 2007)? The "blank screen" is itself a "colourless canvas"—the metaphor used by Levine (2012) to describe the psychic emptiness of patients suffering from failures in symbolic representation. Both images—screen and canvas—convey a two-dimensional flatness, stasis and neutral shading. I want to shift the metaphor of a blank screen—analyst as subdued, almost erased figure—to a more colorful image, moving analytic "function" from abstinence to sustenance, a quality of aliveness in the analyst that is sustaining, rather than a re-presentation of a deadened mother.

In offering a conceptualization of an analytic eroticism, I am speaking of *analytic vitality*, rather than neutrality. It is worth noting that the concept of neutrality derived from Freud's (1915) caution to clinicians to remain "indifferent" to erotic transference. The technical response to this warning seems to have either frozen the analyst or inadvertently contributed to volcanic eruptions of boundary violations when indifference could no longer be maintained. We have not learned how to work *with* our eroticism in an ethical manner. I am proposing that a creative use of our erotic energies provides an aesthetic container for the erotic dimensions of the analytic field.

Contemporary conceptualizations that describe the analyst's activity in contributing to the development of a symbolic narrative, emphasize the analyst's use of her own mind to generate imagery as a key component in helping patients who are limited in this ability (Ferro, 2002, 2006a, 2006b; Civitarese, 2008; de Cortinas, 2009, 2013; Levine, Reed and Scarfone, 2013). Levine (2012) writes that analysts must actively lend our abilities for creative linking to the co-construction of narrative meaning, giving imaginative form to that which a patient may not yet have access; "that form will only be shaped as a result of our analytic efforts" (p. 608). This can be achieved, Levine (2012) states, through:

> acts of spontaneous, intuitive, internal emotional resonance and/or expression (feeling or imagining what the patient may not yet clearly feel or know)" (p. 613) that "must first be created by a work that begins in the analyst's psyche and is then offered and inscribed in the psyche of the patient as part of an interactive, intersubjective relationship and process.
>
> (p. 626)

Analysts do not solely "read the text" presented by a patient in any given session.

Yet, as Harris (2014) astutely points out, in order to be curative, our verbal narrations in the clinical encounter must be grounded in embodied experience and alive with that which is "outside the sentence" (p. 1030) by calling on "our receptivity to the sensuous, embodied aspects of speech and communication" (p. 1030) in order to create "some of the most salient and mutative moments in treatments" (p. 1031; see also Lombardi, 2011; Goldberg, 2012). Speaking to this issue, McAfee (2004) underscored:

> This is Kristeva's point: the symbolic mode of signification is meaningful because of the way the semiotic energizes it. If it weren't for the bodily energy that the speaking being brings to (and puts into) language, language would have little if any meaning for us.
>
> (p. 18)

Writing on the acquisition of language in children, Call (1980) stated: "Some of the most important messages sent between people are beyond words. The poet and creative writer utilize language to create images and to define the wordless territory of subjective experience" (p. 261). De Cortinas (2009) similarly, noted: "The adults that have the faculty of using one or many of these lost sensitivities are the ones that are specially gifted, such as composers, musicians, and dancers" (p. 11). Analysts must also utilize language in this artful way, going beyond, beneath and before the word. "Indeed, the therapeutic situation can be examined as an aesthetic medium through which to engage the dynamics of a clinical creative process fueled by each individual's embodied aesthetic" (Hagman and Press, 2010, p. 210).

I suggest that clinicians become dancers. (This should be no more challenging than the things we ask of our patients.) I trust that the reader will understand that I mean here to be playfully provocative, but with serious intent: If one finds resonance with metaphors involving other art forms, yet does not feel an opening to an identification with a dancing self—might this dis-identification with dance indicate an uneasiness with the more embodied, and therefore potentially erotic aspects of dance? Babies, children, and teens naturally delight in spontaneous movement to music; yet many adults appear to prefer artistic expressions at some remove from the body where the creation is "out there" in the instrument, canvas, clay, etc., rather than "in here, in me, in my body." With Milner's (1950) "On not being able to paint" in mind, a similar reflection on dance might be fruitful.

We see that not only do analysts need to contribute to narrative representation in the symbolic realm, such activity must be registered within *the analyst's*, not solely the patient's, embodied affective responsiveness. The semiotics of analytic eroticism permeated with libidinal energy and creative imagination provide an essential foundation in work with patients in whom early trauma has foreclosed or frozen the development of symbolic capacity. Certainly, the analyst's creative energies are not to be a substitute for the absence of such in a patient, but an enlivening contribution to the analytic encounter, even if, paradoxically, to narrate deadness and de-vitalization.

I want to stress that this capacity in the analyst is an important ingredient in *all* treatments, wherever a given patient might be—frozen or flowing—in relation to this aesthetic dimension of the mind (see de Cortinas, 2009). Each in his or her own way needs the analyst to not merely wait, watch, and applaud; too often there will be no dance created to applaud. We are not the audience to our patients; we need to feel the rhythm, the emotion, the motion, and to co-choreograph a series of movements into a ballet that can be meaningful for many years to come. Even patients with well-developed symbolic capacities—quite capable of dancing and choreographing—want and need an analytic partner who can both follow *and take the lead*. This reciprocal bodily and affective engagement presents a different image of what analysts are doing clinically from the typical conception of providing "a container."

Chora as container

As Wilson (2014) critiqued, conceptualizations of holding and containing have tended toward a disembodied, de-libidinized analytic function: "*Holding, containing, linking*, and the like, risk becoming two-dimensional psychoanalytic slogans, descriptions of maternal experience that seem to come from the outside, as asexual as they are third-person" (p. 106). Goldberg (2012) noted that even in more contemporary models where "the analyst's receptive, responsive functions are richly documented . . . the analyst's inductive or initiating functions—the way he actively engages the patient—have received less systematic attention" (p. 795). In clinical practice, an analyst may still experience containment as rather passive, where one focuses on supporting the patient's expression and is rather inhibited oneself. Similarly, a limited understanding of holding can result in a feeling of being held back as a *self*.

Fortunately, holding and containing are increasingly theorized to be active—though not yet erotic—complex processes on the part of the analyst (see especially de Cortinas, 2009; Cartwright, 2010). Ferro and Civitarese (2015, 2016) view enlarging of the containing function, in both analyst and patient, as synonymous with evolving symbolic capacities to express emotional truth through narrative construction—a joint effort, "(un)conscious narration *à deux*" (2016, p. 137). I add to these newer formulations that it is the erotic that contains, unites the container and the contained, vitalizing the field of clinical engagement. We are connected by, and within, a libidinal matrix. If not, something vital, embodied, is missing.

In contrast to psychoanalytic understandings of the container/holding environment as passive, disembodied, selfless, and static, I highlight the activity of the analyst derived from her erotic self—an inner vibration, a vibrance, a poised alertness, just as a dancer in standing still on stage is poised, not passive, at the ready, full of potential movement, momentum. These are desirable qualities in a clinician: We cannot expect to foster the development of healthy passions in our patients without these aspects of self palpably alive and embodied in *our* presence in the clinical encounter. We are poised receptivity, not a receptacle: We act, respond, and not solely from an intellectualized theory but out of our own embodied, ardent energies—something of the alive moment, momentous.

We tune in to certain strands of feeling that catch our attention, move us to move in a particular manner: to jump in, or sit quietly, to speed up or slow down the rhythm of the session, to develop a theme or motif based on our intuitive leap—striding ahead, circling back, becoming more expansive or carefully balanced, tiptoeing. Sometimes we are still, but still "dancing." Might our analytic container be a womb of conception, a dance of gestation and delivery, where an analyst's embodied Eros pairs with, and facilitates, a patient's ability to feel and express her own personal rhythm?

This ability to improvise from a spontaneous impulse and then to productively shape an emotionally evocative narrative, rich in symbolic meaning, is a choreographic capacity developed in the patient that can then be carried forward out of the consulting room and into life. Such clinical choreographies will need to be works in progress, repeatedly shaping communications that incrementally reach their affective mark with a patient who can feel within the analytic situation the rhythmic flow and movement of the analyst's eroticism as well as his or her own. This creative endeavor of the dyad, sustained and developed over time, promotes confidence, tenacity, and even courage, *in both patient and analyst*. Each member in the clinical dyad must dance to this primal mother–child rhythm in order that either, and hopefully both, can develop and grow.

The erotic in creativity

I want especially to underscore the erotic element in creativity and the creative aspect of the erotic—the central theme of this book. We see the passionate engagement one has with any creative project, with procreation as the biological, sexual prototype. In creative projects an excitement is stirred that can only be described as erotic, an investment that holds, over time— "reliance" (Kristeva, 2014)—even when a project frustrates, stalls, perplexes, one's libidinal energy seeing it through in the face of obstacles, sticking with it, sacrifice, transformation and transcendence. The overarching pleasure derived supports a long-term effort that is often not pleasurable in the immediate sense. Rather than sublimation as renunciation—a sexually submerged experience[10]—I am describing an erotic investment raised up from within oneself and extended outward.

Winnicott (1971) wrote that it is "creative apperception more than anything else that makes the individual feel that life is worth living" (p. 65). Freud (1915) had posited: "Sexual love is undoubtedly one of the chief things in life, . . . one of its culminating peaks" (p. 169). Might we think of the two intertwined—creativity and sexuality—as that which makes *psychoanalysis worth doing*, for both analyst and patient—a spirited union of bodily and psychic engagement. In the history of the analytic literature, sexual energy within the analytic dyad has been quarantined under the rubric of erotic transference and countertransference. However, as Kristeva (2014) theorizes, the semiotic *chora* may be understood as representing a space with potential, with the erotic as the "fuel" to personal creativity and aesthetic living. This potential is embodied and affectively lived through the mother–child dance of development that creates the aesthetic foundation.

A note on creativity, clinical training and professional development

Creating is how we feel engaged. I doubt that analysts could bear to do analytic work if it did not elicit our creative engagement. The analyst has the reward and the fulfillment of developing her own personal expression rather than following a theoretical and technical script. This creative use of self is our gift to each patient and the gift of psychoanalysis to each analyst. It is the path by which our work life becomes richer, more vital, over the years, rather than routinized into a dulling repetition. Many analysts have artistic interests—music, painting, sculpture, poetry, fiction, dance. Have we given enough attention to the influence of these inclinations in a given analyst on the progression of the therapeutic process?[11]

Although historically, analysts have tended to think of patients as shaping the hour, leaving the analyst to interpret what is presented, I believe that analysts are now becoming increasingly aware of how our own creative force shapes a session. Patients often say, "I had no idea we would be talking about this today;" they are correct. A patient typically begins with a direction consciously in mind, but the analyst may take the lead in a direction unanticipated by either. Their combined creative interplay has the potential to develop a meaningful theme that can gather momentum through that session and beyond.

Techniques can be taught; creativity is another matter. Being a talented dancer—able to perform with excellence someone else's combination of steps—does not mean one can necessarily choreograph. What of a clinician? An analyst should not just perform someone else's steps (an occupational hazard of being in supervision). Being a clinician requires that one can choreograph; otherwise one is merely practicing a technique.

Analysts spend many years, in training and beyond, learning the "science" of psychoanalysis; this effort is necessary and important, just as technique in dance (or in any art form) provides a foundation for artistic expression. However, in the arts, it is understood that technique, difficult and taking years to master, is only the basis from which to then move into one's own creative expression. In contrast, psychoanalytic professional development can remain focused on the technical rather than moving into the aesthetic realm. Clinicians continue to try to master increasingly more sophisticated theoretical conceptualizations in the hopes of gaining an ability for more astute technical interventions. Though likely acknowledged tacitly, less attention is given to the idea that developing one's talent as an analyst might involve something ambiguous, intuitive, artistic—something that cannot be taught by or learned from an expert, but only found within one's unique being.

Conclusion

I have suggested that the analyst being in a creative mode is an under-recognized element of how it is that patients get well. Our mode of presence (see Eshel, 2013; Markman, 2017) has its own healing and generative impact. In the analytic space, the analyst needs to dance in the place of expressive movement in order to foster the same in a patient. Otherwise, one might be encouraging spontaneous gestures (Winnicott, 1971) in a patient, but not in contact with them in oneself—a "do as I say, not as I do" model of psychoanalysis. An analyst's capacity to relate within and through a personally creative modality provides a particular environment that supports the patient's access to her own creative self. Such creative aliveness allows one to dance on the tiptoes of a spontaneous melody, living life to the fullest, with passion and zest.

I have proposed that we think of analytic eroticism as stimulating, a stimulus—providing for both patient and analyst a flexible foundation, a springboard with movement, motility, momentum (Elise, 2015b). As with a diving board, there is give and take. It is flexible and firm, something to bounce off, as well as into. Envision those exquisitely anticipatory steps the diver takes in intimate, kinesthetic relation with the board, that bounding leap into and away from, up into space, outward (swan dive as aerial dance), and then back down into the deep, only to surface again and have another go. There would be no diver without that board, no diving board without the diver—mutual reliance.

Invoking maternal eroticism, with its analytic counterpart, we can envision an expansive exuberance—the ongoing creation of a sensually based atmosphere in which we imaginatively experience our bodily and psychic selves, our minds. This lusty experience of being in the world extends beyond the maternal orbit and beyond the purely sexual to a more general joie de vivre, a passion for life in its ups *and downs*. This is of course an ideal picture of what we might hope to be the case, yet often is not. Then we see patients, like Sue, presenting with familiar problems of depression, meaninglessness—loss of joy, vitality, eagerness, and responsiveness. The "diving board" is now just a flat object with no spring; it cannot be made use of; it seems useless to try, indicative of a deadened versus creative relation to the self and one's objects.

Drawing upon the choreography of dance, I have linked this art form with a clinician's creative impulse in shaping the movement of a session. This clinical investment and responsiveness, expressing the unique libidinal connection and excitement of an analytic couple, I refer to as analytic eroticism. The aesthetic dimension of the mind must be rooted in the erotic dimension of the body. The *capacity* to choreograph or compose—in art, in psychoanalysis, in life—requires a confidence in personal expression to give shape to one's inner feeling through creative impulse, spontaneous gesture. I have described how such expressive confidence may greatly increase the effectiveness of the work and the personal reward for both patient and clinician. Each partner in this duet gains increasing access to her own choreographic capacities. When both participants are in the realm of personal creativity, together they co-create the unique choreography of that analysis, allowing the patient eventually to dance her own life.

Notes

1 Certainly males as well as females would internalize maternal eroticism and would embody this quality within a masculine sense of self in their parenting and elsewhere. What would be specific to a paternal eroticism remains to be theorized. See Thomson-Salo and Paul (2017) for an excellent start to that project.
2 See also Target (2015) regarding the link between adult sexuality and infancy.
3 "Like dance for the adult, the social world experienced by the infant is primarily one of vitality affects" (Stern, 1985, p. 57).
4 Each artistic form lends itself to use as an evocative metaphor for clinical process. My intent is to *add* the metaphors of dance and choreography to the evolving literature on creative process within psychoanalysis, not to diminish other forms of creative expression.
5 Piontelli (1987) demonstrated a continuity in prenatal with post-natal life, even in the shape of the baby's personality. See also Liley (1972) regarding the fetus as a personality with agentic mobility.
6 Condon and Sander (1974) have shown that the human newborn moves his body, arms, hands, and feet in rhythmic response to the mother's voice.
7 Tustin (1984) theorizes a "shape-making propensity" (p. 280) of the mind that in normal development facilitates an increasingly complex relationship between self and other: "It seems likely that the normal human infant has an inbuilt disposition to form 'shapes' (p. 279) . . . Normal sensation shapes are the basic rudiments for emotional, aesthetic and cognitive functioning" (p. 280).
8 Freud (1905) was no stranger to such heresy. Having written: "A child's intercourse with anyone responsible for his care affords him an unending source of sexual excitation and satisfaction . . . This is especially so since . . . his mother, herself regards him with feelings that are derived from her own sexual life" (p. 223), Freud then notes that some may consider this idea "sacrilegious."

9 Note that the flat, pen-on-paper metaphor of cartography does not do justice to the two-person, full-bodied interchange that stimulates the libidinal awakening of the infant.
10 Stating that the Freudian theory of sublimation has since its inception been ill-defined, and is now outmoded, Civitarese (2016) aims to reinvent this concept.
11 Knoblauch (2000) notably introduced within Relational theory the manner in which his involvement with music enriches his clinical practice. Ogden (1999) described the resonance of psychoanalysis with poetry, and Peltz (2012) with painting.

References

Alvarez, A. (2012). *The thinking heart: Three levels of psychoanalytic therapy with disturbed children*. London: Routledge.
Balsam, R. (2014). The embodied mother: Commentary on Kristeva. *Journal of the American Psychoanalytic Association*, 62: 87–100.
Call, J. D. (1980). Some prelinguistic aspects of language development. *Journal of the American Psychoanalytic Association*, 28: 259–289.
Carpy, D.V. (1989). Tolerating the countertransference: A mutative process. *International Journal of Psychoanalysis*, 70: 287–294.
Cartwright, D. (2010). *Containing states of mind*. London: Routledge.
Civitarese, G. (2008). *The intimate room: Theory and technique of the analytic field*. London: Routledge.
— (2012). *The violence of emotions:Bion and post-Bionian psychoanalysis*. London: Routledge.
— (2016). On sublimation. *International Journal of Psychoanalysis*, 97: 1369–1392.
Civitarese, G. and Ferro, A. (2013). The meaning and use of metaphor in analytic field theory. *Psychoanalytic Inquiry*, 33: 190–209.
Condon, W. S. and Sander, L. W. (1974). Neonate movement is synchronized with adult speech: Interactional participation and language acquisition. *Science*, 183: 99–101.
Das, A. (2012). *Toward a politics of the (im)possible: The body in third world feminisms*. New York: Anthem Press.
de Cortinas, L. P. (2009). *The aesthetic dimension of the mind*. London: Karnac.
— (2013). Transformations of emotional experience. *International Journal of Psychoanalysis*, 94: 531–544.
Elise, D. (1998a). The absence of the paternal penis. *Journal of the American Psychoanalytic Association*, 46: 413–442.
— (1998b). Gender repertoire: Body, mind and bisexuality. *Psychoanalytic Dialogues*, 8: 379–397.
— (2000a). Woman and desire: Why women may not want to want. *Studies in Gender and Sexuality*, 1: 125–145.

— (2000b). Generating gender: Response to Harris. *Studies in Gender and Sexuality*, 1: 157–165.
— (2001). Unlawful entry; Male fears of psychic penetration. *Psychoanalytic Dialogues*, 11: 499–531.
— (2002a). Blocked creativity and inhibited erotic transference. *Studies in Gender and Sexuality*, 3: 161–195.
— (2002b). The primary maternal oedipal situation and female homoerotic desire. *Psychoanalytic Inquiry*, 22: 209–228.
— (2007). The black man and the mermaid: Desire and disruption in the analytic relationship. *Psychoanalytic Dialogues*, 17: 791–809.
— (2008). Sex and shame: The inhibition of female desires. *Journal of the American Psychoanalytic Association*, 56: 73–98.
— (2012). Failure to thrive: Shame, inhibition, and masochistic submission in women. In Holtzman, D. and Kulish, N. (Eds.) *The clinical problem of masochism*. New York: Jason Aronson, pp. 161–185.
— (2015a). Reclaiming lost loves: Transcending unrequited desires. Discussion of Davies' "Oedipal Complexity". *Psychoanalytic Dialogues*, 25: 284–294.
— (2015b). Eroticism in the maternal matrix: Infusion through development and the clinical situation. *Fort da*, 21(2): 17–32.
Eshel, O. (2013). Patient-analyst "withness": On analytic "presencing," passion, and compassion in states of breakdown, despair and deadness. *Psychoanalytic Quarterly*, 82: 925–963.
Fairbairn, W.D. (1944). Endopsychic structure considered in terms of object relationships. *International Journal of Psychoanalysis*, 25: 70–92.
Ferro, A. (2002). *In the analyst's consulting room*. London: Routledge.
— (2006a). Trauma, reverie, and the field. *Psychoanalytic Quarterly*, 75: 1045–1056.
— (2006b). *Mind works: Technique and creativity in psychoanalysis*. London: Routledge.
Ferro, A. and Civitarese, G. (2015). *The analytic field and its transformations*. London: Karnac.
— (2016). Psychoanalysis and the analytic field. In Elliot, A. and Prager, J. (Eds.), *Routledge handbook of psychoanalysis in the social sciences and humanities*. New York: Routledge, pp. 132–148.
Freud, S. (1905). Three essays on the theory of sexuality. *The Standard Edition*, 7: 130–243. London, Hogarth Press, 1953.
— (1915). Observations on transference love (Further recommendations on the technique of psycho-analysis III). *The Standard Edition*, 12: 157–171.
Goldberg, P. (2012). Active perception and the search for sensory symbiosis. *Journal of the American Psychoanalytic Association*, 60: 791–812.
Hagman, G. and Press, C. M. (2010). Between aesthetics, the co-construction of empathy, and the clinical. *Psychoanalytic Inquiry*, 30: 207–221.
Harlow, H. (1959), Love in infant monkeys. *Scientific American* (June) 201: 68–74.

Harris, A. (2014). Curative speech: Symbol, body, dialogue. *Journal of the American Psychoanalytic Association*, 62: 1029–1045.
Kindler, A. (2010). Spontaneity and improvisation in psychoanalysis. *Psychoanalytic Inquiry*, 30: 222–234.
Knoblauch, S. H. (Ed.) (2000). *The musical edge of therapeutic dialogue.* Hillsdale, New Jersey: The Analytic Press.
Kristeva, J. (1993). *The new maladies of the soul*, transl. R. Guberman. New York: Columbia University Press, 1995.
— (2014). Reliance, or maternal eroticism. *Journal of the American Psychoanalytic Association*, 62: 69–85.
Laplanche, J. (1992). *Seduction, translation, drives.* London: Institute of Contemporary Arts.
Levine, H. (2012). The colourless canvas: Representation, therapeutic action and the creation of mind. *International Journal of Psychoanalysis*, 93: 607–629.
Levine, H., Reed, G. and Scarfone, D., (eds.), (2013). *Unrepresented states and the construction of meaning.* London: Karnac Books.
Liley, A.W. (1972). The foetus as a personality. *Australian and New Zealand Journal of Psychiatry*, 6: 99–105.
Litowitz, B. (2014). Introduction to Julia Kristeva. *Journal of the American Psychoanalytic Association*, 62: 57–59.
Lombardi, R. (2011). The body, feelings, and the unheard music of the senses. *Contemporary Psychoanalysis*, 47: 1–24.
Markman, H. (2006). Listening to music, listening to patients: Aesthetic experience in analytic practice, *fort da*, 12: 18–29.
— (2017). Presence, mourning, and beauty: Elements of analytic process. *Journal of the American Psychoanalytic Association*, 65: 979–1004.
McAfee, N. (2004). *Julia Kristeva.* New York: Routledge.
Meltzer, D. and Harris Williams, M. (1988). *The apprehension of beauty.* Strath Tay, Scotland: Clunie Press.
Milner, M. (1950). *On not being able to paint.* London: Heinemann Educational Books, Ltd.
Mitrani, J. L. (2001). 'Taking the transference': Some technical implications in three papers by Bion. *International Journal of Psychoanalysis*, 82: 1085–1104.
Oliver, K. (1997). Introduction. In Oliver K. (Ed.) *The portable Kristeva.* New York: Colombia University Press.
Ogden, T. H. (1997). Reverie and metaphor: How I work as a psychoanalyst. *International Journal of Psychoanalysis*, 78: 719–732.
— (1999). "The music of what happens" in poetry and psychoanalysis. *International Journal of Psychoanalysis*, 80: 979–994.
Peltz, R. (2012). Ways of hearing: Getting inside psychoanalysis. *Psychoanalytic Dialogues*, 22: 279–290.
Piontelli, A. (1987). Infant Observation from Before Birth. *International Journal of Psychoanalysis*, 68: 453–463.

Ramo, H. (1999). An Aristotelian human time-space manifold: From *Chronochora* to *Kairotopos*. *Time and Society*, 8(2): 309–328.

Ringstrom, P. (2001). Cultivating the improvisational in psychoanalysis. *Psychoanalytic Dialogues*, 11: 727–754.

Stern, D. N. (1985). *The interpersonal world of the infant: A view from psychoanalysis and developmental psychology*. New York: Basic Books.

Target, M. (2015). A developmental model of sexual excitement, desire and alienation. In Lemma, A. and Lynch, P. E. (Eds.) *Sexualities: Contemporary psychoanalytic perspectives*. New York: Taylor and Francis, pp. 43–62.

Thomson-Salo, F. and Paul, C. (2017). Understanding the sexuality of infants within caregiving relationships in the first year. *Psychoanalytic Dialogues*, 27: 320–337.

Torsti, M. (2000). At the sources of the symbolization process: The psychoanalyst as an observer of early trauma. *The Psychoanalytic Study of the Child*, 55: 275–297.

Tustin, F. (1984). Autistic shapes. *International Review of Psychoanalysis*, 11: 279–290.

Widawsky, R. (2014). Julia Kristeva's psychoanalytic work. *Journal of the American Psychoanalytic Association*, 62: 61–67.

Wilson, M. (2014). Maternal reliance: Commentary on Kristeva. *Journal of the American Psychoanalytic Association*, 62: 101–111.

Winnicott, D. W. (1956). Primary maternal preoccupation. In *Through pediatrics to psychoanalysis*, pp. 300–305. London: Hogarth Press, 1978.

—— (1965). *The maturational processes and the facilitating environment: Studies in the theory of emotional development*. The International Psychoanalytical Library, 64: 1–276. London: Hogarth Press.

—— (1971). *Playing and reality*. London: Tavistock Publications.

Chapter 2

Desire and disruption in the analytic relationship

I would now like to consider the impact of desexualization of the maternal on the development of female sexuality. A "chance encounter" suggesting a desire in the female analyst, previously unsuspected, disrupts a female patient's prior sense of homoerotic immersion with the analyst. I contend that a girl's would-be oedipal competition with her mother is encased within a paternalistic structuring of sexuality where the mother is rendered solely reproductive—a pre-oedipal nurturing figure who is not erotically sexual. I examine the meanings for a patient of internalizing a female figure—her analyst—who is viewed as both maternal *and* sexual. I suggest that a female sense of genital inadequacy and inferiority may have a component of not being able to link the mother's (and in the transference, the analyst's) use of her genitals with her use of her mind/maternal function. I begin with the voice of my patient.

Lila tells me:

> In my mind, I talk with you all the time, while I'm brushing my teeth, eating lunch with a friend, making love with my husband, when I wake in the middle of the night—*then* I really have to stop myself because I could go on all night talking to you and never get any sleep. I have to tell myself over and over, like a mantra: you can talk to Dr. Elise tomorrow; you can talk with her tomorrow. I have this intense desire to be speaking to you, almost incessantly. You've become my constant companion. Is this weird, is this what's supposed to happen? Am I abnormal?

Thus began a Monday session with my favorite patient. Yes, I confess—my favorite patient. I hesitate to say "favorite." I imagine readers thinking, "She's not supposed to have a favorite patient; something's wrong with that." The topic of favorite patients, raising many interesting issues, merits attention in itself. The professional persona of generalized care and concern for each patient seems to lead to the belief that having favorites is inappropriate. Yet given the immense variability in connection between any two people, how could it be otherwise? In my clinical example here, I am highlighting the parallel (not equity) in the transference and countertransference in intensity of focus, with the sense of abnormality and confession that often attends such passion. I will address further in Chapter 3 the transgressive element in passion.

So, yes, if truth be told, I almost always have a favorite patient (or two). It makes my professional life feel especially alive, adds excitement and spice to my workday. I am reminded of the crush I had on Scott Courtney all through eighth grade. The academic year was much more fun; every day I looked forward to my encounters with Scott as compensation for the grind of geometry. Now I look forward to seeing Lila.

Lila's focus on me has become especially intense and passionate, and it represents, I believe, an unleashing of her creative energies by the analysis—energies previously held in check but now bursting forth. In addition to my belief that this intensity is a positive development for the patient (and later in this chapter I detail developmental theory, and her own history, in support of this claim), I also just enjoy this energy. I like intense people. I am intense, and this passion for passion is something that this patient and I share. But we are both questioning whether we are allowed to let this amount of desire into our relationship. She is a clinician herself, so she can easily match me in pathologizing our enthusiastic preoccupation with one another. The difference is that she does not know, at least consciously, about my desire for her desire, for her engagement with me. Yet, our analytic field is alive with the erotic.

The mermaid

The initial year of the analysis had involved a slipping into themes of mutual immersion in a watery world. Lila recounted a girlhood game of swimming underwater for as long as possible, imagining herself to be a mermaid, twisting and turning with legs and feet held together in a flutter kick. This memory developed into a transference fantasy that she and I were mermaids, and, similar to dolphins with wet slippery skin, we glided around each other and together swayed in ocean waves and swells. Although we also encountered stormy seas and our share of rocky shores, I viewed this transference fantasy as a productive regression to early, pre-oedipal engagement—a womb-like, oceanic bliss.[1] We swam in the unconscious and in a sea of sensuality and erotic attachment—a primary maternal preoccupation expressing a mutual experience of relational immersion: maternal eroticism.

In Winnicott's (1956) version of primary maternal preoccupation, the erotic connection between mother and infant was not the focus. However, as articulated in Chapter 1, a pre-oedipal erotic environment exists between mother and baby (see also Laplanche, 1970; Wrye and Welles, 1994; Stein, 1998; Bollas, 2000; Kristeva, 2014). I have conceptualized that the nursing couple is engaged in a primal intercourse, with breast-feeding sexually stimulating for infants of both sexes as well as for the mother (Elise, 1998b; see also Kohout, 2004). With mother and daughter, we encounter various levels of female homoeroticism: the early sensuous contact of the nursing couple, elements of which develop throughout the pre-oedipal period and eventually extend into a more focused genital and romantic desire for the mother, traditionally labeled the "negative oedipal complex." I prefer to think of this complex as the primary maternal oedipal situation—given maternal caretaking, first both temporally and in archaic intensity for the girl (as well as for the boy) (Elise, 2000).[2]

In clinical work, we see that mother–daughter eroticism unfolds into multiple and shifting expressions of erotic engagement on many levels. As the work with Lila progressed, I experienced pre-oedipal erotic energies as oscillating, like seaweed in the waves, with a more genital, oedipal level erotic transference. I include in my concept of analytic eroticism this general "atmospheric" quality of eroticism that took shape in the analytic field we created and cohabited—a vitality of engagement that cannot be parsed into traditional understandings of erotic transference and countertransference. Reminiscent of descriptions in Irigaray's (1990) work, we were wet, pressing up against one another in an ebb and flow of excitements in our moist realm. Of course, as in development, this mother–daughter mermaid silkiness was soon to be disrupted, but neither my patient nor myself was prepared for the particular form this rupture would take.

The black man

In an agitated manner, Lila rushed to the couch and began speaking before her head hit the pillow: "I was coming out of a movie theater last night with my husband and two kids. You were walking along holding hands with a tall black man!" After a slight pause, as if waiting for me to account for myself, she continued her astonished accusations:

P: You were wearing a short black skirt, a low-cut top in wild colors and "come fuck me shoes!" He moved his hand around your waist, almost on your butt. I just about screamed to my husband, "*Is that my analyst?!*" And who is that black man? I heard that man say something to you; I don't think he's from this country; he had an accent; he's a foreigner.

After another very brief pause when I again said nothing, Lila began exploring her reactions to this event:

P: I'm astounded; I'd been thinking you might be gay. This experience sure squelches that idea . . . Maybe it wasn't really you. I don't suppose you'll tell me. Could I have been mistaken? Analysts aren't supposed to dress like that. I've never seen you looking like that. You always wear long, flowing things, like the outfit you have on now. Your body is always covered up. I've never been real clear about the outline of your figure. Well that's sure changed! You left nothing to the imagination last night! That *was* you, right? *Unbelievable!* Here I'm leaving a family-oriented animation film while you're strutting your stuff into some divey blues bar.

I noted to myself, beneath the overt astonishment and possible condemnation, muffled tones of both envy and jealousy. Lila went on to recount what she imagined me doing the rest of the evening and night— my having a wild and sexy time. Becoming more subdued, she posed another question:

P: So what *is* your orientation? I don't know anymore if you're homosexual, heterosexual, or bisexual.
A: Just that I'm sexual. And something about *that* is disturbing to you.

Although I sounded calm in this, my first, comment of the session, I was extremely relieved that my patient was on the couch and could not see my face or expression and that I had almost 40 minutes to figure out what my expression would/should be by the time Lila looked at me as she left the session. As I listened to this material, I did not know whether I was being positioned to feel defiant or shamed, self-assured or caught out in some "slutty" behavior that for complex reasons is felt to be completely at odds with my identity as an analyst. Upon considerable reflection, I have decided that I will say nothing here, as with the patient, about whether it was actually *me* who she saw—a parallel ambiguity with which you as the reader might play. In what follows I take up the material, as I did in the treatment, as real in the patient's internal world and in the analytic field.

With the arrival of the foreign black man, so arrived my sexuality—equally foreign—into the treatment and the patient's awareness. Lila had been thinking I "might be gay." I understood this conjecture as not solely her musing on my lifestyle but as significantly influenced by a transference–countertransference dynamic of mother–daughter erotic immersion where my sexuality was experienced as an implicit and muted response to her(s). Now my explicit, adult heterosexuality had intruded to challenge her transference fantasy of our homoerotic coupling.

For my patient, *my* independent desire had come into the room—a desire for this man and my dressing to be desired by him, our sexuality evident, in "public view." A desire in the female analyst previously unsuspected by this female patient was now quite apparent and was disrupting her sense of our prior "gay" immersion in one another. The analyst's desire for someone other than the patient was a passion unforeseen, and most definitely unwelcome. The mermaids were knocked out of the water. I seemed no longer to be one molded piece from the waist down; while I was swishing my tail walking down the street, it seemed clear I would soon have my legs *apart*. My outfit had announced me to my patient, and no doubt more generally, as a woman who has a sexuality. My patient had thought homosexual, sees heterosexual, concludes in favor of bisexual, but undoubtedly I had now become sexual, and that was clearly the most disturbing "orientation." Referring to her wild fantasies regarding the remainder of my evening, Lila acknowledged, "I was awake all night wondering what you were doing!"

It is not uncommon for patients to come into a session saying they have just had sex. What about the analyst; have you or I just had sex? And what difference might it make? The question rarely seems to enter anyone's mind. Why? Lila regularly recounted to me her sexual experiences with her husband as well as fantasies about other men. A subtle assumption prevailed of her having all the men and of me as having none, no one. She had once remarked, "The world is divided into two kinds of people—those who are having sex and those who aren't." "Which group am I in?" I inquired. Taken aback, my patient stammered:

Uhh... I hadn't thought about *you.* I *guess* you have sex, but I can't quite imagine it. It doesn't seem to fit in with my experience of you. But I can't see why you wouldn't be having sex; I definitely think of you as in a relationship. It's weird; I don't know; it doesn't seem to compute somehow.

What does it mean for psychoanalysis and sexuality that the practitioners, especially the women, I believe, are too often seemingly celibate— that the analyst's sexuality is so back-pedaled? Certainly, the way a given clinician experiences herself, and is perceived, will differ depending on individual dynamics in that clinician and in her particular patients. I am trying to identify a generalized lacuna, or selective inattention, on the part of both patients and analysts. What would happen if female analyst and sexy were not, in some general sense, an oxymoron?

Like women more generally, female clinicians are vulnerable to the "dumb blonde" caricature where sex and thinking are split. We think of sexy and thoughtful or intelligent as opposed *in women* but not in men. A *key* subset of the general lack of subjectivity accorded to the mother (Benjamin, 1988), sexy and maternal just do not go together in many minds. Kristeva's (2014) work on maternal eroticism highlights the difficulty that exists in making this charged affective link, returning us as it does to our mother–infant beginnings.

A daughter is in a double bind; in a heterosexual trajectory, she wants to compete with mother for the desire of the oedipal father (Kulish and Holtzman, 2008), yet, as Benjamin (1988) emphasized, she also needs to be able to internalize a sexually empowered mother. Many have noted the absence of positive maternal figures in myths and fairy tales; the "good" mother is often dead or has disappeared, replaced by a witch or wicked stepmother. Rarer still is the active presence of a "sexy mom." In the myth of Persephone and Demeter (see Holtzman and Kulish, 2003) a good mother exists for half the year, but she is not in a sexual relationship, and Hades, a paternal figure, is having sex with the daughter, Persephone.

The phantom father figure

In pursuing the theme of the Black Man, my patient and I uncovered her sense that my sexuality was foreign and located in this man from some faraway country. I now capitalize "Black Man" to indicate a fantasy theme in the case material. In the analysis I was certainly going to take up and work with the patient's material as it unfolded for her. In presenting this material, I want to address directly, versus further entrench, the racism in the familiar sexual stereotype of black men. My patient is white, as am I. Our presumed encounter on the street would likely have taken on a number of different symbolic meanings if either one or both of us were black ourselves.

A long history exists of projecting sex, deemed as bad, onto "lesser," devalued others. Typically, sex has been designated female, dark and foreign. Thus it is especially worth noting that when sex transforms and becomes something good to have—sexual subjectivity and agency—it changes gender and is attributed to men. Among the racial variations of meanings *between* men, typically white men purport to *have* the phallus (omnipotence) as opposed to black men who are devalued as *being* a phallus (part object). Central to my argument here, is a need shared by people in many cultures to project sex away from the "pure white" Madonna-like mother onto *anyone* else. A man of whatever race is "foreign" and "dark" to the familiar glow of mother–child erotic immersion. *Any* third party can be viewed as a "dark" interloper.

For my patient, my companion's unfamiliar accent, language, and dark good looks evoked associations to Zorro, Dracula, and Phantom (of the Opera), each a man of the night. Erotic, scary, enticing, exciting, a sexually powerful male arrives and then departs in the dark (the "Midnight Marauder" as one patient put it; Holtzman and Kulish, 2003). But he may never let you go. My patient recalled being captivated with the film versions of *Bram Stoker's Dracula* and *The Phantom of the Opera*. We noticed intriguing parallels in the plots. The title figure (entitled patriarch) is a threatening but sexually exciting, dark man who is not quite human—who "seems a beast, but secretly dreams of beauty" (*Phantom*; Hart and Webber, 2004a). He prowls only at night, fearful to all but also erotically enthralling to the ingenue. She is caught between the sensible love of a young, paler fiancé, promising marriage and stability, and this mysterious erotic stranger who appears from some underworld that she might disappear to forever, an eternal Bride (of Dracula). Themes of sexuality and death are intertwined; the heroine will give up normal, daily life for dark eroticism in a ghostly world of the undead.

Notably, there is no mother figure in either plot; she has evaporated before the action begins. We find only our heroine torn between two lovers.

She must choose between a "tall, dark, and handsome" phantom of a father, promising an eternal honeymoon of lust and sensuality but for which she will be damned to hell, or a more tempered love with the "boy next door," with marriage and children the imminent outcome. As the seductive lyrics of *Phantom* proclaim, equally applicable in *Dracula*, she must turn away from the life she has previously known and "surrender to dark dreams" (Hart and Webber, 2004b) as she enters a strange new world. In demanding that she only belong to him, this oedipal father bids her say farewell to maternal eroticism. But in spite of the trance-like induction, fears abound in the heroine about the wisdom of this course. Is this the Angel of the Night or a devil in disguise—an erotic union that seems heavenly but that may lead to death and decay?

The Black Man, both in these film manifestations and in my clinical vignette as a character in the analytic field, is scripted to represent the oedipal father who intrudes on the mother–daughter dyad, beckoning the daughter forward in her (hetero) sexual development. But why is it not the oedipal mother who is understood as furthering the daughter's sexual development by introducing maternal genital sexuality in her relationship with the father (or female partner), such that an erotic couple is presented to the daughter *by the mother*. This introduction would present a triangular relationship to the girl and an image of maternal sexuality available for identification, as well as continuing to offer the mother, in addition to a father, as an erotic object for the girl.

Recognizing the mother's desire for the "black man" allows the daughter to identify with a desiring mother, a point central to Benjamin's (1988) work. However, recognition of such a desire is also what shocked and dismayed my patient. Unlike in the films, the Black Man had not come for the daughter, but instead, was *with me*. My sexuality and erotic power had to be reckoned with. This confrontation with maternal sexuality is an affront to the daughter's narcissism but, if left unrepresented, is even more costly in undermining female sexual agency that needs to be based on the internalization of a sexually agentic maternal figure.

The vanquished and vanished erotic mother

In the films discussed, fear, sexuality, consummation, and death are all explicitly linked and illustrate a girl's anxious approach to sexuality when the sexual mother is not present as a third and as a figure for internalization and identification. Psychoanalytic theory typically positions the father as the third intervening in the mother–child dyadic relation and introducing time, sex, and generational boundaries to the child. I suggest, following Benjamin (1988), that it is the absence of the erotic mother—a sexual contender in her own right, functioning as a third—that distorts the daughter's oedipal story. The daughter is left to be forever an eroticized "Daddy's girl," never fully growing up, never fully taking ownership of her own sexuality by internalizing a maternal figure who can do likewise.

Devaluation can attend any representation of a mother who *does* embody her sexuality. When evident, a mother's sexuality may be viewed with suspicion; too often, such a woman loses her status as a "good" mother. For example, a female patient expressed a very negative reaction to a television character who was both a new mother and sexy. The patient reported feeling repelled and critical: "She should be thinking about the baby!" As soon as sexuality is introduced, it can become a challenge to maintain a respectful view of maternality—a bias that Kristeva (2014) was directly confronting with her provocative conceptualization of maternal eroticism. This particular patient struggled to access a positive image of a woman who is both maternal and sexual: "I come up with a blank."

This is not a conclusion to which psychoanalytic theory should lead us. Freud (1905) identified that the sexual researches of children regarding parental sexuality are intimately linked with the development of the mind, with curiosity, learning, and creativity. I am emphasizing, in accord with both Chasseguet-Smirgel (1976) and Benjamin (1988), that the love affair with the phallus—overly idealized paternal figure—serves to defensively distract from envy of the generative primal couple and from envy of the unmistakable power of female sexuality.

Unlike the portrayal of Demeter, a mother does not just want "springtime" with her daughter, nor is she just a mermaid swimming in oceanic oneness with her daughter. As discussed in Chapter 1, such images of maternality deny the reality of the mother's adult sexuality and of her relationship with the father. Those breasts, exposed in the mermaid guise, are not solely to feed and provide sensuous delight to the child—the Good (or Bad) singular, psychoanalytic Breast (see also Stein, 1998; Kohout, 2004). Breasts, twin emblems of desire, form an erotic pair—the mother flaunting her stuff—and, along with legs that are not molded shut but part to engage genital stimulation and incorporative pleasures, encompass the mother's adult sexuality with her lover. Kristeva's (2014) conceptualization of maternal eroticism rests upon the mother's sexual libido appropriately libidinizing her investment in her child.

We can also keep in mind both Meltzer's work on the aesthetic position (Meltzer and Harris Williams, 1988)—the infant's encounter with the unparalleled beauty of the mother—and Chasseguet-Smirgel's (1976) theorizing regarding the omnipotent maternal imago. Both theories speak to the awe of, as well as defenses against, the mother's beauty, power, and sexuality, when facing the enigma that she presents to the child. Originally, it is the *mother* who is Beauty with her "Beast," the mother who is sexual *and* powerful, and whose choice it is to have a relationship with the father/ adult partner in addition to that with the child. A father cannot be recycled to the daughter; *this* union would constitute the denial of generational boundaries,[3] of the reality of aging and mortality, the passage of time, and would indeed shroud the daughter's sexuality in themes of death, removal from life. It is notable that, at the end of both *Dracula* and *Phantom*, the heroine releases the dark beast from his tortured longing for her by kissing him goodbye and going on her way with her generational peer. Too often, however, a daughter, even as an adult, cannot or does not want to free herself from the position of erotic object for a paternal figure.

I propose that an oedipal fantasy where mother and father figure compete for the daughter, as do Demeter and Hades in the Persephone myth, is not truly triangular for the daughter but reflects two dyads split apart. Likewise, the familiar drama of father and fiancé/boyfriend vying for the ingenue daughter is also not triangular for the daughter but represents competing dyads. Both scenarios lack a sexual mother in erotic union with her mate. This theme perseverates because it merges paternalistic assignment of potent adult sexuality to the father (incestuously relating to the daughter figure rather than to the mother) with a daughter's oedipal wish that she be the only sexually desired female. These oedipal scenarios represent *a failure of triangularity*, each involving parallel dyads rather than a daughter being confronted with *another dyad external to herself—a couple that, in relation to, she stands as a third*. Each scenario obliterates the mother as an erotically powerful figure in consort with her adult companion (quite unlike mythic Goddess figures). The primal scene, primal *couple*, is erased from (the daughter's) view.

Boys learn to compete with a sexually powerful father and to identify with the father's phallicism as a powerful aid to their own sexual self-esteem and agency. The boy's oedipal story does not begin with missing, castrated fathers—quite the opposite; Oedipus has to kill his father, the King, in hand-to-hand combat before he can even get to the mother. Thus we cannot take for granted, based solely on the competitive factor, that a child erases in advance the same-sex parent from the narrative. Only girls eliminate the mother without any direct competitive encounter, matching fathers who may as well erase the maternal consort and lose track of the generational boundary in leaping down to the daughter as sexual complement.

The sexy mind

Through chance encounter (whether imagined or real, *vivid* in the patient's emotional reality and within the analytic field), my patient was pressed to contend with me as a sexually agentic being; she thus also expanded her own sexuality. Over the next many months, we explored the meanings for the patient of internalizing a female figure, her analyst, who is viewed as both maternal *and* sexual. This led to an opening up for the patient of her own sexuality in relation to her sense of self, to her husband, and to me.

When Lila began her analysis, she had presented with conflicts related to self-expression in many areas, including sexuality. She tended to doubt her own perceptions as well as the value of her thinking when it departed from those around her. These inhibitions undermined her authority in relation to many people. Although she had access to sexual fantasy and an active sex life, Lila saw herself as the sexually provocative Daddy's girl to be whisked off by various powerful men with their dangerous "dark" sex. Sexual agency was projected onto the male other (definitely not the (m) other), just as she did in our "encounter." She viewed her own mother as a sexually attractive but essentially passive woman in contrast to her father, "a real powerhouse." The mother seemed to have unfulfilled potential and talent in a number of areas, as did my patient. In being unable to internalize a sexually agentic maternal figure, Lila could not integrate ownership of sexual desire into her albeit very sexy self. She fell back from fully inhabiting her capacity for creative expression and passionate engagement.

As the treatment progressed, especially around these issues of maternal sexual agency in the transference, my patient's own sense of agency developed, authorizing her sexuality, but also more generally her mind, her creativity. Like many women, she suffered from a perceived split regarding intelligence and sexuality, mind and genital. She struggled with the idea that, as a woman, you have either got one or the other—not both:

P: Any acknowledgment of my genitals, of my being turned on—"hot"—seems to equate to being stupid. This makes my genitals—what's between my legs—seem dumb.

This line of thinking she and I came to refer to as the "mermaid tail defense." Female sexuality is degraded, and the use of the mind seems to desexualize the female self rather than the possibility that each might inform the other. Quoting my patient:

P: I hesitate to admit this, but I often get my most creative ideas while masturbating. My mind seems to get "turned on" along with my genitals. I get excited by the flow of ideas, and the building of my thoughts, just as my body is getting more excited and building to orgasm. I'd never tell anyone this, but I got my last work idea in consulting to a school program while masturbating. Is this what the term "mental masturbation" means? No, I don't think so. That's pejorative and *not* sexy—de-sexed. What I'm talking about is positive—everything's flowing together, body and mind.

In an expression of the double arrow relation between eroticism, creativity and the expansion of the personality (put forth in this book's Introduction), Lila was able to integrate her sexuality into her image of herself as a therapist and as a thinker. More generally, with her mind and her sexuality no longer split off from one another, she could use her mind to choose what she desired rather than her previous tendency to submit to the desire of the other. I will pursue this theme of sexual agency, rather than subjugation, with further clinical examples in Chapter 9.

This development in Lila occurred in response to her registration of a chance encounter outside the consulting room that "forced" the issue of maternal sexuality. It is quite complicated to consider how a productive disruption of this nature can occur *within the symbolic encounter* in the analytic field of an unfolding treatment. How does maternal eroticism with its parallel of analytic eroticism come alive in a given clinical setting? In what manner might a female analyst embody her sexual agency within the appropriate boundaries of the analytic relationship? It is evident to patients that the analyst uses her mind in an intelligent way; is the analyst's erotic energy also evident or does the analytic field become a desexualized maternal cocoon? A female sense of genital inadequacy, inferiority, may have a component of not being able to link the mother's (and in the transference, the analyst's) use of her genitals with her use of her mind/maternal function.

Unlike men, women have an immense number of decisions to make on any given day regarding personal appearance and how they will present and embody their sexual selves. This cultural reality affects women analysts as well. Attire calls attention to the body and often, especially for women, to the sexual body. If the female body is visible, it is considered inherently "provocative." Encompassed within clothing suitable for work is a range of choices for women that, although often subtle, have significant effect on a felt or perceived sense of sexuality. These choices reflect underlying feelings and then further influence self-concept at a deeper level. It is difficult for these choices to be a non-issue, as almost any decision about attire will say *something*. When it comes to sexuality, a neutral stance will be quite a statement, one that I propose fits in with a transference–countertransference stance that goes unnoticed, unremarked upon by both parties in the clinical dyad, and that is reflective of a deeply recessed wish by mostly everyone to see a maternal figure as a Virgin Mary. In parallel, too often it is comfortable, as well as comforting, for both members of a clinical pair to experience the female clinician as non-sexually maternal.

I underscore that I am approaching this issue of appearance and apparel as the visible surface of female embodiment of sexuality, reflecting a myriad of conflicts in underlying intrapsychic layers. When a female clinician feels she must cloak her sexual self from her patients, her access to an embodied analytic eroticism as a vital aspect of the analytic field may be curtailed. How then does a woman patient gain full access to not only her sexual self, but to the strength of her full personality, in such an environment?

My patient continued to pursue this relationship between my attire and my self. Months after her experience of our encounter on the street, she reiterated these thoughts:

P: You weren't dressed like you are at your office. *Here* you dress *like* your office: neutral, not especially colorful or lively. There's something more to you than I've seen. It makes me feel that your real life is somewhere else, not here with me. Funny, I never thought of myself as not liking this office before, but now it seems too pale. I used to like that. I once saw a therapist who had all this colorful art in her office that was very distracting, including a big picture over her chair of a knife slicing through a piece of fruit—scary! But I think now that your blander colors have allowed me to feel merged with you versus having a sense of difference. I feel some sadness that it is not like that now that I see your more colorful, sexy side. . . . I feel like going to sleep. . .. Didn't I feel this way yesterday too? I can't remember.

We see progression and then, in the face of loss, regression that, for this patient, was only temporary in an overall momentum forward into a depressive position recognition of both loss and gain.

Clinicians tend to develop fine-tuned sensitivity to when our dress, décor, or some less tangible expression of self might "slice through a piece of fruit" and be unnecessarily distracting and unproductively disruptive to a vulnerable patient. We are necessarily cautious out of concern to not harm. We may, however, err in this direction and miss seeing the limitations for our patients and ourselves of our various self-effacements. My patient had now alerted me to this other side.

I became aware that my professional persona and dress were possibly *too* "professional" and lacked certain human aspects—like sexuality. I was intrigued by my attention (and that of my patient) repeatedly returning to the issue of color, both racially, as in people of color, and in the symbolic meanings of the color palette. With the patient seeing my (and her) female sexuality as located in the Black Man, I realized that I needed more palpably to embody ownership of my sexuality and that the muted color of my style of dress, and personality, played an important role in our shared creation of the analytic field.

My continued self-reflection on sexual agency and the colorfulness versus shadowing of my personality resulted in a qualitative change in how I inhabited the analytic field. No longer a pale shade of myself, I became able to allow more of my psyche a place within the clinical venture. At the same time, I also had to work to not *expel* the patient's various ideas of me and my sexuality, to contain the countertransference rather than to jettison the patient's projections. Interpretations can function as subtle corrections.

I attempted to live out as fully as possible the character assigned to me (unconsciously) by my patient, and in interacting with that role, I changed my idea of the self I can bring to my office. That internal journey in my countertransference allowed for transformations in the patient's transference fantasies regarding maternal/female sexuality. Such an evolution of the intersubjective analytic field reflects mutuality in influence and expansion of self for clinician as well as patient: We both changed. I became a more sexy mom, and Lila grew up to be one as well. Our relationship developed passion in more differentiated levels of connection. These issues of embodiment of a sexual sense of self were subtly threaded throughout our sessions over many months, and even years, like a small fiber inextricably woven throughout a tapestry.

The clinical challenge that this "chance encounter" poses to clinicians involves the following quandary: If not forced on the dyad by external circumstances, in what other ways can the positive evolution described in this treatment be integrated into an analysis between a female patient and analyst (and, more broadly, into other gendered pairings)? My goal in this chapter, and in this book as a whole, is to stimulate collective consideration of this issue: In what ways can analytic eroticism enter fully into the analytic field extending beyond a narrow version of erotic transference and countertransference?

Discussion: Oedipal eruption/disruption

We have arrived at a conception of the thinking genital and the "turned-on" mind, both joined in a productive intercourse and leading to further conceptions (see Bion, 1959), on and on. We see the significance of using one's mind to foster one's sexuality and one's sexuality to foster one's mind and creativity. My patient's awareness/recognition of my sexuality had been ushered in by the encounter with the Black Man—an encounter that was disruptive but productive. Such an encounter, usually symbolic, is necessary and will always be inherently disruptive. In my interpreting along the lines theorized in this chapter, I managed slowly to convey to my patient my ownership of my sexuality—a sexuality that belonged to me, no longer located in a foreign man, and no longer seemingly estranged from my intellect. In the face of her reiterated musings about *she* being "the one" to be on the arm of the dark stranger, *I became the one to disrupt* my patient: With the marriage of my intellect and my sexuality, I eventually interrupted, "Ah, but this sexy stranger is *with me!*" In so doing, I confronted her with a parental couple and with my active, sexual participation within this couple.

Because exclusion from the parents' sexual relationship represents a fundamental aspect of reality for the child, as Rusbridger (2004) emphasized, "analysis of the patient's responses to the oedipal situation constitutes the central task of analysis" (p. 731). Although clinicians of various persuasions debate whether analyzing the oedipal crisis is the central task of an analysis, it is important to understand the Kleinian emphasis on the oedipal complex as a fundamental dynamic of the mind, that then structures the mind. Rusbridger (2004) explains "this turns on the subject's response to witnessing a relationship . . . from which he is excluded" (p. 733).

The child's reaction to reality, as represented by the oedipal situation, is what determines his ability to use his mind. Intertwining themes of this chapter concern exclusion from the parental sexual couple and the challenge this experience poses to the perception of reality: "That was you, right? Unbelievable! Maybe it wasn't really you. Could I have been mistaken?" As the patient gradually absorbed the emotional truth of her perceptions, she enlivened her capacity for creative linking on many levels. This clinical material demonstrates how coming to terms with oedipal reality does develop the capacity to use one's mind in a productive, fruitful manner, where thinking is clear and creative, an "intercourse" with one's thoughts.

My particular focus in this chapter highlights unconscious fantasy material regarding oedipal exclusion in its gender-specific, mother–daughter form. Too often in analytic theorizing, the daughter has been viewed solely as competing with the mother for the father. I have elaborated the element of competition with the father for the mother, where desire for, and sense of betrayal by, the mother complicates the female oedipal drama. I hope the reader, regardless of gender, has been drawn into a re-encounter with the emotional impact of the oedipal situation; each sex is confronted by the oedipal crisis with an assault on dyadic relating and omnipotence. I have tried to recreate in as vivid a manner as I can, the startling sense of shock and disruption that ensues.

Ogden (2005) wrote:

> when we read an analyst's written account of an experience with a patient, what we are reading is not the experience itself, but the writer's creation of a new (literary) experience while (seemingly) writing the experience he had with the analysand . . . At the same time, the "fiction" that is created in words must reflect the reality of what occurred.
> (p. 16)

This intriguing play on the concepts of reality and fiction captures a core dilemma of the oedipal situation: What is real? Did I make this up?

Did I find this or create it? A child's personal creativity within transitional space—Winnicott's (1971) conceptualization central to this book—is brought into an encounter with oedipal reality with its challenge to omnipotence. How does one maintain a creative relation to painful realities? How might an analytic field of erotic vitality facilitate such an endeavor?

The emotional experience of oedipal disruption does center on the startling sense of challenge to pre-oedipal (dyadic) "reality," leading to initial denial, a period of confusion, having to think things through, and, eventually, coming to some sort of personal conviction regarding oedipal (triadic) reality that then becomes foundational for going forward. As Rusbridger (2004) underscored, these dynamics are fundamental aspects of the mind coping with an experience of disruption, assaulted by a "new" reality. My patient's "encounter" brings to life—"to the streets"—what is there to be discovered (or not) in the mind.

I analyzed Lila's material as I would a dream in order to retain the ambiguity ("did this happen/was this real/was that you?") that *is exactly the dilemma the oedipal child is faced with* in the unconscious regarding the relation *between* the mother and the father. My intent was to fully engage with the patient's fantasy without collapsing into a concrete relation to external "events" that register as deeply psychic. In not identifying to the patient whether it was actually her analyst that she encountered on the street, my aim was to keep open the symbolic space for the emotional reality of her erotic fantasy life. I believe that good clinical reasons underlie this approach, most exemplified by an understanding of an intersubjective analytic field that is bi-personally shaped and that becomes more than a sum of the two participants' individual personalities (Ferro and Civitarese, 2015); something more all-encompassing is creatively lived out in virtual reality by the analytic pair.

In unfolding this clinical material, I am inviting the reader to step into the dream world that is psychic reality (Bion, 1959; Winnicott, 1971; Ogden, 2005; Ferro and Civitarese, 2015)—the patient's unconscious fantasy regarding the oedipal situation, made accessible by the "encounter," just as it would have been by a dream of such an encounter. In not commenting to the patient on the concrete level (and she did not ask me to do so, being more engrossed in what had been stimulated in her internal world), I hoped to keep her "dream" alive for her and for me to fully inhabit. I believe that I owned my sexual subjectivity much more deeply, than would be the case in a simple disclosure, by staying in the symbolic realm. A living (transference/

countertransference) dream remains affectively intense over time and, ripe with continued feeling, demands ongoing analysis, whereas premature conclusions may foreclose experience and thinking. When asleep and dreaming, we all feel/believe that what is happening is real. Whereas upon awakening psychic reality dims. We soon distance as well from the emotional impact that becomes increasingly remote over time. So what does my patient's "waking dream" tell us about the oedipal situation?

Rusbridger (2004) identified two links, separate in nature, between the three figures of mother, father, and child: the sexual link between the parents, and the link of dependency from the child to each parent. Although the parental sexual link has created the (dependent) child, from the child's perspective the chronology is reversed. First there is (after "oneness") the dependent dyadic link to the mother and then to the father. The sexual link to each parent starts to form as the child develops. It is only then that the child discovers a sexual link between the parents—a normatively "traumatic" discovery, hoped for some time to be a fiction, only imagined, not true.

Specifying a crucial gender difference, Green (1992, p. 141) described the Oedipus complex as:

> [an] open triangular structure in which *the mother occupies the place of the central link*, for she is the only one who has a double bodily relation with both the father and the child . . . What is essential seems to be *situated in the moment* of transition when the fusional relation of the dyad—doubled or complimented by the thought of the father in the mother's mind—is followed by *the moment when he effectively appears in reality.*
>
> (as cited and translated by Van Haute, 2005, p. 1675; emphasis added)

The mother's desire for, and bodily relation with, both partner and child places her, not the phallus, as the central link. The unwelcome reality to the child of not being the sole object of the mother's desire is at first denied. Rupture of mother–child dyadic union is blamed on the "moment" of the father, a moment that takes bodily shape in the image of a powerfully aggressive phallus.

Rusbridger (2004), as well, in discussing oedipal dynamics, speaks of "reactions to moments of meaningfulness" (p. 731). Although we know that meaning is built up over time, recognition of a new, fundamentally important and reconfiguring idea takes place like lightning striking. Momentous change often occurs in a moment, not typically in external reality but in that the feeling of surprise and shock creates a sensation of a traumatic encounter.

Even when well integrated in any given woman, a mother's heterosexuality is an affront to the dyadic omnipotence of the child.[4] Here, "heterosexual" translates in the child's mind to "other (than-with-me) sexuality." The mother's sexual partner being of a gender other than her own is not critical; her partner being other than her *child* is key. The child is not developmentally ready to perceive this "other-sexual" reality for some time, and to do so is rarely a smooth ride. Moving fully into the oedipal situation, and negotiating its challenges toward optimal resolution, requires realization of the sexual independence of the mother's desire, something neither sex is eager to do.

Epilogue: subjects of beauty

At a gathering of clinicians after a presentation of this material, conversation among the women quickly shifted to surreptitious, almost confessional, tones regarding professional wardrobe dilemmas: what is professionally "appropriate" versus "too sexual?" The conversational atmosphere conveyed that this subject was to be kept quiet between women, a private concern, as if even the attention to these issues would be disruptive if voiced more loudly or would be dismissed as trivial "women's issues." The fact that in a profession now "female dominated" so few analytic papers, or even conversations, take up this topic is, I think, indicative of repression of maternal eroticism at the level of group dynamics as well as in the individual psyche.

In many cultures, female sexuality is felt to excite and distort the sensibilities of the male; it then becomes the responsibility of each individual woman to titrate this effect, with attire a critical variable. "Choices" are made in accord with what is considered normative within a given context. Consciously and unconsciously, women take on the project of wardrobe as a regulator of sexual excitement (their own, as well as that of the other). Donning a particular outfit shapes the role one will play (just as actors wear varying costumes to create different characters), and this reality also affects the analytic field and the potential, or not, for analytic eroticism in its many possible manifestations.

Women are viewed as objects of beauty; this truth makes sense given maternal eroticism. When is it that their beauty becomes "objectified" by the gaze of the other? Are women being reduced to "sex objects," or are they being erotically playful and creative with their self-expression in a manner that is significantly curtailed in men (due to fear of being seen as feminine). Are women *subjects of beauty?* Can women be the subject of their own sexual, sensual aesthetic of beauty? Where is the space for the subjective experience and expression of one's beauty, including the erotic, as a woman? How is this engagement with self expressed, embodied, inhabited?

Familiar possibilities include the sensuousness of swaying strands of hair, playful painting of face and nails, colorful materials, flowing scarves, sparkling jewelry (all of which, in some cultures, men choose as well to express themselves; Elise, 2006). Certainly most women everywhere experience beauty as a pleasure for themselves, ideally as a maternal bequest. Even when presented to men, does this display of female beauty necessarily signal oppression? Is it not a form of sexual signaling, a communication to a desired other? Must various female mating "calls" necessarily preclude a communication with oneself as a woman and with other women?

I suggest that female erotic beauty is a communication not solely to men, but between women, within any given woman, and at core (Meltzer and Harris Williams, 1988; Kristeva, 2014) between mother and infant. An aesthetic of beauty, although changing in every society, seems to be an eternal element of human culture given its centrality in the mother–infant relation. The ability to experience, and subsequently express, maternal beauty and sexuality is, one hopes, handed down to and inherited by successive generations of daughters as their birthright. Nor can we as women clinicians expect to foster the development of healthy agentic passions in our female patients without these aspects of self palpably alive and embodied in *our* presence in the clinical encounter. Each woman in the clinical dyad must participate in this primal mother/daughter interplay in order that either, and hopefully both, can develop and grow.

Notes

1 It is interesting to note that, in French, *mer* (sea) and *mère* (mother) are indistinguishable in sound (Tseelon, 1995). Also, that in English, without the accent, the meaning is reduced to "mere"—a minimalization that dovetails with my thesis regarding maternal sexuality.
2 Klein (1928) introduced the concept of oedipal "situations," a formulation that allows for the multiplicity actually present in development.

3 Whereas in Lacanian-influenced thinking (i.e., Chasseguet-Smirgel, 1991, among many others) it is the "law of the father" versus any law of the mother (see Mitchell, 2000) that is viewed as essential to establishing generational boundaries unrecognized in the maternal/infant bond.
4 I want to underscore that the attribution of "slutty" to the "street-walking" analyst is the oedipal child's view of mother's sexual desire going elsewhere—"not the sex I want to see." In a similar attribution, some people view gay couples as "flagrant" and "flaunting" their sexuality when seen holding hands or kissing in public. The particular image of this "sexed-up" woman on the street is not suggested as (or excluded from) a model of female sexuality.

References

Benjamin, J. (1988). *The bonds of love.* New York: Pantheon.
Bion, W. (1959). Attacks on linking. *International Journal of Psychoanalysis*, 40: 308–315.
Bollas, C. (2000). *Hysteria.* London: Routledge.
Chasseguet-Smirgel, J. (1976). Freud and female sexuality: The consideration of some blind spots in the exploration of the "Dark Continent." *International Journal of Psychoanalysis*, 57: 275–286.
— (1991). Sadomasochism in the perversions: Some thoughts on the destruction of reality. *Journal of the American Psychoanalytic Association*, 39: 399–415.
Elise, D. (1998a). The absence of the paternal penis. *Journal of the American Psychoanalytic Association*, 46: 413–442.
— (1998b). Gender repertoire: Body, mind and bisexuality. *Psychoanalytic Dialogues*, 8: 353–371.
— (2000). Woman and desire: Why women may *not* want to want. *Studies in Gender and Sexuality*, 1: 125–145.
Ferro, A. and Civitarese, G. (2015). *The analytic field and its transformations.* London: Karnac.
Freud, S. (1905). Three essays on the theory of sexuality. *The Standard Edition*, 7: 125–243. London: Hogarth Press, 1953.
Green, A. (1992). Oedipe, Freud et nous [Oedipus, Freud and us]. In: *La Deliaison.* Paris: Hachette, pp. 69–149.
Hart, C. and Webber, A. L. (2004a). I remember/Stranger than you dreamt it [Recorded by Peter Manning and Sylvia Addison]. On *The Phantom of the Opera* [CD]. New York: Sony.
— (2004b). The music of the night [Recorded by Peter Manning]. On *The Phantom of the Opera* [CD]. New York: Sony.
Holtzman, D. and Kulish, N. (2003). The feminization of the female oedipal complex, Part II: Aggression reconsidered. *Journal of the American Psychoanalytic Association*, 51: 1127–1151.
Irigaray, L. (1990). This sex which is not one. In Zanardi, C. (Ed.), *Essential Papers on the Psychology of Women.* New York: New York University Press, pp. 437–443.

Klein, M. (1928). Early stages of the Oedipus conflict. *International Journal of Psychoanalysis*, 9: 167–180.
Kohout, E. (2004). The breast in female sexuality. *International Journal of Psychoanalysis*, 85: 1235–1238.
Kristeva, J. (2014). Reliance, or maternal eroticism. *Journal of the American Psychoanalytic Association*, 62: 69–85.
Kulish, N. and Holtzman, D. (2008). *A story of her own: The female Oedipus complex reexamined and renamed.* New York: Jason Aronson.
Laplanche, J. (1970). *Life and death in psychoanalysis*, trans. J. Mehlman. Baltimore: John Hopkins University Press.
Meltzer, D. and Harris Williams, M. (1988). *The apprehension of beauty.* Strath Tay, Scotland: Clunie.
Mitchell, J. (2000). *Mad men and medusas.* New York: Basic Books.
Ogden, T.H. (2005). On psychoanalytic writing. *International Journal of Psychoanalysis*, 86: 15–29.
Rusbridger, R. (2004). Elements of the Oedipus complex: A Kleinian account. *International Journal of Psychoanalysis*, 85: 731–748.
Stein, R. (1998). The enigmatic dimension of sexual experience: The "otherness" of sexuality and primal seduction. *Psychoanalytic Quarterly*, 67: 594–625.
Tseelon, E. (1995). The little mermaid: An icon of woman's condition in patriarchy, and the human condition of castration. *International Journal of Psychoanalysis*, 76: 1017–1030.
Van Haute, P. (2005). Infantile sexuality, primary object-love and the anthropological significance of the Oedipus complex: Re-reading Freud's "Female sexuality." *International Journal of Psychoanalysis*, 86: 1661–1678.
Winnicott, D. W. (1956). Primary maternal preoccupation. In *Through pediatrics to psychoanalysis.* London: Hogarth Press, 1978, pp. 300–305.
— (1971). *Playing and reality.* London: Tavistock Publications.
Wrye, H. and Welles, J. (1994). *The narration of desire: Erotic transferences and countertransferences.* Hillsdale, New Jersey: The Analytic Press.

Chapter 3

Blocked creativity and inhibited erotic transference

An intriguing relationship exists between creativity and erotic transference. As a specific manifestation of eroticism within the analytic field, erotic transference is not solely a resistance to treatment; treatment can involve a resistance to erotic transference, the dynamics of which can have parallels in the inhibition of creativity. Clinical attention often focuses on how active expression of erotic transference defends against other layers of material; less consideration is given to the defensive aspects of *resistance* to erotic desire and romantic love for the analyst. Erotic transference tends to be viewed as representing a problem to be analyzed mainly when it exists, and in *overt* form. The *absence* of erotic transference in many treatments is often taken for granted, not thought of as constituting a problem or as reflecting dynamics in the patient's psyche that might benefit from analysis.

Clinicians are highly in favor of creative expression and value the psychoanalytic process as facilitating this potential, but we are often quite ambivalent about a similar approach to erotic transference. I will elaborate a clinical example involving an erotic transference by a lesbian patient to her female analyst in order to illustrate the connection that I have in mind between erotic transference and creativity. The erotic transference was present, but inhibited. I draw parallels between this inhibition and the patient's difficulty in expressing her creative potential in her career as a writer. Many aspects of the patient's life were derailed and I, as the analyst, came to believe that the block to the patient's creativity was intimately related to the felt presence of erotic transference that was then kept at bay.

The inhibition of erotic transference led to particularly challenging countertransference dilemmas as I deliberated over whether to let the transference desires remain acknowledged, but unelaborated, or to attempt to facilitate the patient's further symbolic expression of these feelings.

Person (1985) described the woman analyst's difficulty in "presuming to be found sexual" (p. 173) by *male* analysands who are likely to ward off awareness of erotic transference due to the power differential in the treatment not favoring the culturally expected male dominant pairing (see also Gornick, 1986; Kulish, 1989). In the case material offered here, I look at the subtle similarities and differences involving sex, gender, and inhibited creativity in work with a female patient. Although I am presenting a female analytic couple where the transference was homoerotic, I believe the larger point I am making has general applicability to any of the gendered treatment dyads.

The clinical material is given theoretical contextualization by considering the fate of a girl's early oedipal desires toward her mother. Unlike a boy's situation where this desire is acknowledged and then forbidden, a girl's desire for the mother tends to be erased, made invisible; it remains an unrecognized desire. When this oedipal desire for the mother—what I have termed the primary maternal oedipal situation (Elise, 2000)—is not recognized in the transference, analysis of erotic themes may be occluded. I will also address what I think of as "couch relations"—the specific, gendered impact of use of the analytic couch on erotic elements within the analytic field. After focusing on the dynamics of the case, I will then discuss more generally certain shared features of erotic transference and creativity, as well as inhibitions on the part of clinicians.

The passion and challenge of psychoanalysis

At a time in psychoanalytic history when almost nothing was written on erotic countertransference, let alone to a patient of the same sex as the clinician, Searles (1965) wrote eloquently about anxieties generated by erotic countertransference to a male patient:

> I was seeing a paranoid schizophrenic man in his middle thirties, a sensitive, highly intelligent, physically handsome man who manifested a gratifying improvement over the course of our work. But after about 18 months, I began growing uneasy at the intensity of the fond and romantic feelings which I had come to experience towards him, and was particularly alarmed during one of our sessions, while we were sitting in silence and a radio not far away was playing a tenderly romantic song, when I suddenly felt that this man was dearer to me than anyone

else in the world, including my wife. Within a few months I succeeded in finding "reality" reasons why I would not be able to continue indefinitely with his therapy, and he moved to a distant part of the country . . . I am certain that it was my anxiety about these recently recognized responses in myself that caused me to find, now, that it somehow made excellent sense for him to leave here . . . I was unable to brave the fondness which now came up in the transference.

(p. 294)

It is apparent from Searles' description that fondness in the *countertransference* constituted the major challenge to bravery.

In another example, Searles (1965) referred to a case later in his career:

I began finding myself feeling surprisingly fond of him, and to be having not infrequent dreams of a fond and sexual nature about him. One morning as I was putting on a carefully selected necktie, I realized that I was putting it on for him, more than for any of the several other patients I was to see that day.

(p. 295)

Searles (1965) admitted to an initial concern that he might have had "an unusual propensity for exploiting analytic patients" (p. 285) in grappling with his own unresolved oedipal issues—a concern that cannot help to arise in any clinician, I believe, when we increase our awareness of erotic transference and countertransference. Searles was writing at a time when, for decades, erotic transference was thought of as an occupational hazard and erotic countertransference was considered a failing on the part of the clinician. Although much has advanced in understanding that countertransference is an important source of clinical information and intuition about the atmospheric conditions of analytic field, much anxiety still attends the erotic.

I have previously described my experience of being rather bowled over by erotic transference and countertransference in a face-to-face treatment with a lesbian patient:

I continued to experience a rather urgent, insistent quality in the transference and an increasing sense of being seduced . . . On one occasion she slowly ran her eyes up and down my body and I thought, "That's it! I can't take this anymore." I had spent weeks feeling vulnerable, sexually aggressed upon, and worried that I was blushing (p. 56) . . . I vividly remember the feelings I had of extreme interpersonal tension at being overtly wooed, feeling seduced, and all the while maintaining (I hoped) a calm, unruffled demeanor . . . I felt psychically undressed by this woman, and worst of all, on one level this feeling was not entirely unpleasant!

(Elise, 1991, p. 58)

The problem of being overwhelmed and flustered by erotic transference and by one's erotic countertransference is certainly formidable, and it is definitely challenging to be able to interpret in the midst of feeling passionately attracted. However, I want to address here the more subtle, and likely trickier, problem of being *underwhelmed* by erotic currents—a situation that also can lead to troublesome feelings that one might be seducing the patient rather than the other way around. My patient Jan, a lesbian in her late thirties, experienced persistent difficulties in bringing her career as a writer to fruition. She clearly had both the talent and skill to be successful, as was evidenced by sporadic periods of meaningful and recognized achievements. However, she was never able to maintain a consistent level of satisfying productivity. Her career languished as she spent more and more time in a low-level depression—like a fog that swirled around her and obscured her path and sense of direction.

About two years into the analysis, I felt that Jan had become quite engaged with me after an initial period of emotional distance and apparent relational apathy. I started to recognize what seemed to be "courting" gestures, i.e., a certain witty repartee, her waiting for me to get to my chair before she laid down on the couch (which required some effort on her part to keep from being obvious since she preceded me into the office). I had been thinking about the presence of an as yet unmentioned erotic transference for a number of months when one day she announced, "I hope this isn't that erotic transference stuff." I was somewhat surprised to hear her use this terminology, and I inquired. She replied that she was aware of the theory of erotic transference and wanted no part in it. When I asked about her objections, Jan remarked that she did not want to be like a little puppy dog or some kind of groupie blindly following me around. Her images were of being belittled, rejected and demeaned; none of this conjured up an attractive picture of herself in her mind and instead left her feeling that any wish she had to have me find her attractive would surely be doomed.

In spite of my best efforts to keep this topic alive, it disappeared from our dialogue for the next many months. Jan seemed to have nothing more to say on the subject. However, I still had the feeling intuitively that she was attracted to me by subtle ways she would interact with me. It was the most muted expression of erotic transference, but I believed it was there just under the surface of our interactions. My conflicts centered on whether I was "making this up"—if it was really *my* erotic feeling, not hers—and whether getting these feelings more to the surface was an appropriate analytic goal or something that would be over-stimulating—a seduction of her by me.

Then at a point where the interaction between us seemed particularly lively, she provocatively proposed that we take a trip to Greece together and boldly quipped: "You seem like a Greek Island kind of girl." The sudden and overt seductiveness of her suggestion to travel away together took me aback. Her reference to me as a "girl," thus changing the power dynamic with her in a more dominant role, felt very seductive to me. I was *most* seduced by the accuracy of her "take" on me and wondered in amazement how she could "know" so much about me on this romantic level: I adore islands and had wanted to go to Greece since I was a teen and saw "Zorba." I love Greek music and dance. In my twenties I had planned a trip to Greece that fell through when I divorced my intended travel companion. A relationship began a number of years ago with the proposal to me that we go to Greece (we never got there). I felt flabbergasted at how much of my history my patient had accidently/ intuitively tapped into and condensed in this one remark of hers. What were the odds of her making a remark—an "offer"—that had so many layers of romantic meaning for me? This intoxicating feeling of being "known" permeates the interactions and subjective experience of new lovers; now this feeling was permeating the analytic field with "signals from the field" (Baranger and Baranger, 2008; Ferro and Civitarese, 2015) going off like fireworks.

When I tried to explore her remark and the fantasied travel together, Jan quickly backed away. On one level it was a *real* proposal: She wanted to put it into action or forget it. She was not interested in symbolically elaborating the fantasy, as fantasy; co-creation of a metaphoric narrative had zero appeal to Jan. Thus, she and I did not go to Greece (in fantasy, in the material) and I was disappointed once again in my desires to visit Greece, even in a clinical session. I recalled that in my own analysis I had had the fantasy of sitting for hours in mutual conversation at a cafe in Italy with my analyst (who, unbeknownst to me at that time, was of Italian descent). I had imaginatively played this fantasy out and elaborated it over the course of many sessions. It was a theme that endured over years. Whereas now, with my patient, no such elaboration unfolded; she stood me up!

As I pondered her failure of imagination and quick abandonment of an exciting fantasy, I was able to link this transference interaction to her foreclosed writing efforts and to her difficulty developing a rewarding love relationship in her personal life. There was little fruition to many aspects of her life and of her desires; *she stood herself up*; she did not show up with her imagination to forward her own wishes. If a wish could not be put into immediate action and quickly gratified, she left the scene in her mind. My countertransference experience of exciting promise and then quick disappointment was key to understanding the fizzling out of her relationship with herself. How could she write or be creative in various ways when she closed down so quickly on her fantasy life?

In slowly being able to explore the underlying dynamics to her transference, it became evident that she avoided oedipal eroticism and was wedded to seemingly non-sexual, pre-oedipal interactions focused on dependent needs for nurturance. She unconsciously envisioned erotic failure with each parent (both of whom had been quite depressed, and each with particular reasons for preferring a boy) if she were to move to expression of oedipal desire, and she believed her earlier dyadic relationship with her nurturing mother would be jeopardized as well. As described in Chapter 1, the early mother–infant relationship ideally has its own erotic life, but this patient's mother in being depressed likely embodied little maternal eroticism. My patient felt that if she were to express deep erotic feeling for me, I would be unaffected, unmoved; she would have no impact, be impotent. She had the conscious conviction that I would "prefer to see a man walk into the room." She recalled her sense of her first two female lovers as being "completely out of my reach" and questioned: "What would it mean to me to give up the idea of you rejecting me?" If she is not rejected and "has a chance," she believes she will "screw it up, fuck it up somehow"— an unusual phrasing for her.

It did seem to me that it was precisely in the arena of sexual relations that she got cold feet and that she preemptively castrated herself to protect against the "castration" of relational failure in a sexual context. Her resistance to the awareness of an erotic transference reflected her thwarted oedipal desires and *the foreclosure of her desire to be oedipal*. She avoided putting herself forward as an erotic competitor. She was only too happy to have me interpret our relationship as a desexualized mother–baby "affair"—dependent attachment denuded of erotic desire. It was as if she was hyperaware of the outcome of triadic oedipal desire (being "dumped" in favor of a superior competitor) and saw this "lack of success" as a personal fate and sign of inadequacy. She was permanently on the threshold of the oedipal complex, feeling erotic desire, quickly imagining inadequacy, defeat and rejection, and then retreating to a seemingly pre-oedipal, dependent position as a defense.

A blind eye

It seemed to me that this patient had been very wounded by oedipal failure in her erotic desires toward her mother that was then reinforced by a similar fate (for different reasons) with her father. Her mother apparently could not erotically cathect her daughter either pre-oedipally or oedipally. A daughter's erotic desire in relation to her mother would ideally integrate early sensual elements into an oedipal romance—the primary maternal oedipal situation. This maternal oedipal configuration (traditionally labeled the female negative oedipal complex) is not to be understood as a "passing phase" of little import, but as crucial to the development of healthy, female, sexual self-esteem. Desire for the mother that is not recognized or that is invalidated can lead to the more general deflation of female desire as specific defense against perceived further loss. I will delve more deeply into these dynamics in Chapter 8. I underscore here that female to female erotic transferences can only be fully expressed, understood, and worked through by recognition of this pivotal experience in female development and desire (see Bergmann, 1995; Burch, 1997; Halberstadt-Freud, 1998). My emphasis is on what is potentially positive about the "negative" oedipal complex regardless of the patient's ultimate sexual orientation.

Although I am at this point discussing female development in relation to the oedipally desired maternal figure, my larger thesis regarding the parallel between inhibited erotic transference and undermined creativity would apply to male patients as well, of any sexual orientation, in treatment with analysts of either gender. As a particular element, inhibited or suppressed erotic transference is one that may be encountered relatively frequently, often unknowingly, by many clinician/patient pairs. This situation reflects an analytic field where certain aspects of analytic eroticism are undercut. Denied desire for the analyst paralleled many foreclosed desires in my patient's life. This dynamic has relevance in working with heterosexual women as well, who because of their conscious sexual orientation may have particular difficulty accessing erotic feelings toward the female analyst (as either a maternal or paternal oedipal figure).

Regardless of sexual orientation, repression of the primary maternal oedipal situation can contribute to inhibition of desire on many levels in women's lives. Both female patients and female analysts may remain unconscious of this oedipal level erotic transference or, if eroticism is noticed at all, reconfigure this transference to a pre-oedipal mother–infant attachment denuded of erotic components.[1] The woman analyst's difficulty with presuming to be found sexual (Person, 1985) extends beyond work with male patients to female patients both heterosexual and lesbian. Unfortunately, the most common analytic pairing of two women is often assumed through heterosexual assumption, to not involve *oedipal* erotic desire for the analyst. Turning a blind eye to female patients' erotic transference mirrors the lack of recognition in the mother of her daughter's desire. Such an analytic field would then replicate a relational experience that does not fully potentiate expression of the multiple erotic dimensions of the mind.

Couch relations

Referring to the first woman my patient found herself attracted to in over a year—one whom she found particularly mature compared to previous possibilities—Jan remarked to me: "How can I get this adult woman to go to bed with me?" I found this statement quite telling in regard to her dilemma with her mother during the oedipal phase, with me in the transference and as extrapolated to any serious interest in a sexual object. The implication is that she is a child. Much analytic material involved her dislike of depending on me for help and her feeling that this dependency infantilized and castrated her.

Several weeks later, I had the following dream: My patient and I are sexually engaged; she is lying on top of me and we orgasm together. I woke up from this dream with eyebrows raised! I mused that Andre Green

(1996) had exhorted clinicians to bring sexuality back into psychoanalysis; well, here it was, though not, I am sure, in the form Green had in mind. However, as Davies (1994) has stated, to be "a full participant in the analytic endeavor the analyst must be willing to feel and process her own somatic states . . . in the erotic countertransference" (p. 161). Full participation both erotically and creatively, by the clinician as well as by the patient, is the overarching theme of this book. My dream seemed particularly striking to me in the context of my generally not feeling very sexual toward my patient; she seemed too young to me—adolescent—not powerful enough. But then I questioned why *my* unconscious, rather than *hers*, could conjure up the dream scene erotically elevating and empowering her. My attention shifted to our physical positions in the dream; I had placed her in the culturally deemed more powerful position that seemed to excite both of us.

Over the next few weeks, with my dream in mind, I started to notice how often she referred to "the position" she occupied in the analysis (pejoratively dependent). I realized that she actually used the word "position" quite often and always to express some disadvantage, inhibition, or disability. A typical comment would be: "I'm not in a position to . . . apply for that job/write that piece/contact that person," etc. I started thinking about the concrete position she was in on the couch. Jan had had a history of impulsively sitting up from time to time or mentioning as she laid down that she did not want to recline, as well as suggesting on a couple of occasions that we both get up and go for a walk. It now became clear to me that she experienced the couch as a cot, crib, or child's twin bed. Both Lewin (1955) and Bollas (1987) have written about the regressive aspects of the couch where the maternal body is felt to hold the sleeping infant. The couch was for Jan an infantilizing, desexualized position that prevented her and I from "coming together" into any erotic connection. My dream depicted her oedipal desire (not just my own!) and restored oedipal vitality to her.

I want to consider now the role of the use of the analytic couch in shaping the erotic life of the analytic field. Westen and Gabbard (2002) noted the lack of attention to this issue:

> Perhaps the least examined way in which the analytic situation inherently structures patients' responses is in its evocation of sexual material. For all gender combinations, the process of lying down in

another's presence is bound to draw associations to sexuality, sexual vulnerability, and related issues. Patients will, of course, put their own stamp on the way these issues are expressed, but the fact that sexual feelings and conflicts are frequently evoked in the analytic relationship is not free of the situation itself.

(pp. 122–123)

Yet, as described just above, use of the couch also may have the opposite effect of dampening libido and may function as a deterrent to analytic eroticism in some pairs. The impact of the couch as an, often silent, force in the analytic field may reflect basic assumptions about what is and is not felt as erotic.

Inhibited erotic transferences in male patients towards female analysts (Karme, 1979; Lester, 1985; Person, 1985; Gornick, 1986; Kulish, 1989; Diamond, 1993; Russ, 1993) have been seen as due to the man being "one-down" in the power differential. Use of the couch—where the patient is literally down—can further entrench this dynamic. A heterosexual male patient began the initial weeks of analysis sitting in a chair facing me. He soon moved into erotic transference material, mentioning examples he knew of patients getting romantically involved with their therapists. He referred with some relish to his understanding that in analysis the patient was expected to fall in love with the analyst. He seemed to be approaching me as a prospective romantic partner and was both excited and nervous about the extent to which our relationship would evolve. In moving to use of the couch, his association during the initial session was of me leaning over him, sucking his penis. I felt some surprise at this abrupt shift to passivity and noticed how quickly the erotic excitement seemed to ebb, accompanied by a proliferation in the material of references to foreclosed sexual approaches to women.

Over the next months it became apparent that the same dynamic of "petering out" characterized his artistic endeavors. He recalled his mother demeaning his painting, saying his work had "no force" to it. This patient was not phallically empowered, and felt controlled by a mother who belittled his art and his anatomy. His penis belonged to Mommy and he could not do anything with it himself. As with the main clinical example above, a similar element characterized both the inhibition of erotic transference (and again the couch position is relevant) and creativity. His feeling regarding an omnipotent maternal figure paralyzed his artistic and his romantic ambitions. The erotic transference became blocked due to his expectation that I would take over and own him and his creations; use of the couch accentuated this transference inhibition.

In contrast, for heterosexual female patients with male analysts, lying on the couch has an almost immediate erotic connotation given its congruence with heterosexual erotic fantasy. The situation of a woman lying on the couch in front of a male analyst requires no imaginative leap at all to call up the sexual for both parties. The female patient can actually feel very *active* in this position to seduce in her "passive" way. Her body position, style of dress, hair on the pillow can all be actively courting and sexually syntonic. The male analyst can gaze down, observe her body, the contour of her breasts and hips, and even mentally undress her. The analytic setting can promote this *interaction* and *think of it as no action at all*, yet a lot can be going on, often unanalyzed, that is expressive of mutual sexual desire. In such a situation, the erotic life of the analytic pair is likely covert, increasing a danger of boundary breaches where eroticism is not worked with ethically.

Whereas when it is the patient who wants to be in the so-called "masculine" or "phallic" position, the analytic geography is not conducive to such expression; the patient may feel forced to either "just lie there" like a baby and give up oedipal erotics, or he *or she* may easily feel that to do anything else does require more overt behavioral action (like sitting up, standing, turning around), that, if acted upon, can lead to another set of boundary problems. Goldberger (1995), in a detailed review of the rather sparse literature on use of the couch, emphasized that patients are more likely to be action-prone during times of affectively intense transference interactions. She described a case where the compliant use of the couch served to defend against an impulse to look at and penetrate the analyst as well as against the wish for the reverse.

My previously published case material (Elise, 1991) illustrated a dynamic in a face-to-face treatment where the patient could be much more "phallic" with penetrating eye contact, running her eyes over my body, leaning forward, seductive smiles—again, all subtle actions that would not easily get the label of overt acting out, yet that erotically electrified the field. My male patient above made much more of an erotic impact on me when he was seated. In contrast, the analytic position on the couch is not sexual to many male patients and possibly not to certain female patients (or to certain female analysts). Although it is important, as Person (1985) stated, for a patient to be able to integrate passive libidinal aims with dependency needs, the analytic setting tends primarily to favor erotic aims that flourish with the patient placed in a supine and subordinate position. Goldberger (1995) reminded analysts to be alert to "the subtle ways in which the couch abets their own avoidance of and defense against strong affects in the transference" (p. 39). Such avoidance is especially an issue with erotic elements in the analytic field.

I am not suggesting that we change analytic arrangements—there are many good reasons for the patient to use the couch—but we could increase our awareness that, when it comes to erotic transference and countertransference, the favorability of the analytic field to eroticism varies for different dyads. Lack of awareness of erotic transference is not purely lack of imagination on the part of certain patients; it may be iatrogenically fostered as a field phenomenon. I wondered if either my male patient or I would have been aware of erotic transference and countertransference if we had begun immediately with the couch. Analysts are so accustomed to use of the couch that we find it difficult to see that these arrangements are not "neutral." The couch can be used to defensively keep eroticism at bay or, conversely, to "heat up" the erotic electricity, with each a performance (Butler, 1990) of gender-coded forms of sexuality—a cultural and couch mandate. Although the couch is not a concrete limitation on erotic fantasy, its use does influence, along with the individual's psyche, the shape of patients' fantasies, as well as how we work through creative inhibitions.

I am highlighting the element of the physical positioning as a microcosm of the gendered power dynamics in the culture. I am particularly concerned with how the experience of desire as expressed in agency, sexuality, and appropriate aggression is forwarded or inhibited in female development in this culture, and in analysis. Females receive multiple reinforcements for becoming the sexual object of someone else's desire, and for many women this does become the template of what feels erotic, but not for all women. I see no reason to require a female patient to assume a stereotypical "feminine" position with regard to sexuality—especially as that position is not particularly associated with agentic expression of desire. The challenge was to get my patient to stay concretely on the couch and to use words to co-create a narrative expression of thwarted desires while symbolically being able to "get (it) up and get it on."

The clinical work required a move into and through symbolic elaboration of her fears and her wishful fantasies. As Davies (1998a) has so eloquently written: "Such fantasies, when allowed to flourish and elaborate themselves, enrich the intimacy of places in which we do act; they fill our lives with an energy and vitality that are invigorating, erotic, and playful" (p. 765). My patient needed to stand up *for* herself in the sense of creatively asserting and elaborating her desires in her mind. Failing this, she had previously been left "standing herself up" both in the sense of abandoning herself in the symbolic realm and in being limited to a prohibited, concrete action (getting up from the couch) which itself was a microcosm of a symbolic action that was felt to be prohibited—agentic oedipal desire.

Creativity and the primal scene

In the clinical vignette above, the patient's inhibition in her career as a writer could be understood on a deeper level when the inhibition of subtly present erotic transference was identified and given narrative expression. A relationship exists between creativity and erotic vitality—a parallel between freedom of expression in sexuality and in creativity, or conversely, inhibition of erotic feeling and of creativity.[2] Analytic exploration of one's (dis)comfort with one's erotic feeling is intimately connected to the freedom to create. Understanding of an obstacle in one area is likely to shed light on inhibition in the other. A similar defensive pattern is likely to inhere. Some felt sense of vulnerability in need of protection seems common to both erotic love and creativity. What is it that feels so vulnerable about creativity? Why does this same quality, and defenses against it, seem to infuse sexual, romantic love? I propose that erotic love and creativity share in common the following features, which I will elaborate in this section: a sense of transgression, a highly charged affective state, and an experience of exposure of a central sense of self.

Analysts from Freud (1905) on have written that to become an adult sexual partner is to transgress against the oedipal prohibition: You *can* symbolically have your parent. One needs to be able to creatively imagine oneself as a participant in the primal scene (Bion, 1959; Meltzer, 1973; Britton, 1989; Feldman, 1989), able to be sexual and to (pro)create with *each* of the parents (Aron, 1995). One needs the potential space of imagined participation and potency in order to carry this feeling into all future creative endeavors (Freud, 1908, 1914; Winnicott, 1971). If blocked from envisioning oneself in the primal scene as other than excluded onlooker, then one will have the experience of passively looking on at others' creative acts, unable oneself to create. If one can imagine active involvement, but in a only limited manner—as the recipient of pleasure, not the initiator (or vice versa), identifying with one parent/one sex versus a bisexual participation—a full range of possibilities essential to creativity will be foreclosed (Aron, 1995; Elise, 1998).

Freud (1905) believed that children's puzzling over where babies come from influences the fate of their curiosity and capacities for learning and creativity. If one cannot tolerate sexual curiosity regarding parental intercourse, future explorations are inhibited as well. Klein (1928) referred to this inquiry into the primal scene as the basis of the epistemophilic impulse. Bion (1959) conceptualized attacks on linking as reflective of anxieties about productively bringing two or more thoughts together in a mental "intercourse" capable of producing new thought. Meltzer (1973) theorized creative capacities as based in identifications with a parental couple engaged in mutually rewarding sexual intercourse. Britton (1989) and Feldman (1989), each focusing on transference implications, emphasized that the ability to link requires the ability to tolerate the primal scene/parental intercourse. A healthy internal model of the oedipal couple allows for identification with a creative activity that can be pleasurably engaged in and consummated. Aron (1995), in writing about primal scene participation, highlighted the psychic achievement of being able to hold two contrasting ideas in mind simultaneously as central to the capacity for symbolic thought and creativity. Rather (2001) described the important resonance between the psychoanalytic process and the creative process, each requiring the capacity for an internal collaboration with an unconscious other.

One needs to be able to put oneself in the picture, not solely as that which is created (a baby), but as one of the creators—able to have sex rather than being an outcome of it, creating (verb/active/subject) rather than being the creation (noun/passive/object). I consider this mental intercourse as an unconscious, internal image of any sexual union where two people co-mingle in reciprocal gratification.[3] Bion's (1959) use of the nipple/mouth connection as the prototype of intercourse (see Elise, 1998) illustrated that this concept need not be limited to penis-in-vagina sexuality. As elaborated in the next chapter, the concept of psychic bisexuality can be utilized to describe a dialectic regarding the penetrating and the penetrated in psychic life. I consider the psychic capacities to be both penetrating and penetrated as essential to creative freedom.

One needs a place to be an erotic participant, (Davies, 1998a, 1998b; Tessman, 1999) being neither in a state of permanent oedipal defeat or of guilt-ridden "victory." Davies (1998b) described this achievement as the creation of a meditative place between "infantile omnipotence and its counterpoint, psychic impotence" (p. 806). Castration anxiety, narcissistic injury, guilt, inhibition, the incest taboo—all aspects of the oedipal prohibition—need to be worked through and *relatively* resolved in order for a mature sexual relationship to be possible. It is important to acknowledge that, of course, this "resolution" is only and always partial, just as in reaching the depressive position, one does not leave paranoid-schizoid dynamics behind, never to return. Erotic elements from all developmental phases (pre- and post-oedipal, as well as oedipal) are intertwined (Cooper, 1998; Davies, 1998a, 1998b; Gabbard, 1998; Hoffman, 1998) rather than representing a linear progression that one passes through in order to reach "normal" sexuality. Putting forward one's sexual excitement will continue to be conflictual, anxiety-laden, risky, *and potentially creative* if one has the courage (Spezzano, 1993). In order to "put two and two together" (linking) one must be able to tolerate the felt sense of transgression against the oedipal prohibition inherent in breaking into the primal scene and in imaginatively participating in incestuous Eros.

A transgression also inheres in the kind of linking that characterizes what we specifically think of as creativity. One does not merely link two things together; one joins two or more things *that usually do not go together—a transgressive combination*. If these specific items are not usually combined, some force is acting against this particular pairing, against this specific link being made; to do so challenges some presently held, accepted, even cherished conception. Such combining may provoke discomfort, even anger; it is an audacious move—daring, bold. Creativity takes courage.

The more one is hailed as producing something truly exciting, the more one risks entering the territory of persecution. New forms of painting, for instance, have usually been extremely controversial, jarring to the current sensibility, and have elicited much negative reaction, provoking outrage as often as excitement and admiration. Creativity engenders tremendous affective response in others and in the self. To the extent one succeeds, one is in peril. Will you survive possible destructive retaliation? Will your creation not only survive but thrive? One is walking a tightrope between exultation and destruction; which way is this going to go—good or bad, terrific or terrible? In fact, this last pairing expresses a central agony—the razor edge balance between success and failure: "That's terrific!" versus "that's terrible!" Both affectively strong, these two words convey exactly opposite meanings—"We love it!" "We hate it!"—by a change in only one small, last syllable. In creating, one is riding that edge. If not in the realm of your production being potentially terrible, you have little shot at it being terrific.

The word "passionate" conveys something strongly felt. Passion is particularly associated with romantic love, erotic desire and creativity (See Freud, 1908, 1915). By its nature, erotic desire is affectively intense—the stronger the desire, the stronger the affect. Creativity is very exciting; there is some mounting tension, as with sexual desire, that has one more and more stimulated, seeking some "orgasmic" outcome; one does not want to be dropped in this endeavor or to have a creative bubble burst before consummation. If one's desire is rejected, one drops precipitously from a very good feeling with movement, vitality, and aliveness to a very bad, static feeling—a state of deflation and deadness. We seek out the former, want to avoid the latter and have a heavy investment in the outcome. If accepted, it is thrilling to desire and to be desired; getting to create the baby with the desired parent, one is potent, omnipotent. If rejected, one experiences a sense of abysmal failure and isolation; one is cast out, castrated, impotent.

Additionally, erotic desire and creative expression each entail a sense of a "core" vulnerability—the exposure of the true self (Winnicott, 1960). Along with the transgressive factor and affective intensity noted above, one is revealing one's most valued, affectively invested self (sexual body, emotional desire, creative mind). The actor Ed Harris (2001) identified with the artist Pollock: "This is where you open up, where you are vulnerable and where all of your hope lives" (p. 50). One is psychically *naked*. The experience of threat extends beyond the possibility that your creation may be controversial; something essential is exposed to view, undefended, unprotected. If *this* aspect of self is rejected, fails to make an impression, it will matter in a central way. As Winnicott wrote, the reason the false self is developed in the first place is to protect the true self, otherwise something essential to the self could be annihilated, gone forever. Yet as

Winnicott underscored, the false self lacks something that is essential to creative originality.

False self efforts at getting positive responses can meet with failure in a manner that can be defended against, and one can go on to make further (half-hearted) attempts. It is the exposure of the true self—so heavily invested—that has many would-be writers/artists stop after initial experiences of cutting rejections (see Kolodny, 2000). One cannot risk that level of rejection of that part of the self very often: "Hurt me somewhere else—not there." We are familiar with how people often act with an attraction (including erotic transference) to a particular individual; covering up their feelings, they are less openly vulnerable with that person than with others where not as much is at stake. People hate to express sexual attraction to another only to get a response that the feeling is not returned. Feeling we have not exposed as much in a platonic request as in a passionate one, we more easily tolerate someone not wanting to be our friend.

In sum, we find in erotic desire and in creativity: 1) a highly positive affective state with intense excitement and fear of affective dropping, 2) a feeling that the true self is exposed, leaving one undefended against rejection of a central sense of self, and 3) a transgressive element that heightens the fearful expectations of punishment/retaliation/castration, insuring that you will not live to create on another day. Creativity, sexual desire, and erotic transference each entail all of these dangers. Defenses against sexual vulnerability will dovetail with defenses against the vulnerability of creativity. One's relationship to creativity likely mirrors one's oedipal complex, with its particular resolution or lack thereof.

With my patient Jan, the dovetailing of anxiety and defense in relation to erotic transference, sexual desire and creative endeavors became evident once I was able to recognize a parallel structure in all three experiences. The analytic task was to make these connections available to the patient's understanding as we untangled her automatic assumptions regarding expectations of failure. This effort required a process of working through the felt sense of humiliation in desiring me such that she could then imagine herself as a viable erotic contender. We were able to challenge Jan's foregone conclusion that the absence of an actualized romantic relationship between us was tantamount to her being inadequate. We were gradually able to dismantle the belief that there could be only one reason for she and I not "consummating" our relationship—that she was not good enough to have me.

My patient was able to develop a psychic stance (to stand up for herself, stand firm) where, although she might not get what she desired in various circumstances, it was acceptable to want it anyway, and to even relish the wanting. Wanting no longer automatically equaled lacking. Desire became a desirable state rather than something to be avoided at any cost (and the costs were great). Jan could entertain, and be entertained by, the possibility that "if we'd met under different circumstances, maybe . . . ". She could consider that many factors in each of our lives played a part in our romance not being consummated: our roles as analyst and patient, the likelihood that I was already in a relationship, and various other external realities. Previously, "unrequited love" was seen as evidence of inadequacy, and rejection seemed to be the only logical outcome. Now, she could play with the possibility that I might also desire her, but have reasons not to act on this feeling. It even entered her mind, that if I was "available," she might find *me lacking* as a good match *for her* in spite of her positive feelings toward me. The erotic economy of our analytic field opened to a new equilibrium as long-held, foundational assumptions loosened.

This kind of shift, relatively easy to articulate here, requires a restructuring of assumptions regarding the self that is not accomplished quickly in the actual treatment, but must be reworked over time. However, this recognition by a patient over time—"*Oh*, you mean there might be some *other* reasons that we are not together" (other than perceived sense of lack of appeal)—is a poignant unfolding. To finally realize that the reason one did not get to "have" your mother/father is because they *are* your parents—a generation ahead and already committed romantically—*not* because you failed to be appealing enough. One can finally let go of the conviction that, if only one had been a more desirable person, it all would have worked out differently.

Tenacity of injured self-esteem is often a reason why a patient can have trouble truly recognizing the generational boundary in the Oedipus complex. The narcissistic wound is sealed over, but not healed, and constitutes an ongoing explanatory fantasy that precludes the rational recognition of reality limitations (including any notion of an incest taboo). The negative generational inheritance of an unresolved oedipal complex frequently involves sustaining significant narcissistic injury such that, against all logical reasoning, the conviction is maintained that personal (in)adequacy is *the sole factor* in whether one's desires are met or unmet.

As these issues were worked through with my patient, and as her self-esteem strengthened, eroticism in the transference was no longer automatically a foray into the realm of humiliation. Our engagement shifted from a somewhat stilted or choppy quality; fantasy could be playfully and erotically elaborated, including her imagining my participation, "but for . . . (various obstacles)." Jan could now envision that I could want her and that I might also experience some frustration and lament in response to the restrictions of reality.

This newly found freedom of being able to esteem herself as a desiring subject (and as a desirable object), and of being able to sustain this feeling over time and in the absence of direct confirmation or gratification, spilled over into her creative projects where the issues of perceived inadequacy and failure were mirrored. She could last longer in her own imaginative scenarios—hold up and hold hope in her internal world—and was freer to go on creating without depending on immediate and continual reinforcing feedback (often unavailable in creative endeavors that require an ability to endure much delayed, and uncertain, gratification). Jan's presenting problem regarding her creative inhibitions had been that, even though she had exciting ideas, she could not sustain creative work. Using the metaphor of writing a play, she described how she was "good with the first and third acts," but could never "hang in there for the second act." Thus, her projects rarely came to fruition. We were able to see how this had played out in the erotic transference—first act, a good opening gambit; third act, a quick and tragic denouement. She had not been able to play out the story line in either realm. As she became able figuratively to write a complete script (several versions, actually!) regarding our relationship, this ability unfolded in her actual writing and in the overall expansion of her personality.

When clinicians help patients to access, express and tolerate erotic transference, we help them to do the same with creative expression: to tolerate, even enjoy, increasing levels of affective intensity that often reach a feverish pitch, without fear of fragmentation, psychic overwhelm, on the roller-coaster from elation to deflation. We hope to strengthen self-esteem so that the lively expression of the true self is worth the risk of rejection and can be more exposed without permanent damage. We aim to lessen the sense of guilt over oedipal transgression so that the fear of retaliation is brought down to reality; one may receive a negative response from the community, but can manage to hold up under this experience rather than feeling castrated by omnipotent parental figures. This accomplishment is marked by:

> the degree to which the patient (and the analyst) comes to know, feel, and own his own desirous states—those that have the potential to be satisfied and those that can only be sustained unmet—without the crushing blows of despair, humiliation, and impotent rage.
> (Davies, 1998b, p. 810)

Such access to one's own states of desire is a crucial aspect of analytic eroticism.

Inhibitions in the analyst

Clearly, an analyst cannot help a patient with inhibited erotic life if the analyst is having trouble with these feelings in the countertransference; both patient and clinician will likely collude in denial and avoidance (Coen, 1994; Davies, 1994, 1998a, 1998b; Kernberg, 1994; Gabbard, 1996; Solomon, 1997). In order to move forward in this complex clinical arena, it is necessary to understand as fully as possible the inhibitions or obstacles to the *analyst's* self awareness in the realm of eroticism.

Thinking about erotic transference requires that clinicians can engage the subject of sexuality; outside of a classical Freudian model, analysts have not demonstrated an impressive ability in this regard, leading Green (1996) to lament the waning of attention to sexuality under the sway of object relations theory. Mitchell (1988) pointed out that there is nothing inherent in object relations theory that needs to limit consideration of sexuality, yet sex has gotten short shrift within this model. Without a theoretical container for clinically fraught material, avoidance is likely, as is particularly evident in the difficulties encountered in negotiating the erotic life of the analytic field.

Often, clinicians have an intuition that erotic feeling is present just below the surface in one or both participants, or have the experience that erotic transference themes appear, and then rather quickly disappear, within the analytic field. This situation leads to a particular type of countertransference anxiety that, in bringing attention to erotic feeling, the analyst is seducing the patient—an anxiety heightened by concerns regarding sexual boundary violations. A strong pull exists toward only analyzing erotic transference when the patient is overtly introducing this material—following the patient's lead, so to speak. This approach is quite in contrast, for instance, to the handling of inhibited aggression; clinicians expect to interpret aggressive themes in the transference when noticed, not to wait indefinitely for an inhibited patient to realized that she or he is actually angry underneath surface passivity, compliance, boredom, etc.

Clinician avoidance of erotic feeling in the material has been attributed to concerns regarding complex issues of self-disclosure and of bodily experience taking over (Benjamin, 1994; Cooper, 1998; Davies, 1994, 1998a, 1998b; Gabbard, 1994a, 1994b, 1994c, 1998; Hoffman, 1998). Yet, analyzing erotic elements of the analytic field touches deeper concerns than the issues considered in the analytic debate regarding purposeful self-disclosure. *Feeling* erotically toward a patient is *itself* disturbing to many clinicians and can also result in unintentional disclosure when this feeling is perceived by the patient, as does happen. Although aggression is also a very bodily experience and may advertently or inadvertently be disclosed, clinicians are not as discomforted by fantasies of strangling patients (even when this is intuited by a patient) as of stroking them.

Spezzano (1993) described sexual excitement as a primary affect. Sexual excitement is also the affect subjected to a primal prohibition: the incest taboo. I suggest that the incest taboo is underemphasized as a central dilemma *for the analyst* in addressing erotic feeling in the clinical hour: conscious awareness of almost any other feeling is tolerated within family life. Families do not condone physical aggression, but aggressive thoughts are quite commonly expressed. In contrast, conscious recognition of sexual feeling toward family members is relatively rare. People might feel guilty over yelling, "I hate you, wish you were dead" to a parent or sibling, but most would be shocked and appalled to encounter even the private thought, "I want you," let alone verbally express it.

Feelings of anger/aggression are *expected* in family life; siblings, as well as parents, fight and tolerate the feeling and verbal expression of hate fairly regularly. The concept of "fair fighting" is popularized within the culture. Clinicians help people to acknowledge familial aggression in appropriate ways and use the transference toward this end. But no parallel clinical agenda exists to have patients start expressing eroticism within the family. This is the dilemma analysts are beset with in the clinical hour: transferences and countertransferences place us back in the family, and we are under the influence of the incest taboo. This taboo works against acknowledging either our own or patients' sexual feelings and permeates the entire topic of sex and sexuality, making clinicians strongly inclined to repress the subject, focusing instead on other issues.

Adding to the clinical complexity, sexual desire or attraction can be a relatively enduring feeling toward another person (versus a mood of a few hours or even days) and may lead to experiencing the relationship as moving into a completely different realm. No other feeling leads to this level of change in the nature of a relationship—anger may lead to the *end* of a relationship—and in how it is defined. Other intense feeling states more often lead to momentary expression and possibly withdrawal. Strong feelings of attraction have the power to categorically change the relationship from the platonic to the erotic.

When a patient, acknowledging his sexual feelings toward me, said in a slow, intimate tone, "Sure, I'd like to become familiar with your body," his remark not only had a definite erotic impact on me but evoked an image in both his mind and mine of a completely changed relationship between us. Our professional relationship out the window, we would now start spending more time with one another than with any other adult. We would not just be "having sex" but would do all the things lovers do: long walks, movies, romantic dinners, etc. Rarely does admission of a feeling have the capacity to alter a relationship so profoundly with such immediacy.

We see an interplay of many factors that inhibit clinicians: In addition to a relative lack of focus in analytic theory and training on erotic life, and the intense concern in the profession at present regarding sexual boundary violations, a feeling subtly permeates our professional identity that we are not as clinicians supposed to be sexual beings. The greater taboo against sexual feeling within the family makes it especially difficult for *either* participant in the analytic dyad to know how to handle erotic feeling in a relationship that has familial undertones.

Inhibitions on the part of the analyst can extend to our participation in a particular professional community where, along with our colleagues, we may act as if we are the parents who never "do it," or at least not in any way ever known to the "children." The professional persona proscribing sexuality contrasts with a relative permission for aggression as seen in the form of professional debates. It seems that we are in the grip of a subtle, but rather pervasive sense of sexual decorum that seems to represent unresolved oedipal issues, not just in our patients, but in ourselves.

Davies's (1998a) paper on the need for recognition of *post*-oedipal sexuality is relevant not only for patients, but for clinicians as well. When in training is there discussion of our own sexuality and how it would be appropriately integrated into our professional lives? The absence of such discussions further reinforces the sense that the eroticism of the clinician is a completely inappropriate topic. Yet it is understood that use of the self is the analyzing instrument. Use of the self to analyze erotic dimensions of the analytic field requires full access to analytic eroticism.

Conclusion

Clinicians often assume it is the explicit presence of erotic feelings on the part of one or both participants that leads to difficult treatment dilemmas, which is indeed often the case. However, all is not necessarily well when erotic feeling appears to be absent or "not an issue." It is important to examine what it does mean when a treatment does not seem to involve erotic transference and countertransference; this significant question is often overlooked in clinical work that, whether going well or not, focuses on other issues. While not every analytic dyad will experience erotic desire for one another, an absence of such feeling should not merely be taken for granted. Absence of erotic transference and countertransference should give rise to as much attention as does the presence of such feelings.

As clinicians, we believe that it is not psychologically desirable for people to rationally decide to experience some emotions and not others. We value awareness of all parts of the self even if certain feelings "cause trouble"—entail conflict, engender a sense of deprivation, loss, narcissistic vulnerability, embarrassment, potential rejection. We want our patients and ourselves to be able to tolerate negative affects that may partner an awareness of our desires. Otherwise, any number of feelings may be preempted or foreclosed before being explored and fully known. It seems unlikely that a healthy "sublimation" or creative redirection ensues for desires that are disavowed; more likely, avoidance and denial lead to a constriction of the personality. In contrast, expansion of the containing capacity, to engage the entirety of psychic life, fosters development of the personality and of the creative self.

In the experience of erotic transference, a patient has the opportunity to get to know a passionate part of the self, as well as all the conflicts that may accompany. People frequently have the sense of discovering themselves when discovering another romantically. Even when such a relationship does not work out, contact is made with a valuable and sometimes surprising aspect of self. One breaks out of a more customary, controlled persona when caught up in desire for another. This experience can be transformative—an enriching of the self that can be retained even if the object of desire is lost. Tessman (1999) referred to the generative possibilities within the analytic dyad of the ever-changing love for the analyst as facilitating a "profound reordering of the inner experience of self and others" (p. 39). Psychoanalysis is, hopefully, a creative endeavor for the clinician as well for as the patient. In examining and working through our own inhibitions to our creative and erotic engagement in the clinical hour, we stand to enrich our experience of the work we do. Psychoanalysis provides for both participants a potent(ial) space for creative elaboration of desire.

Notes

1 See Wrye and Welles (1994) for a sensuously detailed picture of pre-oedipal erotic transference. It is important, however, not to read Wrye and Welles as meaning that all female maternal erotic transference is pre-oedipal. See Russ (1993) for an excellent discussion of the many factors that inhibit women analysts' awareness of erotic countertransference.
2 I am not claiming that this conceptualization constitutes the only way in which to understand the psychodynamics of creativity. Milner (1950) writing on generative emptiness, and Bion (1970) on negative capability, each focused on the ability to tolerate a state of the unknown. Segal (1952) emphasized the capacity to mourn and to make reparation. See Kolodny (2000) for an insightful depiction of a range of psychological factors inhibiting creativity.
3 See Aron (1995) and Schwartz (1995) for a debate on the relative merits of retaining and modifying this classical concept that has often been used to privilege heterosexuality.

References

Aron, L. (1995). The internalized primal scene. *Psychoanalytic Dialogues*, 5: 195–237.
Baranger, M. and Baranger, W. (1961–1962/2008). The analytic situation as a dynamic field. *International Journal of Psychoanalysis*, 89: 795–826.
Benjamin, J. (1994). Commentary on papers by Tansey, Davies, and Hirsch. *Psychoanalytic Dialogues*, 4: 193–201.
Bergmann, M. (1995). Observations on the female negative oedipal phase and its significance in the analytic transference. *Journal of Clinical Psychoanalysis*, 4: 283–295.

Bion, W. (1959). Attacks on linking. *International Journal of Psychoanalysis*, 40: 308–315.
— (1970). *Attention and interpretation: A scientific approach to insight in psychoanalysis and groups.* London: Tavistock Publications.
Bollas, C. (1987). *The shadow of the object.* New York: Colombia University Press.
Britton, R. (1989). The missing link: Parental sexuality in the Oedipus complex. In Steiner, J. (ed.) *The Oedipus complex today.* London: Karnac Books, pp. 83–102.
Burch, B. (1997). *Other women: Lesbian/bisexual experience and psychoanalytic views of women.* New York: Columbia University Press.
Butler, J. (1990). *Gender trouble: Feminism and the subversion of identity.* New York: Routledge.
Coen, S. (1994). Barriers to love between patient and analyst. *Journal of the American Psychoanalytic Association*, 42: 1107–1135.
Cooper, S. (1998). Flirting, post-Oedipus, and mutual protectiveness in the analytic dyad: Commentary on paper by Davies. *Psychoanalytic Dialogues*, 8: 767–779.
Davies, J. M. (1994). Love in the afternoon: A relational reconsideration of desire and dread in the countertransference. *Psychoanalytic Dialogues*, 4: 153–170.
— (1998a). Between the disclosure and the foreclosure of erotic transference-countertransference. *Psychoanalytic Dialogues*, 8: 747–766.
— (1998b). Thoughts on the nature of desires: The ambiguous, the transitional, and the poetic. Reply to commentaries. *Psychoanalytic Dialogues*, 8: 805–823.
Diamond, D. (1993). The paternal transference: A bridge to the erotic oedipal transference. *Psychoanalytic Inquiry*, 13: 206–225.
Elise, D. (1991). When sexual and romantic feelings permeate the therapeutic relationship. In Silverstein, C. (Ed.) *Gays, lesbians and their therapists.* New York: Norton, pp. 52–67.
— (1998). Gender repertoire: Body, mind and bisexuality. *Psychoanalytic Dialogues*, 8: 379–397.
— (2000). Woman and desire: Why women may *not* want to want. *Studies in Gender and Sexuality*, 1: 125–145.
Feldman, M. (1989). The Oedipus complex: Manifestations in the inner world and the therapeutic situation. In Steiner, J. (Ed.) *The Oedipus complex today.* London: Karnac Books, pp. 103–128.
Ferro, A. and Civitarese, G. (2015). *The analytic field and its transformations.* London: Karnac.
Freud, S. (1905). Three essays on the theory of sexuality. *The Standard Edition*, 7: 123–243.
— (1908). Creative writers and day-dreaming. *The Standard Edition*, 9: 141–156.
— (1914). Remembering, repeating, and working through. *The Standard Edition*, 12: 145–156.
— (1915). Observations on transference love. *The Standard Edition*, 12: 157–171.

Gabbard, G. (1994a). Of love and lust in erotic transference. *Journal of the American Psychoanalytic Association*, 42: 385–403.
— (1994b). Sexual excitement and countertransference love in the analyst. *Journal of the American Psychoanalytic Association*, 42: 1083–1106.
— (1994c). Commentary on papers by Tansey, Davies, and Hirsch. *Psychoanalytic Dialogues*, 4: 203–213.
— (1996). *Love and hate in the analytic setting*. Northvale, New Jersey: Aronson.
— (1998). Commentary on paper by Davies. *Psychoanalytic Dialogues*, 8: 781–789.
Goldberger, M. (1995). The couch as defense and as potential for enactment. *Psychoanalytic Quarterly*, 64: 23–42.
Gornick, L. (1986). Developing a new narrative: The woman therapist and the male patient. *Psychoanalytic Psychology*, 3: 299–325.
Green, A. (1996). Has sexuality anything to do with psychoanalysis? *International Journal of Psychoanalysis*, 76: 871–883.
Halberstadt-Freud, H. (1998). Electra versus Oedipus: Femininity reconsidered. *International Journal of Psychoanalysis*, 79: 41–56.
Harris, E. (2001). Interview. *San Francisco Chronicle, Datebook*, 2/18, p. 50.
Hirsch, I. (1994). Countertransference love and theoretical model. *Psychoanalytic Dialogues*, 4: 171–192.
Hoffman, I. (1998). Poetic transformations of erotic experience: Commentary on paper by Davies. *Psychoanalytic Dialogues*, 8: 791–804.
Karme, L. (1979). The analysis of a male patient by a female analyst: The problem of the negative oedipal transference. *International Journal of Psychoanalysis*, 60: 253–261.
— (1993). Male patients and female analysts: Erotic and other psychoanalytic encounters. *Psychoanalytic Inquiry*, 13: 192–205.
Kernberg, O. (1994). Love in the analytic setting. *Journal of the American Psychoanalytic Association*, 42: 1137–1157.
Klein, M. (1928). Early stages of the Oedipus conflict. *International Journal of Psychoanalysis*, 9: 167–180.
Kolodny, S. (2000). *The captive muse: On creativity and its inhibitions*. Madision, Connecticut: Psychosocial Press.
Kulish, N. (1989). Gender and transference: Conversations with female analysts. *Psychoanalytic Psychology*, 6: 59–71.
Lester, E. (1985). The female analyst and the erotized transference. *International Journal of Psychoanalysis*, 66: 283–293.
Lewin, B. (1955). Dream psychology and the analytic situation. *Psychoanalytic Quarterly*, 24: 169–199.
Meltzer, D. (1973). *Sexual states of mind*. Perthshire, Scotland: Clunie Press.
Milner, M. (1950). *On not being able to paint*. Second Edition, London: Heinemann (1957).
Mitchell, S. (1988). *Relational concepts in psychoanalysis*. Cambridge, MA: Harvard University Press.

Person, E. (1985). The erotic transference in women and in men: Differences and consequences. *Journal of the American Academy of Psychoanalysis*, 13: 159–180.
Rather, L. (2001). Collaborating with the unconscious other: The analysand's capacity for creative thinking. *International Journal of Psychoanalysis*, 82: 515–531.
Russ, H. (1993). The female therapist and the male patient. *Psychoanalytic Psychology*, 10: 393–406.
Schwartz, D. (1995). Retaining classical concepts—Hidden costs. *Psychoanalytic Dialogues*, 5: 239–248.
Searles, H. (1965). Oedipal love in the countertransference. In Searles, H., *Collected papers on schizophrenia and related subjects*. New York: International University Press, pp. 284–303.
Segal, H. (1952). A psychoanalytical approach to aesthetics. In *The work of Hanna Segal*. New York: Jason Aronson (1981), pp. 185–206.
Solomon, M. (1997). On love and lust in the countertransference. *Journal of the American Academy of Psychoanalysis*, 25: 71–90.
Spezzano, C. (1993). *Affect in psychoanalysis: A clinical synthesis*. Hillsdale, New Jersey: The Analytic Press.
Tessman, L. H. (1999). A cry of fire, an old flame, the matter of fireplace. In Bassin, D. (ed.) *Female sexuality*. Northvale, New Jersey: Aronson, pp. 33–48.
Westen, D. and Gabbard, G. (2002). Developments in cognitive neuroscience: II: Implications for the theories of transference. *Journal of the American Psychoanalytic Association*, 50: 99–134.
Winnicott, D. (1960). Ego distortion in terms of true and false self. In *The maturational processes*. New York: International Universities Press, 1965, pp. 140–152.
— (1971). *Playing and reality*. London: Tavistock.
Wrye, H. K. and Welles, J. (1994). *The narration of desire: Erotic transferences and countertransferences*. Hillsdale, New Jersey: The Analytic Press.

Part II

Potential space and orientations of the erotic

Chapter 4

Psychic bisexuality and creativity
Gender repertoires

I now want to tease out certain subjective experiences of the body, particularly as elaborated within the sexual encounters of an adult relationship. Integrating a clinical and theoretical focus on sexuality with an emphasis on earliest object relations, I propose to examine the dialectic of the penetrating and the penetrated, beginning with the nursing couple of mother and infant within the reciprocal engagement of maternal eroticism. I view these representations of bodily penetration *as metaphor and microcosm* for intrapsychic experience. I hope to illustrate in this chapter certain ways in which the sexed body veiled by the gendered psyche can lead to a split, and therefore constricted, experience of sexuality—one that can creatively expand, or not, depending on access to psychic bisexuality in the gendered mind of the self and of the partner.

Winnicott (1971), writing about "creativity and its origins," made the statement: "There is nothing new either inside or outside psychoanalysis in the idea that men and women have a 'predisposition towards bisexuality'" (p. 72). While it is true that the concept of bisexuality has had a long history in the analytic literature, for decades this concept fell prey to pathologizing assumptions. Ironically, while analysts often acknowledged the relationship between psychic bisexuality and creativity, creative thinking *about* bisexuality was minimal. Freud (1905) had emphasized: "Without taking bisexuality into account, I think it would scarcely be possible to arrive at an understanding of the sexual manifestations that are actually to be observed in men and women" (p. 220). Although a central concept throughout Freud's work (Stoller, 1972), psychic bisexuality was subsequently neglected in an analytic literature that focused on "normative" development toward heterosexuality. This neglect aligned with the decreasing analytic attention in recent decades to sexuality more generally, in a reversal of what is seen in the culture at large, where sex is fore-fronted.

A thoughtful elaboration of the concept of psychic bisexuality was likely also inhibited by the theoretical focus over several decades on the development of core gender identity. Tyson (1994) put forth that a theory regarding an initial bisexual matrix forecloses a theory of core gender identity in girls.[1] She was responding to Freud's formulation of bisexuality where the girl's earliest sense of her bodily self was theorized not as *bi*sexual, but as male and masculine. This conceptualization of bisexuality did erase recognition of core female gender identity. However, I have theorized that it is possible to include a primary sense of femaleness—a term I have proposed to replace "primary femininity" (Elise, 1997)—within a bisexual matrix. An early sense of self located in a female—or male—body can co-exist with the unconscious fantasy of potential unlimited by gender. In this sense, bisexual matrix refers to an initial *unlimited*, versus *female* or *male*, gender matrix (Fast, 1984, 1990). Thus, the concept of psychic bisexuality addresses the human confrontation with two sexes (Elise, 2000), while understanding that sex and gender representations of self and other *move along a continuum rather than falling into two discrete categories*. We might think in terms of pansexuality.[2]

Fast's (1990) conceptualization of an early bisexual matrix accommodates both the fundamental femaleness of a girl and maleness of a boy as well as the psychological manifestations of bisexuality along a gendered continuum. Early mental representations are influenced by sex and gender in a number of ways—such as anatomy, physiology, identifications with, and treatment by, parents—that can be "gender congruent" rather than Freud's notion that the girl views herself as male, or Stoller's (1972) idea that the boy initially experiences himself as female. At the same time these mental representations are "over-inclusive"—undifferentiated as to gender—and, thus, not limited by one's anatomical sex. Fast's theory highlighted the wish to be both sexes (Kubie, 1974; Wisdom, 1983)—to be bisexually complete—that occurs in females and in males, as well as the conflicts surrounding this wish.

Both Bassin (1996) and Benjamin (1995) did, however, critique the overly rigid resolution of bisexual identifications that Fast's theory depicted as the optimal outcome. Bassin (1996) argued for a post-oedipal recuperation of earlier, unlimited body ego representations and cross-sex identifications, "which can mitigate [a] rigid polarized gender identity" (p. 158). Instead of repression of conflicting representations, use of symbolic ability to engage with, rather than deny, difference allows for creative interplay between "masculine" and "feminine" senses of self. Benjamin spoke of the heterosexual gender complementarity that the oedipal phase organizes—fixed and mutually exclusive positions—as the sacrifice of identifications with difference and a contradiction of the complexity of an individual's desires and identifications.

Core gender identity, object choice and overt sexual orientation are typically only the tip of the iceberg when considering the concept of psychic bisexuality. Difficult to identify underneath surface manifestations of gender consistency and overt sexual orientation are the varied and varying same-and cross-sex mental representations of *self and other* (see Harris, 1991; Benjamin, 1995; Bassin, 1996). As I have written (Elise, 1997), multiple combinations exist intrapsychically that are not bound to the anatomical sex of the partners or to the core gender identity of either. Regarding the use of the term "over-inclusive," I have suggested that gender identity might be better referred to as either inclusive (flexible and integrated) or under-inclusive/exclusive (rigid normative splitting into "feminine" and "masculine") (Elise, 2000).

Recognition of one's core gender identity has been theorized as representing a most basic aspect of reality-testing, which is curious in itself given that the concept of core gender identity, as developed by Stoller (1972), meant conforming to a *designated* sex; one was assigned to a category and expected to stick to it. However, the mind does not like such restraint, has ambivalence about the category and plays tricks with "reality" by unconscious (and sometimes conscious) bisexual fantasies of self and other. The concept of psychic bisexuality should illuminate the wish to *be* both sexes (self-representation) and to *have* both sexes (object choice and representation). Sweetnam (1996) made the important additional point that the concept of bisexuality should also include recognition of the need to be loved and erotically acknowledged *by* both sexes. As I am emphasizing in this book, each child from earliest development on needs an experience of erotic vitality and mutual desire in the relationship with both females and males.

I will now explore certain insights from a bisexual, female patient whose changing experience of sexuality in relationships with men and with women led to variations in her experience of her gendered sense of self. Selected aspects of case material are presented in order to illustrate the experiences of penetrability versus impenetrability within the psyche. The false notion in Freud's work, as well as in much subsequent theorizing, that female sexuality and personality equate with passivity and male sexuality and personality with activity (in spite of Freud cautioning against this dichotomy), has been critiqued (Dimen, 1991; Benjamin, 1995). Here, I explore the dimensions not of activity versus passivity but of a fixed versus a permeable bodily and psychic boundary—the ability to penetrate versus the *ability* to be penetrated. The concept of psychic bisexuality allows for self-representation both as penetrated and as penetrating. I further develop the metaphor of the nursing couple (Winnicott, 1952) as the site of bisexual identifications and as the earliest relation of the penetrating to the penetrated.

My patient showed shifting gender identifications depending on the relational context—the geography of her lover's body and mind. In relation to a woman, she became able to see herself *psychologically* (not just physically) as penetrating, as well as penetrated. In subsequent relations with men, she initially found that this developed ability to be penetrating had "no where to go." I suggest that it is not primarily the penetrability of the body, but *of the mind*, that influences sexuality and relational dynamics in couples. The possibility exists of creative variations in the sexual sense of self when there is fluidity and multiplicity in gendered identifications: This flexibility in gendered experience that I refer to may develop within one's self in tandem with one's ongoing partner, or may be facilitated in a new relationship, be that with a man or a woman.

Clinical material

My patient Keri, heterosexual in her teens and early twenties, had thought of herself as quite assertive and initiating in sexual relationships. However, in a first relationship with another woman, she soon recognized certain assumptions, of which she had been unaware, that she had been operating with in previous relations with men. Having thought of herself as confident in being sexually agentic, she could now see that she had expected a man to be even *more* agentic and initiating in sex. This expectation usually had been met, which had served to keep it unconscious. Keri had "initiated" as an invitation for the man to "take over." Even when she had pursued active stimulation of a man's body while he remained "passive," subliminally this had felt to her "like foreplay and not the real thing"—the "real thing" being his actively doing something to her (most especially penetrating her). Now with this first female lover, with whom ample mutual attraction existed, there seemed to be a gap of sorts in the relational/sexual connection between the two women. Keri realized that she was the one responsible for this gap; she expected the other woman to meet her more than halfway. Her sexual initiative lacked follow-through and the other woman was not responding by automatically taking over in the way Keri had been used to with men. This resulted at times in an unmet potential in the erotic connection between the two women.

Keri went through an experience over the years—in relation to this woman and in another long-term lesbian relationship—that she described as "expanding her gender repertoire." This image expressed a change in her gendered self-concept that affected her participation in sex and in life. Her use of the word "repertoire" captures, I think, the experience of gender multiplicity—the ability to play (in the Winnicottian sense) with varied gendered expressions of self without a threat to sense of self or to core gender identity. This playing out of new parts of the self developed primarily in the context of love-making with a female partner, but extended to influence her sense of self more generally. Keri described herself as developing more of what stereotypically *might* be thought of as a "masculine" identification, but which she referred to as "getting to know the thrill of psychic penetration." She did not lose her "feminine" sense of receptivity, but elaborated a sense of self as one who can penetrate as well.

In Keri's experience of sexuality with women partners there existed not only the exposure (visual penetration) and penetration of the genitalia, but the "penetration" of exposing and touching *many parts* of her lover's body. Another woman could be *psychically penetrated* even when there was no actual penetration of bodily orifices. My patient described the particular example of touching her lover's breasts: "Something about a woman's vulnerability regarding her breasts gives me the feeling as if I am *entering* her." Pursuing this theme, she remarked:

> It's not nearly as thrilling to run your fingertips up the insides of a man's thighs as it is with a woman. It's erotic with a man and you feel he's enjoying it, but with a woman there is such a level of *anticipation*.

When I asked, "Anticipation of what?" she replied:

110   Psychic bisexuality and creativity

> Of going . . . somewhere. With a man, my fingers traveling up his thighs arrive at his penis and, well . . . that's it—there's nowhere else to go. With a woman, my fingers eventually arrive at the opening of her entire body and, even without any literal penetration, there's such an anticipatory vulnerability on her part and thrill on mine—a psychological penetration. It's quite something to feel that powerful in relation to someone!

My patient felt that another woman was more penetrable than she had experienced men to be, not only bodily, but psychologically. She vividly described the excitement of exposing and penetrating a woman, easing the woman's protective impulse, and making her feel safe to open.

In subsequent sexual relationships with men, Keri encountered unexpected blocks to the expression of her expanded sense of self. Male fears of being bodily and psychically penetrated posed an obstacle to certain aspects of her "repertoire." She found that over time her identification as penetrating "shrunk" or was "put on the shelf." She noticed with men an absence of that particular quality of psychological vulnerability—true of women lovers—in being undressed and touched. In earlier relationships with men she had never taken notice of this, but now it seemed odd and in direct contrast to her experience with women. In association she recalled two incidents from high school gym class: In the first, a girl was seen, almost fully undressed, by a boy. The girl gasped in embarrassment, and the boy grinned. In the second situation, another girl walked in on a nude boy. The girl gasped in embarrassment, and the boy grinned.

The lack of parallel structure in these two examples intrigued my patient and expressed her feeling that, "you can literally take a man's clothes off, but you can't really undress him in the more figurative, symbolic sense." Keri elaborated the following comparison:

> You can go "into" a woman in many places of her body, even ones that are not actual orifices, because of the sense of entering psychologically/symbolically. You enter her psyche through many places of her body. You have an effect, an impact, on her. Whereas with a man, I don't feel I really get to him in the same way even though I'm doing the same things to, frequently, analogous parts of his body. Even his penis doesn't seem that vulnerable—it's right out there anyway—and he doesn't have that protective air about it that women have with their

genitals and with their entire body. It's like someone greeting you on their front porch with the door shut behind them. They come right out, quickly visible. You see and talk with them, but you don't go in to where they live; they keep control of what you see and do by coming out to meet you—that's men! It's very different from knocking on a door which the person then opens standing inside, perhaps somewhat shyly, to let you come in—that's women!

With that, my patient concluded her description of the sexual difference between women and men. She might be accused of dichotomizing and essentializing gender dualisms, but her own experience indicated that penetration is not inherently male, and she believed men could be receptive to penetration even though she encountered a certain psychic impermeability in her male lovers. How can we understand her experience?

The primal, 'primal scene'

Kernberg (1991) wrote:

> Erotic desire is a search for pleasure always oriented to another person, an object to be penetrated or invaded or to be penetrated or invaded by. It is . . . [an] intermingling that has a quality both of a forceful crossing of a barrier and becoming one with the other person.
>
> (p. 345)

He went on to emphasize that these "relations between bodily protrusions and bodily openings" should not be confused with masculine and feminine, that polymorphous perverse features are a "crucial aspect of normal sexuality" (Kernberg, 1991, p. 340) and that bisexual identifications are universal. Traditionally, however, analysts tended to view men who were receptive to being penetrated as latently or overtly homosexual and to diagnose women with aims at penetrating as suffering from penis envy or a masculinity "complex" (Lampl de Groot, 1933; Laufer, 1986; Lax, 1994).

Lampl de Groot (1933) pointed out over eighty years ago that there is an identity in a boy's and a girl's active courtship of the mother until the anatomical difference is known, at which time the girl renounces her active sexuality. This renunciation is not easily accepted and Lampl de

Groot (1933) mentioned one little girl who "insisted with astonishing stubbornness 'But I want a little tassel right now'" (p. 497). A girl realizes that without "a little tassel" she will not be accorded the status of one who penetrates. In contrast, male development affirms the penis, "imbued with qualities of power and even assault" (May, 1986, p. 188), as *the* organ of penetration. Diamond (1997) referred to the "universal, 'phallic' gender stereotype of men as active, penetrating and potent" (p. 447)—a phallic ego ideal in which "impulses to penetrate and conquer" (p. 460) illustrate the dominance in the male psyche of defensive phallicism (see also Braunschweig and Fain, 1993; Breen, 1996).

Much of the psychoanalytic literature can be read as the story of the gendered divide of self-experience that was originally equally accessible to both sexes. In contrast, psychic bisexuality can be understood as the recuperation of lost aspects deemed gender inappropriate or possibly even threatening to a coherent sense of self. Thus, psychic bi/pansexuality can be seen to be a healthy, creative, and playful use of potential space (Winnicott, 1971) rather than a pathological delusion of omnipotence and denial of sex differences and generational boundaries. Aron (1995) emphasized this point:

> One omnipotent phantasy, in particular, that has been considered pathogenic and that, it has been argued, requires renunciation is the "bisexual" wish to be both sexes (p. 196) . . . I argue, in contrast that the omnipotent wish "to have it all," to fulfill symbolically the phantasy of being both sexes, can be used constructively and needs to be appreciated as a valuable human motive.
>
> (p. 197)

Aron (1995) described the internalized primal scene as the site of bisexual identifications. The primal scene refers to unconscious phantasies of parental intercourse and includes identifications with each parent. Aron extended the primal scene to include Klein's (1929) concept of the combined parent figure—a more primitive version of the Freudian primal scene with parents locked together in mutual oral, anal, and genital gratification. To the metaphors of the primal scene and the combined parent, I add the metaphor of the nursing couple—the most primal of erotic scenes.

Winnicott (1988) posited a basic "sexuality and fantasy which starts from very early in infancy" and where genital excitation likely occurs in "association with feeding" (p. 46). Chasseguet-Smirgel (1995) further elaborated a picture of the nursing relation as the prototypical intercourse: Erections and vaginal lubrication as well as "coital movement in both sexes have been observed" in nursing infants. The infant's experience of "unlimited penetration by a liquid substance" represents an "elementary expression" of intercourse with "genitality present from the beginning" (Chasseguet-Smirgel, 1995). Nursing within the matrix of maternal eroticism is the primal experience of intercourse for each new human, sexually stimulating for infants of both sexes as well as for the mother (see more recently Thomson-Salo and Paul, 2017).

From Chasseguet-Smirgel's (1995) provocative description, I offer the following: The creative relation to the breast can be seen as containing the basic elements of psychic bisexuality—the ability to imagine oneself in both positions in the relation of the penetrated to the penetrating. The infant is the recipient of the mother's penetration and becomes a penetrator by identification with the mother. Winnicott (1954/1975) gave an evocative image of this dynamic in his description of a three-month-old infant who "put his finger into his mother's mouth whenever she fed him at the breast" (p. 274).

In the potential space of the nursing relation many imaginative possibilities open up regarding sexual anatomy and activities. Everyone has a mouth, tongue, fingers, and anus. The girl has her clitoris-nipple, as well as another mouth in the form of her vagina. So too does the mother have a vaginal space to penetrate, along with her penetrating breasts. The boy's penis is a nipple that can enter the mother's mouth, vagina, anus. The boy's mouth and anus also provide a basis for an identification with the mother's vagina; the boy experiences being penetrated by mother and then desires this experience in relation to father's penis. Kernberg (1991) identified "the deep links between the early relation with mother in both sexes and the enjoyment of the interpenetration of bodily surfaces, protuberances, and cavities" (p. 351) as central to erotic desire. The basic elements of sex and intercourse occur at the mother's breast in a potpourri of possibilities that are the primitive basis for bodily and psychic, same-sex and cross-sex—*pansexual*—identifications and desires.

Aron (1995) described the various traits of the multi-gendered self as patterned and structured on the basis of our internalized primal scene. I propose that this patterning is predated at the most primitive level in the nursing couple, which is directly experienced by a child and so does not rely on Freud's (1918) notion of inherited phylogenetic knowledge. The nursing relation provides the basis in actual experience for being able to elaborate, at more complex levels of development, the sexual interaction of the two parents. Unconscious phantasy of parental sexuality is based in the immediacy of the mother–child "intercourse"—penetration and incorporation, *each active* and in dialectical relation to one another, each creating the other (Ogden, 1989).

In the Freudian version, the primal scene is an oedipal phenomenon and pre-oedipal tones are viewed as regressive. Aron (1995) argued against this division, referring to Klein's (1929) thesis that oedipal issues begin in early infancy. Aron stated that Klein's concept of the combined parent figure "serves a transitional function emphasizing the continual interaction of oedipal and preoedipal issues" (p. 208). I suggest that the nursing couple is that which is transitioned from, and back to, in a progression that includes the combined parent and the primal scene. Aron explicated a developmental process and ongoing synchronic interplay from most primitive to more mature. At increasingly higher levels of development, an internalization of the primal scene—the grandiose phantasy of being and having both sexes—leads to the capacity to hold two contrasting ideas in mind simultaneously, sustaining "the contradiction, ambiguity and paradox that is necessary for the creative process" (p. 213).

Aron (1995) pointed out that the advantage of the metaphor of the combined parent, and I would add of the nursing couple even more so, is that neither a heterosexual primal scene or heterosexuality as a developmental outcome is required as the conceptual basis of thought and creativity: "Psychoanalysis needs to stretch and broaden the primal scene concept beyond the privileging of normative heterosexual genitality to include a whole range of pregenital polymophous sensualities" (Aron, 1995, p. 214). I suggest that the metaphor of the nursing couple—the erotically "combined" mother–infant—can be effectively used toward this end. Now I explore further the realm of maternal eroticism as well as the developing representations of the paternal figure.

Penetration and primitive excitements

A mother penetrates her infant's mouth with her nipple, and her stream of milky fluid flows through the digestive core. Her handling and caretaking ministrations take claim and penetrate the infant's entire body.

Her hands and fingers are on, around and into all orifices: One gives one's body up to one's mother. She lays us on our backs and does "everything" to our bodies including, with our baby legs up and apart, opening up and exposing the genital area. These are the earliest forms of penetration and receptive excitement. These excitements lead to the wish to reverse this experience—to penetrate the mother.

Throughout her work, Klein emphasized that the infant's most profound desire is to penetrate the mother to the exciting contents of her body. The infant "knows" (unconsciously intuits) that it has been *in* the mother's body and has come out. The infant has an inchoate wish to get back inside. Later, a child learns enviously that new babies can grow in the mother's body and that the father's penis is the privileged form of re-entry. Although it is a gratifying bodily experience to be penetrated by the nipple, milk, fingers, it is also psychically exciting *to penetrate;* these experiences together form a basis of curiosity and creativity that has life-long reverberations. For instance, in describing patients' curiosity about the subjectivity of the analyst, Aron (1991) linked the wish to penetrate the maternal body to its psychological equivalent of seeking to know another's internal world.

Through these formulations, we can envision that the mother's body is experienced as penetrating but is "known" also to be permeable to penetration. Lots of exciting things are going on in there! In contrast, the father's body is likely imagined to be impermeable, with no insides for babies, and as solely penetrating with that exceedingly large nipple attached on the outside. Children come to envy the father this ability to penetrate the mother, and they project onto the father an idealized "phallic" penetration that actually is a projection of the experience, much more potent and direct, of the mother's penetration of the self by her breasts/nipples. The father's "nipple" is understandably viewed as his means of penetrating the mother. He is also the one who gets inside mother without any negative side effects such as being engulfed, lost, or controlled. In defense against the seeming omnipotence of the mother, a gender split develops (Chasseguet-Smirgel, 1976; Benjamin, 1988) regarding the ability to penetrate—an ability not inherently male but that comes to be seen as such.

The mixing up of parts and possibilities previously depicted in the nursing couple metaphor is defensively collapsed into a binary categorization where penetration is equated with the penis, then elaborated into "phallus" and into an image of a father who shall not *be penetrated*. In Butler's (1993) words, the father is "the impenetrable penetrator" who:

will never be entered by her [woman] or, in fact, by anything ... if she were to penetrate in return, or penetrate elsewhere, it is unclear whether she could remain a "she" and whether "he" could preserve his own differentially established identity.

(p. 50)

The multiplicity of possible experiences and identifications that should be a rich inheritance from maternal eroticism gets inequitably probated, impoverishing erotic life.

In most descriptions of the oedipal relation to the father, the child—female or male—is passive and penetrated, which is especially of note regarding the boy: Given that he has a penis, it is curious that we do not think of his trying to use it to penetrate his father.[3] In contrast, both sexes are not only penetrated by, but actively penetrating toward the mother. In the "negative," same-sex, oedipal configurations, identification as one who can penetrate is retained by the girl and not by the boy, which may be one reason why homosexuality loses out in the restriction of bisexuality into what McDougall (1986) termed our "ineluctable monosexuality." We taboo any sexual arrangement that does not have the male in the dominant (see Johnson's (1988) analysis of incest) or, I would say, penetrating position.

Love of the father is viewed as passive/feminine because, in a paternalistic culture the father must not be penetrated; this injunction constitutes the definition of patriarchy and the form of sexuality that the oedipal complex has traditionally organized and insisted upon; thus we have no female equivalent of phallus. In connecting sexual penetration with the issue of status hierarchies in ancient Greece, Laqueur (1990) wrote that a penetrated man and penetrating woman were considered "unnatural not because they violated natural heterosexuality but because they played out—literally embodied—radical, culturally unacceptable reversals of power and prestige" (p. 53). Sex performs power. "Masculine" and "feminine" are reciprocally shaped in accordance with a power dualism (see Colombo, 2002).

Although much psychoanalytic theory attests to the mother–infant relation as the prototype of sexual intimacy, with adult sex understood as offering a healthy regression to mother–child union, the oedipal complex is conceptualized as the phase of "true"/genital sexuality. In actuality, the oedipal complex, when establishing culturally encoded gender binaries, becomes the site of the sexualized appropriation of the "feminine" object. The oedipal complex then structures previously existing bisexuality into male dominant heterosexuality (Chodorow, 1978; Benjamin, 1995; Bassin, 1996). Woman is always the penetrated and man is seen as inherently the one to penetrate. Once a girl turns to the father she is limited to being penetrated (Lampl de Groot, 1933) and the boy, in relating to the mother as oedipal object, represses and denies that he ever was, and wanted to be, penetrated by anybody. The heterosexual male rejects being penetrated as a way to distance from infancy and any supposed lack of masculinity (see May, 1986; Diamond, 1997). This theme will be taken up in Chapter 5.

The ability to penetrate, *and not be penetrated*, becomes the definition of "man." We see then the threat to men in being permeable to any penetration, psychic or bodily. Such penetration signals the loss of manhood and does seem to endanger masculine gender identity in a way that the ability to penetrate does not so threaten a female sense of gender, but, instead, adds another aspect that has a basis in identification with the "phallic" mother. Psychic bisexuality may be easier for females as an operation of addition to gender rather than of subtraction. Men's particular difficulty with being penetrated, both sexually and emotionally, leads them to accentuate and to overdevelop their role as penetrators; this defensive stance goes unnoticed because culturally it is taken as a given that people with penises are essentially penetrators with the corollary that people with vaginas are naturally penetrated. This duality seems so obviously linked to one's anatomical equipment that it appears to be a denial of differences and of one's own anatomical sex to want to do otherwise.

In actuality, the penis is a relatively small penetrator of the overall adult woman's body compared to the penetration by the engorged nursing breasts and nipples into the small body of the infant, with milk reaching all through the body and continuing its movement in fecal travels. My intent here is not to make a concrete size comparison, but to illuminate the affective intensity of the infant's experience of being penetrated by the mother. In so doing, I hope to undercut essentialist assumptions regarding sexual intercourse. If we recognize the penis as symbolically substituting for the breast in the child's mind, we should then be able to work backward regarding the image of the "phallic" as a concept that refers to the breast, is initially derived from the relation to the breast, and that provides the reason for why phallic-as-breast would seem particularly well-suited to represent omnipotence—the all-powerful source of food and life.

Although the phallus comes to be associated with the penis, with masculinity, and with the breaking up of the mother–child dyad by the father, Breen (1996) argued that it is possible to think of a phallic "position," existing in the unconscious as a basic configuration and ubiquitous phantasy. She stated that "the phallus represents the state of completeness and of being without need" (p. 650) . . ."like the pot of gold at the end of the rainbow" (Breen, 1996, p. 651). Although Breen did not take this view, these images evocatively depict the nursing couple. Chasseguet-Smirgel (1976) clearly articulated that the theory of phallic monism—the penis as *the* sexual organ—defends against awareness of the omnipotent *mother*. An idealized "domain of omnipotence" (Breen's term for phallic narcissism) becomes a defense against any recognition of lack, and the male's possession of a penis becomes erroneously equated with phallic omnipotence. Thus, what is ideally meant by "phallic"—a sense of completeness—is, in the service of power relations, removed from representations of the mother and females, as well as from erotic life.

Braunschweig and Fain (1993) described "the narcissistic valorization of the penis (which because of this becomes a phallus unfit for pleasure)" (p. 143). For the male, "phallic narcissism is an inheritance which comes from the father, and to a certain extent, like any inheritance, it consecrates the father" (Braunschweig and Fain, 1993, p. 130). Phallic narcissism is also anti-erotic: "A confusion appears between the penis as object of phallic narcissism and the penis as instrument of Eros" (Braunschweig and Fain, 1993, p. 130). Here, Breen (1996) made her contribution regarding the symbolic meaning of "the penis-as-link"—the erotic link between the parents, allowing for recognition of need and incompleteness and, therefore, of sexual desire. Unfortunately, in Breen's formulation, while the penis—symbolized as the linking function—may not (unlike the phallus) be or have everything, it still gets to *do* everything.

Has sexuality anything to do with early object relations?

My subtitle is a play on Green's (1996) rhetorical query in the title of his paper: "Has sexuality anything to do with psychoanalysis?" As touched upon in Chapter 3, Green (1996) deplored the dwindling significance accorded to, and marginalization of, sexuality in analytic theory and practice in favor of (desexualized) early object relations. Green (1996) critiqued theory and clinical practice that "bypasses the sphere of sexuality to address object relationships of a supposedly deeper nature" (p. 873). While Green was correct that sex was receiving less attention within analytic theory—a point made as well by Mitchell (1988)—Green wrote as if sexuality is somehow necessarily apart from early object relations. This is a stance that Mitchell (1988) argued against: "While it is true that infantile sexuality, like sexuality in general, has been underplayed by most major relational-model theorists, this is more a historical artifact than a necessity dictated by the premises of the model" (p. 92). In reality, early bodily pleasure in interaction with others, with its centrality, intensity and endless variation, becomes the organizer of experience: "The dialectics of bodily and sexual intimacies position one[self] in relation to the other" (Mitchell, 1988, p. 103).

As the work of Kernberg (1991), Laplanche (1992), Wrye and Welles (1994), Chasseguet-Smirgel (1995), Kristeva (2014), Atlas (2016) and many others illustrate, early object relations do not need to be viewed as "deeper" than sexuality *or as devoid of sexuality*. The primitive beginnings of sexuality lie here. This understanding is a foundational premise of this book. The body cannot be carved up into sexual and not sexual. The entire skin surface as well as various orifices and protrusions can be understood to be erotically experienced rather than a view that limits the sexual to heterosexual intercourse. Green's (1996) perspective exemplified what is too often an aspect of male sexuality: the encasing of all sexual feeling within the penis and the representation of all sexuality as penetration by the penis.

Green (1996) particularly objected to the nursing relation as the model of sexuality:

> The idea of an object relation starting at the beginning of life raised the breast to a supreme position . . . The breast model extended to the genital phase . . . Needless to say the father's importance in Freud's work is here placed in secondary rank.
>
> (p. 877)

The tone conveyed is that of a jealous father left out of a mother–infant eroticism, which in reality often does occur for a period of time. Braunschweig and Fain (1993), referring to the embodied unity formed by the mother and her baby that is not "beyond sex" in the wide sense of the term, spoke of "the mother's being partially on leave as the father's wife"

(p. 139). They noted the uncertainty surrounding a man's paternity—"a fact which has not stopped him from installing a primacy which has transformed the systems of relationship and done so in a practically irreversible way" (Braunschweig and Fain, 1993, p. 144).

Green (1996) sought to reestablish the father's dominant position in bed and within psychoanalytic theory:

> And for those who like to go back in their theories as early as possible to the first periods of life, do I have to remind them . . . of a very simple fact? If any one of us breathes the air and is alive, it is as a consequence, happily or unhappily, of a primal scene . . . of a sexual relationship . . . between two sexually different parents.
>
> (p. 880)

Yet, from a different perspective, the baby "breathes the air and is alive" (and is happily sexual) because of the nurturing of a sexually embodied mother—maternal eroticism. Although a baby eventually has to come to terms with being excluded from the parents' intimate relation, a father must also deal with the experience of exclusion in relation to the mother–baby intimacy. I agree with Green (1996) that sexuality needs to regain a prominent role in psychoanalysis, both in theorizing and in clinical practice.

Analytic attention to the erotic dimensions of life as they manifest in development and in the analytic field constitutes my overarching conceptual framework for this book. This perspective will not be advanced, of course, by negating maternal eroticism in favor of a paternalistic view of sexuality that includes unexamined assumptions about sexual intercourse and phallic arrogation of penetration. A de-sexualized depiction of the mother–infant relation—in contrast to the descriptions given by Chasseguet-Smirgel (1995) and Kristeva (2014) that I have elaborated—rests on an artificial division of the bodily experience of the sensual and the sexual. Splitting of the sensual and the sexual supports further splitting of gendered roles in sexuality and more generally and thus constricts sexuality and constructs a "gender" that constrains.

Conclusion

We see the possibility of variations in sense of self when the gender of the partner changes, whether that involves the actual sex of the partner or of gendered representations. The sexed body and gendered mind of a lover may reinforce gender-constricted experience or may stimulate development of a rich and varied gender "repertoire." If same-sex relationships can be viewed through a non-pathologizing lens, much can be learned about our inherent bisexuality. McDougall (1995) put forth that heterosexuality is the context for reconnection to bisexual identifications. However, the presence of each sex does not guarantee bisexual recuperation and, in fact, may be an inhibiting factor (Chodorow, 1992; Benjamin, 1995) as was illustrated in my patient Keri's experience. Her same-sex relationships provided the relational context in which she accessed her bisexual expression of self. Although heterosexuality is, as Dimen (1991) quipped, "the object choice of choice" (p. 339), when heterosexual pairing entrenches polarized gender binaries (Butler, 1990; Benjamin, 1995), such gender complementarity becomes what Dinnerstein (1976) referred to as "the diseased norm."

Goldner (1991) emphasized that compliance with the rule of two divided and reciprocally interacting genders activates a "false-self system." As Winnicott (1960) stressed, "the False Self, however well set up, lacks something, and that something is the essential central element of creative originality" (p. 152). Aron's (1995) statement that the "phantasy of 'bisexual completeness' . . . plays a major fundamental and constructive role in creativity and in our capacity to think and symbolize" (p. 201) is in accord with Winnicott's conceptualization that the experience of omnipotence is essential to creativity in the form of the spontaneous, personal gesture. It might be said that creativity is the stimulating relation of the penetrating to the penetrated and that one should not be challenged regarding who is doing what to whom.

Notes

1 See Elise (1997, 2000) for a full explication of the relation between core gender identity and an early bisexual matrix. I clarify that "core" refers to a deeply internalized *psychological* sense of self that may not align with anatomy and that is highly influenced by *designated* sex—how one is viewed and treated; "conviction of bodily sex is not necessarily related to or derived from bodily sex" (1997, p. 497).
2 Questions have been raised in queer theory (see Thurer, 2005) as to why gender is so difficult to establish—why any effort is needed at all. Do we need gender? Why is the acknowledgement and acceptance of one's anatomical sex not

enough as a basis to one's personal expression of self. What would happen/not happen without gender?
3 See Isay (1989) and Lewes (1988) for a discussion of this issue in gay male development.

References

Aron, L. (1991). The patient's experience of the analyst's subjectivity. *Psychoanalytic Dialogues*, 1: 29–51.
—— (1995). The internalized primal scene. *Psychoanalytic Dialogues*, 5: 195–237.
Atlas, G. (2016). *The enigma of desire: Sex, longing and belonging in psychoanalysis*. New York: Routledge.
Bassin, D. (1996). Beyond the he and the she: Toward the reconciliation of masculinity and femininity in the post-oedipal female mind. *Journal of the American Psychoanalytic Association*, 44 (Suppl.): 157–190.
Benjamin, J. (1988). *The bonds of love*. New York: Pantheon.
—— (1995). *Like subjects and love objects*. New Haven: Yale University Press.
Braunschweig, D., and Fain, M. (1993). The phallic shadow. In Breen, D. (Ed.), *Gender conundrum*. London: Routledge, pp. 130–144.
Breen, D. (1996). Phallus, penis and mental space. *International Journal of Psychoanalysis*, 77: 649–658.
Butler, J. (1990). *Gender trouble*. New York: Routledge.
—— (1993). *Bodies that matter*. New York: Routledge.
Chasseguet-Smirgel, J. (1976). Freud and female sexuality. *International Journal of Psychoanalysis*, 57: 275–286.
—— (1995). Studies on hysteria: 100 years after. Presented at the International Psychoanalytic Association Congress, San Francisco.
Chodorow, N. (1978). *The reproduction of mothering*. Berkeley: University of California Press.
—— (1992). Heterosexuality as compromise formation: Reflections on the psychoanalytic theory of sexual development. *Psychoanalysis and Comtemporary Thought*, 15: 267–304.
Colombo, E. (2002). Sexuality and erotism: From sexuality to fantasy. In Widlocher, D. (Ed.) *Infantile sexuality and attachment*. New York: Other Press, pp. 65–95.
Diamond, M. (1997). Boys to men: The maturing of masculine gender identity through paternal watchful protectiveness. *Gender and Psychoanalysis*, 2: 443–468.
Dimen, M. (1991). Deconstructing difference: Gender, splitting, and transitional space. *Psychoanalytic Dialogues*, 1: 335–352.
Dinnerstein, D. (1976). *The mermaid and the minotaur*. New York: Harper & Row.
Elise, D. (1997). Primary femininity, bisexuality, and the female ego ideal: A re-examination of female developmental theory. *Psychoanalytic Quarterly*, 66: 489–517.

— (2000). "Bye-bye" to bisexuality? Response to Lynne Layton. *Gender and Sexuality*, 1: 61–68.
Fast, I. (1984). *Gender identity*. Hillsdale, New Jersey: The Analytic Press.
— (1990). Aspects of early gender development: Toward a reformulation. *Psychoanalytic Psychology*, 7: 105–117.
Freud, S. (1905). Three essays on the theory of sexuality. *The Standard Edition*, 7: 130–243. London: Hogarth Press, 1953.
— (1918). From the history of an infantile neurosis. *The Standard Edition*, 17: 7–122. London: Hogarth Press, 1955.
Goldner, V. (1991). Toward a critical relational theory of gender. *Psychoanalytic Dialogues*, 1: 249–272.
Green, A. (1996). Has sexuality anything to do with psychoanalysis? *International Journal of Psychoanalysis*, 76: 871–883.
Harris, A. (1991). Gender as contradiction. *Psychoanalytic Dialogues*, 1: 197–224.
Isay, R. (1989). *Being homosexual*. New York: Farrar, Strauss and Giroux.
Johnson, M. (1988). *Strong mothers, weak wives*. Berkeley: Univ. CA Press.
Kernberg, O. (1991). Sadomasochism, sexual excitement, and perversion. *Journal of the American Psychoanalytic Association*, 39: 333–362.
Klein, M. (1929). Infantile anxiety situations reflected in a work of art and in the creative impulse. In *Love, guilt and reparation and other works*. New York: Delacorte Press/Seymour Lawrence, 1975, pp. 210–218.
Kristeva, J. (2014). Reliance, or maternal eroticism. *Journal of the American Psychoanalytic Association*, 62: 69–85.
Kubie, L. S. (1974). The drive to become both sexes. *Psychoanalytic Quarterly*, 43: 349–426.
Lampl de Groot, J. (1933). Problems of femininity. *Psychoanalytic Quarterly*, 11: 489–518.
Laplanche, J. (1992). *Seduction, translation, drives*. London: Institute of Contemporary Arts.
Laqueur, T. (1990). *Making sex; Body and gender from the Greeks to Freud*. Cambridge: Harvard University Press.
Laufer, M. E. (1986). The female Oedipus complex and the relationship to the body. *The Psychoanalytic Study of the Child*, 41: 259–276.
Lax, R. (1994). Aspects of primary and secondary genital feelings and anxieties in girls during the preoedipal and early oedipal phases. *Psychoanalytic Quarterly*, 63: 271–296.
Lewes, K. (1988). *The psychoanalytic theory of male development*. New York: Simon and Schuster.
May, R. (1986). Concerning a psychoanalytic view of maleness. *The Psychoanalytic Review*, 73: 175–193.
McDougall, J. (1986). Eve's reflection: On the homosexual components of female sexuality. In Meyers, H. C. (Ed.), *Between analyst and patient: New dimensions in transference and countrtransference*. New York: The Analytic Press, pp. 213–228.

— (1995). *The many faces of Eros*. New York: Norton.
Mitchell, S. (1988). *Relational concepts in psychoanalysis*. Cambridge, MA: Harvard University Press.
Ogden, T.H. (1989). *The primitive edge of experience*. Northvale, New Jersey: Aronson.
Stoller, R. (1972). The "bedrock" of masculinity and femininity: Bisexuality. *Archives of General Psychiatry*, 26: 207–212.
Sweetnam, A. (1996). Babyboomer Bisexuality. Presented at the meeting of the Division of Psychoanalysis (Division 39), New York.
Thomson-Salo, F. and Paul, C. (2017). Understanding the sexuality of infants within caregiving relationships in the first year. *Psychoanalytic Dialogues*, 27: 320–337.
Thurer, S. (2005). *The end of gender: A psychological autopsy*. New York: Routledge.
Tyson, P. (1994). Bedrock and Beyond: An examination of the clinical utility of contemporary theories of female psychology. *Journal of the American Psychoanalytic Association*, 42: 447–467.
Winnicott, D. W. (1952). Anxiety associated with insecurity. *Through paediatrics to psychoanalysis*. New York: Basic Books, 1975, pp. 97–100.
— (1954). The depressive position in normal emotional development. *Through paediatrics to psychoanalysis*. New York: Basic Books, 1975 (pp. 262–277).
— (1960). Ego distortion in terms of true and false self. *The maturational processes*. New York: International University Press, 1965, pp. 140–152.
— (1971). *Playing and reality*. London: Tavistock Publications.
— (1988). *Human nature*. New York: Schocken Books.
Wisdom, J. O. (1983). Male and Female. *International Journal of Psychoanalysis*, 64: 159–168.
Wrye, H.K. and Welles, J. (1994). *The narration of desire: Erotic transferences and countertransferences*. Hillsdale, New Jersey: The Analytic Press.

Chapter 5

Male fears of psychic penetration

My patient Ben spends most sessions going over *and over* obsessional preoccupations, especially regarding sexuality, posed entirely as deliberations over good or bad, right or wrong—a sexual fixation devoid of any true eroticism. He is terrified of sexual/emotional intimacy, of any softening in his sense of self. Ben speaks quickly, with emotional urgency and a palpable need for help. However, he is so anxiously focused on getting a cognitive "answer" to his current dilemma that I often feel that we cannot see through to his underlying emotions. Feeling that I am not allowed to penetrate to Ben's interior, I have gently confronted his need for control and tried to show him how he dismisses as unimportant the very things that are most important. While he puts great energy into his daily concern, he can whip through a recital of the relevant and painful aspects of his upbringing as if this material is "old hat." Ben is a master at isolating his emotional history from his current preoccupations; thus, he remains quite unaware of most of his emotional life. But we have been making progress:

P: I wasn't looking forward to coming here today—that's atypical for me. I'm glad we're having a break (this is the last week before my August vacation). It has to do with moving into an emotional realm where I don't want to go. If I bring up some juicy topic like my argument with my boss, then, OK, but if we continue with stuff from yesterday, then I want to avoid it . . . it's like going into water that's either warmer than I want it or colder. I resist it. It's chaotic. Sometimes when I get in touch with what's really bothering me, it's scary. I'm put in touch with realities I'd rather ignore. I thought on the way here, "Most guys don't do psychoanalysis; what are you doing?!" Whereas last Friday I felt very involved and that this was really important . . .

Maybe this has something to do with your vacation—(abrupt shift): I am becoming more aware of a certain problem that's cropping up at work—

A: (I can tell he's about to launch off, and I interject:) You mentioned having some feelings about my vacation . . . ?

P: Yeah. I haven't really thought about your vacation, but . . . if I were into my obsessions, I'd be upset that you were leaving when I had so much to figure out and find answers for. But this emotional stuff . . . I'm glad you're leaving.

A: There is this thought, "Oh good, she's leaving," rather than any upset feeling about my going away.

P: I'm not having strong feelings about any of this . . .

A: Maybe preparing for me to be away?

P: I guess I don't want to get too close to myself with you being gone. I'm surprised to feel now that it will be a long time . . . I don't know what's going on with me; I'm waiting for the session to end. Can't open up a whole can of worms now (a long pause). When I was young I had feelings of depression. My mother left me with a sitter who ignored me for hours. I don't like to feel depressed. I like to get answers to things. Chaos is very disturbing to me. I try to never have those feelings. If there's even a hint of them I go away on some other track.

A: There's a threat of chaos. I'm leaving you. That's upsetting in itself and my leaving changes your relationship with yourself.

P: I can't have all this touchy-feely stuff; it's not masculine.

A: In not wanting to be touched by your feelings, you put them into a pejorative category, like "not masculine."

P: When I'm in this kind of a mood, I don't know what's going on. I'm a little numb—no prevailing emotion overcoming me. I'm blocking off my feelings so that I don't venture off into any. I could be provoked to anger today in this mood, especially if you were wanting me to have any feelings of loss.

A: Yesterday we talked about your sense of being provoked toward violence in the face of anyone's tears—including your own. Today there's a fear of being left with feelings of depression, and a sense of chaos, with no one around to help manage these feelings.

P: [. . .] Neither of my parents was a good model. My mother was out of control and my father was captain of the ship, keeping things on an even keel, going straight ahead. One time in my teens he was emotionally supportive of me and I thought, "Where has this guy been all my life?" (pause of 2–3 minutes).

A: Are you aware of feeling something in this silence?

P: I started feeling bad for myself as a kid (his voice chokes), but not . . . I'm not comfortable with silence. I feel I need to be getting my thoughts organized and saying something . . . Last time I was back home and about to leave at the end of the visit, my father, sitting across the room and barely looking up from the television, said, "Come back soon, son." That's as close as he can get—as close to me, to his feelings of sadness that I was leaving, to any intimate feelings . . . Yeah, I start to feel sad (tears), but I can't stand that feeling. (Quickly, and apologetically:) I can't do it—can't go with sad feelings. If I start feeling sad, I lose a sense of justice—world order or something. I feel out of control of myself; it's not the safest way to go . . . I had the feeling of slipping into something . . . chaotic . . . like a death, looking at those experiences and feelings. Yeah, I need something to hang onto; I can't be like others who can have sad feelings . . .

A: (softly): Sad feelings have a particular effect on you.

P: It's a warm, but disintegrating feeling that I don't have control over. It draws me, but it's uncomfortable. It also scares me (tears). I'm afraid of losing control. I have to be caught blind-sided and have it overtake me or I avoid it. I can't stand it when Sally [his wife] cries; I get mad . . .

A: Something about a woman crying disturbs you, disrupts you.

P: I feel out of control. Most of the things she cries about, I can't fix. I can't fix it and so I get angry at her. She can mostly resist my "fixes." It frustrates me and gets me angry. If I were ever to get violent, it would be with someone crying. So I guess I have the same problem with myself in some way.

A: There's a way that you do violence towards yourself—towards your feelings—when you feel like crying.

P: (pause) I had this dream last night where you're not sitting back behind me, but beside and above me, and as I'm talking to you I feel a much more direct connection. It seems significant—a stronger bond. There's so much going on in this analysis; If I'd known this analysis was gonna involve so much . . . I was feeling so intense coming over here in the car that I got tearful. This is important to me (tears). I don't get a chance in my relationships to really express how I feel ... Like with my father. But I need to take a risk.

A: You are taking a big risk with me right now in letting me see your inner feelings.

P: I keep thinking, "This is a business relationship and she doesn't really care about me." I hold that in my mind to keep from connecting to you, caring about you too much. It's hard for me to imagine or trust that someone could be there. My mother was never there and my father would be out of the room by now, and because I haven't had that connection, *I'd* be out of the room by now.

Ben's mother's depression and preoccupation with her own concerns left her unavailable to her little son; any maternal eroticism was in short supply. He recalls, throughout his childhood, wanting to catch glimpses of his mother's breasts and being frustrated that his mother and sisters could be nude together while he was "shut out." He seems to have experienced this exclusion as being cruelly left out of a comforting, female "breast world." Instead, he was supposed to harden himself in an identification with his emotionally removed father, becoming a narcissistic extension of the father's injured phallic pride.

Ben anxiously curtails sexual intercourse, feeling that he might "get lost inside"—lost inside a woman, inside his own inner world. He is fixated on breast characteristics connoting perfection and infinite gratification, organizing early, unmet dependency needs around a sexualized image of tantalizing breasts. As with any richer sexual interchange, making an emotional link in his thinking is experienced as extremely threatening, a literal *melt*-down, and, thus is warded off. Instead, a labyrinth of cognition—a sterile mental masturbation—has had him wandering in circles, endlessly retracing his steps. This dynamic might be thought of as *per-verse*: a destruction of the language of maternal eroticism—the 'mother tongue'—where libidinal vitality is twisted into deadness. Eros devolves into Thanatos. And yet, in the potential space of the maternal erotic connection to his analyst, the tears will not be held back.

In Chapter 4, I proposed that the original basis for identifications as penetrator and as penetrated is not gender de-limited: males, like females, have an early experience in relation to the nursing mother of being receptive to bodily and psychic penetration. A woman is the first penetrator and the stimulating experience of being penetrated is *enjoyed by both sexes*.

Males tend to lose access to this experience, fearing penetration as antithetical to a masculine sense of self. Phallicism as a fortress of emotional self-sufficiency—what I describe as a "citadel complex" (Elise, 2001)—can become a matrix of a subjective sense of masculinity. My use of the term "citadel complex" might be thought of as parallel to Freud's conception of the "masculinity complex" in women; I am describing a masculinity complex in men. An impermeable bodily and psychic boundary—the ability to penetrate without *the ability* to be penetrated—collapses a necessary dialectical tension that can affect men's experience of sex and of love and that may shape and limit their desire and curtail access to their fullest creative and erotic potential.

In classical psychoanalytic theory, male fear of symbolic penetration (a frequent theme in analyses) tended to be viewed as conflict over latent homosexuality—wishes for, and fear of, penetration by the analyst. In that formulation, psychic penetration is *by a male*. Eissler (1977) noted that wishes to penetrate and to be penetrated "are not as sex-specific as one might expect" given their "biological mission" in male and female sexuality (p. 37). Later approaches focused not on tabooed homosexual wishes, but on fears regarding loss of masculinity (Wisdom, 1983; Kaplan, 1991; Hansell, 1998). Being penetrated was then viewed as equivalent to femininity and thus an issue of gender rather than of sexual orientation. Fogel (1998) and Hansbury (2017), recognizing that "[s]plit-off parts [of the self] have a tendency to haunt both psyche and soma" (Hansbury, 2017, p. 1013), significantly forward theorizing regarding the need for inclusion of a sense of interiority in males.

I am proposing that the vulnerability of being emotionally penetrated can be experienced by men as a threat to a heterosexual identity, a threat to a sense of masculinity and, potentially, to a sense of a separated and individuated identity—a consolidated sense of self. In defense against these threats, a masculine sense of self (especially in heterosexual males) may come to be based on, *dependent upon*, an impermeable psychic boundary that is *not* to be penetrated. As theorized in Chapter 4, it is not primarily the penetrability of the body, but of the mind, that influences sense of self, gender, sexuality, and relational dynamics.

Men may avoid their internal life through an overemphasis on work—phallic projects characterized by intense absorption in solitary activity (Axelrod, 1994). The difficulty that a man might experience with psychic permeability can also manifest with other men as co-workers and friends

(Kaftal, 1991), in gay relationships (Hansbury, 2017), in heterosexual pairings (Chodorow, 1978; Rubin, 1983), in relation to their children (Diamond, 2007), in the resistance men have to entering and engaging in treatment (Kaftal, 1991; Axelrod, 1997; Real, 1997; Ducat, 2004) and in resistances that male analysts may experience to certain transferences (Renik, 1990; Hirsch, 1997). A man can fear having an inner receptive space—an internal space that can be penetrated and known—where something about the private self can be discovered and revealed. Working through this fear is an important aspect of adult male development and a needed focus in analytic treatment.

Psychic vulnerability in males as threat to gender identity and sense of self

In the previous chapter, I described a bisexual, female patient whose sexual experience in relationships with women expanded her gendered sense of self. In this woman's subsequent relationships with men, male fears of being bodily and psychically penetrated posed an obstacle to certain aspects of her expanded gender repertoire. She remarked, "you can literally take a man's clothes off, but you can't really undress him in the more figurative, symbolic sense." The cultural construction of masculinity can interfere with a man's capacity to be receptive to opening his inner self to another. My conceptualization of male psychic permeability and receptivity rests on the creative potential of bisexual identifications that permit fluidity and multiplicity in a secure sense of self.

In viewing the nursing relation of maternal eroticism as the primal experience of intercourse, sexually stimulating for infants of both sexes (Chasseguet-Smirgel, 1995), I have elaborated the following theoretical formulation: The basic elements of bisexuality are contained within the creative relation to the breast which involves the relation of the penetrated to the penetrating and the ability to imagine oneself in each/any position (Elise, 1998). The infant is the recipient of the mother's penetration and becomes a penetrator by identification with the mother. The nursing relation is a form of potential space allowing for many imaginative possibilities regarding sexual anatomy and activities. The interpenetration of bodily surfaces is central to erotic desire and is deeply linked for both sexes in the early relation with mother (Kernberg, 1991). To penetrate and to be penetrated form a nexus of sexual excitement as psychic and physical boundaries are crossed.

I utilize the metaphor of the nursing couple to represent the earliest matrix of bi/pansexual self and object representations situated within the semiotic *chora* of maternal eroticism. My formulation concerns the exciting interplay involving experiences of putting into/taking in that occur normatively for the nursing couple and that are "the stuff" of maternal eroticism. What I have in mind is akin to a description by Bollas (2000): "There is a type of lust in the breast to be suckled that meets with an increasing lust in the infant to suck, and this initial intercourse is deeply fulfilling to both figures, who achieve a type of mutual orgasm" (p. 87).

Juliet Mitchell (2000) considered the normative, but potentially traumatic aspects of the mother–infant interchange:

> Human beings are unusual in that any and everyone can be penetrated—this vulnerability makes penetration always a threatening possibility . . . Because of our utter dependency on the carer in infancy . . . the baby can feel life-threatening risk and simultaneously have a focus of sexual excitement in the experience of penetration and incorporation.
> (p. 138)

I do not view the experience of being psychosomatically penetrated by the mother as necessarily imbued with threat at these early stages unless as a response to pathology in the mother. Penetration is a healthy aspect of maternal eroticism. A sense of threat would be a later development that is then retroactively ascribed (*Nachtraglichkeit*). The threat to the infant is in *losing the mother's erotic presence*. Mitchell's (2000) thinking coheres with mine when she stated: "A baby's sexuality would seem to be really the surplus of pleasure and satisfaction it gets when it is being fed and cared for" (p. 140)—a view that resonates with Kristeva's (2014) eloquent depiction of the infant's earliest erotic encounter with the mother as based in bodily interaction and mutual pleasure (see also Wrye and Welles, 1994).

My conceptualization of the nursing couple speaks to a reciprocally engaged, erotic matrix that *facilitates and stimulates* development, (rather than being normatively traumatic as Laplanche (1992) and Mitchell (2000) theorize), and that only *later* becomes problematic for males when "masculinity" seems to proscribe receptivity. The belief that boys would need a more definitive separation from the relational field of maternal eroticism in order to "achieve" masculinity has been overemphasized within both familial and earlier psychoanalytic understandings of male development (Fast, 1984, 2001; Benjamin, 1995). Too often father identification has been deployed as buttress to repudiation of the bond with the mother. Such a developmental trajectory forms a fragile foundation for sexual wishes toward the mother at the oedipal phase and for adult relationships with women, both sexually and emotionally. A ban on "feminine" identifications in boyhood can also undermine sense of self in gay men (Hansbury, 2017). These intertwining developmental experiences take place within a cultural context that shapes a desired form of masculinity into a constricting mold. *Masculinity, like femininity, is a field phenomenon*—a "dominant fiction" (Silverman, 1992).

Christiansen (1996) proposed that, "psychoanalysis has simultaneously exposed and defended against its own discoveries regarding male development" (p. 101). He argued that, "Gender-specific defensive structures have been institutionalized in the normative psychoanalytic account of human development" (Christiansen, 1996, p. 105). Furthermore, Christiansen (1996) emphasized that, "male identity formation is perpetually pressured by the passive currents upon which it is problematically built" (p. 101). Passivity is confused with femininity and with homosexuality, and then masculinity as it is culturally constructed brooks no integration of either femininity or homosexuality.

Friedman (1996) underscored the need to include in our definitions of maleness "more of the 'inner space' repudiated by men and projected onto women" (p. 249). He stressed the need for men to deal with anxieties regarding their own "dark continent" of their inner body (Friedman, 1996, p. 249). Grosz (1994) suggested that, "perhaps the great mystery, the great unknown, of the body comes not from the peculiarities and enigmas of female sexuality . . . but from the unspoken and generally unrepresented particularities of the male body" (p. 198)—the riddle of masculinity (Chodorow, 2005).

Just as females can come to experience anxiety about entry into their body, with a sense of vulnerability and loss of control, males too can experience this anxiety. Males, however, must also contend with an additional anxiety, fearing that if they *are* penetrated they will then be unable *to* penetrate—an outcome understandably equated with loss of masculinity. Multiple pressures result in a powerful pull for a male to represent the self as *not* permeable. We see that boys may both envy procreativity and greatly fear the basis in their own psychic and physical experience for identifying as penetrable, receptive and internally generative. Too frequently, being the one *to penetrate* becomes the singular goal whether that be in sex, athletics, or outer space. The mystery of exploration is comfortably "out there"— penetration into somewhere or someone else, not into the self and certainly not into the male body.

I have been underscoring the mother's penetration of the infant in the nursing relation. As a reciprocal expression, an intense, early desire to penetrate the mother's body arises in the infant. However, as development proceeds toward individuation, along side this primitive desire to penetrate the mother a fear of being engulfed, being lost inside and controlled by her (Klein, 1928) generates a pressure to escape from the archaic mother. As we saw in Chapter 4, eventually a small child may come to view the father's penis as the privileged form of access to the mother, as well as separation from her. Children envy a father's ability to penetrate the mother; he is the one who gets inside mother without being overtaken and entrapped by her.

In defense against the draw of the maternal erotic surround, now feared as threatening to re-engulf the separating child, an idealized image of "phallic" penetration and autonomy is projected onto the father; penetration is equated with the penis and then elaborated into "phallus." A phallic ego ideal presides over male development (Diamond, 1997) and the penis is imbued with magical qualities of power (May, 1986) as the organ of penetration. Phallicism also defends against a loss of the mother that takes a specific form for a boy in the repudiation of identification with her. Rey (1994) described how the penis can be used in a manic defense against mourning the intolerable loss of the mother. Denial of the lost maternal object is achieved by the creation of the "manic penis" (Rey, 1994, p. 220): The penis becomes omnipotent, and a boy in identification becomes omnipotent as well. Rey (1994) stated:

> The boy's initial turn away from his mother, in part out of hurt and envy when he discovers that he cannot *be* a mother, is for many men the kernel of a character style involving the denial of hurt, the compensatory assertion of power, and an aversion to the "feminine" qualities

of attachment and tenderness. This attempt to demean and subdue the female presences in one's internal world [leads to] . . . the alternative achievement of control through fearful identification with a more powerful male.

(p. 189)

Benjamin (1995) noted that the boy's relationship with his father may have a quality of "desperate urgency . . . as if it were the bulwark of the boy's representation of gender as identity (his sense of self-cohesion . . . implicitly aligning the father with the self-cohering object)" (p. 60). Benjamin emphasized that a boy should not have to choose between the father and mother, in the sense of forgoing maternal identifications. Yet, this foreclosure has been typically what has occurred in order for a boy to be deemed masculine. Furthermore, a boy's mourning for this maternal loss (and loss of a part of the self) usually goes underground—an ungrieved grief.

The citadel complex

Manninen (1992) identified that a key factor in a boy's development concerns the building of an identification with a loving father over that with a magic phallus. When a father has not resolved his own relationship with his father, a generational transmission of masculine gender trauma ensues (see also Diamond, 2007). Narcissistic injuries to a sense of masculinity and personhood can lead to "compensatory phallicism as a weapon and fortress for the sake of the security of his self. When the phallicism thus increases, the black side of it, fear of castration, also grows in force, and a vicious circle is created" (Manninen, 1996, p. 73)—a citadel of self-sufficiency that precludes vulnerability or dependency.

"Citadel" is defined in the dictionary as a fortress overlooking a city "intended to keep the inhabitants in subjection or to form a final point of defense during a siege . . . any strongly fortified place, stronghold" (Webster's, 1992). I regard a citadel structure of masculinity as a reliance on being the one to penetrate and an avoidance at all costs of the experience of being penetrated. Such a definition of masculinity requires, as well as obscures, the emotional sacrifice and psychological pain of a harsh separation from the mother, from one's feelings and from intimate connections with others. Boys are frequently encouraged to "play through pain"—to be active and achievement-oriented in the face of painful experiences that they are pressured to keep submerged. Real (1997) referred to this definition of manhood—withstanding physical and emotional pain—as a form of "emotional amputation" (p. 133). Masculinity is defined in the negative, as that which is *not* feminine: "For most boys, the achievement of masculine identity is not an acquisition so much as a disavowal . . . a negative achievement" (Real, 1997, p. 130). This repudiation of "feminine" feeling has significant ramifications, particularly in adult love relationships.

In adult sexuality, erotic desire ideally would be based on the *mutual interpenetration* and intermingling of the partners (Kernberg, 1991). The crossing of bodily and psychic barriers involves the capacity for multiple identifications, including with active incorporation and penetration and with the receptive experience of being penetrated. The simultaneous identification with each possibility temporarily erases the boundaries of the self and has its basis in the early mother–infant interplay; adult sexuality revisits maternal eroticism. Such reciprocity can be especially challenging for men when perceived as not only a loss of masculinity, but of a cohesive sense of self.

Person (1980) referred to a compulsive quality in men's pursuit of intercourse whereby "relative gender fragility in men fosters excessive reliance on sexuality" (p. 57) that serves to consolidate and confirm gender. Sexual penetration serves as a mainstay in a phallic identity. Sex can also confirm male power over women especially when dependency needs and vulnerability are both covertly met, *and denied by*, the very form that sexuality may take. This confirmation of male gender and power (seen as synonymous) is most apparent in the preoccupation that some heterosexual men can have with sex as penetration of the woman and as very little else.

Tooley (1977) described the heavy responsibility that the penis carries for an adult man "for the whole range of self-esteem and pleasure possibilities" (p. 191). I would specify that it is the ability of the penis to penetrate that is most emphasized and that this focus significantly shapes the object relational possibilities for each partner. When a collapse occurs in the dialectical tension regarding the ability to penetrate and to be penetrated, a collapse of desire may soon follow, leading to sexual boredom for both partners. Tooley (1977) noted that in sex therapy a man is specifically forbidden to engage in intercourse in order to explore a range of sexual possibilities and to remove "the internal demand to *prove* himself in a sexual athletic competition" (p. 192).

Sexual excitement is dimmed when mutuality in experience and a range of relational possibilities are collapsed into a rigid, gender polarity—a literal *sex* role—where a man has one type of physical and psychic experience and a woman a complementary opposite. Fixed complementary roles limit the repertoire of each participant, and sex tends to become perfunctory and perseverative. One scenario is continually reenacted, a likely indication of a compromise formation at work. A tendency for one particular sexual scenario to repeat, due to its defensive value for a male—as a primary form of "safe" "intimacy" with a woman—contributes, I suspect, to a high potential for female "frigidity" in heterosexual relationships. A diminishment of desire may show up more readily in a woman given the vulnerability and risk versus defensive value of being physically and psychically penetrated. Over time a woman may become guarded about and even resentful of having her body—if no longer her psyche—penetrated if there is little reciprocal vulnerability on the part of a man regarding his interiority.

We are familiar clinically and anecdotally with women's expressions of frustration at trying to get inside men emotionally. Perhaps the apparent diminishment of sexual desire in some women may express, in part, their reaction to being thwarted at getting inside erotically—in both bodily and psychically penetrating their male partner. The inhibition of women's desire, well-noted in the literature, may represent not so much an inherent female tendency toward frigidity, but a loss of passion and erotic excitement *in and between* both partners that may go unnoticed in a male given the valence that sexual penetration of the female has for men psychologically (as well as biologically).

Clinicians witness a certain male psychic impenetrability to be a significant aspect of marital unhappiness in heterosexual couples. The psychological inaccessibility of many males that women commonly complain about has been too often a problematic reality given masculine character structure in male dominant culture. Male fears of psychic penetration are also evident in a greater difficulty in opening to an analytic process that, by definition, focuses on a dyadic exploration of the inner self. Analysis asks a man to let go of a structuring of self that is deeply identified with masculine self-esteem. I now want to offer a second clinical vignette to illustrate what I am referring to as a citadel complex. With many possible case examples that could be included, Rob is particularly expressive regarding his subjective experience of fortress-like qualities in his sense of self.

Rob is a relatively high functioning professional from a white, middle class family in which he experienced considerable well-being as a child. His mother was actively engaged in work both in and outside the home; his father was a successful engineer. Rob, age 37, sought analytic treatment when he began to feel that something was threatening his marriage of five years. He was not sure what the problem was, but he was increasingly aware of a tension between he and his wife. She seemed to be expressing more and more dissatisfaction with their level of emotional intimacy. It took a number of months of work before he and I could articulate what might be undermining the marriage. During that period I found him to be a likeable man, but a rather challenging patient in a subtle way, given his difficulty with introspection. I too found it difficult to deepen our intimacy within our analytic field; any analytic eroticism seemed muted.

During one session, Rob had been describing to me a recent argument with his wife that once again centered on the issue of how close they were (or were not). He was quite agitated as he spoke and eventually exclaimed, "but I don't let her get to me." The contradiction between his palpable emotional state and his statement about himself captured my attention and I found myself recalling how often I had heard him use the phrase, "I don't let it get to me." This phrase, used as it was to cap any further exploration of his emotional life, would tend to evoke in me a sense of my being warded off, shut out. In this reflection, I started to be able to identify in the "feel" of the analytic field a likely source of his wife's feeling that they lacked a certain closeness; I felt kept at "arms length" myself.

In response to his comment, "but I don't let her get to me," I asked: "Where would she have to get *to*, to get to you?" As Rob tried to take in my question and spatial metaphor, the intonation of his protracted "uhhhh . . ." conveyed the impression that he was thinking, but not saying, "Hey lady, is this one of those weird analyst-type questions" or equally plausible, "Hey analyst, is this one of those weird female-type questions?" I definitely felt in those few moments of silence that he didn't want *me* "getting to him."

At the point where he could mentally breath and actually begin to think about my query, Rob stated, "OK, so you're asking where am I; where does the real me reside that someone would have to get to—to reach—in order to get to me." After a few minutes, he continued with uncharacteristic self-revelation:

> I guess I'm sort of walled off in a certain way; it's not that easy for me to show my feelings—to *know* my feelings for that matter. I don't let my emotional guard down very often. I think guys are generally kind of protected in that way . . . (a few minutes of reflective silence). You know, this sounds kind of stupid, but I remember as a kid—you know how kids are—being totally into building forts, castles with moats, that kind of thing. My friends, we all did this for hours, looking for the enemy through the turrets at the top with our guns pointed out, ready for an attack. It definitely wasn't a dungeon; no, I was on top looking out—a "room with a view," you might say . . . but not easy for anyone to see in or get in. I was in control of that with the moat . . . (pausing).

I softly commented, "remote." After a "pregnant pause," Rob slowly continued:

> Yes, and now it's difficult to open myself up even if I want to . . . Sex is dicey: I feel really close to my wife then and like I could be vulnerable to her in a way I'm not sure guys are supposed to be. I certainly don't have any sense that to "get to" my wife I have to go through anything like this in reverse; she's just there, out and about in the world. Funny—it looks like I'm out in the world what with sports and all, but that's physical stuff; emotionally I'm not "out and about" at all! . . . We want kids, but would I be like this with them? And if I have a son, is it OK to *not* be like this?

Building on my one word comment—a seed, Rob gestated his own link between his childhood pastime and his current internal state of being emotionally guarded; thus, the permeability and generativity of the field expanded.

As illustrated by my patient, the boyhood game with forts and castles is no mere game, but the projection of an internal psychic configuration. Male development repeatedly seems to require a mental barrier against emotional closeness, especially when maternal longing might be re-awakened. A boy's fearful dis-identification from the mother and defensive counter-identification with the paternal imago can form a fragile foundation for the sense of self, gender identity and sexual orientation. This fragility can influence various developmental stages and the nature of many relationships. Emotionally intimate relationships can make men vulnerable to feeling re-traumatized regarding the original loss of the mother. When love seduces, "laying down the shields...[and] yielding to love would make the self helpless" (Manninen, 1996, p. 83).

Fogel (1998) viewed the phallic defense as a hardening of the heart that protects from the "dangers of exposing softer and more tender inner organs and psychical sensibilities" (p. 679). In a similar vein, Real (1997) described typical male development as the clamping of a band around the heart, where boys are "systematically pushed away from the full exercise of emotional expressiveness and the skills for making and appreciating deep connection" (p. 23). Males are generally forced out of an expressive-affiliative mode:

> Men do not have readily at hand the same level of insight into their emotional lives as women, because our culture works hard to dislocate them from those aspects of themselves. Men are less used to voicing emotional issues, because we teach them that it is unmanly to do so.
> (Real, 1997, p. 82)

Kaftal (1991) noted a tacit form of emotional communication common among men that "demands that one's emotional life be unlabeled and un-described" (p. 307). One of Kaftal's patients put it this way: "I know that I'm really close to somebody when I can go on a three-hour car ride with them without saying anything" (Kaftal, 1991, p. 307).

Kaftal (1991) identified that the "heroic model of manhood is an attempt to strengthen and stabilize the gendered self-representation" (p. 305). He viewed the absence of fathers from the *nurturing* matrix as critical to the instability of masculine gender identity. Instead of being nurturing and empathic towards their sons (and wives and daughters), historically too many fathers have tended to poke and prod the next generation of males into "manhood." If a father devalues emotional expressiveness and connection, his son will fear being denigrated if he engages in these "feminine" ways. Diamond (1997, 2007), in articulating the need for fathers to have the ability to hold and contain the mother–infant dyad, identified interiority as a crucial aspect of the paternal function. Real (1997) pressed even further:

It becomes clear that boys don't hunger for fathers who will model traditional mores of masculinity. They hunger for fathers who will rescue them from it . . . Sons don't want their fathers' "balls;" they want their hearts. And for many the heart of a father is a difficult item to come by.

(p. 159)

In my first clinical vignette, Ben gave poignant expression to this longing, underscoring the need for paternal eroticism, along with maternal eroticism, as an essential aspect of the developmental matrix.

Treatment must gently dismantle phallic defensive structures. Only when adult men are able to soften in relation to women, children, other men, *and to themselves*, can they and their partners feel relationally fulfilled. Otherwise relationships are undermined, and children likely learn that masculinity is about being emotionally and interpersonally walled off. The fact that we are as a culture so "successful" in eradicating tears from male emotional expression is to my mind one of the single most blatant examples of the closing up of the male psyche. Just this one example alone speaks volumes about what we do to a person to make him into a man.

Penetrating the analytic field

It is not solely a male patient who needs to open himself to a receptive introspection. Analytic eroticism poses significant challenges to a clinician to be libidinally present within the analytic field in one's receptivity to being penetrated. Aron (1996) critiqued Freud's portrayal of the phallic analyst, "thought of as the fearless and adventurous male who seeks to uncover, expose, and penetrate the feminine 'unconscious'"(p. 258). Aron's explication of a relational perspective emphasized the need for an analyst (male or female) to allow a patient to penetrate the analyst's subjectivity and for an analyst to be comfortable with, and allow access to, his own interiority. Similarly, Kaftal (1991) spoke of the need in treatment for affective interpenetration, "a sense of 'sharing' one's inner and private self with another without undue anxiety and with relative confidence that one will remain in possession of one's own body and mind" (p. 311). Affective *interpenetration*—what I term *analytic eroticism*—would ideally not only be free of undue anxiety, but would be imbued with embodied excitement, an erotic "spark" of genuine emotional contact.

Renik (1990) described the difficulty male analysts may experience in being receptive to specifically sexualized penetrations in the form of patient fantasies toward the analyst. He gave a case example of a woman who had strong desires to sexually penetrate him, which she then repudiated as being impossible. Renik pointed out that male anxieties about being the object of a female patient's desires to be sexually penetrating may have the analyst collude with the patient's defenses against recognition of these wishes:

> In order to address a woman patient's conviction that he cannot be penetrated, impregnated, and excited by having these things done to him, a male analyst must disagree with that conviction in the first place! We know that every male analyst has resistances to acknowledging his femininity...
>
> (Renik, 1990, p. 43)

We must also attend to a male clinician's anxieties, *and excitements*, in being penetrated by a *male* patient.

Clinicians are aware of a homosexual "*panic*" that can underlie brittle masculinity and hyper heterosexuality—a subterranean fault line threatening to shake up the entire personality. As Ducat (2004) stated,

> some men can experience any effort to understand them at a deep level as a kind of threatening homoerotic intrusion... defenses against having felt small, helpless, and humiliated as a child are so brittle that the vulnerability, trust, and transient regressions associated with being in psychotherapy are too unbearable to even contemplate.
>
> (p. 242)

Hirsch (1997) cautioned that, in mutually affirming a sense of heterosexual masculinity, a male analytic dyad may collusively "avoid the conscious experience of homosexual anxiety and the vulnerability of regressive dependency" (p. 479). Engaging analytic eroticism in this male clinical pairing is especially challenging!

Conclusion

Within the reciprocal engagement of maternal eroticism, male (as well as female) infants can enjoy the stimulating experience of being penetrated. In penetrating, the mother is erotically active in a manner that is culturally deemed masculine and phallic. Just as it is important to allow "phallic" qualities to a mother, it is invaluable to be able to attribute "feminine, womb-like" qualities to a father and for fathers to be comfortable embodying these qualities. While very young children may be "over"-inclusive in their attribution of gender characteristics to self and others (Fast, 1984), adults are too often *under-inclusive* in their gendered expression of self. I have described a particular difficulty that various men may face in developing a sense of self that is penetrable, internally receptive and generative. The experience of being psychically penetrated is then imagined to be somewhat analogous to a balloon being "penetrated": This socially constructed masculine sense of self would burst if it were to be "punctured" in this manner. When the capacity for intimate relatedness is seen to entail a receptivity that is equated with being feminine rather than with being human, male fear of psychic penetration results.

References

Aron, L. (1996). *A meeting of the minds: Mutuality in psychoanalysis*. Hillsdale, New Jersey: The Analytic Press.

Axelrod, S. (1994). 'Impossible projects:' Men's illusory solutions to the problem of work. *Psychoanalytic Psychology*, 11: 21–32.

— (1997). Developmental pathways to masculinity: A reconsideration of Greenson's 'disidentifying from mother.' *Issues in Ego Psychology*, 19: 101–115.

Benjamin, J. (1995). *Like subjects and love objects*. New Haven: Yale University Press.

Bollas, C. (2000). *Hysteria*. London: Routledge.

Chasseguet-Smirgel, J. (1995). Studies on hysteria: 100 years after. Presented at International Psychoanalytic Association Congress, San Francisco.

Chodorow, N. (1978). *The reproduction of mothering*. Berkeley: University of California Press.

— (2005). The riddle of masculinity. Panel, Winter Meeting, American Psychoanalytic Association, New York.

Christiansen, A. (1996). Masculinity and its vicissitudes: Reflections on some gaps in the psychoanalytic theory of male identity formation. *Psychoanalytic Review*, 83: 97–124.

Diamond, M. (1997). Boys to men: The maturing of masculine gender identity through paternal watchful protectiveness. *Gender and Psychoanalysis*, 2: 443–468.

Diamond, M. (2007). *My father before me: How fathers and sons influence each other throughout their lives*. New York: W. W. Norton.

Ducat, S. (2004). *The wimp factor: Gender gaps, holy wars, and the politics of anxious masculinity*. Boston: Beacon Press.

Eissler, K. (1977). Comments on penis envy and orgasm in women. *Psychoanalytic Study of the Child*, 32: 29–83.
Elise, D., (1998). Gender repertoire: Body, mind and bisexuality. *Psychoanalytic Dialogues*, 8: 353–371.
— (2001) Unlawful entry: Male fears of psychic penetration. *Psychoanalytic Dialogues*, 11: 499–531.
Fast, I. (1984). *Gender identity: A differentiation model*. Hillsdale, New Jersey: The Analytic Press.
— (2001). Boys will be boys! A contested aspect of gender development. Presented at the meeting of the Division of Psychoanalysis (Division 39) of the American Psychological Association, Santa Fe, NM.
Fogel, G. (1998). Interiority and inner genital space in men: What else can be lost in castration. *Psychoanalytic Quarterly*, 67: 662–697.
Friedman, R. (1996). The role of the testicles in male psychological development. *Journal of the American Psychoanalytic Association*, 44: 201–253.
Grosz, E. (1994). *Volatile bodies: Toward a corporeal feminism*. Bloomington: Indiana University Press.
Hansbury, G. (2017). The masculine vaginal: Working with queer men's embodiment at the transgender edge. *Journal of the American Psychoanalytic Association*, 65: 1009–1031.
Hansell, J. (1998). Gender anxiety, gender melancholia, gender perversion. *Psychoanalytic Dialogues*, 8: 337–351.
Hirsch, I. (1997). On men's preference for men. *Gender and Psychoanalysis*, 2: 469–486.
Kaftal, E. (1991). On intimacy between men. *Psychoanalytic Dialogues*, 1: 305–328.
Kaplan, L. (1991). *Female perversions*. New York: Doubleday.
Kernberg, O. (1991). Sadomasochism, sexual excitement, and perversion. *Journal of the American Psychoanalytic Association*, 39: 333–362.
Klein, M. (1928). Early states of the Oedipus complex. *International Journal of Psychoanalysis*, 9: 167–180.
Kristeva, J. (2014). Reliance, or maternal eroticism. *Journal of the American Psychoanalytic Association*, 62: 69–85.
Laplanche, J. (1992). *Seduction, translation, drives*. London: Institute of Contemporary Arts.
Manninen, V. (1992). The ultimate masculine striving. *Scandinavian Psychoanalytic Review*, 15: 1–26.
— (1996). The supremacy of evil. *Scandinavian Psychoanalytic Review*, 19: 73–96.
May, R. (1986). Concerning a psychoanalytic view of maleness. *The Psychoanalytic Review*, 73: 175–193.
Mitchell, J. (2000). *Mad men and medusas*. New York: Basic Books.
Person, E. (1980). Sexuality as the mainstay of identity: Psychoanalytic perspectives. In Stimpson, C. R. and Person, E. S. (Eds.), *Women: Sex and sexuality*. Chicago: University of Chicago Press.

Real, T. (1997). *I don't want to talk about it: Overcoming the secret legacy of male depression.* New York: Scribner.
Renik, O. (1990). Analysis of a woman's homosexual strivings by a male analyst. *Psychoanalytic Quarterly*, 59: 41–53.
Rey, H. (1994). *Universals of psychoanalysis in the treatment of psychotic and borderline states.* London: Free Association Books.
Rubin, L. (1983). *Intimate strangers.* New York: Harper and Row.
Silverman, K. (1992). *Male subjectivity at the margins.* New York and London: Routledge.
Tooley, K. (1977). 'Johnny, I hardly knew ye:' Toward revision of the theory of male psychosexual development. *American Journal of Orthopsychiatry*, 47: 184–195.
Webster's new universal unabridged dictionary, (1992). New York: Barnes and Noble.
Wisdom, J. (1983). Male and female. *International Journal of Psychoanalysis*, 64: 159–168.
Wrye, H.K. and Welles, J. (1994). *The narration of desire: Erotic transferences and countertransferences.* Hillsdale, New Jersey: The Analytic Press.

Chapter 6

Reclaiming lost loves
Transcending unrequited desires

In this chapter I address the multidimensionality embedded within the oedipal phase of development and underscore that the elaboration and working through of unrequited oedipal longings within the potential space of the analytic field is one of the most profound gifts of an analysis. The oedipal child's confrontation with thwarted desire (generationally) for either parent is central to the development of the mind, the personality, and one's erotic life. I also contend that the experience of oedipal exclusion becomes not solely a response to a generational boundary but to a gender boundary discouraging same-sex love. I favor retaining a conceptualization of an oedipal *complex* that does not obscure the complexity of individual experience. In describing our oedipal lineages for erotic life as resting upon an interwoven tapestry of maternal and paternal desires, my aim is to further a project to rehabilitate the oedipal concept from heteronormative presumptions and from being (mis)understood in a reductive manner that alienates rather than engages.

Oedipal negativity

Historically, the oedipal complex has too often not been presented or understood in its richness and variability, but reduced to a formulaic depiction of heterosexual development based on the presumed psychology of the boy. Not surprisingly, many have reacted "negatively" to this limited view, resulting in a negative conception of the oedipal concept. Understandable objections arise to the privileging of male development and of heterosexual ("positive") object choice, with homosexuality ("negative") relegated to a weak second, a dark inverse, a passing phase on the way to normative "health." Yet, as Davies (2015) pointed out, a "wholesale extradition" (p. 269) of the oedipal complex would be an unfortunate outcome. Instead, basic assumptions *within* this concept need to be excised.

Chodorow (1999) stressed the need to keep in mind the cultural embeddedness of psychoanalytic theories in order to see how they are shaped in a particular manner rather than being universal truths: Freud's framing of the oedipal complex reflected ties to a culturally and historically-specific, male dominant family structure, evident in "Freud's neglect of the introjection of *maternal* values in the formation of the conscience and possibly in the Oedipal resolution" (Obeyesekere, 1990, p. 252). Similarly, Bollas (2000) stated that inner structures derive in part from "a culture's transmission of its own interpretation of maternal and paternal orders" (pp. 85–86). Chodorow elaborated how we projectively enliven aspects of cultural meanings and social identities making them personally meaningful and deeply felt "truths."

Much recasting and elaborating of the oedipal concept has been done over decades by many analytic thinkers in each of the major psychoanalytic models. The continued centrality of the oedipal constellation both in development and in analytic treatment is attested to by contemporary analytic theorists from various theoretical perspectives. Certainly this holds for Contemporary Kleinians and Freudians. Many relational theorists have reworked this key concept to include the role of culture as it is embedded within family dynamics (among them, see Benjamin, 1988, 1998, 2004; Greenberg, 1991; Chodorow, 1992; Aron, 1995; Davies, 1998, 2003a, 2003b, 2006; Corbett, 2001; Harris, 2005; Gonzalez, 2012). The list of authors putting forth a sophisticated critique and sensitive rendering of the oedipal world would fill a page or more of citations. To dismiss the oedipal complex altogether is to not avail oneself of a significant body of our psychoanalytic literature built up over decades, lively still, and far from a simplistic formulation that has been associated with Freud.

Analysts have long since moved past the "nutshell" schematic of the oedipal complex now viewed as inadequate to describe the full dimensions of anyone's development. Children do not want to eliminate one parent or the other, nor is their desire limited to one (opposite sex) parent; children are attached to and needing both parents, desiring both and, yes, aggressively competitive at times with each. Re-conceptualizations of this triadic constellation in girls' development (see especially Kulish and Holtzman, 2008) have led to a more nuanced view of boys' oedipal experiences as well. It is evident to psychoanalytic developmental theorists that for each child varying aspects of attachment are layered within the unfolding of their erotic life. As Davies (2015) underscored, attachment and sexuality interweave from the beginning of development and throughout life; they are not separate or sequential systems.

The oedipal complex has also been astutely critiqued and significantly re-conceptualized in its homoerotic dimensions, illuminating the previous dark negative of the erotic picture (Lewes, 1988; Isay, 1989; O'Connor and Ryan, 1993; Goldsmith, 1995; Burch, 1997; Magee and Miller, 1997; Corbett, 2001). Taking oedipal dynamics out of the closet, dusting them off and bringing them into contemporary life, Davies (2015) has revisioned positive and negative oedipal configurations, thinking, instead, in terms of which configuration in a given individual is primary/foreground and which is secondary/background. I like the use of these two words, foreground and background, conveying as they do that *both* same and "opposite" sex object choices should be in the theoretical, developmental and clinical picture. The pursuit of this project to rehabilitate the oedipal concept from a heteronormative formulation has formed the trajectory of much of my own work (Elise, 1997, 1998a, 1998b, 2000a, 2000b, 2000c, 2001, 2002a, 2002b, 2002c, 2007, 2008, 2012a, 2012b). In the developing theme of my papers over the past 20 years on female psychosexuality, my aim has been to resuscitate the female "negative oedipal complex"—the daughter's erotic wishes toward her mother—from where it has languished in the analytic literature.

Davies (1998, 2003a, 2003b, 2006, 2015) in particular has demonstrated the richness with which oedipal issues can be explored clinically. In putting clinical flesh on the bones of the oedipal concept, she has worked to restore its centrality within relational psychoanalysis—"its status as a treasure trove of clinical understanding" (2015, p. 269). Such understanding within an unfolding analysis can greatly help patients, of any gender identification or sexual orientation, alleviating a sense of shame and pervasive inhibition, and leading to greater freedom and playfulness within erotic life.

Most people struggle in one manner or another with thwarted oedipal wishes, the subsequent feelings of inadequacy often resulting in a failure to actualize desire. A full elaboration and working through of unrequited oedipal longing within the analytic field makes use of what distinguishes psychoanalysis: a deep understanding and appreciation of the unconscious and of infantile sexuality within an intersubjective matrix. Such an offering is not easy to receive.

Psychic bisexuality: bedrock and shock

An analysis may bring to the fore erotic desires that have remained unexplored, even unrecognized. One's conscious adult sexual orientation represents the erotic path taken, while at the same time it often obscures the alternative. Our "Consent for Treatment" forms might need to include: "BTW—analysis may result in unexpected sexual orientations emerging." For people whose sexual orientation has always felt congruent with lived experience—matching up with their actual choice of partner(s)—psychic bisexuality may pose quite a shock.

Certainly, a significant number of people feel no such congruency between sexual orientation and overt partner choice; they are not necessarily living out their predominant oedipal configuration, but, instead, an alternate. Many with bisexual life experience are aware that the gender of their romantic partner in a long-standing couple may not match up with their predominant orientation. Living in a heterosexual marriage, they may feel that they are truly gay, or that in a same-sex marriage, they are actually heterosexual. This conundrum gets at a difficulty in how one thinks of a "primary" sexual orientation: Are we speaking about what is felt most strongly, deep in one's soul, or about whom one is actually sleeping with/married to?

A person is usually defined by what one *does*, what is visible to others. People who are consciously bisexual likely keep their psychic bisexuality more actively in play—and possibly more comfortably integrated—in their minds, lives, and sexual experiences. But we see that this area of potential space is rife with potential torments that are disturbing to many in one manner or another. Caught by surprise at desires not previously recognized—in terms of the gender of the desired—patients tread cautiously in this fraught realm. Yet, along with the possible terrors and conflicts, the benefits of being able to access one's psychic bisexuality are manifold.

Most often we see psychic bisexuality restricted (Freud, 1905) into monosexuality (McDougall, 1986). It is usually homosexuality that is foreclosed (Butler, 1995), though I contend that, developmentally, female homoeroticism—originating in the primal sensual bond with the mother—tends to be "closed" *after* the fact. Immersed in an erotic relation with her mother, a girl is typically oedipally "redirected" to her father, whereas a boy is generally discouraged in advance (foreclosure) from erotic approach to the father. This sequencing of oedipal desires has fateful consequences.

Our bi/pansexual potential is channeled into a singular sexuality (Schafer, 1974) that typically is consciously felt to be inherent—"natural," comfortable, unquestioned. Yet the first "sexual orientation" of most humans is, what might be termed (drawing on the terms matrilineal and patrilineal) *matrisexual*—directed to the mother as object of desire—with *patrisexuality* layered upon and drawing from this maternal foundation. These are our oedipal lineages for erotic life.

Desire for the maternal

I want to look more closely at the developmental piece of the oedipal puzzle. As Davies (2015) noted, "There must, I think, be a beginning . . . that unique psychic space in which desire is born, in which sensual delights are first experienced" (p. 266). In a developmental line—a temporal sequence—typically mother is first, primal, primary; Her sensual care—maternal eroticism—enlivens her child's sexual body (Laplanche, 1992; Stein 1998; Bollas, 2000; Kristeva, 2014). As described in earlier chapters, this development of sexuality is taking root within the early, relatively undifferentiated self-other matrix of the nursing couple. For development to proceed, this early dyadic matrix needs to give way to encompass the presence of a third—someone (or even something) that is competing for the mother's attention. Both sexes must relinquish the fantasy of sole possession of the mother.

A child will likely move into the triadic, oedipal level of development with the mother as the initial focus of sexual desire, and may (as seen in lesbians and heterosexual males) continue to focus erotically on the mother throughout this new, more complex, triadic level of development. Or the focus of oedipal desire may shift to the father as it does predominantly with gay males and heterosexual females. Either way, each gender will need to confront, and will lament, not being the one chosen in return. Unless an oedipal "victor," one necessarily faces defeat. One needs to compete for the desired parent, eventually relinquish this wish to "marry" either parent, and later find one's own generational partner (of the desired sex).

Girls and boys, regardless of eventual object choice, have certain commonalities in their oedipal experience if the conceptual focus is kept on the first love object—the primary care-taker, usually a woman. As I have written (Elise, 2000c), these commonalities become much more apparent if one thinks of oedipal situations (Klein, 1928, 1945) in terms of a primary maternal—first temporally and in archaic intensity—and then a secondary paternal oedipal situation, rather than a positive and negative oedipus complex. This latter conceptualization is a view through a heterosexual lens that obfuscates important realities. Thinking in terms of an interwoven sequencing of maternal and paternal oedipal desires follows more closely the developmental reality for most children of early female caretaking (Chodorow, 1978) and stays with Freud's emphasis on the centrality of bisexuality.

Ideally, development includes erotic components that unfold in the preoedipal dyadic relationship and then gain momentum in the more complex, triangular oedipal configuration where various erotic strands intricately intertwine. As a child moves through the oedipal phase, the intermixing of desired objects typically leads to what Davies (2015) described as an eventual foregrounding of a predominant sexual orientation with other choices likely moving into the background. I would emphasize, however, that too often the path not chosen is forced *underground*, completely disavowed and no longer in the picture seemingly at all. This effort at banishment is costly both erotically and more generally, in what Winnicott (1971) would think of as creative living.

We need to remain especially aware when considering the fate of oedipal desire for the mother that the archaic relation to the mother, where infantile dependence and Eros deeply embrace, eventually results in the formation of an omnipotent maternal imago (Chasseguet-Smirgel, 1976). In relation to this "omnipotent" maternal figure, a deep substrate exists of erotic longing, dependent attachment, *and* subsequent fear of engulfment, impingement, loss of a boundaried sense of self in erotic "union." These dynamics of intense ambivalence surfacing in relation to a female sexual partner are well known to analysts in working with heterosexual men; as detailed in Chapter 5, sexual intimacy with a woman threatens regression to this early matrix of maternal eroticism. Thus, erotic transference from male patients to their female analysts is often resisted and remains out of awareness (Person, 1985). Yet, erotic longing for the maternal object can result in a sense of threat for persons of any gender or sexual orientation when accessing desire for a woman.

Erotic transference as a riptide in the analytic sea

What may be underground in adult life (desire for a woman in gay men and in heterosexual women) is foregrounded developmentally (desire for the mother). The eventual outcome ("resolution") of the oedipal complex leading to an adult sexual orientation does not usually reveal the full erotic picture developmentally. In deep analytic work, patients can feel quite shocked to unearth within the analytic field erotic desire for the maternal figure. This desire toward a female may not primary for these patients in terms of conscious sexual orientation, but *is* primary in my conceptualization of the (unconscious) maternal oedipal situation. Put another way, latent desire for a woman, surfacing and conflicting with manifest object choice, is ego-dystonic and can lead to heterosexual and homosexual "panic," in gay men and heterosexual women respectively. As detailed in Chapters 4 and 5, longing for the maternal figure "panics" heterosexual men, as well.

Davies' (2015) analytic work with Sam illustrated how these fears can manifest in a gay male relationship with the *male* partner unconsciously viewed as feminine/maternal. Paternal desire was the seemingly singular ground of Sam's sexual orientation; he disavowed that maternal desire was *ever* part of his erotic development. These repudiated desires were then projected entirely and vehemently onto the analyst/mother and experienced as forced back upon him as *her* desire.

In Davies' second vignette, Samantha, also had mother trouble in her erotic life, while married to a man and manifestly heterosexual. This situation would not surprise Freud (1931), noting as he did how regularly a woman transfers to the husband her relationship with her mother. In her adult oedipal triangle, Samantha made sure with her affairs (turning passive into active) that *she* was the focus of desire (like mother), not the excluded third party (see Josephs, 2006). However, like Sam, her rigid defensive organization was toppled by an erotic dream toward the analyst, so graphic, vivid, and threatening that it could not be ignored.

Both Sam and Samantha had basically the same dream, a "seduction" by their female analyst that resonated in alarming ways with the maternal configuration. The surety of their sexual orientation lost ground when swept into the deep currents and undertow of the analytic relationship and the erotic transference. In each patient, when this unconscious maternal oedipal constellation (re)emerged, it was profoundly destabilizing.

Erotic transference (and/or countertransference) can be thought of as a riptide, catching one completely by surprise, overwhelming all efforts to swim toward shore. One minute you are fine, the next, in the grip of a force so strong it cannot be combated with will. This dramatic change of scene is evident in Davies' (2015) eloquent depictions of riveting clinical encounters with her two patients. Sam tried to regain a hold on dry land, yelling, "I am a gay man, a GAY MAN" (Davies, 2015, p. 274). But as Davies noted, the ferocity of his instantaneous denial of *his* desire for her was telling. Samantha was a bit more willing to take the maternal erotic plunge into the flood of yearning and horror, recognizing "the urgent craving desire in her own body" (Davies, 2015, p. 280).

Of course, the discovery of erotic longing for a man/paternal figure, in heterosexual men and lesbians, can also be quite destabilizing given the lack of congruence with the consciously identified sexual orientation. This expression of desire (patrisexual) is likely not as regressive an undertow as is matrisexuality. But here too, the sheer force of banished oedipal desires exerts a tremendous and very frightening pull. Clinicians usually understand that the only way through erotic transference is to wade into it. Yet with a riptide, one must "relax" (while fearing for one's life!), let the tide take you out quite a ways, before then being able to swim sideways and eventually back to shore (hopefully). Clinicians, as well as patients, may decide to remain "on shore."

I particularly appreciate Davies' (2015) passionate engagement of *oedipal* desire in the transference from her patients. Davies is clearly a strong "swimmer" and knows her erotic seas. I have written (Elise, 1991, 2002c) about the problematic tendency in the literature and in everyday clinical work to "pre-oedipalize" oedipal level erotic feeling, especially in the female dyad, into a de-sexed mother–infant cocoon. Certainly it is common for women in treatment with a woman to access deep longings, including the erotic, for a woman—the maternal figure. Analytic exploration of these "negative" oedipal dynamics reveals a rich layer of development that unfolds from the matrix of maternal eroticism. As stated in Chapter 3, this maternal oedipal configuration is not to be understood as a passing phase of little import, but as crucial to the development of healthy sexual self-esteem.

The complex within the complexity

I do wish to retain a conceptualization of an oedipal *complex* without losing any of the complexity of individual experience. It is truly unfortunate that this triadic phase of development would be understood in a reductive manner that alienates rather than engages. In his unpublished *Didactic Statement of Child Development of 1962*, Winnicott stated:

> Without the Oedipus complex psycho-analysis could not have been founded, because it is the most difficult area in the emotional growth of healthy persons, and we ought not to do the treatment of persons who are disturbed at stages prior to that of the Oedipus conflict unless when we get them forward we can carry them over the Oedipal conflicts when they arise in the transference.
> (cited in Giannakoulas, 2005, p. 62)

Winnicott was attesting here to the clinical importance within *every* treatment of addressing oedipal issues. In noting that these conflicts will arise in the transference, he was speaking to the immediacy of the analytic relationship—what can now be thought of as the analytic field—as the context for the working through of this complex.

Freud's choice of the word "complex" argues against a narrow formulation, referring instead to a multi-faceted, interrelated set of emotionally charged feelings and impulses that are usually repressed. The complex represents a basic structure of object relationships and the way in which the subject positions himself or herself in it (Spezzano, 1993). The oedipal crisis, within an intricate web of object relations, reflects the child's confrontation with thwarted desire for either parent, a confrontation with significant implications for the development of the mind and one's erotic life.

Contemporary Kleinians have extensively theorized the necessity of a developing capacity to tolerate the experience of oedipal exclusion (see Chapter 2). In recognizing the sexual relation between the parents, a child must engage in a complex task of facing a boundary, yet not relinquishing a desiring self. The capacity to keep desire alive—what Davies (2015) referred to as "pleasurable anticipation" (p. 267)—in the face of obstacles and disappointments, forms the complex that we all struggle with as our oedipal inheritance. This encounter with developmental angst will reverberate throughout one's life.

Oedipus *refused* to be excluded from the parental couple, and his romantic wishes for his mother were actualized and returned by her. Oedipal victory is a tragedy. Whereas the experience of "failure" to obtain the oedipal object, though *feeling* tragic, is paradoxically a potential source of vitality and vibrancy. As Davies (2015) stated, what matters in "our fate as lovers . . . regardless of object choice" is our capacity "to sustain passion and eros in our most intimate relationships, to continue to desire that which we can't possess . . ." (p. 268).

As is evident in my discussion, the life lesson of this complex is further complicated for homoerotic desires, given the lack of affirmation for same-sex oedipal configurations typically expressed within the heterosexual family, as well as within society more generally. As Schafer (1974) emphasized, we insistently shape each sex's psychosexuality, steering children "from their infancy toward procreative male and female roles" (p. 471) in nuclear families (see also Chodorow, 1978, 1992). Freud (1931), while recognizing the girl's erotic relationship to her mother, could only conceptualize the girl as a little man; he could not quite get his theory of bisexuality fully into his own language possibilities. Schafer (1974) noted that:

> it is not inaccurate to attribute to Freud a relative neglect of bisexuality . . . for his theory of development the important thing was to get the girl to become feminine and ready to receive love and babies passively from an active man . . . he needed a sustained phallic perspective. But that perspective is not inclusive enough for his own psychoanalytic discoveries.
>
> (p. 477)

It becomes apparent that the experience of oedipal exclusion becomes not solely a response to a generational boundary, but to a gender boundary discouraging same-sex object choice.

The poet and the mermaid: transcending oedipal obstacles

I would like to illustrate the power of the complex within the oedipal situation with a ballet: I hope to evoke the richness of the oedipal drama as it was offered in the San Francisco Ballet's 2011 production of John Neumeier's "The Little Mermaid" (then broadcast on PBS and put on DVD). Typically not known, this children's story represents an erotic love letter from one man to another: Hans Christian Andersen writing to the man who rejected him, Edvard Collin. In the story, a man—the Prince—is lost to a love of a woman—the Princess. The Little Mermaid herself is Andersen's embodied evocation of the pain of unrequited love across a chasm so wide that one cannot cross by any means, no matter the strength of the wish to do so.

The advertising for this ballet indicated that this would not be a story for children (though as analysts we see that it is indeed a children's story, developmentally), but instead, would be expressing complex themes. One of those themes was male homoerotic longing, the other, the degree of sheer pain—psychic wounding—in unrequited love. The Program for the 2011 performance gave an account of Andersen's thwarted love for another man, portrayed in the ballet by the addition of the "Poet" who shadows the Mermaid throughout the narrative. Neither Poet nor Mermaid can have the object of their desire. Both are tortured by longing for a foreclosed love of the "Prince." The Program Synopsis (Neumeier, 2011) stated:

> Mourning his separation from Edvard, a tear rolls slowly down the Poet's cheek, falling into a sea of memories and fantasies . . . At the bottom of the sea, the Poet's longing for Edvard takes the form of a little Mermaid. This lovely sea creature . . . [the story unfolds, and then ends:] The Little Mermaid is left alone. Her pain reflects the Poet's own painful situation. Each seems the shadow of the other—each abandoned by the object of their intense love. They are one—creator and creation.
>
> (p. 33)

This stage production was so emotionally powerful, so stark and searing, that by the closing scene of this oedipal ballet, when both Mermaid and Poet are boxed in by increasingly narrowing confines (that they somehow also transcend), one is left absolutely stunned. Neither is "equipped" to obtain their love object, continually yearned for across an unbridgeable gulf. Watching the ballet, one realizes we are each of us poets and mermaids: sensitive creatures with fierce desires. Such desire may be thwarted, but it remains a turbulent undertow to our sexuality and romantic wishes.

In the Program Notes, Choreographer Neumeier (2011) described the ballet's central theme: "But the story teaches us . . . that no matter how strong our love may be, it doesn't obligate the object of our love to love us in return" (p. 34). Two ballerinas each performing the title role spoke eloquently. Regarding the character's pursuit of unconditional love, Yuan Yuan Tan (2011) noted: "People dream about it. And [the Mermaid] tries to pursue it, and fails, but still believes in it" (p. 36). Sarah Van Patten (2011) revealed:

> It's so scary to do a part like that and be fully honest. It's very exposing . . . Say you felt that much pain in your life, or that much loneliness or feeling of being excluded, being cast outside . . . Or having such a broken heart, or loving somebody so much and not getting that in return. [Dancing this role] makes all those emotions surface again. And then to experience that over and over again . . .
>
> (p. 36)

Out of the mouths of ballerinas, come some of the most poignant descriptions of the oedipal crisis as it unfolds in early development and as it can be painfully re-contacted in an analysis. These descriptions resonate deeply with what I find to be one of the most challenging, profound and rewarding of analytic journeys: recognizing our experiences of felt rejection, unrequited love, and yet not giving up on our future as desiring subjects. I believe this ballet captured both levels of thwarted oedipal longings. First, the *generational* boundary with which every human being must contend (your parents love you, but won't "consummate" oedipal erotic love with you; this is also the central issue in working through erotic transference longings). Second, the additional *gender* barriers encountered in same-sex erotic love, both across the generational divide (childhood) as well as within one's own generation in adulthood.

Although there is no object mother directly represented in this ballet (the "Sea Witch" is, interestingly, a male character), the mother–child "sea of sensuality" is conveyed by the extensive underwater scenes, a beautiful evocation of the "environmental mother" (Winnicott, 1965). As Choreographer Neumeier (2011) stated regarding the Mermaid: "She is in her element— gorgeously, beautifully, and belonging . . . She knows this world, and yet she has a desire to go beyond that" (p. 37). The Mermaid looks up to the ship above where the Prince is playing a very different game. The Poet and the Mermaid, excluded from the wedding party of the royal pair (primal scene), each look on, unseen, not chosen, devastated and forlorn.

Freud (1905) wrote that "the Oedipal complex . . . represents the peak of infantile sexuality, which through its after-effects, exercises a decisive influence on the sexuality of adults" (p. 226). Oedipal defeat in relation to either parent can undercut the capacity to desire through a generational and also a gendered experience of castration. This psychic "mutilation" with its bodily register—a tearing of one's being—is conveyed quite graphically when the Mermaid loses her tail.

As analytic clinicians we hope that our work within the analytic field can transform a patient's sense of rejection, inadequacy and shame. To regain a sense of personal value and access to one's authentic self, can lead to a profound feeling of transcendence in the face of oedipal adversities of feeling dismissed, scorned, forsaken by the one desired. The Synopsis of the ballet ends: "Courageous, they [the Poet and the Mermaid] search for a new world" (2011, p. 33). This is the search we each must find the courage to pursue.

Conclusion

Whether foreground, background, or underground, the fate of various oedipal desires can be viewed from different vertices. Expanded theoretical conceptualizations can extend what is included clinically in developing more fully the picture of any given patient's erotic repertoire. Yet, we must also appreciate that, in engaging oedipal desires, we are entering dangerous waters of longing and loss—the emotional truth of erotic life. We see how difficult it is to be in full, honest emotional contact with oneself, let alone with any other human. To risk, as Stein (2003) put it, that the "totality of one's being could be unbearably shaken" is not for the faint of heart.

In our clinical engagement with our patients' passions, and with our own, clinicians must not be "faint of heart" in meeting patients' experience of catastrophic change (Bion, 1965) in the sense of self, erotically and otherwise. We must be willing to reach for truth in order to help a patient confront change and bear up in the face of a threatening sense of loss. Such a transformative journey is, as Davies (2015) stated, "essential to a fully robust and resilient" erotic life, and to a "uniquely individual erotic signature" (p. 269). I heartedly concur.

References

Aron, L. (1995). The internalized primal scene. *Psychoanalytic Dialogues*, 5: 195–238.
Benjamin, J. (1988). *The bonds of love*. New York: Pantheon.
—— (1998). *Shadow of the other*. New York: Psychology Press.

— (2004). Beyond doer and done to: An intersubjective view of thirdness. *Psychoanalytic Quarterly*, 73: 5–46.
Bion, W.R. (1965). *Transformations: Change from learning to growth*. London: Tavistock.
Bollas, C. (2000). *Hysteria*. London: Routledge.
Burch, B. (1997). *Other women: Lesbian/bisexual experience and psychoanalytic views of women*. New York: Columbia University Press.
Butler, J. (1995). Melancholy gender: Refused identification. *Psychoanalytic Dialogues*, 5: 165–180.
Chasseguet-Smirgel, J. (1976). Freud and female sexuality: The consideration of some blind spots in the exploration of the 'Dark Continent.' *International Journal of Psychoanalysis*, 57: 275–286.
Chodorow, N. (1978). *The reproduction of mothering*. Berkeley: University CA Press.
— (1992). Heterosexuality as a compromise formation: Reflections on the psychoanalytic theory of sexual development. *Psychoanalysis and Contemporary Thought*, 15: 267–304.
— (1999). *The power of feelings*. New Haven: Yale University Press.
Corbett, K. (2001). Nontraditional family romance. *Psychoanalytic Quarterly*, 70:599–624.
Davies, J.M. (1998). Between the disclosure and foreclosure of erotic transference-countertransference: Can psychoanalysis find a place for adult sexuality? *Psychoanalytic Dialogues*, 8: 747–766.
— (2003a). Falling in love with love: Oedipal and post oedipal manifestations of idealization, mourning, and erotic masochism. *Psychoanalytic Dialogues*, 13: 1–27.
— (2003b). Reflections on Oedipus, post-Oedipus, and termination. *Psychoanalytic Dialogues*, 13: 65–75.
— (2006). The times we sizzle and the times we sigh: The multiple erotics of arousal, anticipation and release. *Psychoanalytic Dialogues*, 16: 665–687.
— (2015). From Oedipus complex to oedipal complexity: Reconfiguring (pardon the expression) the negative Oedipus complex and disowned erotics of disowned sexualities. *Psychoanalytic Dialogues*, 25: 265–283.
Elise, D. (1991). When sexual and romantic feelings permeate the therapeutic relationship. In Silverstein, C. (Ed.) *Gays, lesbians and their therapists*. New York: Norton, pp. 52–67.
— (1997). Primary femininity, bisexuality and the female ego ideal: A re-examination of female developmental theory. *Psychoanalytic Quarterly*, 66: 489–517.
— (1998a). The absence of the paternal penis. *Journal of American Psychoanalytic Association*, 46: 413–442.
— (1998b). Gender repertoire: Body, mind and bisexuality. *Psychoanalytic Dialogues*, 8: 379–397.

— (2000a)."Bye-bye" to bisexuality? Response to Layton. *Studies in Gender and Sexuality*, 1: 61–68.
— (2000b). Woman and desire: Why women may not want to want. *Studies in Gender and Sexuality*, 1: 125–145.
— (2000c). Generating gender: Response to Harris. *Studies in Gender and Sexuality*, 1: 157–165.
— (2001). Unlawful entry; Male fears of psychic penetration. *Psychoanalytic Dialogues*, 11: 499–531.
— (2002a). Blocked creativity and inhibited erotic transference. *Studies in Gender and Sexuality*, 3: 161–195.
— (2002b). The primary maternal oedipal situation and female homoerotic desire. *Psychoanalytic Inquiry*, 22: 209–228.
— (2002c). Being bad on the side: Commentary on paper by Eric Sherman. *Psychoanalytic Dialogues*, 12: 667–673.
— (2007). The black man and the mermaid: Desire and disruption in the analytic relationship. *Psychoanalytic Dialogues*, 17: 791–809.
— (2008) Sex and shame: The inhibition of female desires. *Journal of the American Psychoanalytic Association*, 56: 73–98.
— (2012a) The danger in deception: Oedipal betrayal and the assault on truth. *Journal of the American Psychoanalytic Association*, 60: 679–705.
— (2012b) Failure to thrive: Shame, inhibition, and masochistic submission in women. In Holtzman, D. and Kulish, N. (Eds.) *The clinical problem of masochism*. New York: Jason Aronson, pp. 161–185.
Freud, S. (1905). Three essays on the theory of sexuality. *The Standard Edition*, 7: 130–243. London, Hogarth Press, 1953.
— (1931). Female sexuality. *The Standard Edition*, 21: 225–243.
Giannakoulas, A. (2005). Childhood sexual theories and childhood sexuality: the primal scene and parental sexuality. In Caldwell, L. (Ed.) *Sex and sexuality: Winnicottian perspectives*. London: Karnac, pp. 55–68.
Goldsmith, S. J. (1995). Oedipus or Orestes? Aspects of gender identity development in homosexual men. *Psychoanalytic Inquiry*, 15: 112–124.
Gonzales, F. J. (2012). Loosening the bonds: Psychoanalysis, feminism, and the problem of the group. *Studies in Gender and Sexuality*, 13: 253–267.
Greenberg, J. (1991). *Oedipus and beyond: A clinical theory*. Cambridge: Harvard University Press.
Harris, A. (2005). *Gender as soft assembly*. Hillsdale, New Jersey: Analytic Press.
Isay, R. (1989). *Being homosexual*. New York: Avon Books.
Josephs, L. (2006). The impulse to infidelity and oedipal splitting. *International Journal of Psychoanalysis* 87: 423–437.
Klein, M. (1928). Early stages of the Oedipus conflict. *International Journal of Psychoanalysis*, 9: 167–180.
— (1945). The Oedipus complex in light of early anxieties. *International Journal of Psychoanalysis*, 26: 11–33.

Kristeva, J. (2014). Reliance, or maternal eroticism. *Journal of the American Psychoanalytic Association*, 62: 69–85.
Kulish, N. and Holtzman, D. (2008). *A story of her own: The female Oedipus complex reexamined and renamed*. New York: Jason Aronson.
Laplanche, J. (1992). *Seduction, translation, drives*. London: Institute of Contemporary Arts.
Lewes, K. (1988). *The psychoanalytic theory of male homosexuality*. New York: Simon and Schuster.
Magee, M. and Miller, D. (1997). *Lesbian lives: Psychoanalytic narratives old and new*. New Jersey: The Analytic Press.
McDougall, J. (1986). Eve's reflection: On the homosexual components of female sexuality. In Meyers, H. C. (Ed.), *Between analyst and patient: New dimensions in transference and countertransference*. New York: The Analytic Press, pp. 213–228.
Neumeier, J. (2011). *The little mermaid*. San Francisco Ballet, Program 8, Encore Arts Programs. Seattle, Washington State: Encore Media Group.
Obeyesekere, G. (1990). *The work of culture: Symbolic transformation in psychoanalysis and anthropology*. Chicago: University of Chicago Press.
O'Connor, N. and Ryan, J. (1993). *Wild desires and mistaken identities*. New York: Columbia University Press.
Person, E. (1985). The erotic transference in women and in men: Differences and consequences. *Journal of the American Academy Psychoanalysis*, 13: 159–180.
Schafer, R. (1974). Problems in Freud's psychology of women. *Journal of the American Psychoanalytic Association*, 22: 459–485.
Spezzano, C. (1993). *Affect in psychoanalysis: A clinical synthesis*. Hillsdale, New Jersey: The Analytic Press.
Stein, R. (1998). The poignant, the excessive and the enigmatic in sexuality. *International Journal of Psychoanalysis*, 79: 259–268.
— (2003). IARPP-Colloquium Series: No. 2, *What happens when love lasts? An exploration of intimacy and erotic life*.
Winnicott, D.W. (1965). *The maturational processes and the facilitating environment: Studies in the theory of emotional development*. The International Psycho-Analytical Library, 64:1–276. London: The Hogarth Press and the Institute of Psycho-Analysis.
— (1971). *Playing and reality*. London: Tavistock.

Part III

Women and desire
Erotic dysphorias

Chapter 7

Sex and shame
The inhibition of female desires

In this third section of the book, delving more deeply into female experience, I begin with a developmental narrative that centers on bodily-based narcissistic injury and sense of shame in response to unrequited oedipal longings. In Chapter 6 we saw that unrequited erotic wishes pose a significant challenge to each individual. In heterosexual family structure, a girl must typically negotiate her way from the intensity of mother–daughter erotic life to an oedipal relinquishment of this relationship that is both quite profound and yet usually unacknowledged. Through an experience of oedipal "defeat" in relation to both mother and then father, a female sense of inadequacy and shame may be internalized and accepted as one's identity, in contrast to a male phallic-omnipotent trajectory. The demise of genital narcissism in females can underlie various expressions of pervasive inhibition and failure to actualize desire. I will be building upon this theme in each of the three chapters of this section on female erotic dysphorias.

Inhibitions to female desire and an undermined sense of agency have been approached within separation–individuation theory as a mother–daughter problem in terms of lack of individuation. Chodorow's (1978) influential thesis regarding a daughter's gendered identification with her mother let loose a flood of literature conceptualizing female inhibitions in terms of the pre-oedipally-based identificatory tie to the mother. Merger in the mother–daughter relationship has been a major lens through which to view female lack of autonomy and agency in sexuality, aggression, competition, achievement, power and authority—all aspects of desire subsumed in the wish to secure relational bonds (see Benjamin, 1988; Holtzman and Kulish, 2000, 2003).

Such object relational thinking was a major advance in conceptualizing gender differences and female psychology from a perspective not based on assumptions of genital inferiority and penis envy as the central explanatory paradigm. Yet, going forward we can continue to consider what may be added to a separation–individuation perspective that might further deepen our appreciation of the complexities of the female psyche. As I have been emphasizing throughout this book, the focus within object relations theory on the internal object world has tended toward a relative neglect of the sexed body of the child and of sexuality per se. More recently, growing interest in a comparative approach allows for an integration of the strengths of various psychoanalytic models. Detailed attention to the sexual *body* has been a continued strength of contemporary Freudians. It is particularly the sexual body—"anatomy as destiny"—in relation to the oedipal crisis that I focus on in this chapter. I find it intriguing to take up again certain of Freud's propositions, but within an intersubjective, object relational matrix, in the service of our attending more fully to multi-level erotic aspects of the analytic field.

The body ego

Freud (1923) put forth that the ego is "first and foremost a bodily ego" (p. 26). Experience arising from the physical sensation of the body is the original template from which an infant develops a sense of self. This shape of the self would include one's genitals, especially intense in focalized sensation, and thus, the body ego draws upon sexual specificity. Bernstein (1990) argued that, "the girl's body, her experiences with it and conflicts about it are as central to her development as the boy's body is to his" (p. 152).

To make this concept more vivid to our adult minds, one might imagine being very small and, after finding fingers and toes, etc., locating the genitals: that place feels *particularly* good! For boys that feeling is sensed as emanating out from the body, the most intense pleasure a few inches out from the torso. In holding the penis, they feel its extension outward, somewhat separable from the rest of the body. Girls locate both a feeling and an organ that is flush with, and infuses, the torso and that seems to have some inner potential (Mayer, 1985; Tyson, 1994).

The elaboration of genital structure into mental structure is a concept most familiar in Erikson's (1950) description of children's play; boys tended to build towers and girls preferred enclosures. I agree with Bassin (1982) that, though this concept—used prescriptively and without recognition of cultural influences—has been appropriately critiqued, there is something in it to appreciate. Sensate experience of one's genital structure has the potential to lend shape to one's ego—to make particularly salient certain configurations as a sort of internal mapping of the body, the self, and the world. It is obvious that the sexism of the culture has privileged phallic intention: linearity, following the straight and narrow, expansion into the world, penetration of outer space. Women have often been viewed as wandering around in circles, not having a straightforward view of situations, and of getting nowhere fast. The list of genitally related metaphors is so long, pervasive, and inequitably valued, that the list itself makes the point regarding the power that genital geography exerts on the human mind.

Consideration of the sexual body and its potential impact on ego formation has been relatively missing in an object relational conceptualization of the mind as developing separately from a sense of genital definition or shaping (see Fonagy, 2008). Unfortunately, earlier psychoanalytic theory, aligned with the cultural surround, tended to see females as having inherently problematic genital structure (see Chapter 8)—a bias that was then extended to a view of female psychological structure. Addressing this sexism, Bassin (1982) called for the need for new language categories to describe female experience, beyond the traditional roles and reproductive functioning. A subsequent panel on phallocentric language (Long, 2005) explored how language shapes and confines thinking and perception. Especially as clinicians speaking to patients, we need to be aware of how language limits what we can think and how limited thinking constricts our language and what we can say (Goldberger, 1999).

In more recent decades, with the concept of "primary femininity," contemporary Freudian theory acknowledged that, very early in development, little girls know and like their bodies, rather than experiencing themselves to be failed males (Blum, 1976; Richards and Tyson, 1996). An attempt was made to describe the girl's earliest sense of her female body. It is a line of thinking that links development of the ego—one's sense of self— with the mental representation of the body. I proposed (Elise, 1997) that we use the phrase "primary sense of femaleness" to highlight the focus on early bodily awareness—a bodily sense of self that corresponds to the sexed body one inhabits as a female (see also Kulish, 2000).

I now want to explore particular influences on female development at the juncture of the Oedipus complex that deserve more attention. At about three years of age, a strong upsurge occurs in genital focus, traditionally labeled the "phallic phase" (Jones, 1933). Around that time, exploration of the genitals shifts to masturbation per se—stimulation with the goal of creating ongoing pleasure (Marcus and Francis, 1975). The phallic phase coincides with later stages of separation–individuation and with entry into the oedipal period—a crisis where intense genital stimulation and pleasure dovetail with triadic whole-object relating. The child gains an awareness of threesomes; a relationship exists *between* the parents, not just with each parent in dyadic relation to the child. A wish arises to romantically win over one or both of the parents—more colloquially expressed as, "I want to marry Mommy/Daddy." As we know, this wish regularly meets with profound disappointment: "carried out with tragic seriousness, [it] fails shamefully . . . a permanent injury to self-regard in the form of a narcissistic scar" (Freud, 1920, pp. 20–21).

I will discuss the impact of oedipal defeat/relinquishment that can lead to a sense of shame and inadequacy for both sexes, but with a very different follow-up for girls than for boys. I will then use this thesis as a lens through which to examine the pervasiveness of inhibition in female personality that I believe can center in sexuality and then extend to many other areas of failure to actualize desire.

I want to underscore that I am investigating one strand of development with both conscious and unconscious elements; in focusing on the psychosexual stages, particularly the "phallic" phase, I do not mean that development involves distinct phases in strict linear sequence. It is evident that in the overarching trajectory of development, children are involved in an ongoing, oscillating process of maturing and regression. I am attempting to give a picture—a child's eye view—of how a child likely experiences the effort to get "bigger and bigger."

Sex and shame

Echoing Freud regarding oedipal wishes, Davies (2006) identified "our surrender to those unparalleled dangers of wild romantic passion and to the idealized others who steal our hearts . . . as the pivotal moments that mark our lives" (p. 667). In romantic passion we "expose our desires, and our exquisite vulnerabilities. But desire is also inextricably linked with pain . . . intolerable moments of humiliating and unanticipated rejection by those adored others" (Davies, 2006, p. 667)—what I take up here as the shame of unrequited love, involving rejection and loss at pivotal moments in early childhood by which we are marked. A child's heart is easy to steal, as is his or her self-esteem. I aim to expand contemporary thinking on female psychosexual development by elaborating the experience of shame and by articulating what I believe is one of the central reasons shame comes to be so associated with sexuality.

Shame—a feeling of inferiority, inadequacy, incompetence, helplessness; a sense of self as defective, flawed, leading to a pervasive sense of failure, unworthiness, and to an experience of being scorned, unloved, and forsaken. These are descriptions we find in psychoanalysis for what is viewed as a searing affective experience, also referred to as embarrassment, humiliation, and mortification. Shame leads to a wish to hide, to keep the flawed sense of self secret and to avoid any interpersonal context that might reveal one's inadequacy and lead to further rejection (Morrison, 1989; Lansky, 2005). Shame is a two-person experience; one is shamed in the eyes of another, even if that person is no longer literally present.

Shame has been addressed in self psychology as primarily a pre-oedipal issue in dyadic relationships, coinciding particularly with anal phase issues and contrasted with guilt and conflict in Freud's oedipal focus. Guilt and castration anxiety arise in an experience of active oedipal transgression whereas shame has been seen as an earlier dynamic reflecting passivity and a sense of defect of the entire self involving need and failure in the oral and anal phases rather than oedipal longings (Morrison, 1989). While this division helps to explain the dynamics of narcissistic personality disorder, we can look at shame on an oedipal level, and as not limited to people with narcissistic character structure. I focus specifically on the relationship of shame to libidinal drives, unrequited love, and the fate of healthy narcissism in the oedipal romance. This aspect of shame can be quite intense and may lead to long-lasting effects, particularly regarding sexuality, that are then often generalized to the entire self in gender-specific ways that I will elaborate in this chapter. Freud (1933) thought of shame as a "female characteristic par excellence" in reaction to "genital deficiency" (p. 132). I believe males are no less vulnerable to shame at the oedipal level or to a sense of genital deficiency, though they may defend against such shame in a different manner as discussed in Chapter 5. Shame affects us all.

Consider the following definition by Morrison (1989): "Shame is a reflection of feelings of the whole self in failure, as *inferior in competition or in comparison* with others, as inadequate and defective" (p. 12, emphasis added). This description is applicable to various developmental levels, including shame that follows narcissistic defeat regarding sexual longings at the oedipal level. At that level, shame represents the relationship of the self to another in *unrequited love*, an experience of lost erotic attachment to a highly cathected object. The experience that one has failed to capture and keep the attention, admiration and desire of one's "significant other"—the idealized oedipal parent—leads to a belief that one's libidinal longings are unacceptable and can result in undermined or even shattered self-esteem.

Morrison (1989), following Chasseguet-Smirgel (1985), linked shame with the inability to live up to the ego ideal, one's narcissism and grandiosity sinking to a sense of worthlessness and dejection and to a wish to conceal an unacceptable self. This experience of failure in relation to the ego ideal is, I believe, regularly/normatively triggered by the oedipal object(s) being unattainable, understood by the child as a failure due to defect in the self—being small, inadequate—literally "falling short." Schafer (1967) wrote that, "an *ideal self-representation* is an image of oneself as one would be if one had satisfied a specific ideal" (p. 15). Certainly a highly invested ideal image is that of a desired/accepted suitor of the oedipal object. In pursuing the concept of self-representation in relation to the ego ideal, Morrison (1989) emphasized that "failure to approximate the shape of the ideal self" (p. 35) leads to shame. The use of the word "shape" reminds us that mental representation of the self is developed through the body ego. One embodies one's ego ideal; an ego ideal failure is felt most basically to be a failure of *the body*. What is it about the body that fails in the oedipal romance? It is too *small*. What specific part of the body is especially "flawed" in its diminutive size?—*the genitals*.

The sexual body inflated and deflated

Anatomy should be ecstasy. The mother's physical caretaking of the infant's body stimulates body-surface eroticism. Parents seduce physically as well as enigmatically (Laplanche, 1992; Stein, 1998; Bollas, 2000; Kristeva, 2014), which, combined with the child's maturation, culminates in the phallic/early genital phase, but with a major lack of gratification in the oedipal crisis. The oedipal child is "all turned on" with nowhere to go. Not only is the mind and erotic fantasy expansive, the sexual body is engorged, tumescent—an erection of the penis, and of the clitoris and vulva as well (all of which literally swell with stimulation and blood flow). This would-be oedipal contender is "pumped up and ready to go," only to find little or no reciprocal confirming, affirming response to these desires. The small child encounters a dilemma: "Where am I going to put this thing, this part of my body that feels *so good*?" The oedipal child is left to deflate; there is no where to go but down. Both sexes are forced to contend with a big/little polarity that now has sharp consequences regarding one's sexual body and romantic aspirations. Children feel shamed, and often are shamed, for thinking big romantically and erotically and then being exposed inevitably as little—not a contender. About to be put to bed, one little girl ardently expressed her conviction that she would marry Daddy. Her father haplessly replied that he was already married and that she would marry someone else when she got big. Stung, she demanded to be taken to bed by her mother and retorted, "no one with a penis is putting me to bed!"

Corbett (2001) has critiqued the turn in psychoanalytic theorizing on masculinity away from consideration of healthy phallic states and penile pride. Phallicism has been demoted as a defensive retreat from intimacy, its manic bubble pricked by attachment theory. Corbett made a compelling point, and one that I believe is also applicable to girls. I am not sure that psychoanalysis has ever adequately theorized healthy genital exhibitionism for girls (see Balsam, 2012). Schalin (1989) detailed the positive versus defensive nature of phallic narcissism in both sexes. Healthy exhibitionistic expression of phallic intention takes the form of wanting to make a positive impression upon another person and includes the bodily component of wanting to "press in"—to penetrate. In Chapter 4, I conceptualized the ability to penetrate, bodily and psychically, as an enlivening aspect in female as well as male psychology. Following this line of thinking, the "phallic phase," while a problematic term based on the male genital, and typically seen as correctly applied only to boys, does actually capture something that I think is important not to lose regarding genital pride for both sexes (see Fogel, 1998).

Suggestions to rename this period the early genital phase (Parens et al., 1976) redress the sexism, but tend to eclipse the aspect of engorgement both genital and psychic. There is an advantage to making explicit the tumescence of genital and mind and the exhibitionistic glee which phallic narcissism does convey. As Freud felt girls could be phallic, I think he was getting at a quality of sexual experience that is essential in understanding how shame comes to be so attached to sex (and that Freud did connect to girls' genital shame, deflation, and departure from sexuality). We likely need to have a concept of healthy *inflation* accessible before a problematic sense of *deflation* can come into focus. Then we can more fully account for the wide extent of narcissistic injury that shows up regarding the sexual body and then about sex itself.

Genital exhibitionism—"Look at me!"—may be squashed out of parents' own anxiety and discomfort with grand(iose) displays. Inadvertent or even active shaming by parents can undermine the child's sense of bigness, when previously big was positively reinforced. Active shaming may have been employed regarding lack of oral and then bowel and bladder control in familiar experiences of spilling one's milk, soiling one's pants, being "a baby" versus being "big." Children want nothing more than to be big, and parents often trade on this wish to get desired behavior: "Don't you want to be a big girl/boy?" Early development is, in the child's mind, all about getting big and being proud of it—getting the spoon or cup to one's mouth, getting one's bottom to the toilet. Yet, with "phallic" aspirations, the previous, relatively straightforward developmental trajectory toward "bigness" seems to collapse. Now the parents may appear to want the child to be small, or smaller. Just when the child especially wants to be big and to have some sense of genital mastery, such ambitions are blocked and the child is left to feel small—without gratification, let alone mastery. Genital "swelling," in concert with oedipal intentions, stirs up problems for parents and other adults that are unlike any other. Adults are in very peculiar territory when it comes to contending with childhood sexuality (see Davies, 2006; Fonagy, 2008).

As an example, a three year-old boy, taking no notice of the adults gathered, went around with a toy toolbox full of electrical cords that he busily and gleefully plugged into wall sockets. After some time, he suddenly took notice of one of the women with whom he seemed to become enchanted, gazing at her with an enraptured expression. Wasting little time, he directly approached her and unabashedly placed his little hand suggestively in her lap and exclaimed, "Would you like to see my pee-pee!" This delicate moment, not atypical for the oedipal child, raises a question: How does he or she handle the fact that no such viewing will take place, as well as the eventual recognition that the "pee-pee" the adult *is* interested in "viewing" is that of another adult, a *big* "pee-pee." Hopefully, these moments are handled in a tactful manner and the entire object relationship supports the child's narcissism and self-esteem to counterbalance the inevitable sense of oedipal defeat. Unfortunately, parents' anxieties regarding their children's lust and longing, as well as with narcissism more generally, can lead to shaming (whether intended or not) or even to humiliating ridicule of the oedipal child.

Consider the phrase, "too big for your britches." This is a "put down" meant to shame, to make a child's sense of self get smaller. Notice that, as with "smarty-pants," the item of clothing is not a hat or coat, reflecting I believe an unconscious reference to, and wish to inhibit, *genital* narcissism. The image of bursting out of one's pants is clearly meant to be pejorative rather than having any positive connotation regarding genital expansiveness and prowess. Along with "swell-headed," "full of yourself," and "don't get carried away," these common family epithets function to squelch expansiveness, healthy omnipotence and grandiosity, which at this stage is specifically genital, as well as more global.

A child then emerges from the oedipal period shamed for being too small and forced to stay "small" (sexually) for at least another decade. This potentially humiliating defeat is experienced within the context of sexual fantasy of the oedipal relationship and is registered as both 1) a failure of the entire self in relation to the ego ideal, and 2) a genital flaw quite specifically. We see in adults that the frequent focus of ongoing, seemingly intractable sexual shame centers on the perceived small size of penises or breasts. Ego ideal failure is not only bodily but gendered, leading each sex to feel deficient in anatomically specific ways. A beautiful, young patient referred to what she dejectedly felt were her now drooping breasts: "They still feel good, but they don't deserve to." We are all too familiar with the pained focus on sexual body "defects"—too small, soft, sagging, not firm, hard, erect; premature ejaculation, impotence, frigidity, the inability to "get it up"—the deflated body as abject for *both* sexes. Quite a bit of damage has been sustained in the place where it hurts the most. As Bader (2002) emphasized, it is important that we "understand the deep level at which shame, rejection and helplessness extinguish sexual desire" (p. 81).

Clinical illustration

I will now present a clinical example that focuses specifically on a woman concerned with a sense of shame that inhibited her enjoyment of certain sexual activities. My patient had quite a bit of difficulty discussing these matters with me as shame was then activated in the transference relationship and permeated the analytic field that we inhabited. Tess felt certain sexual positions, although she engaged in them enthusiastically, were shameful, potentially humiliating in relation even to her lover, let alone anyone else who might suspect her of such "undignified" activities. This subject first arose when Tess managed with great reluctance to discuss with me the subject of rear entry intercourse. It was difficult for her to even mention the words and she stumbled over a number of different awkward phrasings. She felt conflicted about what emerged as her robust enjoyment of this form of sex, feeling also that she was "reduced to being an animal." She felt that she specifically, unlike the man, was in the demeaned position—on all fours, her buttocks, vulva, and anus exposed—literally presenting a full view of her sexual body. "Like a monkey," she thought. "What kind of position is this for any self-respecting adult! How do I go from a 'power suit,' or any attire for that matter, to this indignity?" Being visually exposed so totally had associations not only to being an animal but to being diapered:

> When else would my "private parts" be on such full view? Okay for an infant with its mother, but an adult woman with a man? And why me and not the man? He doesn't have *his* butt in the air, and his penis and balls, visible all the time, aren't really that "private."

The feeling of being shamefully infantile was, Tess felt, allocated to her alone.

Over time, I explored with my patient her feeling that certain aspects of sexuality as a woman seemed somehow inextricably linked to being demeaned as too young, small, not grown up enough, with an accompanying expectation of humiliating inadequacy and rejection. This sense of being "babyish" did not cohere with an image of a sexually appealing woman. The sense of shame that infused any attempt at addressing these areas of sexuality posed quite a challenge to our capacity to keep the erotic alive in the clinical exchange. Tess would feel quite avoidant. I would feel concern that I was actively humiliating her in my remaining attentive to this topic rather than being drawn away into other areas of the analysis. I had to manage my sense of disquiet that I was forcing this sexual exposure of Tess, while at the same time I hoped to enlarge the container—the psychic space—for us to develop a narrative articulating her erotic distress.

When Tess and I were able to work through and alleviate some of her feelings of discomfort, she was eventually able to further let go in sex and even relish her experience of vulnerability in "infantile, animalistic" sex with her man, even without this exposure feeling reciprocal: "Why limit pleasure and excitement for both of us just to prove I'm not less than him? He knows that, and now, so do I on a much deeper level." That deeper level concerned her sense of self and her female sexual body—each injured in her oedipal defeat with her father.

Tess recalled feeling scoffed at as "just a little girl," "the baby of the family," when at around age five she wanted to be included in the father's activities with her two teen-aged sisters. I pursued this oedipal material with her and underscored how much she had longed to be her father's favorite when he did not seem to be interested in a small girl. For this patient as an adult, the shameful sense of feeling small, demeaned, "regressed," was evoked by a particular sexual position rather than attached to a sense of a "small" body part. Her references to being a (supposedly asexual) baby conveyed a sense of oedipal defeat, of being "sent back" to a "lesser" developmental stage. This "sent back" feeling was evoked by, and also interfered with, her adult sexual relationship. A central contribution of the analytic process was to sort out, within the context of the analytic field, this complex, confusing, and inhibiting set of images and associations.

Tess then described a particular sexual encounter that had been very compelling for her and her man. As before, this material was approached haltingly, with much embarrassment and uncertainty about whether this was even "an appropriate topic in analysis." However, the benefits of our previous work allowed her to go further with me, as she had with her lover. She described that although in the "standard" missionary position, she uncharacteristically had allowed her legs to rise completely above the man's back—first her knees, then her feet and finally her entire legs splayed out in a V. She reported that she had been used to keeping her legs wrapped tightly around her lover's legs or back. On occasion he might raise her legs somewhat further by putting his arms under her thighs, but she kept them wrapped around his body, uneasily aware that any spreading, let alone raising, of her legs felt shamefully exposing. She participated without any obvious inhibition, but was always aware of a niggling sense of embarrassment.

The idea that she would now voluntarily raise her legs and let them flail about in the air felt again to be strongly associated with a shamed sense of "being a baby." The now familiar doubts surfaced again: "Isn't sexy sex supposed to be between seductive adults? How seductive are babies and diapering? How can I possibly be appealing in this position?" Again, she experienced the same shame and conflict over her sense that this "infantile" posture was no position for any adult to be in. We see here the erasure from conscious awareness of a maternal erotic matrix as a valued aspect of adult sexuality.

We continued pursuing the gender specificity of these issues. Tess observed that men did not seem to "have any trouble pushing their genitals in your face" in pursuit of erotic pleasure; they even seemed to gain from it, their masculine pride enhanced—nothing small or babyish there. Whereas my patient felt that the more robustly she "went at" sex, the more she entered a realm where she felt potentially demeaned. Somehow, full exposure of the vulva can seem tainted with indecency, inadequacy, insufficiency, leaving a woman in a state of conflict right in the midst of active pursuit of sexual pleasure.

Let me note that I am focusing on a heterosexual pairing here because, while certainly not in every couple, heterosexuality has generally been the site of hierarchical gender polarities; as detailed in Chapter 4, female submission develops and lives in a mutually reinforcing relation to male dominance. How much a woman or a man in a same-sex relationship carries over, rather than transcends, these issues would have to be examined on an individual basis, just as heterosexual women and men would vary as individuals.

As I am emphasizing, shame attached to oedipal defeat is almost unavoidable developmentally. Aspects that infuse sexuality, viewed pejoratively as "infantile—not sexy," lend themselves to an experience of shame as a frequent element of the human sexual condition and give rise to a wish to hide from exposure. The gaze of the other and the visual image of the self become highly charged territory abounding with anxieties about how one is viewed, both concretely and symbolically. For each sex, oedipal defeat means that the gendered ego ideal is not realized, but how the two sexes typically contend with such shame tends generally to follow very different trajectories. As we see with my patient, her active exposure of her female body and of her lust felt particularly shameful, and this contrasts quite sharply with prideful phallic exhibition and activity more frequently accessible to men.

Males typically experience shame over being unable to "perform;" the penis is supposed to be able to *do* something rather than something being done to it. Looking and being looked at also tend to break down into gendered divisions along the lines of an active subject and a passive object. Women as a sex are more on sexual display. Shame leads to a wish to not be seen, but gaze functions differently in male and female sexuality, with heterosexual men having a strong desire to view the female body (Dio Bleichmar, 1995). Women as the objects of male sexual gazing are often passively, anxiously, on exhibit as opposed to being actively and confidently exhibitionistic. As in my clinical example, access (both visual and tactile) to the female body in various sexual positions that have infantile associations may often be unmatched in heterosexual males.

Sexual anxieties and insecurities tend to become gender specific in their shaping: He can't "get it up;" she didn't "catch his eye." Likewise, defenses become gendered: men likely turn passive into active, while women seem to sink into an acceptance of shame and a need to hide. How do the two sexes tend to end up in such different places from what I have described thus far as a similar developmental experience?

A gendered fork in the developmental road

To begin, there is a profound difference for the two genders in the oedipal period itself. The boy gets to keep his original object—the mother—in the sense that it is at least someone of his sex that his mother desires. The boy is defeated due to his generation, not his gender; he is not pressed to change his sexual "orientation." That the mother is typically the primary caretaker in pre-oedipal life (Chodorow, 1978) leads to the likelihood that she will be the first oedipal object—focus of erotic desire—for *both* sexes (Freud, 1931). A girl's initial confrontation with oedipal defeat is also in relation to the mother, and she learns a very different lesson from the boy: Her mother does not desire someone of her sex—a gender defeat. She then likely turns to the father, only to experience the generational defeat commonly associated with the oedipal crisis. It is this *double* oedipal loss for the girl that I believe is significant, especially in relation to her mother.

Kernberg (1991) noted that in heterosexual family structure a girl would "gradually become less aware of her own genital impulses" (p. 356) in response to the mother's subtle and unconscious negation of sexual excitement between the two. Schalin (1989) also addressed this point: "the realization that only men can marry women may mean a libidinal catastrophe for the daughter. Gradually, the girl realizes that 'the penis is the key to a woman's heart'" (p. 44; see also Lax, 1994; Frenkel, 1996). Lampl de Groot (1927, 1933) identified the parallel nature of the boy's and the girl's active courtship of the mother until the anatomical difference is known, at which time the girl renounces her active sexuality. Without "a little tassel," (Lampl de Groot, 1933, p. 497) a girl's erotic desire for her mother likely feels blocked. A girl may suffer a serious defeat in her first, most intense erotic love affair, and she is likely to register this defeat as her inadequacy on a bodily level. The oedipal loss of the father can deepen this sense of failure. A girl can come to feel that her body is inferior to *everyone's* (Barnett, 1966).

Males, though, are certainly not immune from oedipal defeat and a sense of shame regarding impotent desire. Such shame is initially experienced (as is so for a girl) in relation to the mother. Males tend to defend against this shame in a manner that might be thought of as counterphobic: instead of shrinking away from mother, a boy will attempt to triumph over her. In this effort, he will use identification with the father who seems to be in the desirable position—in the position to desire. A boy will attempt to become "big" like Dad and to make mother "small." As Corbett (2001) so eloquently put it, the effort to be a big winner, not a small loser, is a central boyhood trope—a phallic illusion:

> an insistent, illusory display of bigness and agency that is coupled with an equally unrestrained contempt for smallness and lack. In the spirit of 'boys will be boys,' bravado, aggressive protest, and illusory phallic narcissism have become defining, normative attributes of masculinity.
>
> (p. 6)

As described in Chapter 5, denial of the lost maternal object is achieved by the creation of the "manic penis" (Rey, 1994, p. 220). The penis becomes omnipotent—a magic phallus—and a boy in identification becomes omnipotent as well. This strategy is not a return to healthy narcissism—the genital inflation I have described above—but a dependence on *over-inflation* of both one's genital and one's sense of self. As a corollary, the mother and her female genital must be devalued;

maternal eroticism is subjected to disavowal. A generalized manic defense in males is bolstered by society's greater valuation of males, making the penis into a larger than life phallus—"the mythic, permanently erect archetypal monolith of masculine omnipotence" (Ducat, 2004, p. 2). A phallic ego ideal reflects the dominance in the male psyche of defensive phallicism (Diamond, 1995, 2004; Fogel, 1998). As put forth in Chapters 4 and 5, the ability to penetrate (and not be penetrated) becomes the definition of "man."

Whereas males manically over-inflate their genitals and desire in hopes of immunity from an experience of castration, I suggest that females, unconsciously motivated and with much support for this maneuver from the culture, may depressively embrace the *deflation* of their genitals and desire. This feminine form of defense against being castrated—rendered impotent—is parallel to, but opposite in form from, the masculine strategy of phallic omnipotence.

Lerner (1976) pointed out that the lack of adequate information given to a girl regarding her sexual body often leads to anxiety, confusion, and shame regarding her sexuality. I propose that the marker "absent" regarding female genitalia and desire may be a female form of camouflage, sexual and more generally. The female body lends itself—and is unconsciously used by females with the aid of the culture and, until relatively recently, psychoanalytic theory—to this specific defense. I emphasize that this "protection" is based on *inhibition* (rather than male exhibition), and rests on the idea that if you *don't* "use it," you won't "lose it." A belief takes hold that it would be more shameful to try and to fail than to not try at all and that desires are best held on to as unfulfilled fantasies. Problematically for women, defensive deflation undermines one's agency, whereas inflation as a defense in activity, even if overblown, directs one out agentically into the world. We need a route by which the female "no-thing" genital (Slap, 1979; Kalinich, 1993) can be represented (Schiller, 2012) and used as a "something" genital with potent capacities of incorporation, expansiveness and penetration—capacities that can extend to, infuse, and inform the sense of self.

If only male, as opposed to female, anatomy represents the shape of potent action, then women will have trouble fitting themselves into these qualities—they will not be able to "embody" them, literally. It is a problem *in language*, not with the female body, that agency is masculinized. We need vocabulary grounded in the female body (Goldberger, 1999; Balsam,

2001; Kulish, 2003; Long, 2005; Schiller, 2012), and language not based solely on the incorporative, interior quality of the vagina and uterus, but that includes *the expansive exterior of the female sexual body.*

Both in concrete anatomical reality and in the felt sense of sexual desire, the female body sticks out, stands out, as does the male body. I have described earlier in this chapter the sensation of genital swelling—engorgement—that is strongly registered even if not visually noted in the female. Consider also the pregnant belly (glowing in the 2004 Olympic Opening Ceremonies pageant in Athens), clearly registered visually and making quite an impression as it expands out into space (Balsam, 1996, 2001, 2003, 2012). Balsam (2012) underscored that the psychoanalytic literature, in contrast to its fascination with phallic icons, tends to neglect female sexual prowess as evidenced in the exterior contours of the pregnant female body: "The vast belly, the bounteous breasts, and the swayback posture of pregnancy create an arresting new outline . . . It requires hard work to ignore a pregnant woman" (p. 55). Yet female erotic prowess has been ignored within analytic theorizing. And what is its fate within the analytic field of each clinical dyad?

As a further example of potent, female exteriority—going out into the world in a penetrating manner—I have emphasized, following Klein (1932), that breasts are the original "phallic" objects. Feeding breasts and nipples have an erect, penetrating quality and form the "erotic epicentre of the self's relation to the other" (Bollas, 2000, p. 47; see also Sarlin, 1981). In the psychoanalytic erasure of the female form and of maternal eroticism, breasts—plural, powerful, and erotic—tend to be singularized into a desexualized Good or Bad breast. Scarfone (2013) noted that:

> as Laplanche points out, it is highly surprising that the basic fact of the breast[s] as a powerfully erogenous zone for the maternal other should have been overlooked in the theory of the mother–child relation, as well as in the theory of libidinal stages and erogenous zones!
> (p. 553)

It is indeed "highly surprising" given the anatomical facts, but not surprising given the provocation that maternal eroticism poses (Kristeva, 2014). What is meant by "phallic"—sexual power—has been removed from the maternal and from females as a sex—an amputation rendering the female body devalued and seemingly impotent.

I want to underline here, as I do throughout this book, the importance of the positive awe rather than defensive devaluation of the mother's sexual body as something that needs to be maintained as an accessible image of female potency. At the beginning of life, a strong aesthetic impression is made as a mother's beauty penetrates the infant's senses and mind (Meltzer and Harris, 1988; see also Elise, 2006). This aesthetic-erotic experience should ideally be a source over time of positive identification for girls and integrated into healthy narcissism. As one patient put it: "I urgently wanted to know what it was like to have big breasts myself. Mother's breasts were great . . . awesome . . . like the universe or something" (Balsam, 1996, p. 419). Positive representations of the female body are needed to give voice to a woman's body, her sexual desire, and to her agency in various realms. And each sex needs not to be confined to their own concrete body in representing self; as identified in Chapter 3, bi/pansexual identifications open up creative erotic possibilities and need to be accessible. A clinical focus on psychic bisexuality, as well as on oedipal shame that is generationally generated and then gendered, can be useful in elucidating aspects of patients' material that may be missed by more familiar formulations whether those be Freudian or object relational.

Creative penetrations: keeping the erotic in the field of clinical engagement

I will now offer a second clinical vignette involving a woman patient's fear of writing and public speaking in the context of professional ambition and desires for achievement. Writing is the epitome of needing to authorize one's own thinking, one's own mind: to put forth an idea, to send it out into the world, to penetrate into unknown realms for purposes of discovery and creation, to produce something new. To write is to assert oneself. In public speaking, one does not solely write one's own unique perspective but lets this thinking be heard and responded to by the group; thus one exposes a core, highly valued and vulnerable aspect of self, as described in Chapter 3. Fear of public speaking is often ranked close to, or even above, the fear of death, especially by women. People tend to think that only men should stand up and speak their minds (Riviere, 1929), impregnating the feminine audience with their seminal thinking.

My patient, a bisexual woman, is extremely bright and creative, with strong anxieties regarding separation–individuation from her mother that have been the focus of much of the analysis. But attend to the sexual bodily metaphors in this condensed material that, although familiar to analysts with a Freudian-based model as reflecting penis envy, are here understood as generational anxieties that may *masquerade* as penis envy. Lynn has a contract to write her first book. She reports feeling "lonely and cut off" when home writing. When I inquire about this sense of isolation (typically thought of in terms of separation and individuation), Lynn notices that she does not feel isolated when she is home alone reading. I comment: "—*taking in* someone else's ideas." She responds:

> What I'm writing is so big, I feel inadequate, not up to the task. Besides, I'm afraid it will have no impact whatsoever, or worse, be mocked. That's what you get for sticking your neck out. I'll never be able to show my face again. I should just close up shop.

A sense of shame is evident. She avoids her writing and spends a lot of time eating, another "taking in" activity.

Later, Lynn says:

> If I'm going to be an author, I have to act like I really know something—be an authority—but I'll feel like a fraud. I'll have to be able to fight for my perspective when I'm challenged; the men in my department are cocky and can be very aggressive.

Viewing "cockiness" not only as defensive pretense, but also as a healthy female potential for expressing "masculine" confidence, I ask: "Can you be as well?" Yes, Lynn replies, that's the question:

> Can I play ball with the big boys; can I compete? I can't just melt into the crowd, get lost in the group; it's going to be clear how I differ from the others, what my individual approach is. And what if I succeed? Writing is powerful; you can have quite an impact on a lot of people. How will I handle success, what will people expect of me then? What if they resent me? Will I be able to blend back into the group or end up all on my own?

Here, separation–individuation themes continue to oscillate with genitally based material.

Lynn's anxiety intensified exponentially when she had to give a departmental presentation, "I know I have to be able to assert my thinking, state my ideas and stand behind them; I have to forward my argument, but I'm so anxious I feel like a wet noodle." She makes reference to what may be seen as a deflated/pejorative sense of the female genital/vulva. She fears attack for presuming that she has any ideas worth paying attention to; not only will her thesis itself be demeaned, but more painfully, the belief that she has anything to offer will be scoffed at and ridiculed: "Who do you think you are? Is that it, is that all?" Lynn states that she imagines "being laid low and slinking away with my 'tail between my legs.'" I viewed this reference as not so much to a penis per se, but to a state of genital deflation and narcissistic injury.

As the presentation loomed closer, anxiety approached panic. My patient feels it is actually dangerous to stick out in a crowd, and imagines:

> being physically smashed, my teeth knocked out; . . . my argument will have no teeth either—a public humiliation—I'll feel like sinking through the floor in shame. I won't be able to think; I'll just go limp. I'll never be able to stand up in front of people again if my ideas don't stand up.

Here she speaks to the internal obstacles, projected outward, to maintaining a sense of healthy inflation.

This material moved explicitly into the transference. Do I think she has anything to offer, has what it takes? Would I take her seriously if I read her work, came to her presentation? She expresses the wishful fantasy that she could impress me with her ideas. Maybe I would use her ideas in my own writing. Or would I envy her and want to cut her down; could she actually compete with me to "woo an audience?" What if she reads a paper of mine, admires it, but then feels deflated about her own abilities? We see here the intermingling of wishes to woo *me*—to offer me something I would "take seriously" and not dismiss—with more analytically familiar material about envious competition with the maternal object. Eventually, making use of a positive maternal transference identification, she recognized the possibility that if she imagined admiring my work, it might actually make it easier for her to write. "If you can do it, so can I—we can each "strut our stuff." This idea led to a dream: "I'm so excited, I'm flying through the sky on a rocket. I offer you a ride and you hop on. I feel really full of myself! I'm bursting with excitement. It's great!"

Among a number of possible interpretations, I saw this patient's dream as a powerful and charming illustration of mother–daughter eroticism—both mother and daughter genitally empowered in creative intercourse with one another and with the world. I am suggesting that this "phallic" quality does not here stem from a fantasy of a truncated penis, but can be expressive of female genital and breast engorgement and inflation. As Fogel (1998) has stated, "'phallic' power is available in varying degrees and symbolic transformations to both sexes" (p. 685). A sense of female potency that is expansive, enlarged, soaring, can support experiences of enthusiasm, excitement, and exhilaration that are essential momentum to sending any project forward. Aron (1995), writing about narcissistic inhibitions in the process of writing, stated that "it is not necessary to overcome, give up, or abandon our omnipotent phantasies, but rather . . . to appreciate them, celebrate them, and integrate them into our overall sense of self" (p. 196). In inhibiting or eliminating access to one's grandiosity, "people deprive themselves of an important prerequisite to the creative process" (Aron, 1995, p. 196). I have argued here that women are the people especially likely to deprive themselves of genitally based narcissism, and that women need to regain a sense of grandeur grounded in the female body (see Balsam, 2012).

I have been showing that women have anxieties about embodying the role of penetrator: Standing out—being outstanding—has likely *become* body-ego dystonic due to the oedipal dynamics described above rather than being inherent to a concrete, penis-less state. Subsequent developmental issues can further entrench these earlier oedipal dynamics. Women then worry about not having what it takes, about being mocked for thinking that they have something to show or are impressive in any way. Women fear being exposed as having nothing to offer; someone else's ideas are bigger, better (themes traditionally understood as penis envy). Criticism is dreaded as annihilation—psychic castration—and women imagine being sent away in shame, never to show up again.

I am detaching "phallic" aspirations from the penis to speak about experiences of self that are important in the female psyche. As stated above, I believe these self-representations have a female bodily correlate that is, as yet, unnamed. While I would like a term based in female anatomy, I do not find it thus far, and I am speaking of qualities not evoked by vaginal incorporative powers. A breast-related term has appeal, yet it is doubtful that mammary or mammilla ("any nipplelike process or protuberance" [Webster's, 1992]) would ever "catch on" as a female equivalent to phallus and phallic ('mammillic?'). It is interesting, however, to note the anatomical definition of phallus: "the penis, the clitoris, or the sexually undifferentiated embryonic organ out of which either of these develops" (Webster's, 1992). This bisexual definition would support my usage in this paper of *phallic* as a term re-appropriated to the female body.

Phallic metaphors and metaphors of impotence or castration elicit charged affective and somatic responses that have emotional "punch" and that open up material for women on many levels (see Fogel, 1998). As Vivona (2003) has noted, "Forgotten bodily experience is implicit in metaphor" (p. 56). Anxiety associated with "sticking out" especially pertains to women's, as well as to men's, wish for (genital) potency. At the oedipal level, these anxieties represent fears of narcissistic injury, genitally and more general, based in a sense of defeat, rather than reflecting fantasies of an illusory penis (masculinity complex) leading to the *delusion* that one can be castrated. In encountering the reality of unrequited oedipal desires, what may be "cut off" is one's self-esteem regarding one's (female) genital and sense of (sexual) potency and prowess. How clinicians hold these ideas in mind makes a significant difference in how one registers and works with these erotic dimensions of the analytic field.

Hopefully the reader gleans in this brief case material the anxiety, ambivalence, and inhibition regarding agency, aggression, competition, power, achievement and authority that women can experience in basically any form of self-assertion. In order for girls, and then women, to have a sense of agency as females we need to facilitate, not restrict, these various forms of "phallic" behavior (see Elise, 1991; Hoffman, 1996; Seelig, 2002; Holtzman and Kulish, 2003; Harris, 2005). We know that these attributes are needed in many life pursuits—professional ambitions, creative endeavors, athletic prowess, etc.—and I would apply my theorizing to each of them as an additional level in understanding the derailment of female desires.

I have delineated a developmental account that emphasizes the centrality of intersubjective influences in shaping the sense of self and of one's body. My formulation, while recognizing the girl's difficulty in standing separate with her own individuated identity from the mother, directs our focus to oedipal sexuality. What I do take from Freud (1920) is his profound insight into the intense romantic passions of small children "carried out with tragic seriousness" toward their parents and failing "shamefully" (p. 21) and his recognition that the mother is the first focus of desire for each sex. I depart from Freud in that I do *not* attribute a female sense of inadequacy and inhibition, sexually or more general, to a supposed anatomical fact: that it is inherently problematic and disappointing to be without a penis.

I am arguing instead that oedipal defeat in relation to each parent results in a castration that originates as a generational rather than as a gendered experience. With or without a penis, children feel that their "big" genital (which feels "great") "suddenly" becomes a puny genital—not worth much. A sense of disappointment and deflation ensue regarding one's sexed body and one's romantic aspirations. It is only then that the heterosexual developmental course for the sexes divides with the penis being the ticket *within patriarchal social structures* to manic restitution and an overinflated masculinity. For females, living out a dejected, deflated stance (classically understood in a limited way as penis envy) sends them in the direction of inhibition instead of toward healthy exhibition.

Conclusion

It is poignantly painful that individuals of each sex, and along a continuum of gendered identities, can come to feel such a sense of shame and inadequacy around their bodily and gendered sense of self. We think of ego ideals as positive for development, and in many ways these representations do contribute in a positive manner. But it is evident both in clinical work and more generally that the ego ideals set up by the culture to construct gender do so in a way that is often very undermining of personal wellbeing. Dinnerstein (1976) in *The Mermaid and the Minotaur* articulated even in her title how each sex becomes half human—able to express and embody only half of what should be available to each and every person.

Ideally, psychoanalysis creates a transitional space for the transformation of shame where a new relationship between the ego and the ego ideal is achieved. A significant portion of shame is gender-related. The capacity to do battle with shame-ridden aspects of the personality is a developmental accomplishment that benefits one's entire personality, not to mention one's sex life. Analysis—like sex, interestingly—entails risking exposure of a sense of shame with the hope that the interpersonal outcome will not deepen or confirm an experience of humiliation but ameliorate it. Optimally, the negative self-concept is disconfirmed; when that occurs exposure can be connecting. Exposure uncovers a vulnerability of the self that is attractive; the toxicity of shame has been triumphed over by both members of the couple within the analytic field, directly or vicariously. In helping our patients to "detoxify shame and add a playfully transgressive freedom to internal experience" (Davies, 2006, p. 680), we as clinicians—women and men—may also be able to access a transformative integration of our own gendered experiences of shame.

Object relations and relational theorists have generally paid less attention to the body-centered psychosexual stages, the oedipal complex, and childhood sexuality than is optimal. Freudian-based models have underemphasized intersubjectivity and the impact of object relations on the experience of the body. Bringing multi-layered erotic themes into creative engagement within the vitality of the analytic field—analytic eroticism—is an ongoing process. Thinking advances from the integration of valuable perspectives from multiple orientations. A strong foundation in object relations theory and intersubjectivity allows for the use of classical themes in drive theory in a compelling manner that I hope to be demonstrating in this book. As Fonagy (2008) stated:

> Neither drive theory nor object relations theory in their pure form offers a satisfactory formulation of psychosexuality (p. 17) . . . We need a truly developmental model of the evolution of personality and interpersonal relationships that retains a substantive place for sexual feelings and behavior within the context of unfolding object relationships.
>
> (p. 18)

It is my aim to contribute to that integrative effort in placing these interweaving perspectives on development and sexuality within the clinical context of analytic field theory.

I have conveyed in this chapter that a "laying low" of female sexual agency is a microcosm of pervasive trends in female personality. Females may inhibit themselves more generally due to a representation of self as "not having what it takes" genitally, and then bodily and psychically. An appreciation for the impact of the sexual body—unavoidably registered through both object relational and cultural filters—underscores its contribution not only to sex-specific shaping of the mind, but to the affective intensity with which gendered identifications are felt. I believe we then have an enriched palette with which to comprehend more fully how female inhibitions, even though railed against by women, can become so entrenched. In the following chapter, I will focus further on the way in which a girl's genital structure may be imbued with certain meanings given her object relational experience within our particular culture, and on the manner in which her anatomy may dispose her to certain imagery regarding her relations with objects.

References

Aron, L. (1995). The internalized primal scene. *Psychoanalytic Dialogues*, 5: 195–237.
Bader, M. (2002). *Arousal: The secret logic of sexual fantasies*. New York: St. Martin's.
Balsam, R. (1996). The pregnant mother and the body image of the daughter. *Journal of the American Psychoanalytic Association*, 44 (Suppl.): 401–427.
— (2001). The integration of female and male identifications in a woman's gender identity. *Journal of the American Psychoanalytic Association*, 49:1335–1360.
— (2003). The vanished pregnant body. *Journal of the American Psychoanalytic Association*, 51: 1153–1179.
— (2012). *Women's bodies in psychoanalysis*. New York: Routledge.
Barnett, M. (1966). Vaginal awareness in the infancy and childhood of girls. *Journal of the American Psychoanalytic Association*,14: 129–141.
Bassin, D. (1982). Woman's images of inner space: Data towards expanded interpretive categories. *International Review of Psychoanalysis*, 9: 191–203.
Benjamin, J. (1988). *The bonds of love*. New York: Pantheon.
Bernstein, D. (1990). Female genital anxiety, conflicts and typical mastery modes. *International Journal of Psychoanalysis*, 71: 151–165.
Blum, H., (Ed.) (1976). Female psychology. *Journal of the American Psychoanalytic Association*, 24 (Suppl.): 1–454.
Bollas, C. (2000). *Hysteria*. London: Routledge.
Chasseguet-Smirgel, J. (1985). *The ego ideal*. New York: Norton.
Chodorow, N. (1978). *The reproduction of mothering*. Berkeley: University of California Press.
Corbett, K. (2001). Fagot=loser. *Studies in Gender and Sexuality*, 2: 3–28.
Davies, J. (2006). The times we sizzle, and the times we sigh: The multiple erotics of arousal, anticipation and release. *Psychoanalytic Dialogues*, 16: 665–686.
Diamond, M. (1995). Someone to watch over me: The father as the original protector of the mother-infant dyad. *Psychoanalytic Psychotherapy*, 12: 89–102.

— (2004). The shaping of masculinity: Revisioning boys turning away from their mothers to construct male gender identity. *International Journal of Psychoanalysis*, 85: 359–380.
Dinnerstein, D. (1976). *The mermaid and the minotaur*. New York: Harper & Row.
Dio Bleichmar, E. (1995). The secret in the constitution of female sexuality: The effects of the adult's sexual look upon the subjectivity of the girl. *Journal of Clinical Psychoanalysis*, 4: 331–342.
Ducat, S. (2004). *The wimp factor: Gender gaps, holy wars and the politics of anxious masculinity*. Boston: Beacon Press.
Elise, D. (1991). An analysis of gender differences in separation-individuation. *Psychoanalytic Study of the Child*, 46: 51–67.
— (1997). Primary femininity, bisexuality and the female ego ideal: A Re-examination of female developmental theory. *The Psychoanalytic Quarterly*, 66: 489–517.
— (2006). Beauty and the Aesthetic Impact of the Bejeweled Mother. *Studies in Gender & Sexuality*, 7: 207–215.
Erikson, E. (1950). *Childhood and society*. New York: Norton.
Fogel, G. (1998). Interiority and inner genital space in men: What else can be lost in Castration. *Psychoanalytic Quarterly*, 67: 662–697.
Fonagy, P. (2008). A genuinely developmental theory of sexual enjoyment and its implications for psychoanalytic technique. *Journal of the American Psychoanalytic Association*, 56: 11–36.
Frenkel, R. (1996). A reconsideration of object choice in women: Phallus or fallacy. *Journal of the American Psychoanalytic Association*, 44 (Suppl.): 133–156.
Freud, S. (1920). Beyond the pleasure principle. *The Standard Edition*, 18: 7–64.
— (1931). Female sexuality. *The Standard Edition*, 21: 225–243.
— (1923). The ego and the id. *The Standard Edition*, 19: 12–66.
— (1933). New introductory lectures on psychoanalysis: Lecture XXXIII: Femininity. *The Standard Edition*, 22: 112–135.
Goldberger, M. (1999). Obsolete terminology constricts imaginative thinking. *Psychoanalytic Quarterly*, 68: 462–466.
Harris, A. (2005). *Gender as soft assembly*. The Analytic Press.
Hoffman, L. (1996). Freud and feminine subjectivity. *Journal of the American Psychoanalytic Association*, 44 (Suppl.): 23–44.
Holtzman, D. and Kulish, N. (2000). The feminization of the female oedipal complex, Part I: A reconsideration of the significance of separation issues. *Journal of the American Psychoanalytic Association*, 48: 1413–1437.
— (2003). The feminization of the female oedipal complex, Part II: Aggression reconsidered. *Journal of the American Psychoanalytic Association*, 51: 1127–1151.
Jones, E. (1933). The phallic phase. *International Journal of Psychoanalysis*, 14: 1–33.

Kalinich, L. (1993). On the sense of absence: A perspective on womanly issues. *Psychoanalytic Quarterly*, 62: 206–228.
Kernberg, O. (1991). Sadomasochism, sexual excitement, and perversion. *Journal of the American Psychoanalytic Association*, 39: 333–362.
Klein, M. (1932). *The psychoanalysis of children*. London: Hogarth Press.
Kristeva, J. (2014). Reliance, or maternal eroticism. *Journal of the American Psychoanalytic Association*, 62: 69–85.
Kulish, N. (2000). Primary femininity: Clinical advances and theoretical ambiguities. *Journal of the American Psychoanalytic Association*, 48: 1355–1379.
— (2003). Panel: The changing language of female development. APsaA 92nd Annual Meeting, Boston.
Lansky, M. (2005). Hidden Shame. *Journal of the American Psychoanalytic Association*, 53: 865–890.
Lampl de Groot, J. (1927). The evolution of the Oedipus complex in women. *International Journal of Psychoanalysis*, 9: 332–345.
Lampl de Groot, J. (1933). Problems of femininity. *Psychoanalytic Quarterly*, 11: 489–518.
Laplanche, J. (1992). *Seduction, translation, drives*. London: Institute of Contemporary Arts.
Lax, R. (1994). Aspects of primary and secondary genital feelings and anxieties in girls during the preoedipal and early oedipal phases. *Psychoanalytic Quarterly*, 63: 271–296.
Lerner, H. (1976). Parental mislabeling of female genitals as a determinant of penis envy and learning inhibitions in women. *Journal of the American Psychoanalytic Association*, 24 (Suppl.): 269–283.
Long, K. (2005). Panel Report: The changing language of female development. *Journal of the American Psychoanalytic Association*, 53: 1161–1176.
Marcus, I. and Francis, J. (1975). *Masturbation; From infancy to senescence*. New York: International Universities Press.
Mayer, E. L. (1985). Everybody must be just like me: Observations on female castration anxiety. *International Journal of Psychoanalysis*, 66: 331–347.
Meltzer, D. and Harris Williams, M. (1988). *The apprehension of beauty*. Strath Tay, Scotland: Clunie Press.
Morrison, A. (1989). *Shame: The underside of narcissism*. Hillsdale, New Jersey: The Analytic Press.
Parens, H., Pollock, L., Stern, J. and Kramer, S. (1976). On the girl's entry into the Oedipus complex. *Journal of the American Psychoanalytic Association*, 24 (Suppl.): 79–107.
Rey, H. (1994). *Universals of psychoanalysis in the treatment of psychotic and borderline states*. London: Free Association Books.
Richards, A. and Tyson, P., (Eds.) (1996). The psychology of women. *Journal of the American Psychoanalytic Association*, 44 (Suppl.):1–555.
Riviere, J. (1929). Womanliness as masquerade. *International Journal of Psychoanalysis*, 10: 303–313.

Sarlin, C. (1981). The role of breast-feeding in psychosexual development and the achievement of the genital phase. *Journal of the American Psychoanalytic Association*, 29: 631–641.

Scarfone, D. (2013). A brief introduction to the work of Jean Laplanche. *International Journal of Psychoanalysis*, 94: 545–566.

Schafer, R. (1967). Ideals, the ego ideal and the ideal self. In *Motives and thought*. Psychological Issues Monograph, 18/19: 131–174.

Schalin, L.J. (1989). On Phallicism: Developmental aspects, neutralization, sublimation and defensive phallicism. *Scandinavian Review*, 12: 38–57.

Schiller, B. (2012). Representing female desire within a labial framework of sexuality. *Journal of the American Psychoanalytic Association*, 60: 1161–1197.

Seelig, B. (2002). The rape of Medusa in the temple of Athena. *International Journal of Psychoanalysis*, 83: 895–911.

Slap, J. (1979). On nothing and nobody with an addendum on William Hogarth. *Psychoanalytic Quarterly*, 48: 620–627.

Stein, R. (1998). The poignant, the excessive and the enigmatic in sexuality. *International Journal of Psychoanalysis*, 79: 259–268.

Tyson, P. (1994). Bedrock and beyond: An examination of the clinical utility of contemporary theories of female psychology *Journal of the American Psychoanalytic Association*, 42: 447–467.

Vivona, J. (2003). Embracing figures of speech: The transformative potential of spoken language. *Psychoanalytic Psychology*, 20: 52–66.

Webster's *New universal unabridged dictionary*. New York: Barnes and Noble, 1992.

Chapter 8

Erasure of the female erotic

Let's consider a masturbatory experience of a female patient. This woman and the man she had been involved with had just broken up. The couple had separated on a number of previous occasions and so Zoe was familiar with what to expect in her emotional reaction. After a few tearful hours of grief and agitation, she started to masturbate in what she knew would be a fairly successful, though short-lived, attempt to ward off depression. Zoe reported to me what she had found to be a rather surprising train of thought while masturbating. As she became more aroused she did experience the sought-after sense of well-being. However, she found that the natural drift of her fantasy towards awareness of vaginal sensation, an image of a penis—her boyfriend's penis—and then the desire for intercourse with him, "spoiled" her attempted escape from the experience of object loss.

Right in the middle of an effort to self-soothe, Zoe was confronted even more vividly, on a bodily, sexual level as well as emotionally, with painful loss and emptiness. She realized that an awareness of vaginal arousal, connected as it was with an image of his body and the desire for intercourse, made her miss him all the more. She found herself consciously shutting down vaginally and retreating to a focus on purely clitoral sensations. In this way, her "depression remedy" worked: If her focus was clitoral, she could have pleasure and a sense of well-being without him. If she allowed for vaginal sensation and imagery, she missed the absent man. Zoe concluded to me: "I don't want to have any sexual image of my vagina because it leads to an image of his penis and that's gone!"

Now clearly it was her boyfriend attached to his penis that Zoe was missing—not the penis as a part-object. This patient has great depth of feeling for this man. Her relevant history and area of vulnerability do involve paternal object loss and, what was in her view, a sexual dysfunction.[1] When she was four her parents divorced and she saw little of her father after that time. At age 25 she married a man she felt she truly loved and was loved by. She was disturbed however to be unable to have an orgasm induced through intercourse. She enjoyed love-making with her husband, but remembered feeling "bothered" by any form of penetration when she was sexually excited as this seemed to "distract" her from arousal that she experienced as clitoral. She felt that it was completely unimaginable to her why intercourse, which she did feel was erotic and a general bodily and emotional pleasure, ever lead to orgasm for a woman. This marriage ended when Zoe was 31 due to a combination of dissatisfactions on the part of each spouse. After a year of being single and some casual dating she met and fell in love with the current man.

As this new sexual relationship unfolded Zoe realized that she was having a sense of vaginal arousal that was new to her. She described incremental elaborations of vaginal responsiveness that led "to a whole new image of my vagina as a site of sexual stimulation." Although she continued to be unable to orgasm during intercourse without manual clitoral stimulation, she now experienced penetration as adding to rather than detracting from her arousal. As Zoe and her man became closer to one another emotionally, she perceived herself to be literally opening up to him sexually, vaginally. It no longer seemed mysterious to her that a woman could climax through intercourse.

In looking back at her experience in her marriage, Zoe felt that although she had engaged rather enthusiastically in intercourse, in actuality, "I had no real picture in my mind of my vagina as erotically alive—it was passive, passively receiving the penis in something more like an affectionate hug than an exciting, hungry, actively seeking kind of experience." She did have a mental representation of her vagina, as most women do, developed in adolescence (Plaut and Hutchinson, 1986), but it was as a desexualized, predominantly reproductive organ. Her comment might be understood as reflecting the difference in subjective experience between an image of a vagina that actually desires and goes after the penis (and other forms of stimulation) rather than merely passively accepting penetration.

This clinical fragment points to multiple layers in the erasure of female desire. The patient became conscious of one layer—the wish to disavow vaginal longing in order to defend against object loss in relation to an adult male partner. Within the analytic work, she could connect this defensive effort to her experiences of loss in relation to her father at the oedipal stage. Recognition of a deeper maternal layer of erotic loss was much more difficult to access as a remembered experience and could only surface over time in the transference configuration within the analytic field. I offer this vignette as preface to a discussion of female desire as it has been theorized within psychoanalytic theory. My goal is to shed further light on theoretical "erasures" that have confused the developmental and clinical understanding of female erotic life and its vicissitudes.

Clinically, it is apparent that the sexual realm remains fraught for many women despite a cultural facade of sexual sophistication. Underlying feelings of uncertainty and lack of self-assurance often prevail, infusing female sexual subjectivity with an underground uneasiness that itself feels shameful. How might clinicians facilitate within the analytic field a mutual exploration of the female erotic, especially in an age when we like to think we are past confusion and insecurities? Do clinicians as well collude with an assumption that sexuality is no longer "an issue" for women (or for men)? Has the analytic field as clinical terrain been erotically neutralized? Can we instead foster thoughtful inquiry into this crucial subject? I want to underscore the clinical importance of an analytic context where questions can be posed for analyst and patient to explore together in generating a meaningful narrative elaboration of a woman's erotic sense of self. Such dialogue is supported by questioning assumptions about female sexuality permeating decades of psychoanalytic theorizing.

Why women may *not* want to want

Possibly the central and most perplexing question in the history of psychoanalysis has been, "What does a woman want?"—almost a lament as initially posed by Freud (1925), who seemed frustrated enough with this quandary to hand it over to female colleagues and future generations of theorists. This question led to numerous responses and further questions, with a most cogent reply by Benjamin (1988) that women *want to want*, to have a sense of agency and desire—sexual subjectivity. Yet, questions regarding women's erotic life continue to abound.

Woman—does she want? If she does not, why not? If she does, what is it she wants? Why is it not clear what women want? The persistence of this question illustrates that something renders female desire opaque both with regard to its existence and its object. Zak de Goldstein (1984) pointed out that some of Freud's own metaphors—such as a "dark continent"—worked to obscure further the subject of female sexuality, "thus a priori making the key question 'what does a woman desire?' difficult or even impossible to answer" (p. 180). Some element of mystery seems to prevail; women's desire is veiled, has a hidden, shrouded quality. Can we imagine asking the question "What do men want?" and have it take up a century of theorizing? Yet, is the answer regarding male desire so obvious? How is it that what men want is considered to be self-evident?

As brought forth in Chapter 5, male desire has its own complexities and hidden realms. Males may pursue sex even when it is not clear that sex is what they are actually after but, instead, some other experience they may be less able to acknowledge directly: emotional intimacy, affection, reassurance, power, aggression, feelings of aliveness, and anxiety reduction. Dimen (1991) wrote that desire is "dualistically organized, such that desire is gender syntonic for men, dystonic for women ... women are represented to be without desire" (p. 343)—to be the "targets" of male desire. Thus, male desire is presumed to have a clarity that stands in contrast to the seeming opacity and ambiguity of female desire.

Yet women must have some central motive to be complicit and compliant in sustaining the myth of mystery and lack regarding their desire (Riviere, 1929; Torok, 1970; Irigaray, 1990). In the last chapter, I proposed that the marker "absent" denoting female genitalia and desire might be understood as reflecting a female form of protection against "castration" of sexual desire; males inflate whereas females may deflate their genital representation and desire. I suggested that the female body lends itself—and is unconsciously used by females, with the aid of the culture and, until relatively recently, psychoanalytic theory—to a specific form of protection of female desire, *unfortunately though, a protective deflation that may turn into an erasure*. In this chapter, I intend to pursue this theme of hidden desire, hidden so well that a given woman may be unable to locate her own desire.

I am theorizing that early in development a girl's desires can be quite focally sensed and directed, and that the sensation of desire—erotic hunger—can be intensely experienced, and in certain circumstances uncomfortably so. I will consider the way in which a girl may respond to a particular experience of erotic object loss by forming a mental representation of her sexual self and of her body, specifically her genitalia, as empty, not full, not filled—a "void." In relation to her female body, a girl can fear being genitally open when it is the object to whom access is lost.

The presence of erotic hunger is then defensively turned into a seeming absence of desire: sexual anorexia.

Silences, gaps, and lacks: "girls don't have what it takes"

Following the psychoanalytic literature on female sexuality written through the decades, one notices references throughout to inexplicable silences regarding female erotic life. Certain complexities in female experience were eclipsed and transformed into the unknown, unquestioned, and un-thought. Some believed that the vagina has been ignored; others, the clitoris; and still others, the vulva—the external genitalia as a whole. Erikson (1974) felt that the female experience of an inner space was clinically "so obvious that generations of clinicians must have had a special reason for not focusing on it" (p. 349). Bassin (1982) wrote that available language categories were inadequate to the task of articulating female eroticism. Similarly, Irigaray (1990) put forth that "women's desire most likely does not speak the same language as man's desire" (p. 346).

As noted above, Freud (1925) started with a *question*: "What does a woman want?" A true question openly acknowledges that there is something to be explored and understood, that as yet may elude clarity. A silence in the literature regarding female desire slyly skips over the suggestion that there is anything to question. A statement in the negative (one that explicitly or implicitly positions female desire as inherently lacking) overtly shapes the negative pole of the question into the answer. Braunschweig and Fain (1993) referred to a misrecognition of female sexuality that "remains impregnated with the initial mistake" (p. 142). Psychoanalytic theory and the clinical literature, situated within and influenced by the culture, have been in large part (though always with exceptions) actively involved in this negative evolution regarding women's desire. My observation is that historically the classical psychoanalytic literature overall (d)evolved from, initially, a question being asked—indicating a difficulty in understanding female desire—to a number of silences or gaps in inquiry, to finally a description in the negative that reified the supposed absence of various valued qualities. What was originally an open field of inquiry slid into non-inquiry and then into a static, pejorative account.

It is interesting in the context of these silences and omissions regarding women's desire to look further at the assumptions that have permeated the literature. Regarding female genital image and representation, analytic theorizing has often depicted female bodies as a catalogue of absences, no-things and have-nots. Over many decades, attention tended to focus on how a girl's actual body creates difficulties for her and on what the girl can*not* do with her genitality that the boy *can* do with his. The girl's genitalia cannot be easily seen, cannot be easily touched, are not focal enough in stimulation, cannot be controlled adequately; the girl's genitals keep disappearing or failing in some respect. Can we conclude that a girl's *body* creates these difficulties for her rather than the object relational and cultural context in which she comes to terms with her body?

Freud (1931, 1933) saw female sexual anatomy as a not-penis genital and put forth the belief that the vagina plays no role in girls' development until adolescence when it should take over in female sexual experience from the inadequate and immature clitoris. Much of the subsequent literature, in reaction, focused primarily on the vagina's role in sexuality, yet sees the vagina as inert, passive, a receptacle for the penis. Clitoral pleasure has often been maligned and undermined. A vast amount of the literature is devoted to female "frigidity" usually defined as the inability to orgasm through penetration.

Girls have been seen as not likely to masturbate owing to a supposedly lightweight libido or—the opposite—girls are viewed as overwhelmed by masturbatory intensity. Alternatively, there is an absence of focus on girls' masturbation and its role in their sexual development and experience of desire. Frequently, when female masturbation is mentioned in the literature, not much is detailed about the experience—its quality, impact and, especially, the fact of the female capacity to experience (multiple) orgasm beginning *in childhood*. Further attention is needed to the role of female masturbation in early childhood, latency, adolescence, and adulthood.

Counter to the view that the girl is dissatisfied with her genitalia and that in her early development she has no knowledge of an inner space, the literature on "primary femininity" evolved with a focus on the specificity, adequacy, and gratification of the girl's anatomy (Mayer, 1985; Tyson, 1994; Richards, 1996). Even so, in searching for different sources of female genital anxieties other than penis envy (Bernstein, 1993), often girls' genitals were viewed as hidden, threatened by penetration, with sensation too "diffuse" —not focalized enough—a series of deficiencies. Consider the different quality that would be conveyed if female sexual sensation were to be described as *extensive*, rather than as diffuse.

The number of references within the analytic literature to the female genitalia as invisible is staggering. For the most part, females consistently "come up short" when it comes to the representation of their genitals and sexuality in the psychoanalytic literature.

Yet, as mentioned at the outset of this chapter, this particular traversing of the terrain of female desire could not occur without the unconscious complicity of women themselves; as women internalize cultural views, it is to be expected that they would be implicated in their fate. Analytic field theory emphasizes that participants in a field both shape and are shaped by that field. Women, including analytic theorists and clinicians, have themselves been conscripted into the dominant motif allowed to them in the cultural discourse. But what is it internally that motivates women to eclipse themselves, to accept the "silencing of the female first person sexual voice?" (Wolf, 1997, p. xxii).

The sleeping vagina

Freud (1925, 1931, 1933), as we know, focused on the girl's sense of missing, not *some*body, but *a body part*—the penis. Believing vaginal sensation to be dormant until adolescence, Freud (1931) also maintained that the clitoris "with its virile character" (p. 228) is masculine. In fact, Freud considered *all libido* to be masculine. When the girl discovers that she is inadequately equipped in this masculine domain, she turns to the father in the hope that he will give her a penis for her very own. The awareness of her vagina plays almost no role in Freud's depiction of the girl's early development and Oedipus complex.

Horney (1924, 1926, 1933) was one of the first to challenge this formulation, stating instead that the vagina is sensed at an early age by the girl; the original desire for the penis is not as an anatomical part to be *added* to the girl's body, but for the penis *in* the vagina in phantasied intercourse with the father. She argued that a girl's wish to have a penis as part of her own body was a secondary and defensive response to the unconscious, vaginally-based and instinctually comprehended, desire to incorporate her father's penis in intercourse. This unconscious wish expressed the desire for sexual, bodily consummation of the love felt for the father and wished for in return.

Over the years many analytic writers have supported the thesis that early vaginal awareness does exist; the presence of internal sensation is registered by the girl, leading to an image of an opening and of "the inner space under the [body] surface" (Hagglund and Piha, 1980, p. 258). Writers vary in the extent to which they emphasize a primary penis envy; for many, however, penis envy is seen not solely as a primary reaction, but as a defensive formation with the aim of repressing vaginal awareness and attendant anxieties. Barnett (1966) pointed out that, "a great deal of energy would have to be expended by a girl to keep awareness of her vagina (as the source of diffuse sensations) out of consciousness" (p. 131).

This literature then led to a consideration of female genital anxieties that might be experienced by a girl in relation to her own anatomy—what she "has" versus what she "has not" (Mayer, 1985). Breen (1993), in an excellent discussion regarding the links between body and psyche, stated: "If the body cannot be ignored, and I do not believe it can, what is the role of the female body in the structuring of the feminine unconscious?" (p. 22). Bernstein similarly (1990) argued that the body is centrally involved in children's psychic development: "As the bodies are different, the nature of the resulting anxieties . . . must be different as well" (p. 152).

Within the psychoanalytic literature, numerous female genital anxieties have been proposed and seen to lead to repression of vaginal awareness buttressed by envy of the penis. Although some recognition has been given to the disappointment of unfulfilled erotic wishes in relation to the mother and then the father, my impression is that the factor of *object loss* for a girl has been underemphasized as a source of female genital anxiety. The mother is *presumed* to be erotically insignificant to the girl based on sameness of sex. When the father, as the "appropriate" oedipal object, is recognized as unavailable in his own way, this loss for the girl has often been viewed in a generalized manner as a factor of the generational difference and the impossibility of fulfillment of incestuous desires. These unexamined assumptions obscure what I consider to be a girl's particular potential for subjectively experiencing objects as erotically unavailable.

Aligned with Freud's (1931) observation, several earlier authors did note the ways in which a girl fares less well than a boy in her early "love life" (Kestenberg 1956b; Barnett, 1966; Chasseguet-Smirgel, 1970; Grunberger, 1970; Montgrain, 1983), with the result that all subsequent substitute objects "become doubly charged with significance for the little girl"—a reminder of "the mother in her absence" (Montgrain, 1983, p. 172). Long ago, Barnett (1966) observed that when a girl recognizes the impossibility of realizing her desires towards her mother, her father then seems to be the only attainable love object. Yet how attainable does a girl experience her father to be? And what is the impact on female sexuality of a sense of oedipal "failure" with the father following upon that with the mother? We are in the conceptual terrain of attempting to identify how a girl's giving up of the mother as erotic love object (if indeed she does) may cast a shadow on her passage through the oedipal romance.

As in Chapter 7, I wish to highlight experiences of erotic loss in relation to the mother and then to the father that are very specific to a girl and that are not solely an outcome of the generational and incest barrier. In the literature on female genital anxiety, Wilkinson (1991) was closest, in my view, to including the factor of object loss in a girl's development regarding her sexual body: "Mourning the absent phallus may substitute for a more profound response to the loss (real or imagined) of the father. Or a mother's unconscious rejection of her daughter might be counterbalanced by the girl's longing for a phallus" (p. 342). Experiences of object loss in conjunction with the girl's anatomical structure lend themselves, I believe, to displacements onto orality and penis envy, both of which may serve vaginal repression and may act as a disguise for object hunger that otherwise might be experienced as vaginally incorporative longing.

Females have bodily-based differences from males in the way they mentally represent their experience of the object world and of genitality. They also perceive their bodies (as do males) through the lens of their object relational experience. Body and object relations co-construct one another. Little sense of the body is likely to exist separate from the impact of object relations nor would object relations develop in isolation from the body; each is interpreted and further developed through the other within a cultural context.

Mother hunger and the inflated penis

Analytic writers, beginning with Freud (1905) and extending forward more than a century to Kristeva (2014), have recognized the sexual foundation of the mother–infant relation—what I refer to throughout this book as the nursing couple within the matrix of maternal eroticism. Multiple bodily and emotional components of infant care contribute to the intensity of the experience with the mother as first erotic love object for both boy and girl. What has been less acknowledged is the nature and degree of the impact for a girl in being pressed to give up her mother as her erotic love object as she moves from pre-oedipal development through the various oedipal stages. For most infants, object loss and hunger occur first in relation to the mother and are focalized in the experience of "weaning." Girls, however, are not solely weaned from the breast as a source of milk and comfort. If their future is to be heterosexual, they are not going to get the breast back as a source of sexual gratification. Unlike a boy, who of course is also weaned, a girl loses the nipple, and her mother as erotic/sexual object, in a much more profound manner.

Orality is the predominating experience of the first year of life. Data indicates that suckling is sexually stimulating to infants of both sexes (Thomson-Salo and Paul, 2017); in the case of girls, vaginal stimulation and lubrication result (Kestenberg, 1956a, 1956b, 1982; Kleeman, 1976). Kestenberg (1956a) viewed the mouth as the model by which all other bodily orifices are mentally represented; in girls there is a "spontaneous overflow of excitation from the oral to the vaginal zone . . . so that a local response of vaginal "sucking" may develop in association with oral sucking" (p. 261). Vague awareness of vaginal sensation is experienced as "an inside pressure, a feeling of emptiness, a desire to be filled" (Kestenberg, 1956a, p.464). Hagglund and Piha (1980) also theorized orality as a precursor and prototype of the girl's inner genital space such that the vagina can be experienced in many ways including as an "empty place longing to be filled" (p. 263). As oral desires are situated within the intensity of maternal eroticism and are intimately connected to a girl's experience of vaginal sensation, the bodily-based imagery of a hungry empty cavity yearning to be filled seems especially pertinent to female experience with objects.

Several authors (Barnett, 1966; Torok, 1970; Kestenberg, 1982; Montgrain, 1983; Laufer, 1986; Lax, 1994) have described girls' erotically desirous relations to their mothers as well as the resulting wish for a penis when a girl discovers that her genital is "the wrong one" to pair with her mother. Laufer understood a girl's desire to have a baby with her mother as her primary libidinal aim. However, "at some point in her development she must give up the fantasy of being able to keep her mother's love to herself" (Laufer, 1986, p. 265) because, unlike the boy who possesses "at least the potential of a potent penis" (Laufer, 1986, p. 266) the girl must recognize that the father (and even the boy in his future) can gratify the mother in a way that she can "never hope to replace" (Laufer, 1986, p. 265).

Lax (1994), referring to the negative oedipal phase, identified that masturbation fantasies in two- to three-year-old girls focus on the mother as the erotic object (p. 286). At some point however, the girl realizes, "that the boy has the potential she lacks for the type of relationship with mother she would like to have" (Lax, 1994, p. 287). Depression over perceived maternal object loss is "evoked when the erotic longings and fantasies which the little girl has directed toward her mother are confronted by the reality of the mother's unattainability as an erotic object" (Lax, 1994, p. 291).

I emphasize that Laufer and Lax were not referring to the mother as unattainable due to generational and incestuous boundaries, but due to confrontation with the mother's heterosexuality which favors the penis—the father and the boy (at least in fantasy)—and eliminates the girl's possibilities with the mother even on the level of fantasy: "someday, later, when I grow up . . . ." A girl suffers an erotic defeat in her first, most intense love affair, and she is likely to register this defeat as her inadequacy on a bodily level; she is "rejected" for her genitals. As stated in Chapter 7, this double loss is a powerful combination. Due consideration has not been given to the possibility of a girl's sense of genital inferiority as derived from her encounter with her mother's heterosexuality. Upon this template of a subjective sense of failure, a second may be superimposed in relating to the father that has the potential to repeat and seal the sense of inadequacy.

Freud (1905) emphasized that the first and most basic anxiety is that of object loss. It has been acknowledged throughout the analytic literature that girls fear object loss more than any other factor, while boys are most fearful of castration—the loss of a body part. Anxious focus on objects has been viewed as an almost essential female condition, along with dependency and vulnerability to depression (Elise, 1991). Not enough thought has been given to what it might be in a girl's object relational development that leads to uncertainty regarding the reliability of objects.

Freud was clear that the first thing a girl wants is her mother. However, as I have been emphasizing, unlike the boy's situation where desire for the mother is acknowledged and then forbidden, a *girl's desire* for her mother is typically negated and rendered as non-existent (in parallel to the diminishment of her genitals). Often a woman, in relating to a male partner, has internalized heterosexual assumption and presumes erotic desire to be a non-issue with a daughter. That a girl wants her mother is generally not seen or registered by the mother or by anyone else; it remains an unrecognized desire. The belief that heterosexuality is the only "natural" sexuality has operated as a given in the traditional nuclear family, in our culture, and within psychoanalytic theory.

Challenging the notion of innate heterosexuality, Zak de Goldstein (1984) pointed out that the infant receives precise instructions through the mother's gaze: "Her gaze summarizes expectations and wishes that order and define the sexual profile of each (p. 182) . . . She receives from a distance her father's sexual instructions as well" (p. 183). Dio Bleichmar (1995) also underscored the libidinal role of the father's gaze in "the psychogenesis of the girl's heterosexual desire" (p. 331). Kernberg (1991) considered the undermining impact on the girl of the "mother's subtle and unconscious rejection of the sexual excitement which she would freely experience in relation to the boy" (p. 356). Describing this situation where the girl is a non-erotic/oedipal object for the mother, Olivier (1989) wrote that, as a result of her mother's lack of reciprocal desire, a girl can come to feel that she is "unsatisfactory, incapable of satisfying" and later is "never satisfied with what she has or what she is" (p. 44; see also Bergmann, 1995; Halberstadt-Freud, 1998).

The girl is simply not a boy—a person with a penis whom a heterosexual mother can cathect in a particular erotic fashion. A girl is pressed to forego her desire for her mother. In Butler's (1995) terms, the daughter's desire for the mother is foreclosed in a never-never land of the "sexually unperformable" (p. 178). I mention one example described by Frenkel (1996) of a little girl who, after being reasoned with by her mother that the mother had not shown any preference for boys, responded tearfully that, "the mother was lying because if she really loved girls more, she would have married one" (p. 152).

Generally, Winnicott's ordinarily "good enough" mother would provide the sensual foundation for erotic desire to develop and flourish; maternal eroticism (Kristeva, 2014) is a primal "paradise." Paradise is lost when desire that is stimulated in a daughter for her mother is then deemed nonsexual or is viewed as having a life only in relation to the father. Heterosexual assumption can result in a deficiency of maternal eroticism in relation to the growing girl. Considerable variation would occur across mother–daughter pairs regarding the relative balance of stimulation and disavowal/deflection; the unfolding of maternal eroticism is highly specific to each mother–child dyad. Certainly it is a potential implicit within maternal eroticism for a heterosexual mother to erotically cathect her daughter. However, doing so requires that a mother enthusiastically relate (even if only unconsciously) to the homoerotic aspect of her psychic bisexuality, especially as her daughter reaches the oedipal stage. It would still be a delicate task to deal with the blow to a daughter's erotic confidence, and to her desire for her mother, dealt by the mother's ultimate choice of a male partner.

Freud (1931) did notice that in the turn to the father as erotic object, something comes to a halt in female sexuality that was *previously in motion*. A girl "takes refuge" in being the passive object of the father's desire; Freud noted that this shift is unlikely to occur completely or without conflict; the oedipal relation to the father inherits qualities of the original relationship with the mother, and women are often looking to re-find their mothers in their husbands. Let's look further at what might be unfolding in a girl's oedipal relation with her father.

Turning (in)to heterosexuality

Although much overlap occurs in relating to mother and father both pre-oedipally and oedipally, in heterosexual development a girl *resolves* the oedipal complex with her father as her sexualized love object: She relinquishes her mother as her primary erotic focus and "turns to the father" thus establishing her heterosexual orientation. What might be understood about this particular oedipal trajectory? What is the fate of a girl's experience of desire in relation to her father and how does a girl fare when she "tries again" to pursue her erotic wishes.

The form that fathers' affective involvement has traditionally taken has been that of an exciting, but sporadic, presence. Fathers often offer a high level of stimulation that is quite tantalizing, yet experienced as intermittent. An oedipal girl has to wait for what can seem like a very long time for Daddy to come home again. Even while involving themselves more actively in parenting than in earlier decades, most fathers continue to work full-time with women still providing the majority of early child care. Additionally, gender differences in relational styles, although shifting, may lead a girl to experience her father as less emotionally close than she has felt her mother to be. Even with a father who feels himself to be genuinely present, the manner in which his engagement is affectively expressed with a daughter may feel less palpable to her than the emotional and physical closeness she has (hopefully) known with her mother. Of course, individual mothers and fathers vary greatly in their capacities for emotional and embodied presence with their young children. It is entirely possible that a given father is much more relationally connected than is that particular mother. Yet, there are general trends established within a cultural norm that influence and are influenced by gendered tendencies in relational patterns.

Kernberg (1991) identified the complex step that a girl takes in shifting her love object from mother to father (see also Ogden, 1987). He referred to the girl's "bravery" or relational courage in leaping to the more distant father for love and acceptance. Kernberg (1991) proposed that this "early exercise of trust" (p. 357) leads to a greater capacity for relational commitment in women. However, a female emphasis on commitment may also reflect anxious uncertainty regarding the outcome of relationships. The expectation that small girls manage emotional and/or physical distance of their adult fathers places a serious demand on small girls' relational capacities. While this situation might encourage the development of certain relational strengths, I am focusing on the potential costs to a girl, particularly on how such costs may manifest within her erotic life.

I am considering a potential for anxiety to derive from fear of rejection and abandonment by the paternal (superimposed on the maternal) oedipal object. In turning to the father, a girl may feel that her relationship with her father does not (ful)fill the relational space opened up by the erotic loss of her mother; I propose that this lack of sexual and relational gratification may be schematized by a female as her body being empty of something. The relational void in giving up the mother as love object can lead to an internal self-representation of a "hole" to be filled, like the mouth sucks the pacifier in the absence of the nipple. This image may then be extended to the genital representation. Vaginal repression may serve to disguise object hunger that might be experienced as vaginal longing. Erotic longing that begins *in relation to the mother* is subsequently repressed/defended against through a "shrinkage" of female sexual desire.

As a subset of the more general deflation and erasure of female genitality, a negative mental representation of the vagina may develop in association with unfulfilled libidinous and object relational desires. Erasure (or desexualization) of the mental representation of the vagina might seem preferable to a consciously maintained sense of longing and hunger. Vaginal eroticism can be repressed, with a subsequent displacement onto "penis envy." Focus on a part-object—"I want one too"—then represents the endpoint of failure in love, not the beginning of a girl's sense of herself as female. Freud theorized that the girl turns to the father not primarily out of erotic desire (which should be understood as inherent in psychic bisexuality), but due to narcissistic injury regarding her supposedly inadequate genitals.

I concur that a basic feeling of lacking genital capacity holds, but with a different meaning than that supplied by Freud: Symbolically, a girl lacks a penis *for* her mother and *in* her vagina in relation to her father. I propose that this subjective experience of lack of sexual and relational gratification may be schematized by a girl as her body being empty of something—not because she is inherently lacking, but because the nature of the vagina is to take in, to actively incorporate. The mouth is associated with hunger for the nipple; in parallel formation, the vagina is a "hungry" genital. Agentic female desire would be *voracious*—a term that has been viewed solely as pejorative, a pathological excess of sexuality in contrast to positive images of male virility and potency.

Erotic dysphorias

If we accept that there are male and female forms of genital anxiety (Klein, 1932; Bernstein, 1993; Richards, 1996), then it follows that specific forms of male and female genital defense would develop. As emphasized in Chapter 7, while males inflate their genitals and desire in hopes of immunity from various experiences of castration, females, unconsciously motivated and with much support for this maneuver from the culture, may deflate their genitals and desire. Female sexuality pulls in and disappears into itself, closing up into its own internal labyrinth. Just as a maze or labyrinth can protect a private place from exposure and conceal secrets and treasures, the female genitals support this particular strategy of female genital defense. The counterpart to the very visible, overextended phallus is the mysterious, the secret, the disavowed—the vulva rendered "invisible" and "non-existent," not represented in language.

The male embellishes his sex; the female secludes hers. The penis erects, extends. The phallus symbolizes this trajectory. The clitoris retracts, disappears into the hood of the prepuce. Vaginal contractions pull in, suck in, incorporate; female sexual sensation is less visible (Irigaray, 1990). Aligned with the cultural need to disavow a powerfully agentic female sexuality (Chasseguet-Smirgel, 1976; Dinnerstein, 1976), a female may use for defensive purposes these specifics of her anatomy that allow for magic disappearing tricks.

A woman's strategy may be to hide herself (even to herself), to slip behind the scenes rather than displaying a macho bravado, to be passively elusive, silent, slippery. This female defensive mobilization is rendered invisible—part of its power to be effective—and then women themselves, culture, and analytic theorists all believe the quality of absence to be an inherent fact about the female genital and about women's seemingly flimsy desire. This cultural mythology must in some part reflect the actuality of the two bodies—"the specific modes of materiality of the 'page'/body must be taken into account" (Grosz, 1994, p. 156). Anatomical qualities are extended into culturally relevant anatomical metaphors that then lead to a particular view of the body as a "reality" of anatomy, "a reality which is not a truth . . . but a group error erected into reality" (Braunschweig and Fain, 1993, pp. 141–142). The cultural depiction is an extension of the two bodies that circles back around to inaccurately define and confine the body.

Destiny is created from anatomy in that a psychic geography evolves that is specific to each sex. A male protects himself from threats of castration by a continued affirmation: "I have a penis. See, here it is." He does not seem to fear that pointing it out might be tempting fate. This same narcissistic assertion manifests in the culture as well: We affirm erections. In contrast, a female protects herself from castration by "pretending" to be (already) castrated: "See, I have nothing; I want nothing" (Lewin, 1948; Slap, 1979; Kalinich, 1993). She has nothing to take or to harm, nothing to perform with that poses any threat or demand (Torok, 1970; Richards, 1996), nothing worth looking at (Mayer, 1985; Irigaray, 1990; Krausz, 1994) or to speak of (Lerner, 1976; Lacan, 1972–73). Her sex, her desire, is little, "dainty," insignificant, maybe even nonexistent—the feminine object. Yet, as Irigaray (1990) articulated, "the role of 'femininity'. . . corresponds only slightly to woman's desire, which is recuperated only secretly, in hiding, and in a disturbing and unpardonable manner" (p. 349).

As in any defensive strategy or compromise formation, flexibility is given up to protect against anxiety. In sexual defensive strategies for both women and men, range of motion, both literally and figuratively, is foreclosed in order to have fixed complementarity between the partners. Fluidity and multiplicity in self-experience is limited in favor of "safe" sex. When this defensive elaboration threatens to collapse on the cultural level, we see concrete expressions of its reinstatement, including in the extreme of female genital mutilation (Lax, 1994; Joseph, 1996; Wolf, 1997). Olivier (1989) argued that if a woman "takes the liberty of naming her desire, her partner's chance of successful performance may be correspondingly reduced. There is no greater threat to a man than the express desire of the woman" (p. 96).

We continually hear in clinical work that women feel that they do not get enough of what they can identify that they do want from men: more tenderness, affection, mutual gazing, kissing, emotional exchange, whole body touching, the right kind of touching (typically labeled foreplay as if it is not the "real thing"), more of the right kind of stimulation, orgasm more reliably, and more orgasms. Women want an experience originally based in a relationship with a woman—their mother—who did, or provided the basis for, all of the above in a very effective and gratifying manner: maternal eroticism.

Dinnerstein (1976) wrote that men literally re-experience the original embrace with the mother—with a female body—in sex with a woman. In adult heterosexuality, the male returns to the mother in phallic omnipotence; he penetrates the maternal body with all the archaic eroticism and gratification experienced at her breasts and with all the emphasis now on what his penis can do to her and for him. He now actively controls his own stimulation.

Women as well may wish to reencounter maternal eroticism and yet may have reasons to bury this desire. If a more active wanting were to be revived, females might be in touch with wanting specific experiences first known with the mother. Such desires could painfully revive the earliest experience of wanting and not getting (to keep) her mother and of seeming to have the wrong body/genital. Any wish to re-experience the early sensual atmosphere with the mother might seem ill-fated as well in relationship to a man. For a woman, sexual desire may be once removed: "She must evoke and forget her first experience of *jouissance* and impotence and laceration" (Zak de Goldstein, 1984, p. 185). It becomes easier to take refuge in being wanted, in being the passive recipient of a man's attentions.

Conclusion

The cultural veneer suggests that sexual life has changed in a progressive direction—"you've come a long way, baby" —such that we are no longer beset by all the old "hang-ups." However, clinical practice reveals a time-lag in female sexuality "catching up" to sexual "liberation;" when clinicians look closely, we see difficulties and inhibitions that women still encounter in getting sex to work for themselves. This reality should not surprise us.

When one considers that in her oedipal desires for her mother a girl may experience her body as inadequate and her object choice as wrong, the impact cannot be insignificant. It seems that it is primarily on the strength of bisexuality (see Chapter 6)—the ability to redirect sexual object choice—that girls continue on a sexual trajectory. We have bisexuality to thank for female heterosexuality and, thus, for a fulfilled male heterosexuality. The question remains: What promotes a fulfilled female heterosexuality? I suggest that a woman wants an erotic experience that does not lack in the qualities of desire that she initially experienced in the sensuous bodily contact with her mother.

As Chodorow (1992) challenged:

> How do we reconcile a theory that heterosexual preference is innate with our observations and theory concerning the pansexuality of infants and children and . . . with our knowledge that virtually everyone's initial bodily erotic involvement is with their mother?
>
> (p. 273)

Halberstadt-Freud (1998) saw the mother's central place in a woman's life as meaning that "she is born and continues to live with the legacy of a homo-erotic bond" (p. 42) that has significant implications for her sexuality. Freud recognized that women look to re-find the maternal in a husband.

When a woman, expressing (sexual) disappointment, denigrates her husband as "not enough of a man," might she not be understood as saying that he is not enough of a *woman*? As long as the gender specificity of this criticism remains unconscious, it can never be resolved; the "war between the sexes" continues. A woman can quite consciously negatively compare her husband to her father—as *less* of a man, but to the extent that maternal longings remain out of awareness, she will be unlikely to accept her husband on his own terms *as a man*. Analytic attention to the unconscious layers of female erotic loss, especially in relation to the maternal object, holds the possibility of repair to narcissistic injuries that permeate sexual life and diminish the happiness of adult couples. Increased emphasis on the role of subjective experiences of erotic object loss in relation to both parental figures can broaden exploration of female erotic life within the analytic field of the consulting room.

Most likely, difficulties stemming from a woman's unconscious erotic disappointment and injury to her sexual self-esteem in relation to the maternal figure will only be accessed in the transference-countertransference configurations of the analytic field. The "Sleeping Beauty" of female erotic life waits to be awakened not by the kiss of "the Prince" but by the "kiss" of maternal/analytic eroticism. Analytic treatments typically are conducted within the constraints of available analytic theory. Without a concept of maternal eroticism, analytic theory does not offer a large enough container for comprehending female erotic life. Without a concept of analytic eroticism, analytic technique is not sufficiently expansive in engaging the full erotic dimensions of a treatment. When a female patient herself "erases" the maternal layers of her erotic life, disavowing as well any *erotic* longing for her female analyst (or for the maternal in her male analyst), forward movement relies upon the clinician not colluding with this foreclosure of the work.

As underscored at the beginning of this chapter in regard to the vignette presented, female erotic loss operates on many levels. Conscious sexual fantasy with a partner or in masturbation provides a way into recognizing and working with these complexities. Masturbation fantasies are especially telling—a "royal road" to erotic life. In auto-erotic activity, one relies solely on the contents of one's mind for additional stimulation beyond the physical. Do our patients tell us these fantasies? Do we ask? Analysts in recent decades may have shied away from such exchanges that were once considered crucial to an analysis. In directing attention to realms of the erotic, clinicians offer patients a therapeutic process with unique potentials for diminishing erotic dysphoria in favor of more rewarding experiences of sexual life.

Note

1 Fisher (1973) concluded a lengthy and comprehensive analysis of female sexual response in his sample of nearly 300 middle class, married women by stating that, "orgasm difficulty in women is fundamentally a function of anxiety about the lack of permanence of love objects" (p. 281). Women in Fisher's study who had difficulty with orgasm represented no one personality type, but did express insecurity over dependability of relationships and a concern with object loss: "It is as if she assumed that union with someone else could not be counted on to persist, but rather to be ultimately terminated unexpectedly" (Fisher, 1973, p. 233). See Elise (1998) for a full discussion of "frigidity."

References

Barnett, M. (1966). Vaginal awareness in the infancy and childhood of girls. *Journal of the American Psychoanalytic Association*, 14: 129–141.
Bassin, D. (1982). Woman's images of inner space: Data towards expanded interpretive categories. *International Review of Psychoanalysis*, 9: 191–203.
Benjamin, J. (1988). *The bonds of love*. New York: Pantheon.
Bergmann, M. (1995). Observations on the female negative oedipal phase and its significance in the analytic transference. *Journal of Clinical Psychoanalysis*, 4: 283–295.
Bernstein, D. (1990). Female genital anxiety, conflicts and typical mastery modes. *International Journal of Psychoanalysis*, 71: 151–165.
—— (1993). *Female identity conflict in clinical practice*. Northvale, New Jersey: Aronson.
Braunschweig, D. and Fain, M. (1993). The phallic shadow. In Breen, D. (Ed.), *The gender conundrum*, London: Routledge.
Breen, D. (Ed.) (1993). *The gender conundrum*. London: Routledge.
Butler, J. (1995). Melancholy gender: Refused identification. *Psychoanalytic Dialogues*, 5: 165–180.
Chasseguet-Smirgel, J. (1970). Feminine guilt and the Oedipus complex. In Chasseguet-Smirgel, J. (Ed.). *Female sexuality*. London: Karnac, pp. 94–134.
—— (1976). Freud and female sexuality: The consideration of some blind spots in the exploration of the "Dark Continent." *International Journal of Psychoanalysis*, 57: 275–286.
Chodorow, N. (1992). Heterosexuality as a compromise formation: Reflections on the psychoanalytic theory of sexual development. *Psychoanalysis and Contemporary Thought*, 15: 267–304.
Dimen, M. (1991). Deconstructing difference: Gender, splitting, and transitional space. *Psychoanalytic Dialogues*, 1: 335–352.
Dinnerstein, D. (1976). *The mermaid and the minotaur*. New York: Harper & Row.

Dio Bleichmar, E. (1995). The secret in the constitution of female sexuality: The effects of the adult's sexual look upon the subjectivity of the girl. *Journal of Clinical Psychoanalysis*, 4: 331–342.

Elise, D. (1991). An analysis of gender differences in separation-individuation. *The Psychoanalytic Study of the Child*, 46: 51–67.

— (1998). The absence of the paternal penis. *Journal of the American Psychoanalytic Association*, 46: 413–442.

Erikson, E. (1974). Womanhood and the inner space. In Strouse, J. (Ed.) *Women and Analysis*. New York: Dell, pp. 333–364.

Fisher, S. (1973). *The female orgasm*. New York: Basic Books.

Frenkel, R. (1996). A reconsideration of object choice in women: Phallus or fallacy. *Journal of the American Psychoanalytic Association*, 44 (Suppl.): 133–156.

Freud, S. (1905). Three essays on the theory of sexuality. *The Standard Edition*, 7: 125–243. London: Hogarth Press.

— (1925). Some psychical consequences of the anatomical distinction between the sexes. *The Standard Edition*, 19: 248–258. London: Hogarth Press.

— Female sexuality. *The Standard Edition*, 21: 225–243. London: Hogarth Press.

— New introductory lectures on psychoanalysis: Femininity. *The Standard Edition*, 22: 5–182. London: Hogarth Press.

Grosz, E. (1994). *Volatile bodies*. Bloomington: Indiana University Press.

Grunberger, B. (1970). Outline for a study of narcissism in female sexuality. In Chasseguet-Smirgel, J. (Ed.), *Female sexuality*. London: Karnac, pp. 69–83.

Hagglund, T.B. and Piha, H. (1980). The inner space of the body image. *Psychoanalytic Quarterly*, 49: 256–283.

Halberstadt-Freud, H. (1998). Electra versus Oedipus: Femininity reconsidered. *International Journal of Psychoanalysis*, 79: 41–56.

Horney, K. (1924). On the genesis of the castration complex in women. *International Journal of Psychoanalysis*, 5: 50–65.

— (1926). The flight from womanhood: The masculinity complex in women, as viewed by men and by women. *International Journal of Psychoanalysis*, 7: 324–339.

— (1933). The denial of the vagina. *International Journal of Psychoanalysis*, 14: 57–70.

Irigaray, L. (1990). This sex which is not one. In Zanardi, C. (Ed.) *Essential Papers on the Psychology of Women*. New York: New York University Press, pp. 344–351.

Joseph, C. (1996). Compassionate accountability: An embodied consideration of female genital mutilation. *Journal of Psychohistory*, 24: 2–17.

Kalinich, L. (1993). On the sense of absence: A perspective on womanly issues. *Psychoanalytic Quarterly*, 62: 206–228.

Kernberg, O. (1991). Sadomasochism, sexual excitement, and perversion. *Journal of the American Psychoanalytic Association*, 39: 333–362.

Kestenberg, J. (1956a). On the development of maternal feelings in early childhood. *The Psychoanalytic Study of the Child*, 11: 257–291.
— (1956b). Vicissitudes of female sexuality. *Journal of the American Psychoanalytic Association*, 4: 453–476.
— (1982). The inner-genital phase: Prephallic and preoedipal. In Mendell, D. (Ed.), *Early female development: Current psychoanalytic views*. New York: Spectrum Publications, pp. 81–125.
Kleeman, J. (1976). Freud's views on early female sexuality in the light of direct child observation. *Journal of the American Psychoanalytic Association*, 24 (Suppl.): 3–27.
Klein, M. (1932). The effects of early anxiety situations on the sexual development of the girl. *The Psycho-Analysis of Children*. London: Hogarth Press.
Krausz, R. (1994). The invisible woman. *International Journal of Psychoanalysis*, 75: 59–72.
Kristeva, J. (2014). Reliance, or maternal eroticism. *Journal of the American Psychoanalytic Association*, 62: 69–85.
Lacan, J. (1972–73). God and the *jouissance* of the woman. In Mitchell, J. and Rose, J. (Eds.), *Feminine sexuality*. New York: Norton, 1982, pp. 138–148.
Laufer, M. E. (1986). The female Oedipus complex and the relationship to the body. *The Psychoanalytic Study of the Child*, 41: 259–276.
Lax, R. (1994). Aspects of primary and secondary genital feelings and anxieties in girls during the preoedipal and early oedipal phases. *Psychoanalytic Quarterly*, 63: 271–296.
Lerner, H. (1976). Parental mislabeling of female genitals as a determinant of penis envy and learning inhibitions in women. *Journal of the American Psychoanalytic Association*, 24 (Suppl.): 269–283.
Lewin, B. (1948). The nature of reality, the meaning of nothing, with an addendum on concentration. *Psychoanalytic Quarterly*, 17: 524–526.
Mayer, E. L. (1985). Everybody must be just like me: Observations on female castration anxiety. *International Journal of Psychoanalysis*, 66: 331–347.
Montgrain, N. (1983). On the vicissitudes of female sexuality: The difficult path from 'anatomical destiny' to psychic representation. *International Journal of Psychoanalysis*, 64: 169–186.
Ogden, T.H. (1987). The transitional oedipal relationship in female development. *International Journal of Psychoanalysis*, 68: 485–498.
Olivier, C. (1989). *Jocasta's children: The imprint of the mother*. London: Routledge.
Plaut, E. and Hutchinson, F. (1986). The role of puberty in female psychosexual development. *International Review of Psychoanalysis*, 13: 417–432.
Richards, A. K. (1996). Primary femininity and female genital anxiety. *Journal of the American Psychoanalytic Association*, 44 (Suppl.): 261–281.
Riviere, J. (1929). Womanliness as masquerade. *International Journal of Psychoanalysis*, 10: 303–313.

Slap, J. (1979). On nothing and nobody, with an addendum on William Hogarth. *Psychoanalytic Quarterly*, 48: 620–627.
Thomson-Salo, F. and Paul, C. (2017). Understanding the sexuality of infants within caregiving relationships in the first year. *Psychoanalytic Dialogues*, 27: 320–337.
Torok, M. (1970). The significance of penis envy in women. In Chasseguet-Smirgel, J. (Ed.) *Female sexuality: New psychoanalytic views*. London: Karnac Books, pp. 135–170.
Tyson, P. (1994). Bedrock and beyond: An examination of the clinical utility of contemporary theories of female psychology. *Journal of the American Psychoanalytic Association*, 42: 447–467.
Wilkinson, S. (1991). Penis envy: Libidinal metaphor and experiential metonym. *International Journal of Psychoanalysis*, 72: 335–346.
Wolf, N. (1997). *Promiscuities*. New York: Random House.
Zak de Goldstein, R. (1984). The dark continent and its enigmas. *International Journal of Psychoanalysis*, 65: 179–189.

Chapter 9

Failure to thrive

Masochistic submission in women

A deflated sense of sexual subjectivity in women can lead to a propensity for masochistic submission. To acknowledge and actively pursue one's desire is the opposite of masochistic submission where one subjugates one's will—one's desire—to the will/desire of the other (see Benjamin, 1988). I will approach masochistic submission in women— a "failure to thrive"[1] —from the perspective of undermined female desire.

In order to delineate one particular aspect of the underlying foundation for masochistic submission, I want to extend my prior discussion of female development at the juncture of the Oedipus complex. In considering the fate of the girl's oedipal wishes for her mother, I have elaborated the potential impact of an "erotic failure" that is unique to the girl. The path to heterosexual object choice determines that a girl's first erotic object choice—her mother—will not result in a "successful" oedipal pairing. I view compromised confidence regarding obtaining and keeping one's sexual love object as the heritage of what has been classically referred to as the female negative oedipal complex: the girl's oedipal level erotic desires toward her mother. One consequence can be masochistic submission— a symptomatic expression of an insecure oedipal attachment involving a fear of loss of love that is recognized as a stronger anxiety in girls by many theorists throughout the history of the analytic literature. I want to directly link masochistic submission in females—as the expression of a felt need to secure relational bonds—to elements of the girl's oedipal experience that heighten insecurity regarding the capacity to obtain and retain one's erotic object.

In order to account for inhibitions in female personality that promote dynamics of masochistic submission, I will be focusing on the manner in which shame *as a female* leads to women becoming not only invested in but often wedded to self-destruction rather than "self-construction."

Masochistic submission is seen from the perspective of gender-based shame that predisposes (too often) to lack of self-assertion, sexually and more generally, as described in detail in Chapter 7. Two clinical vignettes will be presented to illustrate female inhibitions in agentic expression of self in sexuality, in love relationships, and in professional aspirations as understood within the framework presented.

The derailment of female erotic agency

Kulish and Holtzman (1998) noted the emphasis in the literature linking girls' conflicted pre-oedipal relationships with the mother "to later difficulties in owning and enjoying their sexuality . . . agency over sexual pleasure [is] a capacity often conflicted for many women" (p. 66). Along with other authors, Kulish and Holtzman (1998) also stressed the "importance of the girl's tie to the mother in the shape, progression into or resolution of the girl's Oedipus situation" (p. 68). Rather than a struggle for power and authority seen in males, in the contrasting female oedipal story, "the maintenance of intimate relationships takes centre stage" (Kulish and Holtzman, 1998, p. 69). In order to preserve closeness with the mother, females can defensively abdicate ownership of sexual desires, and "aggression is in the shadows" (Kulish and Holtzman, 1998, p. 69).

It is evident that having to separate from *and compete with* the primary object can be highly threatening and a potential contributor to fear of object loss in girls. This fear of losing the (m)other fosters a prioritizing of connection to the object over ownership of one's own impulses and wishes; such accountability to and for oneself is disavowed. These female dynamics regarding separation from the object originate pre-oedipally and then infuse the entire experience of progression into oedipal life.

Linking these two phases, Loewald (1978) underscored that, "oedipal attachments, struggles, and conflicts must be also understood as new versions of the basic union–individuation dilemma" (p. 775). Already seen earlier in the phase of separation–individuation, now oedipally an "active urge for emancipation comes to the fore" (Loewald, 1978, p. 757). The mastering of the Oedipus complex, that will take place over a lifetime, requires a wresting of authority from the parents: "By evolving our own autonomy . . . we are usurping their power, their competence, their responsibility" (Loewald, 1978, p. 758). Such mastery requires a self-confidence that can only flourish when there is confidence in the relational bond.

Loewald (1978) placed strong emphasis on the need for "self-responsibility," for agentic action and autonomy rather than masochistic punishment: "Becoming independent, taking responsibility for the conduct of his own life" (p. 756) . . . entails "appropriating parental authority" and "owning up to one's needs and impulses as one's own" (p. 761). Loewald (1978) articulated:

> to develop a sense of self-identity, means to experience ourselves as agents . . . When I speak of appropriating our desires and impulses—which of course are active forces in themselves . . . I mean allowing, granting them actively that existence . . . being responsive to their urgings, acknowledging that they are ours [rather than] self-destruction . . . self-inflicted or "arranged" punishment [that] is one form of corruption.
>
> (p. 761)

In a paragraph on dynamics of submission in relation to the father in *male* development, Loewald (1978) paid particular attention to a boy's deleterious identification with his "mother's passive-receptive attitude toward father" (p. 760). Note that, throughout the analytic literature, a *girl's* identification with a mother's passive-receptive attitude toward father is often thought to be unproblematic. Loewald (1978), echoing Freud, went on to remark: "If we add to this the less-well-explored intricacies of the feminine oedipal conflict, the complexities of the Oedipus complex tend to become overwhelming" (p. 760). By contrast, Kulish and Holtzman (1998), undeterred in tracing the intricate tapestry of female development, identified that, "what is unique to the feminine positive oedipal organization derives from the fact that rivalry occurs with the same-sexed parent, the mother, who is generally the primary caretaker" (p. 68). Unique facets of female oedipal life, though complicated, can be delineated (Holtzman and Kulish, 2012).

Pursuing this exploration, I want to lift out and disentangle the thread, not of oedipal *competition* with the mother, but of oedipal *desire for* the mother in the context of the challenging change of *erotic* object expected in the heterosexual oedipal trajectory that a girl typically traverses. As detailed in previous chapters, the complexity of giving up her first erotic object is, like rivalry with the primary caretaker, unique to the girl's positive oedipal configuration. There is no parallel in the boy's development.

Viewing masochistic submission in females from the vantage point of these specific "complexities" of the *feminine* oedipal conflict allows for a conceptualization of why "the assumption of responsibility for one's own life" (Loewald, 1978, p. 757) may be particularly challenging for women. We can develop further an appreciation for why so many women fail to thrive to the full extent of which they are, or should be, capable.

Of course, females and males vary immensely in any individual propensity for masochistic submission. Complex factors that contribute to or work against masochistic submission are multiply determined and will find unique expression in any given person. Yet the general demise of healthy narcissism in girls and women is a pronounced tendency that undermines female erotic agency and predisposes toward masochistic submission.

Freud (1931) noted that with a girl's turn to the father and circuitous winding into femininity she relinquishes (not without a struggle) her sexuality, her desire, her activity, and her mother as love object. This developmental *outcome* was misconstrued in early analytic thinking to conclude that the female is "naturally" given to masochism (Deutsch, 1930; Bonaparte, 1952). Freud (1931) saw the girl's sexuality as permanently injured; "there is to be observed a marked lowering of the active sexual impulses ... they have proved totally unrealizable and are therefore abandoned" (p. 239). This halt is coexistent with the turn from mother to father as primary, sexual love object, and Freud (1931) identified that this shift is complex:[2]

> Her relation to her mother was the original one, and her attachment to her father was built up on it, and now, in marriage, the original relationship emerges from repression. For the main content of her development to womanhood lay in the carrying over of her affective object attachments from her mother to her father.
>
> (p. 231)

We see in Freud's theorizing the recognition that the *erotic* relationship with a girl's mother is the foundational substrate for all that follows with her father and with later love objects in adulthood.

I want to return to the powerful role of shame in development, now as a potential determinant of masochistic submission. I am extending the title of Morrison's (1989) classic text in suggesting that shame is the underside of masochism (as well as of narcissism). It is clinically evident that the potential for masochism in females is high. Shame ends up functioning differently in males and females. As described in Chapter 7, a male will most typically attempt to reverse the gendered power imbalance experienced with his mother, narcissistically elevating himself and devaluing the female. This devaluation of the female can then set the stage for a masochistic-narcissistic relational pairing seen in adult couples. Female inhibition becomes wedded to male exhibition. Rather than self-promotion and aggrandizement, this feminine defensive strategy is self-defeating and belittling: masochistic. Such devaluation of self derives from and furthers an anxious focus on the potential for object loss, here understood as loss of the *object's* desire.

In the gaze of the (m)other

I am now going to offer case material from an analysis of a female patient that illustrates a pronounced, though not rare, sense of shame regarding sex, an image of herself as inadequately small, and an inhibition, repudiation, even repulsion toward active female desire. These dynamics are not overtly masochistic in the more pathological sense, but reflect a fairly common feminine diminishment of self that expresses submission to a relinquishment of erotic pleasure in favor of maintaining an object relationship.

Consider Sara who, after a few years in analysis, arrives uncharacteristically late: "I'm late today because I want to bring up a new topic. Well, I want to talk about it, but, then again, I don't. It's about sex . . .." When I ask Sara what had made it difficult to bring sex up earlier in our work, she at first denies the subject's importance to her. But then she acknowledges how she has avoided—even hidden—her concerns by occasional and seemingly comfortable references to sex designed to put me "off the track." She then confesses a preference for masturbation over sex with her husband:

> I feel a freedom masturbating; it's all mine; I can fantasize whatever I want with no concern about someone else. By myself, no one can see me. I fantasize about myself when I was younger and more attractive. Orgasm is so reliable in masturbating, but with my husband it's not. It feels like sex is for him, and masturbation is for me. I have to talk myself into sex with him. When it's just me, I feel that urge and just go for it.

Noting that she had avoided any specifics about her body, I inquire.

Sara painfully catalogues bodily "defects":	I wouldn't do cosmetic surgery, but there isn't a week that goes by that I don't think, fix these (she gestures to her eyelids), lift these (breasts), erase these stretch marks (belly). In my fantasies, my body looks great.
Sara continues:	I've spent a lot of time feeling I'm supposed to *love* sex, be super sexy in bed, be a fabulous experience for the guy. But it doesn't lead to orgasm for me; I'm always so focused on what I can do for him, being sexually superlative; it's all an act.
I respond:	All this effort to be pleasing interferes with focusing on your own pleasure.

She agrees. Although men have seemed very pleased with Sara as a sex partner, her sexy self is a persona, one that gives her *narcissistic gratification but not much bodily pleasure*. The need for self-esteem and securing the relationship trumps sexual gratification—a trade too frequently made by women.

Sara conveys to me that her focus on the man's pleasure includes her preoccupation with *his* pleasure at her having a perfect, young body. In masturbatory fantasies, she can arrange this scenario with elements involving sexy lingerie and orchestrated sexual positions. In actual sex, her husband does not necessarily arrange the scene to create the sexy visual of her body, so she experiences sex as the context in which her flaws are exposed, and she wants to avoid this shame. In our exchanges, the symbolic exposure to me of her flawed body/self furthers, in the analytic field, Sara's sense of shame, deficiency, and inadequacy. I feel a discomfort with the palpable sense that I am forcefully subjecting her to a degrading experience. It is tempting for me, as well as for her, to move away from this material. Just how long she had delayed discussion of this topic, when it was regularly on her mind, is significant regarding the vulnerability to a sense of sexual shame even in relation to another woman.

Note that sex as a topic had not been markedly absent in a way that would, or should, typically alert an analyst. Periodic references to sex and descriptions of some dissatisfaction with marital sex life had obscured the fact that the real issues had "slipped under the radar." Unfortunately, sex may slip away in this manner too frequently in present day clinical work. Although sex is front and center in the cultural milieu, with patients frequently presenting as if sex is not that much of an issue (unless they aren't having it), much angst is hidden below the surface. In an interesting reversal from Freud's time when psychoanalysis shocked Victorian sensibilities, we now have a "shock-proof" public when it comes to erotic life, yet patients are still struggling with many inhibitions, including in discussions with their analysts. As I have been underscoring, clinicians themselves may share this inhibition about sexuality becoming a central focus of clinical work. Countering this tendency is a central aim of this book.

After Sara's and my initial foray into this shame-infused realm, a massive avoidance set in that was difficult to alleviate and that proved to be session after session a rather impenetrable obstacle to attempts on my part to link back to what had been revealed. Sara recounted a trip to the zoo as a girl: "Two animals mated, the male mounted, the female seemed stuck there, trapped, looking both degraded and bored." In addition to being a rather grim, masochistic image of female sexuality, this association seemed to depict her feeling in relation to me as her analyst. I had the corresponding experience that I was using her for my own clinical desires. The analytic field felt like a sado-masochistic realm where I could "get off" (analyze her) at her expense. It was difficult to develop a shared narrative that could identify these dynamics without our each feeling captive to an enactment of the very experience we were trying to articulate.

As I continued to attempt to elaborate with Sara how the experience of shame led to a feeling that avoidance was the best option, she did eventually reopen the topic: "My friend Pam is overweight and rather pear-shaped; she looks way better with her clothes on, but she seems to feel fine about herself."

A: How do you understand that—her not being critical of her imperfect body?
Sara: I guess she doesn't have the same standards I do for myself.
A: Why do you think you have them?

Sara: That's the six million dollar question, isn't it.

After a pause, I then interpret to her: Something leads to a sense of your being under the shadow of this impossible standard. And you are not actually *in* your body or experiencing the immediacy of a sexual encounter. You are outside, observing, listing flaws and judging yourself as inadequate, not worth much, not worthy of pleasure, submitting to the man's pleasure. Flaws seem a cause for rejection. Fear of rejection leads to a vulnerable, anxious focus on flaws and a need to hide them.

Sara: I can't imagine someone not being critical of my bodily flaws; if they look and see imperfections, it's ugly, not sexy . . . (long pause). With one man I did have great sex; I felt totally free. And accepted.

A: What do you think made the difference?

Sara: I sensed how much he cared for me. During sex he looked straight into my eyes with an intense feeling of connection.

A: That close eye contact reassured you he wasn't standing back scanning you for flaws—evaluating, assessing, judging, criticizing.

Sara: It's not that the men I've been with have actually done that; no one has that I can think of . . . (extended pause) well, my mother. . .[Sara gives numerous examples from girlhood of feeling physically scrutinized by her mother in a way that made her feel "small."] I felt . . . well, not quite right, dismissed somehow. And then in my later puberty development, I really *was* small—the little skinny one, with two bumps on my chest, knock-kneed; I didn't think I was ever gonna be a woman. Other girls were voluptuous, wearing grown up women's shoes. I was wearing kiddy shoes; my feet were so small. My mother seemed sympathetic, but she couldn't really relate; she had always been full-figured. Some guys thought I was "cute," but cute seemed little, diminished, not sexy. When I did see guys looking at my body, I guess I thought I had finally filled out and wasn't the scrawny little kid anymore.

I said: Something in the way you registered your own body seemed to block the knowledge that you'd filled out until the gaze of others really communicated this new sense of yourself to you.

There was no mention of Sara's father in this material. She seemed preoccupied with a sense of inadequacy in relation to her mother, but not only in the standard formulation of oedipal competition for the father. Instead, Sara's desire to show up—"fill out"—in *the approving gaze of her mother* seemed central.

Eventually, Sara revealed fantasies of being seduced, overpowered, wishing not to be responsible for her own sexual desires. Thinking about my own concern that I had been overpowering Sara, "seducing" her into this sexual arena of the analysis, I ask her what it means to be responsible.

Sara: When I think about women being turned on—I can hardly say the word "horny"—I'm repelled. When Pam says she got "wet," it makes me cringe. Any bodily evidence of being turned on, "wanting it" is repulsive. Men can take off sexually on their own. You could be "dead" underneath them and they can carry on, come and feel just fine about themselves. But as a woman, no matter how jazzed you are, if you get all carried away, well, the man can "drop out," and you just can't keep on going without him/his excitement. You're left high and . . . well, I was gonna say, high and dry, but actually it's worse—you're left high and wet!

We laugh.

Sara continues: They should change that saying. Something about being the only one feeling horny seems shameful, degraded, for a woman, like you're ridiculous to be all "hot and bothered"—now there's a saying we can keep! A woman alone in lust is a subject of ridicule, humiliated; a man, a proud phallic animal looking for a conquest.

The session ends.

Due to a sense of shame predominantly experienced in relation to her mother, Sara inhibits her own desire and "submits" to a sexual relationship with her husband that is not sado-masochistic in the usual sense but that does involve psychic masochism in the giving up on the pursuit of direct sexual pleasure for herself. The relinquishment of pleasure (sexual fulfillment) in exactly the place one should expect to find it can be quite psychically painful, even if in a dull, deadening manner. These dynamics can infuse the analytic field as well, with a clinical couple teetering on the edge of re-enacting sado-masochistic dynamics of shame-filled exposure. It is a challenge to find a way through to a creative communication rather than remaining locked in a repetition that becomes a stalemate.

Kulish and Holtzman (1998) have written of women's "greater inhibition in the ability to take responsibility for their sexuality" (p. 66); they explicated through the Persephone myth a tendency in women to view sexuality as something forced upon them and from which it is difficult to escape. To take responsibility sexually means being willing to validate one's own pursuit of pleasure rather than having the sole aim of pleasing the other. The prospect of not pleasing a man gets right to the heart of a fear of object loss with explicit links to oedipal defeat that, as I have been indicating, is likely a redoubled experience for girls. Paraphrasing Freud (1893) regarding normative unhappiness, we might think of the common masochism of everyday life that often goes "under the radar" in women's sexual relationships. Women can foreclose their potential to be potent sexually and as a person.

Concern about failing to engage or out-stripping male libido can dampen female libido. Yet, oedipally, it is *female* libido—the mother's—that the girl likely fails to engage. Rather than being embedded in a reciprocal erotic oedipal relation with her mother as well as with her father, a girl is too often left alone without a partner. What may be "cut off" for the girl, in encountering the reality of unrequited oedipal desires, is her self-esteem regarding her sexual body as well as her sense of potency and prowess. How clinicians hold these ideas in mind, especially in considering a gendered sense of shame as a substrate of masochistic submission in women, makes a significant difference in how one hears and works with analytic material. But working in the realm of the erotic requires more than the holding of ideas—psychoanalytic theories—in mind; a clinician must be *fully present* in the manner that I conceptualize as analytic eroticism: embodied contact with one's own libidinal being, including with erotic anxieties and inhibitions, in a manner that has the potential to bring vitality and commitment to the erotic enterprise of the analytic work.

The trophy husband

With the next patient I will present, masochistic submission manifests throughout the entirety of the marital dynamics. Yet, once again, shame, a devalued sense of self, and fear of object loss, lead to inhibition and submission rather than agentic assertion and self-responsibility. A sense of oedipal failure is reiterated in the marriage and within the analytic dyad and proves difficult to transform. The patient's submission to another is often quite covert, taking cover under the disguise of idealized "love."

Kate has seen her husband as superior to her in almost every way, admiring him and feeling deficient herself. In reality, her husband is exceedingly narcissistic and much less emotionally mature than Kate. The idealization that had her thinking of him as a "good catch" has been slowly giving way in the analysis, and Kate is starting to question the basis for her feelings of intimidation in relation to her husband.

Kate: I realize how really scared I am to assert what I want in my marriage and professionally as well. I see that I believe I can't get the kind of mature relationship that I want because I'm not that mature myself.

She speaks of her emotional reactivity and volatility—disregulated states that we have done much work to stabilize and that she can now reflect upon.

A: What is it that compels your emotional reactivity?
Kate: A lack of ground under me; when I'm able to move from a more mature place in myself, it comes from a sense of having a ground under me.

Kate gives some examples of maturity that have been evolving in her parenting.

Kate: I see that I have maturity *there* that I don't usually recognize in myself more generally.
A: Through misrecognition or even an erasure of your strengths, you're not making full use of your developing maturity.

I am aware of how Kate keeps herself small and seemingly incompetent in relation to me. She is quite troubled by her fear of losing me, but is less conscious of her anxiety that her *progress* in the analysis will lead to her being *ready* to leave me.

Kate continues: "Now I'm pulled back into my childhood: I was much younger than my sisters, but I felt from an early age that I was *more mature*—'older'." We discuss how Kate needed to disavow her strengths, especially as her parents seemed quite immature themselves; she jettisoned her mature aspects in order to bolster her objects so that she could have a sense of relating to "strong" people. This masochistic submission— *being "less than"* in order *to be with*—has left her feeling that she has nothing to offer to someone she would actually think of as a healthy match. Kate: "I feel like a nobody—just floating around in the universe."

I ask how as a child Kate held her sense of being more mature than her family members *and* like "a nobody."

Kate replies: When I'd look in the mirror as a kid, I saw myself as just a dumb, little kid—totally unappealing. For a long time I saw this as a fact, not just a feeling state—a fact. Everyone could see it.
A: Your negative view of yourself matched how you felt mirrored by your parents and older sisters.

Kate can also easily project this negative reflection of self into the mirror of my gaze; if I am not experienced as overtly affirming, she concludes that I am negatively evaluating her. I regularly feel ensnared in this bind.

Kate: This all goes along with my feeling of being vulnerable, embarrassingly young—'a dirty puddle.' It's not good to show vulnerability.
A: Can you say more about what it means to you to be young and vulnerable?
Kate: You wouldn't want to be partnered with me; it would be a total embarrassment to you if anyone knew you and I were together.
A: In what ways would I be embarrassed?
Kate: The fact that I was clinging onto you—the opposite of a 'trophy wife'—a small ball of snot.
A: A tiny little girl wanting to be close, to be together, with her mother. This little girl who wants to 'cling on' feels dumb and unappealing, embarrassingly young/vulnerable, not at all desirable.

Here, the impact of a developmental collapse of maternal eroticism is evident as this dynamic infiltrates the analytic field and poses a challenge to analytic eroticism to inhabit and yet transform this experience.

Kate: I'm thinking about the qualities I'd want in a partner/friend; I realize how I go after "trophy" relationships so I'll look better; I do this with Tom (her husband): "He's great and he's *with me*."

I speak to Kate about how her pairing up with a trophy spouse does not actually "transfer" these wished for qualities to her devalued self, but instead further drains her agentic sense of self. Kate has sought a borrowed self-esteem by relational proximity that has actually undermined her sense of self worth.

I say to Kate: In fact, the more mature qualities that you do possess are obscured from view, kept unrecognized and underdeveloped. You continue to look in the mirror and misrecognize yourself, seeing yourself as without resources of your own that you can appreciate and develop.

Kate ponders: What am I afraid of? What the hell keeps me doing this? I'm not feeling self-accusatory, just feeling the impact of how persistent this all is . . . I don't know why, but I'm thinking about a television show about Dracula that my daughter was watching.

Thinking about my growing familiarity with the character of Dracula appearing in the analytic field formed with my female patients, I merely ask: "Any thoughts about that?" Kate, equally brief, states: "blood suckers," and we experience an extended pause.

I start to register images and thoughts that may provide a stimulus for our elaboration of this metaphor of blood sucking, erotic perversion; I say: "Vampires live off the blood of others left drained of vitality, limping along soon to be the 'undead.' Yet, the ingénue 'victim' initially sees Dracula as powerful and erotically compelling— a trophy husband." Kate and I both laugh. I continue: "But the desire to submit to, in order to unite with, his power actually drains her of any strength." After a long pause, Kate joins in on our newly forming scenario of erotic decay:

I can keep alive—less sucked on—if I pretend I'm already dead. He will never let me go. This dynamic—toxic and sickening—is so huge inside me, it would take an exorcism or a blood transfusion. It's so deeply rooted—I see it, but I can't let go of it.

The Dracula theme is used to identify an internal dynamic from which it is difficult for Kate to extricate herself without external help. Without foundational provisions of maternal eroticism invigorating and sustaining her, our "ingénue" falls victim to erotic perversion. The nutritional vigor of analytic eroticism is needed in steady supply to generate a store of personal vitality that can combat the draw into an unhealthy union.

A: You would have to be ready to go forward on your own strength; that's a lot to be ready for . . . We need to stop.

Kate: I just had this unusual, strange thought about the session: Did I do this right?

Kate sounds doubtful.

One can see in this material the impaired mother–daughter erotic relation reflected in a specific expression of erotic transference where Kate feels not just little and (sexually) inadequate, (a failed oedipal contender), but completely unappealing and repellent (pre-oedipally abject, "snot"). In the progression of the analysis, Kate's depleted self-esteem had become even more evident as she began to contact erotic wishes to be romantically partnered with the analyst. The sense of shame and inadequacy showed up in relation to me as an inhibition in elaborating her libidinal longings, both pre-oedipal and oedipal, for a maternal figure (to be close to me erotically, as well as more generally). Erotic transference wishes could be referred to, but resisted deeper elaboration and were most often diluted or circumvented in being split off to objects outside the analytic dyad. As Kate once expressed, "What would be the point of going into these feelings? I'd just be stuck." She imagined that expression of these erotic wishes would lead to a masochistic submission to her analyst that would result in a stasis (like her marriage) and deplete her, obstructing analytic progress. However, as seen in this session, Kate does have the growing belief that she has increasing maturity in certain areas of her personality and that she might recognize and further develop her strengths in her own right rather than by relational submission to a trophy husband (or analyst), attempting to borrow strength by proximity and narcissistic extension.

The image of Dracula as the ultimate trophy husband—handsome, powerful, vigorous (as he enters the scene in various films) portrays the marital dynamic Kate is embroiled in, her need to idealize interwoven with her husband's narcissistic issues. The relationship bedevils her, maintaining an addictive lure from which it is very hard to separate and individuate as she is even further depleted of nutritious narcissistic supplies ("blood"). She sees herself as having few internal resources that would sustain her; thus, maturing and individuating from an oedipal dynamic of submission feels impossible. Just as depicted in films, for the blood-sucked victim to free herself from Dracula always takes incredible force and the efforts of many in order to "save" the woman from erotic enthrallment.

This vampire representation of a sado-masochistic relationship, both sexually and more generally, is recognizable as a familiar feminine, romantic fantasy, as described in Chapter 2. The iconic Dracula tale parallels themes in the Persephone myth, but with erotic enthrallment and masochistic submission highlighted. For Loewald (1978), such a "romance" would represent a failure to work through the passive-submissive attachment to the oedipal object toward a more mature, individuated object relationship. I emphasize that a passive, submissive oedipal stance is likely the result of deficiencies in maternal eroticism beginning in pre-oedipal development.

The Dracula theme provides a metaphor for dynamics, both pre-oedipal and oedipal, of narcissistic depletion in the self vis-à-vis a hungry object; the hungry self is wedded to an object even hungrier than the self. A failure of maternal eroticism derives from and leads to libidinal starvation and loss of vigor. Masochistic submission can be understood as reflective of wounded narcissism, a loss of robust vitality in both self and other. When a girl is not fed enough narcissistic supplies in the mother–daughter relationship (including in the early oedipal situation), then she is vulnerable to relating to a narcissistic oedipal figure in masochistic submission. In an adult relationship where it is difficult to be clear who is feeding off of whom, a masochistic-narcissistic union—a particular form of pair-bonding—continues to deplete a healthy narcissistic investment in the development of self. Individuation is a relational threat in the masochistic-narcissistic couple.

To go in the direction of the developing self is believed to be at the cost of maintaining the tie to the narcissistic oedipal (as well as pre-oedipal) object; this threat of loss in the internal object world may be lived out in the external world if the adult life partner cannot develop in tandem. An object relation of masochistic submission is internalized so as to avoid triggering the other's narcissistic injury, retaliatory rejection and abandonment. One either submits or loses the connection/attachment. One loses either way, but submission keeps the object relation in place. With a partner whose fragility and potential for narcissistic injury is high, submission cannot be refused without a breach in the relational "security."

For such a patient, to strike out "on one's own" feels as if it means "going solo" indefinitely, which feels intolerable, especially with a weakened sense of self. This emotional situation has resonances with what a child would have to surmount in deciding it is necessary to leave home—not a choice most children could make. Instead, one most likely attempts to make do with a bad situation, continuing to subsist on relational malnutrition, getting weaker and weaker, unless "supplies" can be located from some source external to the primary bond. Yet since the nature of such a relationship ensures limited development of external supports both personal and professional, extricating oneself can be very difficult.

These basic assumptions about securing connection infuse the analytic situation as well. The clinician is called upon to both experience and resist the seduction of a patient's submissive idealization, then to start to represent the dynamic pull of the analytic field in a developing narrative in which a patient truly can feel her agency and creativity as co-author. Otherwise, patient-focused interpretations from a knowing, seemingly un-implicated clinician will serve to reinforce the polarized roles to which the analytic dyad becomes subjugated (Ogden, 1994, 2004).

Feminine masochism in females

Masochism can be viewed as a disorder of desire. I have conceptualized masochistic submission as a relinquishment of one's own desire, motivated by a fear of object loss. Shame and a depleted sense of self worth lead to inhibiting one's own desire, trying instead to fulfill the desire of the other and typically failing to do so. Without "self-construction," self-destructive actions or inactions predominate. This disorder of desire takes its initial form in failures of maternal eroticism that undermine pre-oedipal development and that set a fragile foundation for oedipal progression.

I have proposed that a girl's experience that, because she *is* a girl, the first oedipal object—her mother—is not "accessible" now, or later, may also play a role in generating a relational strategy of masochistic submission as a fearful "grasp" on the object. Oedipal failure for the girl qua girl in relation to the mother as first erotic object choice begins her heterosexual journey: The expected turn to the father occurs at the *site of her failure* to "win" her mother. In relation to first the mother, then the father, active frequently turns to passive, and "femininity" as a relational strategy sets in and takes hold. One *becomes* feminine.

Schafer (1974) identified that in Freud's theory of development, "the important thing was to get the girl to *become feminine* and ready to receive love and babies passively from an active man. . ." (p. 477; emphasis added). Getting a girl to become feminine was not merely a conceptual strategy in Freud's theoretical model; Freud was describing something that he observed in female development, supported by cultural expectations, also famously depicted by de Beauvoir (1952).

We have long known (Broverman et al., 1970) that the stereotypic characteristics of femininity (passive, timid, coy, pleasing, docile, submissive, dependent, etc.) align with masochism (Elise, 1997). These gendered traits, not far removed from masochism, led Freud (1924) to identify the second of his three forms of masochism as "feminine masochism." Freud was analyzing "feminine" masochism in males, making it evident that feminine masochism is not inherently female; something has to account for its development in males *and in females*. Feminine masochism refers to passivity, whereas Freud's first form of masochism—erotic masochism—refers to sexual pleasure in pain. Feminine masochism might be seen as "pleasure" (perceived security) in relational passivity—an *anti-erotic* masochism.

Steyn (2009) asked, "Is feminine masochism a concept worth reviving?" (p. 867) and answered in the affirmative. I agree with Steyn that this term can be usefully employed, that it signals a specific defense in flight from oedipal sexual conflicts, and that careful attention needs to be paid to the word "feminine." The intent is not to convey that masochism is inherent in female nature, but instead to refer to a masochistic position taken up by females (or by males) that aligns with a culturally entrenched gender role internalized at a very deep level through early object relations. Feminine masochism is a maneuver enacted for purposes of defense against oedipal anxieties. The specific anxiety that I am addressing is the fear of not getting, or of losing, the object's desire. Female eroticism can be abandoned in favor of feminine masochism.

In discussing male development, Steyn (2009) noted that a mother who discourages separation and differentiation "encourages a feminine development," (p. 871) that undermines sexual desire and assertion in the child.[3] She continues: "What Freud described in feminine masochism was the way in which a certain identificatory position was adopted to stunt development out of anxiety" (Steyn, 2009, p. 872). I suggest that this conceptualization can be productively applied to a *girl's* (as well as a boy's) flight from sexual desire, individuation and agency. Girls, too, can employ femininity in the service of defense against oedipal anxieties that include fears of narcissistic injury, impotence and rejection.

Marital dynamics

In looking at masochistic submission in adult couples, one sees that the internal object worlds of two individuals intertwine. Sara and Kate each *interpreted* her relationship with her husband to *require* a submissive stance sexually, and more generally. Most likely each woman paired with a man who actively contributed to this dynamic. Female masochism easily resides with male narcissism. Even so, neither woman was able to use her considerable communication skills and relational capacities to the advantage of herself, her husband or of the marital bond. Instead, both Sara and Kate continued the internalized parental object relation that led them to feel inadequate sexually, interpersonally, and in aspects of life outside the marriage. In tandem with masochistic submission to a narcissistic husband, these women, like many others, have encountered significant inhibitions in their work life (see Applegarth, 1976). The inhibition of professional development then returns them to, and reinforces, a submissive stance in relation to the husband. The marriage becomes a "declaration of dependence" (Symonds, 1971).

With these and several other women patients I have treated, masochistic submission as a particular marital dynamic served to reinforce on multiple levels varying degrees of overt masochism in each of the women. Instead of thinking in terms of a sado-masochistic pairing, I am discussing what can be thought of as a maso-narcissistic union. This conceptualization allows for thinking about masochistic submission in couples without attributing to the partners the degree of pathology that the term sadism usually connotes. A "failure to thrive" dynamic was evident in each of these women and was a clinically useful conceptual model that could be directly discussed without being taken as condemnation and further humiliation. The jointly developed capacity within the analytic field to articulate, understand, and transform obstacles to thriving, fostered oedipal individuation in each woman and an ability to "stand on her own" *within* a healthier marital context. Helping women and men to extricate themselves from these restrictive dynamics that inhibit both the individual self and the health of pair-bonding facilitates the development of the personality in the context of an erotic life which then benefits as well.

In writing about maturing object relations, Loewald (1978) emphasized:

> In the process of becoming and being an adult, significant emotional ties with parents are severed . . . a form of taking over actively what had to be endured passively in the beginning (p. 756). What will be left if things go well is tenderness, mutual trust, and respect—the signs of equality . . . [whereas evasion] is a way of preserving libidinal-dependent ties (p. 758). In mature object relations . . . the self engages, in a return movement as it were, with objects that are differently organized . . . [leading to] novel ways of relating with objects . . . a sea-change on the plane of object love.
>
> (p. 763)

When such transformations do not occur, repetitive oedipal dynamics are reiterated, impeding the creative process needed to achieve novel resolutions.

In wanting a relationship with a man, many heterosexual women are pressed not solely by a partner, but more importantly by internalized cultural assumptions insinuated into marital dynamics, to shape the relationship and themselves in a particular way. Both men and women are inducted into these polarized roles of male dominance and female submission and accommodation through the internalization of early object relations (Benjamin, 1988). Given these cultural and familial expectations, full recognition and expression of women's desire can threaten this highly valued love relationship for women; thus, women may back-pedal on one form of desire (self-assertion and erotic pleasure) to achieve another (relational "security"), often finding themselves in a masochistic trap of growing proportions. This strategy is a manifestation of the need in men and women alike to see the male as superior. Female desire poses a threat to the power balance accepted and expected in a paternalistic culture regarding heterosexual gender roles (Chasseguet-Smirgel, 1976; Person, 1980; Benjamin, 1988; Johnson, 1988). Woman's sexuality, and more general agentic expression of self, cannot come into its own until its expression is not felt to threaten the attainment of the desired love bond with a partner.

Conclusion

Multiple determinants of a submissive stance can be deeply embedded within the object relational world of the female. Most importantly, I wish to highlight the foundational role of maternal eroticism as elaborated by Kristeva (2014). Female erotic life most likely begins in relation to the mother. If things go well there, a girl will have a robust sense of her erotically embodied self; her libidinal vitality can flourish. If the relationship with her mother is libidinally undermined, erotic vigor will suffer, confidence will shrink. Recognition of these complex developmental factors located within the object relational matrix illuminates more fully how female inhibitions, though often railed against by women themselves, can become so masochistically entrenched. In the derailment of female desires, being "small" may become a way of life.

Notes

1 I am borrowing the phrase used when infants do not grow in a robust manner.
2 See Harris (1991) for a famous case in point.
3 See Torok (1970) and Elise (1991) for an analysis of this dynamic in the mother–daughter relationship.

References

Applegarth, A. (1976). Some observations on work inhibitions in women. *Journal of the American Psychoanalytic Association*, 24 (Suppl.): 251–268.

Benjamin, J. (1988). *The bonds of love*. New York: Pantheon Books.

Bonaparte, M. (1952). Some biopsychical aspects of sado-masochism. *International Journal of Psychoanalysis*, 33: 373–384.

Broverman, I. K., Broverman, D. M., Clarkman, F. E., Rosencrantz, P. S., and Vogel, S. R. (1970). Sex role stereotypes and clinical judgements of mental health. *Journal of Consulting and Clinical Psychology*, 34: 1–7.

Chasseguet-Smirgel, J. (1976). Freud and female sexuality: The consideration of some blind spots in the exploration of the "Dark Continent." *International Journal of Psychoanalysis*, 57: 275–286.

de Beauvoir, S. (1952). *The second sex*. New York: Alfred A. Knopf, Inc.

Deutsch, H. (1930). The significance of masochism in the mental life of women. *International Journal of Psychoanalysis*, 11: 48–60.

Elise, D. (1991). An analysis of gender differences in separation-individuation. *The Psychoanalytic Study of the Child*, 46: 51–67.

— (1997). Primary femininity, bisexuality and the female ego ideal: A re-examination of female developmental theory. *The Psychoanalytic Quarterly*, 66: 489–517.

Freud, S. (1893). The Psychotherapy of Hysteria from Studies on Hysteria. *The Standard Edition*, 2: 253–305.

— (1924). The economic problem of masochism. *The Standard Edition*, 19: 157–70.

— (1931). Female sexuality. *The Standard Edition*, 21: 225–243.

Harris, A. (1991). Gender as contradiction. *Psychoanalytic Dialogues*, 1: 197–224.

Holtzman, D. and Kulish, N. (2012). *The clinical problem of masochism*. New York: Jason Aronson.

Johnson, M. (1988). *Strong mothers, weak wives*. Berkeley: University of California Press.

Kristeva, J. (2014). Reliance, or maternal eroticism. *Journal of the American Psychoanalytic Association*, 62: 69–85.

Kulish, N. and Holtzman, D. (1998). Persephone, the loss of virginity and the female oedipal complex. *International Journal of Psychoanalysis*, 79: 57–71.

Loewald, H. (1978). The waning of the Oedipus complex. *Journal of the American Psychoanalytic Association*, 27: 751–775.

Morrison, A. (1989). *Shame: The underside of narcissism*. Hillsdale, New Jersey: The Analytic Press.

Ogden, T. H. (1994). The analytic third: Working with intersubjective clinical facts. *International Journal of Psychoanalysis*, 75: 3–20.

— (2004). The analytic third: Implications for psychoanalytic theory and technique. *The Psychoanalytic Quarterly*, 73: 167–195.

Person, E. (1980). Sexuality as the mainstay of identity: Psychoanalytic perspectives. In Stimpson, C.R. and Person, E.R. (Eds.) *Women: Sex and sexuality*. Chicago: University of Chicago Press.

Schafer, R. (1974), Problems in Freud's psychology of women. *Journal of the American Psychoanalytic Association*, 22: 459–485.

Steyn, L. (2009). Is feminine masochism a concept worth reviving? *International Journal of Psychoanalysis*, 90: 867–882.

Symonds, A. (1971). Phobias after Marriage: Women's Declaration of Dependence. *American Journal of Psychoanalysis*, 31: 144–152.

Torok, M. (1970), The significance of penis envy in women. In Chasseguet-Smirgel, J. (Ed.) *Female sexuality: New psychoanalytic views*. London: Karnac Books, pp. 135–170.

Part IV

Erotic betrayal and poisoned desires

Chapter 10

Infidelity and the betrayal of truth

Now in this fourth and final section of the book, we turn to damaging and damaged desires. It is well known that one of the most excruciating experiences for many people in our culture is the confrontation with a spouse or partner's sexual infidelity—what is curiously referred to as "cheating." Whether as lay people or as clinicians, we are all too familiar with the emotional devastation brought about by this sort of betrayal. A tsunami of jealousy, rage, and grief sweeps one along in a nasty current, all available energy expended in the effort to avoid being dragged down and under. Most succumb. Months, even years, may go by before the debris is cleared away and any equilibrium restored. Some couples seem to weather the storm, but it is unclear that their relationship is stronger in the face of such destruction or merely able to persevere with the damp chill. For many couples infidelity is often the end of the road, the relationship damaged beyond repair, whether that is apparent immediately or not.

It is evident that the piercing sense of pain involved in infidelity penetrates to the hearts of both women and men. Few are immune. In "The Impulse to Infidelity and Oedipal Splitting," Josephs (2006) located the deepest roots of these dynamics in the oedipal complex. The oedipal child of either sex feels betrayed by the realization that the desired parent has "run off" with the other parent. Josephs delineated a defensive organization where, in adulthood, passive is turned into active as people are *motivated* to cheat. Instead of being the "cheated upon" oedipal child, one becomes the "cheater" in one's adult relationship. This pattern of defense involves a reversal as one identifies with the "cheating" parent.

Although Josephs illustrated his thesis with a female case example, I suggest that the defensive pattern he described has traditionally tended to be more likely a male response to oedipal wounding. While U.S. statistical data on rates of infidelity in heterosexual couples show that women are "catching up" with men, the trend has been toward a long-standing, cross-cultural gender asymmetry in infidelity. In contrast to Josephs, I am considering the direct *repetition*, rather than *reversal*, that has more typically characterized female experience: A woman has been more likely to *re-experience* being cheated on—a repetition of the original oedipal injury in being the passive recipient of betrayal. As she likely felt as a small girl, she has been "dumped" for someone more desirable. Once again she has lost not only her love object, but her self-esteem. As I will illustrate, she may also feel that she has lost her mind.

Men as well can certainly experience being distraught to the extent of fearing the loss of one's mind. While I hope to illuminate this element of being on the receiving end of infidelity in using a female case example, this aspect of my thesis is not specific to one gender. However, I also wish to consider particular aspects of the heterosexual female oedipal trajectory brought forth in earlier chapters in light of how they might bear upon the experience of adult infidelity. A multitude of complex determinants involved in gender development and sexual object choice, both pre-oedipally and beyond, will of course play a significant role in defensive styles, in propensity toward infidelity, and/or in a vulnerability toward losing trust in one's own mind. Due to the complexity of addressing various oedipal configurations and sexual orientations, I will limit my focus throughout to heterosexual dynamics. My attention will be on the direct repetition of the experience of deception that is fully registered, not obscured by defensive denial or attempts at omnipotent reversal.

My specific emphasis is on the dual nature of the girl's erotic object choice: the mother as the first object of desire before the addition of the father in what is (heterosexually) a refocusing of desire (Freud, 1933; Halberstadt-Freud, 1998). As I have theorized, a girl's oedipal desire for her mother, traditionally referred to as the negative oedipal complex, is better thought of as the primary maternal oedipal situation to reflect its developmental timing and intensity (see Chapter 6). The desire for the father—the so-called positive oedipal configuration—is *added* in what is typically a secondary paternal oedipal situation intertwining with the girl's already established love affair with her mother. In taking seriously the duality of the girl's oedipal picture, one sees that she has two "opportunities" to be "dumped."

Investigating these particularities of the female oedipal configuration, I have in preceding chapters conceptualized that, through an experience of oedipal defeat in relation to both mother and father, a female sense of inadequacy and shame can be internalized and accepted as one's identity. This more typically female response to a sense of shame in perceiving oneself as an oedipal "loser" stands in contrast to what is more likely a male phallic-omnipotent defensive pattern. An extensive analytic literature on gender development, beginning with Freud (1924, 1925, 1931, 1933), has addressed the prevalence of phallic-narcissistic and active trends in males, passivity and inhibition in females. Kernberg (1991, 1995), especially, emphasized the greater tendency for boys to turn passive into active and for inhibition in girls, as erotic desire unfolds in relation to the stimulating, yet oedipally unobtainable mother.

As detailed in Chapter 7, for both sexes oedipal defeat in relation to either parent results in a sense of disappointment and deflation regarding one's sexed body and one's romantic aspirations. However, as much psychoanalytic gender literature identifies, defenses against injured narcissism tend to become gender-specific: Instead of accepting defeat, a male will likely attempt to triumph sexually. Such attempts at reversal usually require multiple repetitions. For females, living out a dejected, deflated stance (classically understood in a limited way as penis envy) sends them in the direction of inhibition and failure to actualize desire, as we also saw in Chapter 9.

I want to highlight specific potential precursors to women's experience of partner infidelity as these particular dynamics unfold within the oedipal crisis—the "betrayal" by the oedipal objects—plural. While not the single relevant factor, this *doubling of deception* is, I believe, especially pronounced for a girl as she is likely to inhabit more fully her bisexual potential in negotiating the expected shift of object choice from mother to father. The potential for "doubled deception," inherent in psychic bisexuality, can be evident in boys' development as well; however, homoerotic oedipal object choice is much more discouraged in boys than in girls. Girls are expected to shift away from the already established homoerotic tie with the mother; in male development, oedipal choice of the father is normatively foreclosed.

As each child moves into the oedipal phase, he *or she*, comes to recognize not only his or her own desire for the mother, but the mother's desire for the father. This recognition of the mother's desire going elsewhere can feel to the child like a betrayal by the mother: "I thought you were mine alone, but now I see that you've been involved with him all along!" For both sexes, deception first takes place in relation to the maternal object who is, as Freud (1933) put it, a "faithless" seducer (p. 123).

In following a heterosexual trajectory, a boy has to "master" this situation *in relationship to the mother* (Kernberg, 1991, 1995). Josephs (2006) holds, correctly I believe, that the usual pattern is for the boy to turn passive into active—to *become* the betrayer—in order to tolerate continued desire for a female as his internalized oedipal object. A boy will more likely use unconscious identification with the maternal figure as the unfaithful object in order to ward off future betrayals by a female—a vindictive as well as preemptive strategy. The boy can also directly identify with a sociocultural image of the paternal figure as the one to "play the field," thus using a gendered, generational transmission to ratify a defensive approach to relating. *He* will be the one to do any deceiving.

I am, however, particularly interested in thinking about how a girl might register a sense of erotic betrayal by her mother. Unlike a boy, who will likely evidence some protest, a girl is expected to swallow the betrayal by her mother. It is supposedly a non-event. As articulated in prior chapters, this erasure is culturally supported by denying the intensity of her erotic desire for the mother and by redirecting her to the paternal object. As Schafer (1974) emphasized, societies insistently attempt to steer each generation of children along a heterosexual path: "And this learning will be very much under the influence of some care-taking presence" (p. 470). Kernberg (1991) referred to the development of the girl's "tacit understanding of the 'underground' nature of her own genitality" (p. 356). Altman (1977) wrote of the girl's giving up of her mother as first love object as an "act of renunciation" that prepares her for renunciation in the future "for which there is no counterpart in the boy" (p. 48). In turning to the father, a girl then has to traverse the entire experience of oedipal desire and betrayal all over again in relation to the father—a "double whammy."

Kernberg (1991) described the daughter's "leap to the father" as requiring greater relational trust in that the father is an object less known than the mother. We might consider what this greater trust would be based upon—wishful thinking, a fantasy that "this one will be mine?" Kernberg (1991) identified a "secret hope of eventually being accepted" by the father (p. 356). But the father is already with the mother; a girl knows this oedipal fact from her experience of her mother's betrayal. Not only can she feel "dumped" by the mother, she is sent off to consort with her father who she knows *in advance* will never be hers alone.

I think of this dynamic as the *harem mentality*: an unconscious, passive resignation in the female to "accept" and endure male infidelity/non-monogamy. The girl registers on a deep psychic level that she is defeated in advance, and yet she sets forth anyway. This is her heterosexual trajectory, and much both culturally and in internalized early object relations supports this path. While hoping for a new outcome, she is unconsciously prepared to submit to the inevitable. I suggest that the experience of betrayal by the mother may set the stage for this dynamic of submission, which usually is understood solely at the level of culture in terms of patriarchal power and privilege. Given this early shaping of internalized object relations, in an ironic twist of gender, *the father may be the original "other woman."* It may be "matriarchal" power—the mother's desire for, and choice of, the father—that is key in understanding female submission to male infidelity. Such submission does not imply any lessening of conscious distress when confronted with an actual or feared infidelity.

As I have indicated, my aim in this chapter is twofold: 1) to investigate the impact of infidelity in its assault on the mind that is a risk/vulnerability for both genders, and 2) to analyze this tormenting drama in adult relationships, underscoring unique elements of the female heterosexual oedipal configuration. Investigation of this oedipal situation, though focused in the female direction, should nonetheless help us in dealing clinically with the trauma of the adult experience of betrayal in either gender. Although gendered trends exist, the experience of any individual is unique and may or may not fall along gendered lines. I do believe, along with Josephs (2006), that much of the trauma for adults in dealing with sexual betrayal has to do with the resurfacing of oedipal wounding. Much of what is painful in the present and/or dreaded in the future has already occurred in the archaic history of our erotic object relations. A deeply buried devastation from the past is mapped onto the present or onto the feared future.

I now move to a clinical example that will put a human voice to what can be consciously accessible in an adult. Direct, conscious recall of oedipal betrayal would be rare, especially as such betrayal by a mother would have occurred for a girl at a very young age and then be overlaid by extended experience with the father. Yet this clinical material does lay out the phenomenology of the experience of adult betrayal, especially

Lived reality becomes fiction

I was stunned one day to hear myself being vehemently accused of "cheating on" one of my female patients. Eva spit out her rage at me: "I feel totally betrayed by you; you've been seeing *her* [another patient] all along! I feel like you've been lying to me all along, and for how long, I don't even know." What made this declaration even more startling was the fact that this patient is not psychotic, as it might well seem, but a well-grounded, warmly related professional. We were three years into an analysis of predominantly neurotic conflicts carried out within a generally positive transference. The reader will of course wonder what had provoked this outburst of outrage that seemed to be taking the form of a psychotic transference regression in an otherwise quite sane patient. What had driven her "insane?"

A change in our schedule one day resulted in a "collision" between Eva and this other female patient in my waiting room. In agreeing to see Eva at an earlier hour that day, I had inadvertently set the stage for her to arrive just when this other woman was leaving. It turned out that they recognized each other from their jobs in a rather large corporate world, where Eva felt they "eyed" one another from a distance on a regular basis. Now for a moment they had stood a few inches apart, face to face, staring at one another before each moved on.

I was quite unprepared for the powerful impact of Eva's reaction to the realization that I was working with this known "other woman." The felt sense of the *sexual* nature of the betrayal became clear as she continued her accusation: "It's as if my husband cheated on me!" She well knew of course that I have other patients, some of them other women. This knowledge in no way diminished the shocked reaction she had to actually seeing this other patient in what was a brief and, on the surface, generally unprovocative encounter. To Eva it was very provocative, "sickening knowledge," as she put it; "I felt like I might vomit, or even faint."

In working to comprehend the emotional intensity for Eva of what had occurred—a felt sense of catastrophe—the reference to her husband cheating on her sexually called my attention to oedipal dynamics and the question of whether I was a paternal or a maternal figure at this point, or both. The family history included the reality that her father had an affair when Eva was about seven. Even at her young age, Eva gleaned a fair amount about the nature of her mother's distress. Thus, with his affair her father symbolically cheated on Eva and cheated her out of a secure home and family, as well as out of a positive identification with a mother loved faithfully by her husband.

Additionally, as I am theorizing, the less consciously accessible emotional reality of feeling cheated upon by *both* parents in the oedipal drama played a part in her reaction. The transference within the analytic field reflected this bisexual multi-layering. In the somewhat more accessible gender link between husband and paternal figure, I represented the oedipal father cheating on her with another woman. This connection placed the other patient as the "other woman," whether mother or mistress. On a deeper level, I represented the maternal oedipal figure cheating on her with the father. Here the other patient figured as the parental couple's "love child"—the patient's sibling rival. In her associations, Eva could recall that at age four, shortly after the birth of her sister, she announced to her mother, "When I grow up, I'm going to marry *you!*" Her mother "looked strange" and replied, "Girls don't marry their mothers." Eva reflected: "I felt something . . . quite bad; I would now say crestfallen . . . confused, and alone."

Adding to the mix, there also existed further crucially relevant history in Eva's adult life. In her late twenties, prior to her marriage in her mid-thirties, Eva had been in a relationship for four years when she discovered that her boyfriend had been having an affair for a number of months. The couple had stopped at local drugstore. Eva's boyfriend went into the store while she remained in the car listening to the radio. As she leaned forward to switch stations, she noticed the corner of a piece of paper wedged deeply between the seats. Extracting this document from its hiding place, she saw it was a letter from a woman who clearly had accompanied the boyfriend on his recent trip to Los Angeles. The rest of the letter's contents conjured up images of hotels, restaurants, beaches, a naked woman, sex.

Eva vividly described this moment as "beyond horrible—a moment that had no end, no next moment;" it was "beyond words," she said:

> As if my breathing had stopped. Something in my chest or stomach was bursting, caving, imploding; to say popping is not enough, more like those movies when the nuclear reactor is melting down—there's

panic, a threat of time pressure and annihilation, everything's shaking apart with increasing ferocity. And then I realized, it wasn't the woman, the sex, the trips, all of which were horrible, but the truly devastating knowledge was the realization of a reality that I hadn't been aware of, but that was true and that had been happening over some time.

As Eva paused, I commented, "your past was no longer your past." She replied, "No, it wasn't; I'd been lied to for some time and *my* reality that I'd *lived* was *not* true— it was dissolved in seconds, shaken apart, as if my memory banks were melting down." In response to Eva's profound experience of cognitive and emotional dissonance, I simply acknowledged, "What had been *real* was no longer true."

For Eva, lived truth turned out to be a fiction and was replaced with a horrible nightmare that *was* true. Over time she made continued attempts to find words to describe this powerfully traumatic experience:

Eva:	I will never forget that moment, like when people have near-death experiences where their life narrative unfolds before their eyes while time "stands still." Something about shock, impending annihilation, sudden realization—all seemed to have the power to change or even stop the normal passage of time. In one moment, I realized I had been deceived over a substantial period of time. This knowledge was much more disturbing than even those brutal images of the sexual infidelity—my boyfriend and some other woman in bed together.
I said:	You didn't think, before, that anything could be worse than that.
She replied:	No, and I had also always thought that I'd *know* if something on that level was wrong long before any actual sex. I'd have clues, hints that things between us were dulling out, that some emotional distance had set in, or that my boyfriend seemed to be going through some kind of crisis affecting his self-esteem. I'm aghast to have been so absolutely unaware, and yet people will say, "Oh, there must have been signs; you just looked the other way."

	But I don't think that is it. I felt cheated of the truth, deceived regarding reality; it's not solely about sex. People always refer to cheating as the sex.
I commented:	It's the infidelity with the truth that feels most devastating.
Eva said:	Yes, and I never would have believed I would be saying this.

In offering this focused case material, I hope to call attention to the sense of mental confusion that can result from the discovery of a lie about what has been taking place over time. The fact that affairs have usually been occurring for some time leads, upon discovery, to a need to rewrite one's personal history. In being cheated of the truth, something one has lived has no longer taken place; how can that be? This unraveling of history—a retroactive reconfiguring—is profoundly disturbing to one's sense of reality testing and leads to doubt, often crippling, about the ability to determine what is true. This assault on truth can be as disruptive as the sexual intimacy with a third party, or even more so. I believe it is this aspect of infidelity, destabilizing to both women and men, that often eludes clear recognition by patients, and even by clinicians: One loses trust not only in the other's love, but in one's own mind, in one's hold not only on the object but on reality.

Before discovering her boyfriend's affair, Eva had believed that her stance on infidelity was such that she would never be able to come to terms with a sexual intimacy between her man and another woman—the relationship would be over, period. She had felt she would never recover from vividly upsetting images of other women she could not erase. But when Eva was actually confronted with the reality of her boyfriend's affair, it was the assault on her sense that she could trust her own mind to tell her what was, and was not, real that proved to be the biggest stumbling block to any reconciliation. To her great surprise, Eva found herself, though extremely distressed, able to cope with the sex involving the other woman. She could actually take in and believe that the other woman was not that emotionally significant to her boyfriend and that he was willing to give up the affair, clearly wanting to continue the relationship with Eva. Even though it "gave her the creeps" to imagine her boyfriend and this woman in bed together, "him touching her naked body, making love to her," this distress slowly abated over the next months.

What held fast for much longer, becoming the actual downfall of the relationship and now a continued source of anxiety and "paranoia" for Eva in her marriage, was a fear of being cheated on again because she could not detect the truth. This fear of the future shadows her marriage though she is with a man who from all impressions is loving and devoted. That is the core question: how much does loving and devoted count? Since Eva had not suspected the first time, what would or could she rely on to tell her if anything similar was occurring? If she had, indeed, had "her head in the sand" the first time there would be something to work through and change regarding her denial. But her four-year relationship with her boyfriend had shown no signs of deteriorating or of emotional flatness; sex was gratifying and quite often passionate.

Eva's boyfriend had not seen his affair as emotionally meaningful. Having grown up in a cultural context where, not uncommonly, it was taken for granted that even married men would not "limit" themselves sexually to one woman, he did not show either the emotional distance or guilt that might have been the "tip-off" in another man. He did not act guilty, because he did not actually feel much guilt, and the circumstances of his work life offered plenty of opportunity for infidelity without any apparent change in the pattern of his relationship with Eva. In his worldview, he was truly quite connected with Eva and genuinely distraught when she left him. There had been no identifiable clues to alert her, warn her in advance, and hopefully to allow her to avert a potential affair.

Eva lamented: I have never been so confident or arrogant that I assumed that an infidelity couldn't possibly happen to me, but I had always believed that I would see a shift in the emotional "weather" of the relationship in order to be able to predict trouble—like hurricane warnings. I was totally hit by surprise, and I still don't feel I could go back and do it any differently.

I acknowledged: That experience of profound surprise created a sense of being crazy, unmoored from reality, with no sense of how to tell what was really happening.

Eva concluded: And when a woman does start to suspect the truth, she's usually told, "you're crazy!" by the man. The whole thing's a mind fuck. He's not just fucking some other woman, he's messing with your mind.

The inextricable nature of sexuality, triangularity, and infidelity

This case material portrays quite vividly what it can be like to be on the receiving end of adult sexual deception. Of course, we have one woman speaking, and a full understanding of her reactions would have to include consideration of her particular history and the complex determinants of her character. I propose, however, that there is something to attend to here that illuminates what often is present yet obscured in people who have been deceived. To address this more general relevance, I want to return to a consideration of the oedipal situation.

As introduced in Chapter 2, in contemporary Kleinian theorizing the oedipal complex is understood as a fundamental dynamic of the mind that then structures the mind (Britton, 1989; Steiner, 1989). Exclusion from the parental sexual couple poses a foundational challenge to the perception of reality. The child, "witnessing a relationship . . . from which he is excluded" (Rusbridger, 2004, p. 733), is faced with the recognition of a new, centrally important and reconfiguring idea; his or her mother is "involved" with someone else. Green (1992) described the Oedipus complex as an open triangular structure in which the mother is the central link in relation to both the father and the child.

Rusbridger (2004) identified the sexual nature of the link between the parents and the link of dependency from the child to each parent. Although the parental sexual relation has created the dependent child, from the child's perspective the chronology is reversed. First is the dependent dyadic link to the mother and then to the father. As the child develops, the sexual link to each parent starts to take form. It is only then that a child truly understands the sexual nature of the parental couple.

I emphasize that for both sexes the erotic link to the mother—maternal eroticism—takes increasingly more complex form as the child transitions from dyadic into triadic (oedipal) level relating (see Ogden, 1989a, 1989b). When the child discovers the sexual link between the mother and her mate, the oedipal father "arrives." In the substrate of the mind, a startling sense of shock and disruption ensues. The unwelcome reality to the child of not being the sole object of the mother's desire is at first denied.

This traumatic[1] though developmentally normative discovery is for some time hoped to be a fiction, only imagined, not true. The difficulty in differentiating reality from fiction captures a core aspect of the oedipal situation concerning what is real and true. Contending with ambiguity constitutes a crucial unconscious dilemma facing the oedipal child regarding the sexual relation between the parents, experienced as a betrayal, an "infidelity," committed by the mother.

Rusbridger (2004) referred to "reactions to moments of meaningfulness" (p. 731) in the child's confrontation with the oedipal drama. Although meaning is built up over time, recognition of a new, fundamentally important and reconfiguring idea hits in an instant, creating a sensation of a traumatic encounter. Rupture of the mother–child erotic dyad is blamed on the "moment" of the father's oedipal arrival. For the girl as well as the boy, the moment of the father represents a primal "castration" in breaking up the experience of all-encompassing union with the mother, a "displacement from the centre of the world" (Rusbridger, 2004, p. 735). The relationship both to time and to one's personal history is de-stabilized. *Meaning cascades backwards*, seemingly washing away what has gone before.

Oedipus and après-coup

No learning is more crucial than is coming to terms with developmental surprises. Life offers many surprises, some quite unpleasant. We think of separateness, exclusions (gendered and generational), and the limitations on time inherent in mortality (McDougall, 1986), each imposing a new understanding of self and other. Oedipal betrayal, especially, constitutes a surprise with the power to confer complex, retroactive meaning regarding object ties.

In Sophocles' *Oedipus Rex* we see just how powerfully retroactive meaning can assail the mind. Oedipus, in a blinding realization, undoes in a moment the history he believed he had lived; everything is changed, the nature of all actions, all relationships. This ancient drama exquisitely captures certain aspects that Freud identified as crucial to the normative developmental crisis he named after its tragic hero. Freud, in a primarily one-person psychology, focused on the registration of guilt for one's incestuous desires. Object relations theory allows for a more developed conceptualization of the experience of the wrongdoing of others: being "lied to and cheated on" by one's parents. I am focusing on oedipal "retroactivity" as an assault on the as yet unsteady foundation of the mind.

I see in oedipal betrayal a subjective experience of temporality where meaning travels backward and suffuses one's object relational past, creating a *new history* that is now personally registered, (though not "remembered"), as immensely painful. "Tricks with time" are at play in, and plague, personal subjectivity. The non-linearity of time in psychic life results in a bi-directionality such that in various circumstances past meaning can be reconfigured, re-transcribed, by retrospective attribution.

With the classical *Nachträglichkeit*, a later event in life gives new, traumatic (sexual) meaning to a past event, registered as disturbing at the time it occurred but not understood then in its full implications. In this process, when translated and expanded as *après coup*, "a rewriting of the past occurs when new understanding leads to an altered comprehension of history . . . Rather than causal connection and linearity [between earlier and later *events*], there is realization" (Pine, 2006, p. 251). In yet another conceptualization of the strange workings of non-linear psychic time, Winnicott (1974) focused on the additional element of a fear of the future as the only way to represent a breakdown in the past.

Winnicott (1974) identified a fear of a future breakdown as a disguised registering of a past breakdown that "*has already been*," (p. 104) where the ego-organization has been threatened. Because a patient confuses the past with the future, the fearful event "cannot get into the past tense" and the patient "must go on fearing to find what is being compulsively looked for in the future" (Winnicott, 1974, p. 105). Although Winnicott was addressing "psychotic core" dynamics surrounding primitive agonies before there is a "unit-self," I believe this anxious mixing up of past and future can also be operative at oedipal levels of development when once again the ego is threatened and maturational processes may suffer regression. As Freud (1937) identified, "The transposing of material from a forgotten past on to the present or on to an expectation of the future is indeed a habitual occurrence in neurotics no less than in psychotics" (p. 268). However, the concept of the repetition compulsion (Freud, 1914), traditionally used to explain neurotic, oedipal conflicts where the past is unconsciously recreated and relived in the present, does not usually get at the inchoate sense of a deep threat in one's future that Winnicott illuminated.

Eva could not work through her fear of a future betrayal by her husband until the trauma in her recent past with her boyfriend's infidelity was understood in light of her childhood experience of oedipal trauma—something that could not be directly recalled, but only reconstructed after being experienced in the present tense of the analytic field. As Winnicott (1974) stated, it is only when the threat to the ego is fully felt in the transference that "this past and future thing then becomes a matter of the here and now" (p. 105)—the here and now of the analytic field. For Eva, the felt sense of threat was triggered by the waiting room experience that I, her female analyst, was cheating on her. The ambiguity of her conscious association, "*as if* my husband cheated," left room for links to both paternal and maternal oedipal betrayals.

I am emphasizing that with oedipal betrayal and subsequent adult deceptions, the *truth* is the traumatic event and does reconfigure one's personal history rather than necessarily referring back to any previously registered, concrete event. As Perelberg (2009) stated: "The oedipus complex retrospectively retranslates earlier experiences in terms of *après coup*" (p. 137)—an oedipal restructuring of earlier life where one had been innocent of the knowledge that any painful "event" was taking place. I would say that, for adults, *deception constitutes foreclosure of the possibility of registering* events as problematic. Truth becomes the trauma in that it refers back to an absence of any earlier event that would have undone the deception. Deception constitutes a trauma based on a non-event—something that *did not occur* in the individual's *experienced* history, an "absent event"—where the revelation of the deception is the event that is traumatic.[2]

The painful realization of oedipal truth sends further pain flooding back into the past, thus spoiling far more than the present moment and future prospects. This strange sequencing can occur with betrayals at both the time of the oedipal crisis and later, in adulthood. As the oedipal reality of the triadic and sexual nature of the relationship to the parents unfolds and the primal scene is comprehended, the child realizes that the parents' adult sexuality has been right there all along. Known reality is reconfigured: "Oh, is *that* the nature of your relationship? I didn't realize you were involved *sexually*. I thought it was just we two."

We see film representations of this scene in the infinite repetitions of an adult walking in on a lover in bed with another. In this agonizing circumstance, incredible violence frequently takes place. "Crimes of passion" constituted a legally recognized form of "temporary insanity" where one is driven mad by sexual betrayal. In these situations, sexual jealousy and competition are center stage, yet the thwarted wish to be the only one is not the sole problem. Tucked into this riveting scene is the shock to one's sense of reality—the crushing attack within one stunning moment on one's understanding of one's history with a loved other. This attack on the sense of reality constitutes a level of threatened danger to the psyche different from that posed by sexual jealousy, narcissistic injury, and the resulting sense of shame.

Danger situations

Josephs (2006) identified parental "unfaithfulness" as a betrayal trauma and as a universal danger situation (Freud, 1926) in the form of narcissistic injury and humiliation. The danger is to one's sexual self-esteem in the face of parental disloyalty. I am following Josephs in including oedipal betrayal as a basic danger situation, though my emphasis differs regarding the nature of the danger. Josephs focuses on the fundamental doubts about the loyalty of the loved one; I focus on fundamental doubts about the capacity of one's mind to detect danger and on the threat to one's mind—one's mental functioning—of such danger. One is contending not solely with an injury to one's sexual self-esteem—a bruised ego—but with a deeper threat to one's trust in one's own sanity.

One can lose the object, the object's love, even self-love; none of these losses is as threatening as a fear, or felt sense, of losing one's mind. We rely on signal anxiety built up from past experiences (Brenner, 1982). Some ability to predict the future and to protect oneself, at least to some extent, is based on a sense of good reality testing in the past. The inability to tell truth from falsehood, reality from fiction—equivalent to a quasi-psychosis where one is "losing" one's mind—would constitute a most fundamental danger situation.

It appears that even as adults, an assault on truth has the capacity to disrupt our minds—our going on being (Winnicott, 1958)—if only for a few moments and that this assault can be quite destabilizing. We see with Eva that the sudden realization of a reality of which she had been unaware created a sense of reality dissolving, "shaken apart, as if my memory banks were melting down." As she evocatively described, the boundaries of time seem to dissolve as one hovers in an endless moment—a sense of time "standing still." Dislocated in time and space, one temporarily loses hold on the coordinates of one's being. Green (2009) refers to such disorganizations of temporality—where traumatic factors impede integration or even elude representation—as that of an exploded time (*"temps éclaté,"* p. 17). We think of the common expression of being "blown away."

As I am indicating, questions regarding reality are central to the oedipal task and need to be worked through over time. The oedipal child must come to grips with the grim realization that the parents, though they do love the child, have indeed "cheated" on him or her by their "affair" with one another. It is a very confusing situation. Perplexing questions abound. The child is left to wonder, painfully ponder, how much does having a loving and devoted parent count in protection against betrayal. We can see that these are the very quandaries adults struggle with in the face of a sexual betrayal.

Moving fully into the oedipal situation, and negotiating its challenges toward optimal resolution, rests on the fundamental recognition of the sexual independence of the mother's desire (an unwelcome aspect of maternal eroticism), something neither sex is eager to accept. Simply put, the mother's adult sexuality, when comprehended, is an affront to the child's wish to erotically possess the mother. Here, maternal "heterosexuality" translates in the child's mind to "other (than with me) sexuality." The mother's sexual partner being of a gender other than herself is not here the issue; her partner being *other than her child* is key. The child is not developmentally ready to perceive this "other-sexual" reality for some time, and to do so is rarely a smooth ride. Eventually, it is hoped that each child will come to some sort of personal conviction regarding oedipal (triadic) reality that then becomes foundational for going forward. But first quite a lot of psychic work must be done, and in times of stress this work can be undone, and vulnerable individuals can become "undone."

In situations where one is confronted with infidelity in an adult relationship, oedipal dilemmas are revisited, often traumatically. The ability to determine, "Did this betrayal really happen, or am I crazy and making it up?" is challenged once again. Questions of how to proceed in responding to a suspected infidelity generate strong feelings of anxiety and self-doubt. Determining truth against a series of logical dismissals rests on trust in one's "intuition"—an emotional conviction such that one is not dissuaded by clever denials.

Many adults shore up their defenses against contending with oedipal level threats: Denial shows up as a refusal to see or register the meaning of what is right in one's face. Many couples go along in a marriage where infidelity is intuitively known, but not directly acknowledged as they both agree to look the other way. Josephs (2006) delineated the defensive strategy of preemptively doing to others what you do not want done to you (again). I have been exploring the situation where one is *not defending against, but experiencing anew*, the original trauma. Unconscious fantasy regarding the oedipal situation is evoked, and typically becomes a waking nightmare as the adult relationship devolves into a repetition.

Gender, danger, and deception

I have suggested that particular aspects of the female heterosexual oedipal configuration—the dual nature of erotic "betrayal" more likely encountered—may be an additional factor shaping women's experience of erotic deception. This specific patterning of early object relations, combined with many other aspects of gender development and powerful socio-cultural forces, may contribute to a female propensity toward being in the position to re-experience, rather than defensively reverse, the pain of oedipal betrayal. It is in the re-experiencing (for either gender) that the full impact of the assault on truth is laid bare. These most powerful dynamics regarding sexual exclusion unfold within the primary maternal oedipal situation. Both boys and girls are confronted, affronted, by the mother's sexual desire going elsewhere, most typically to the father. Within a heterosexual trajectory this defeat is one the boy must *surmount*, the girl *accept*.

For the girl, the mother's desire for the father, represents not only desire for another, but for another sex altogether. Often a new sibling is the incontrovertible evidence of a mother's infidelity (Freud, 1910, 1919), intensifying the sense of injury in a most poignant manner. The girl realizes that her wish to have a baby with her mother is doomed. And unlike the situation of a boy, this disappointing matter cannot be attenuated by the phantasy of a future adult capacity to impregnate the mother. Freud (1931), surprised by the degree of activity in the girl's early relation to her mother, noticed that it is once she turns to the father that passive trends prevail.

When a girl does take her father as her oedipal object (likely overlapping her wish to retain her mother as her oedipal object), confusion is compounded. She is redirected from the mother to the father *in the immediacy of the disturbing realization of parental "infidelity."* The girl may feel she cannot obtain *either* object. With the oedipal father arriving "later" in development, from outside the maternal orbit and in the context of evident parental sexuality, he is more likely to be suspected already of being a "known womanizer." I am suggesting that these oedipal particularities for the girl may be an aspect of why women can be relatively "accepting" of infidelity in men—they are somewhat inured to male infidelity by their experience with the oedipal transition in object choice. Being inured speaks to an experience of subjugating oneself to a situation that feels unavoidable, not to an absence of emotional distress. For instance, one would not conclude that women in a *seraglio* were happy about sharing a husband.

Unlike the boy, the girl moves on to a second, less archaic object toward whom the girl is already alerted to *his* lack of faithfulness: "I know you're involved with my mother. I found that out when she betrayed me with you." The oedipal girl is less able to maintain the innocence needed even to generate the unconscious phantasy that she is her father's *first* love. The daughter may hope for a new commitment of faithfulness from the father, but this wish is likely registered as on shaky ground, at best. Doubt regarding self and other is the context in which she *begins* the oedipal relation to her heterosexual object, with faith in her mind's ability to determine reality already shaken. This path is quite distinct from the one traveled by the boy.

Josephs (2006) noted the "widespread double standard that makes it more permissible for men than women to have affairs and more permissible for betrayed men than betrayed women to openly avenge themselves against their unfaithful lovers" (p. 429). I agree with Josephs that gender-specific cultural sanctions (based on patriarchal power relations) play a crucial role in shaping incidence of, and reactions to, infidelity. These socio-cultural influences gain in strength as they become internalized in the deepest strata of the psyche through developing object relationships. Altman (1977) linked oedipal development to gender asymmetry in a "steadfastness of commitment" to love (p. 47) that requires a capacity for "renunciation of alternative possibilities" (p. 48). I, too, address oedipal aspects of this double standard that potentially further entrench gender asymmetry in responses to sexual betrayal.

Josephs (2006) gave an eloquent description of people who "would rather undo the narcissistic injury of their own betrayal traumas by turning passive into active than by acknowledging their own hurt, humiliation, impotent rage, and paranoid dread of being betrayed once again" (p. 429). While this portrayal can certainly apply to either gender, it resonates in the masculine direction. The defensive organization detailed by Josephs (2006) is based on the *evasion* of "full awareness of the exquisite human vulnerability to the trauma of seduction and betrayal in our most intimate and trusting relationships" (p. 435). My conceptualization rests not on the evasion of awareness of one's vulnerability to betrayal, but on the human struggle to come to terms with the threat posed by this awareness.

Issues in clinical treatment

For a number of women in my practice, the reaction to news of an infidelity focused at first on the sexual betrayal and threat to the relationship. But far more pronounced and prolonged over time was the anxious preoccupation with a need to "reconstruct" *past* reality. Efforts to go back in time, approximating the duration of the affair, focused on intensive searches through phone records, credit slips, e-mail logs, appointment books, and the like. Various occasions were reconsidered in their new significance: "Oh, when *we* were there, he had just been with *her*; when he gave *me* that gift, he had just bought something for *her*." Such research, and contemplation of the resulting data, was excruciatingly painful, yet continued to have a sense of vital urgency.

These women could not go forward until each had revisited the past and brought what she thought had been occurring into alignment with what had actually been the case. This entire period of time absorbed in this effort was one of great anxiety and mistrust blanketing all object relationships and permeating the analytic field. It was as if each woman had stepped "off the page" that everyone else, including myself, was on in order to pursue an obsession for which only she understood the crucial need. It was only when I could appreciate and interpret the imperative to regain a grasp on the past, in order to restore a confidence in a personal sense of reality testing, that this fact-finding mission was able to gradually abate. But this eventual restoration was preceded by a grueling period of intrapsychic chaos.

I am not proposing that this experience is the same for each woman or man when betrayed. The passionate nature of the couple and of their personal temperaments, the libidinal intensity of erotic desire for the partner (and earlier, for the oedipal parent), all play a part in the intensity of the felt sense of betrayal. The degree of wounding in the injured love will surely depend on the vitality of the felt sense of connection to the love object.

I do want to emphasize the vulnerability in even the most psychologically healthy to a significant degree of regression and destabilization in the face of such betrayal. This perspective gives another level of insight into the severity of various breakdowns related to infidelity, including murderous rage, psychotic depressions, phobic anxieties, and compulsive fact-finding missions that seem never to end. I am theorizing, in keeping with Freud (1926), that oedipal calamities hark back to the most primal anxieties and can render almost anyone vulnerable to regression to a primitive core. With adult erotic deception—so destabilizing due to its oedipal roots—it is important to remember that those roots rest in pre-oedipal soil.[3] Confidence in one's mind, the normal sequence of time, and the reality of one's personal history, all can come into question. A painful event in an adult relationship, back-lit by oedipal dynamics, gives rise to and determines the shape of one's fear of an anticipated future repetition. Not only can repetition replace the remembering of oedipal history (Freud, 1914), fearful anticipation can as well: "I hope this never happens to me (again)." Instead of nameless dread (Bion, 1962), here the dread is named, but still with no conscious link to one's childhood—until, as we see with Eva, one further detail is put most profitably into place in the clinical drama as it is brought to life within the analytic field.

Eva's fear of the future, in terms of (mis)trusting herself, her husband, and her analyst, could not be alleviated until the trauma with her boyfriend was affectively recognized for its roots in her past. A narrative construction of oedipal injuries in relation to mother and father, which for the most part could not be directly recalled, was accessed only when those injuries surfaced in the analytic field, making their presence felt in an urgent manner to both patient and analyst. For a period of time, our dyad had to survive in an atmosphere of erotic betrayal. Transformation of mental anguish to a more solid sense of personal security was achieved only by acknowledging the power of betrayal as lived out in the intersubjectivity of the analytic relationship.

Although Eva was quite "unhinged" in her waiting room encounter with my other patient, she retained hold on the "as if" nature of the experience: It was *as if* I had cheated on her. The containing capacity of our analytic field, though threatened, remained intact. It was primarily in her associations to her prior "meltdown" after her former boyfriend's betrayal that this relatively healthy woman was able to give evocative expression to powerful states of affect in the face of traumatic realization. Eva's history had unraveled, not her mind. Instead, her highly developed capacity to symbolize intense subjective experience allowed her to articulate quite poignantly what might be imagined to be the oedipal child's challenge at the cusp of dyadic to triadic relating where the ego is wobbly even in the healthiest people. Such experience occurring so early in development is not easily accessible to conscious recall. However, once betrayed as an adult, the "paranoia" and vigilance regarding a feared repetition is given force by the unleashing in adult life of what has lain dormant (repressed) from the oedipal phase. Such "unleashing" can quite powerfully overtake the analytic field, destabilizing the analytic couple as well.

While unconscious processes do not proceed in accord with linear time, unconscious contents can be modified over time and are not immune to change (Hanly, 2009). When healing can take place, painful experiences from the past, frozen in time, "can take their place in the temporal sequence of the individual's life. . ." (Hanly, 2009, p. 31). This re-placement in time allows a traumatized individual to move into the present with their future truly in front of them rather than as a mirage of the past.

Conclusion

Undermined trust in one's mind in relationship to one's objects has far-reaching consequences. The rebuilding of trust, often referred to after marital infidelity, is usually understood to mean *trust in the partner* to care enough not to cheat again, not to wreak any further such havoc on the relationship. By contrast, I have emphasized the much more difficult and complex task of rebuilding *trust in the self*—specifically, trust in one's mind, one's capacity to differentiate truth from fiction, to detect deceit.

Clearly, both women and men suffer greatly in this area. It is in how these anxieties and powerful passions are handled that certain gendered patterns may show up. Although counter examples are plentiful and cultural variations are significant, gendered trends exist. Men are just as anxious as women about being cheated on, but may gain more of a sense of conscious control through defensive identification and reversal. Men tend more often to be preoccupied with a fantasy of self as the one to cheat even if never acted on. Women seem to be more vulnerable to continual conscious anxiety regarding a feared repetition of being cheated on and to a sense of not trusting their own mind.

As each of us has had the normative developmental experience that our oedipally desired parents have all along been selling us a "bill of goods" pretending they were ours alone, this trust in one's mind to detect deceit in loved and loving objects is on a fundamentally shaky foundation. This fault line of doubt is attested to by the anxiety and insecurity the issue of fidelity raises in so many people. Having begun with the metaphor of a tsunami, I find that I have now come to images of an earthquake. The issue of infidelity, with its oedipal substrate, does indeed seem to be something of a "natural disaster" with its seismic capacity to shake the bedrock of our being, to knock our feet out from under us. It is true in nature that an earthquake often leads to a tidal wave of massive proportions. Similarly, in development the fault line of oedipal betrayal and doubt can lead to an adult wave of destruction— the danger in erotic deception being the assault on truth.

Notes

1 In conceptualizing normative oedipal trauma, we might think of the analogy to healthy muscle development where weaker tissue needs to be broken down and temporarily "damaged" by exercise in order to build back stronger.
2 Parents now tell children from earliest years that they are adopted; this is not traumatic knowledge. In prior decades, revealing this knowledge later in development was a revelation found to be so disturbing that parenting practices changed. Otherwise, one's closest people—parents—were felt to have deceived with a lie encompassing one's entire past life. Then the truth became traumatic.
3 Kleinians do not think in terms of a pre-oedipal phase, placing as they do the oedipal complex very early in development. I am speaking to a more general psychoanalytic understanding.

References

Altman, L. (1977). Some vicissitudes of love. *Journal of the American Psychoanalytic Association*, 25: 35–52.
Bion, W. R. (1962). The Psycho-Analytic Study of Thinking. *International Journal of Psychoanalysis*, 43: 306–310.
Brenner, C. (1982). *The mind in conflict*. New York: International University Press.
Britton, R. (1989). The missing link: Parental sexuality in the Oedipus complex. In Steiner, J. (Ed.) *The Oedipus complex today*. London: Karnac, pp. 83–102.
Freud, S. (1910). A special type of object choice made by men (Contributions to the psychology of love, 1). *The Standard Edition*, 11: 163–176.
— (1914). Remembering, repeating and working through (Further recommendations on the technique of psycho-analysis, II). *The Standard Edition*, 12: 145–156.
— (1919). 'A child is being beaten' A contribution to the study of the origin of sexual perversions. *The Standard Edition*, 17: 175–204.
— (1924). The dissolution of the Oedipus complex. *The Standard Edition*, 19: 173–179.
— (1925), Some psychical consequences of the anatomical distinction between the sexes. *The Standard Edition*, 19: 248–258.
— (1926). Inhibitions, symptoms and anxiety. *The Standard Edition*, 20: 75–172.
— (1931). Female sexuality. *The Standard Edition*, 21: 225–243.
— (1933). New introductory lectures on psychoanalysis: Femininity. *The Standard Edition*, 22: 112–135.
— (1937). Constructions in analysis, *The Standard Edition*, 23: 257–269.
Green, A. (1992). Oedipe, Freud et nous. In *La deliaison: Psychanalyse, anthropologie et literature*. Paris: Hachette, pp. 69–149.
— (2009). From the ignorance of time to the murder of time. In Fiorini, L. & Canestri, J. (Eds.), *The experience of time: Psychoanalytic perspectives*. London: Karnac, pp. 1–19.
Halberstadt-Freud, H. (1998). Electra versus Oedipus: Femininity reconsidered. *International Journal of Psychoanalysis*, 79: 41–55.
Hanly, C. (2009). A problem with Freud's idea of the timelessness of the unconscious. In Fiorini, L. and Canestri, J. (Eds.), *The experience of time: Psychoanalytic perspectives*. London: Karnac, 21–34.
Josephs, L. (2006). The impulse to infidelity and oedipal splitting. *International Journal of Psychoanalysis*, 87: 423–437.
Kernberg, O. (1991). Sadomasochism, sexual excitement, and perversion. *Journal of the American Psychoanalytic Association*, 39: 333–36.
— (1995). *Love relations: Normality and pathology*. New Haven: Yale University Press.
McDougall, J. (1986). Eve's reflection: On the homosexual components of female sexuality. In Meyers, H. (Ed.), *Between analyst and patient: New*

dimensions in countertransference and transference. New Jersey: Analytic Press, pp. 213–228.

Ogden, T. H. (1989a). The transitional oedipal relationship in female development. In *The primitive edge of experience.* New York: Aronson, pp. 109–140.

—— (1989b). The threshold of the male oedipal complex. In *The primitive edge of experience.* New York: Aronson, pp. 141–168.

Perelberg, R. J. (2009). The first narrative, or in search of the dead father. In Fiorini, L. and Canestri, J. (Eds.), *The experience of time: Psychoanalytic perspectives.* London: Karnac, pp. 133–153.

Pine, S. (2006). Time and history in psychoanalysis. *International Journal of Psychoanalysis,* 87: 251–254.

Rushbridger, R. (2004). Elements of the Oedipus complex: A Kleinian account. *International Journal of Psychoanalysis,* 85: 731–748.

Schafer, R. (1974). Problems in Freud's psychology of women. *Journal of the American Psychoanalytic Association,* 22: 459–485.

Steiner, J., (Ed.) (1989). *The Oedipus complex today.* London: Karnac Books.

Winnicott, D.W. (1974). Fear of breakdown. *International Review of Psychoanalysis,* 1: 103–107.

—— (1958). The capacity to be alone. *International Journal of Psychoanalysis,* 39: 416–420.

Chapter 11

Betrayal and the loss of goodness in the analytic relationship

In this chapter, I will be addressing the situation of patients who have had an experience of traumatic betrayal by a clinician whom previously they had trusted. The nature of the betrayal can range along a continuum from overt boundary violations—with the patient, or as revealed to have occurred with another patient—to various ethical lapses and to more ambiguous clinical errors that contribute to impasses and to broken off treatments. Regardless of the particular aspects of any given betrayal, a unifying factor for these patients is the traumatic disruption to their sense of trust in a good object. My focus will be on the *subjective experience of the patient*, not on an attempt to delineate the specific nature of the betrayal.

I write from the perspective of the subsequent analyst sought out in the wake of a felt betrayal and a disrupted termination. This next analyst encounters a situation with particular implications for the transference-countertransference matrix as situated within the analytic field. The analyst is challenged to assist the patient with a task that is exceedingly complex *for them both*. This analyst is charged, as witness to the loss of a clinical relationship between two others, to aid the patient in her or his confusion over the disappearance of a good object. The analyst must help the patient to look back, to sort out experiences of good and bad, and to "dream" a goodbye.

In the film, *Imagining Argentina* (2003), the protagonist Carlos has prescient, waking dreams about the fates of lost loved ones who have "disappeared" and with whom no goodbye has been possible. As person after person comes to Carlos with their painful query about their missing person, he dreams a response. There is actual death in these disappearances, but also symbolic death through tyranny and betrayal as most of the missing have been taken away by corrupted political powers that should have been in place to protect the people. Instead, loved ones have been abducted, likely murdered, maybe imprisoned, leaving only a desperate hope that they are in hiding and will at some point return.

In providing a context in which to say goodbye, Carlos's dreams offer a process of closure to those who cannot move forward until they have looked back and found the truth of what has occurred—that their loved one will not be returning. The film emphasizes that when a loved one has disappeared it is imperative to look back in order to mourn. Though painful, this process stands in stark contrast to the fate of the bereaved left in limbo. Without a third person standing outside of, but deeply concerned with, the fate of the original relationship between two others, a process of grieving is obstructed.

The role of waking dreaming by a third in facilitating the mourning of one person for another has its parallel in the analytic situation: "The past cannot become memory without a dream-work furnished by the analyst" (Botella and Botella, 2005, p. 32). Ogden (2005) described the analyst as "participating in dreaming the patient's undreamt and interrupted dreams" (p. 2; see also Ogden, 2000, 2004, 2017). Civitarese (2016) emphasized that awake dreaming "expresses the deepest psychological capacity that human beings possess for making sense of experience" (p. 91). When confronted with the symbolic loss of a former analyst due to a betrayal, a patient needs to be able to look back, to make the past the past, and he or she needs help in order to accomplish this painful task. The ability of a next analyst to dream what the patient as yet cannot rests, I suggest, on the analyst's intimate connection to his or her erotic vitality—*analytic eroticism*—that paradoxically can be used in the service of a process of mourning that unfolds within the analytic field.

As evocatively depicted in *Imagining Argentina*, when loved ones are abducted by corrupt political powers, a separation between good and bad can be maintained. Loved ones are gone, but they are still good; badness lies with the abductors. By contrast, when one is betrayed *by* a loved one, good and bad come to reside in the same person and one loses not only a loved person in one's life, but a good object in one's mind. In the analytic community—with ethical violations[1] and lapses of integrity that lead to a felt sense of betrayal for a patient—good and bad are inextricably intertwined. This crucial element imposes a complex demand on the process of grieving the loss of this trusted relationship.

Although splitting is, at least for a time (often a long time), a possible and likely defense, the most disturbing element for any patient confronted with this experience of betrayal is the registering of a "lost" good analyst who "turns into" a bad object; loss of the good and intrusion of the bad are occurring within the representation of one object. Neither side of this split is viable, yet it is extremely challenging to integrate the two, to retain for oneself what was good about the treatment relationship with the former analyst, while also being able to trust one's experience about what was problematic and harmful. Resolving this dilemma takes considerable effort. This task of integration is what is at stake in any subsequent treatment. In looking back over an expanse of thirty years, Dimen (2011) articulated what this protracted struggle encompassed for her.

In her compelling narrative about a sexualized boundary violation, Dimen (2011) revealed the complexity of the psychic task entailed in the effort to come to terms with a betrayal by a trusted other: one's analyst. Her entire text affirms the crucial need to look back in contending with deception, betrayal and loss. With a vantage point of three decades and a very changed sense of self, Dimen (2011) utilized her considerable scholarship and talents as a writer—most especially her impressive capacity to theorize—to form a retrospective realigning of her views of Dr. O, who "broke his compact and my heart" (p. 39). She pulled into focus what she could see at the time but could not make sense of, grasp emotionally, or be willing to integrate into her conscious understanding of Dr. O and her relationship to him. She shares her journey with us.

Yet for many years— "until I wrote about it and had the exchange afforded by writing and speaking with the psychoanalytic community and others," (2011, p. 37) —Dimen (2011) found herself in silence, "attempting to manage this painful flood alone" (p. 37). Without a third engaged as witness and container, "feeling could not be contained . . . knowledge . . . could not coalesce, nor could there evolve an 'I' to hold the self-shards together" (Dimen, 2011, p. 37): She "lacked the internal structure to engage full-on the heartbreak, anger, and disillusionment that would have rushed in" (Dimen, 2011, p. 62) had she relinquished her still idealized view of her former analyst. What then of patients who have to contend with an immediate, unavoidable dismantling of the relationship with their analyst and without the resources readily available that Dimen subsequently had at her deft disposal? And what is the fate of patients, *themselves clinicians*, where defensive patterns such as denial and isolation may not be tenable in today's clinical climate where heightened attention to boundary violations now pervades the larger analytic field of the professional community.

Although absolutely painful and damaging, silence and dissociation were, as protective strategies, a possibility for Dimen for many years. As Dimen (2011) underscored, her analysis was occurring at a very particular historical juncture where the analyst's authority and wisdom remained unquestioned. She was also a young adult and not yet a clinician herself, and gendered dynamics regarding sexuality and power—a woman patient with a male analyst—were at play as cultural basic assumptions. One could more easily cling to idealization as a way to blur the analyst's culpability. Today, the intense scrutiny that has now been brought to bear on the psychoanalytic relationship makes it more likely that patients (regardless of age or gender), and clinician-patients *especially*, will register that *something* is wrong, and has been for some time, when confronted with an inappropriate action or problematic stance of the analyst.

An announced ethical violation occurring with another patient will certainly trigger an avalanche of pain that is virtually unavoidable for any patient. While momentarily silenced as one is bludgeoned by the impact and reeling with shock, silence is not usually possible for long. The reality and egregious nature of such a violation is even less likely to be occluded when the patient is also a clinician. Though, in an effort to protect the good object and to refuse the reality of the loss, certain patients, including those who are clinicians, may still yield to rationalizations put forth by the analyst. This situation may include continuing in treatment with a clinician who is publicly known to have committed a violation.

More ambiguous infractions embedded within an analyst's countertransferential stance may also be more likely detected by a clinician–patient who can make use of her training to form an opinion, however shaky, that an impasse is not solely to do with her own difficulties. Regardless of the actual nature of the clinical breakdown across a spectrum, my attention here is particularly directed to clinician-patients as a group, though much of what I will discuss is applicable to any patient who feels betrayed.

As Dimen (2011) looked back, she could clearly identify *many* aspects of her analyst's approach to her that, while un-integrated at the time—"I failed to connect the dots" (p. 54)—she could, many years later, see as both sexually inappropriate and as narcissistically motivated acting out. In addition to imposing the sexual kiss represented in the title of Dimen's paper, "*Lapsus linguae*, or a slip of the tongue?", her analyst was inappropriate in innumerable ways. Referring to women patients on the couch, he commented to Dimen, "I get to look at their legs" (2011, p. 55). A line drawing of a prone naked woman hung at the foot of the couch. He regularly held forth on pet theories. Using his patient's rapt attention to puff himself up as "Doctor Knows Best," he enacted rather than analyzed the oedipal dynamics in their analytic field. It is truly lamentable that a patient would be subjected to such improprieties in a treatment and, furthermore, that she would not be able to register at the time that she had the grounds to object. Such a situation constitutes a perversion of analytic eroticism, poisoning the erotic into something that is sickly and defiled.

Yet, despite current increased awareness of clinician fallibility, in certain compromised treatments it can still be difficult to discern any obvious "errors" even with hindsight. In trying to assess what is within the scope of appropriate practice, a patient may get lost in shades of grey. Even when an overt violation by one's analyst with another patient becomes a known fact, this news intrudes into a treatment that might have seemed to be going well (enough). In such a situation, a patient may have had a good experience of her analysis, unaware that anything was amiss on the part of the analyst.

Nonetheless, whether violations occur within or outside of one's own treatment, when betrayal *is* registered, a patient's experience of a felt good object is brutally confronted with information that reveals her analyst to be a bad object. How are these two views able to cohere in one's mind when they come into crushing collision with one another? This colliding of good and bad is particularly difficult to resolve when the new information or realization cannot be linked initially, nor often for a protracted time, with any "aha moments" looking back. What if one can find no "dots" to connect with any certainty? The discrepancy between one's lived history and what is newly revealed is at its most dystonic—a tormenting, cognitive and emotional dissonance. The experience of being deceived by another is profoundly disorienting, as I have illustrated in Chapter 10 regarding sexual infidelity. Particularly disquieting is the added fear of having deceived oneself, of having been "blind" to a situation one "should" have somehow perceived.

In problematic treatment situations where no explicit ethical violation is evident, perceiving clinical infractions can be a very clouded endeavor for a patient, even a clinician–patient. An analyst's character/countertransference problems, embedded within the intersubjective analytic field, are not easy for a patient to identify *with confidence*. Feelings of uncertainty abound, "Did I know something was 'off'—yes, no?" The analyst has not committed a boundary violation in any overt, clearly recognizable sense. Instead, the analyst's narcissistic rigidities and subtle lapses in clinical integrity contribute to a treatment stalemated or broken off with a patient left traumatized.

Such character difficulties in the clinician can include inappropriate ways of handling a patient that antagonize, humiliate or otherwise undermine the patient's state of mind. An overinvestment in adherence to a particular theoretical model and wedded technical approach can result in abuses of interpretive power, with interpretations functioning as accusations. Clinician defensiveness can be cleverly disguised by lines of interpretation that, although they may be accurate, obscure an entrenched countertransference stance that persistently does not recognize or acknowledge the clinician's contribution to an impasse. Although patients can and certainly do play their part in impasses, it takes two to *tangle* (see Kantrowitz, 1992; Elkind, 1994; Harris, 2009)—the analytic field is jointly constructed (Ferro and Civitarese, 2015).

As Levin (2014) underscored, in a "tragic betrayal of the psychoanalytic spirit" (p. 195) narcissistic boundary violations by clinicians contribute heavily to impasses, stalemates, and to inadequate, even tormented, terminations. Levine (2010) defined narcissistic boundary violations as "nonsexual forms of misuse of the analyst's power and authority" (p. 43).[2] Either willingly or unwittingly, an analyst makes narcissistic use of a patient; such misuse is motivated by "personal self-aggrandizement [that overrides] an appropriate subordination of self-interest" (Levine, 2010, p. 43) to the analytic task. The atmosphere of the analytic field becomes toxic. A patient may not have the self-assurance to differentiate analytic authority in the service of *her growth* from an authoritarian arrogance on the part of the analyst that pulls for submission.

Confronted with these more ambiguous lapses in her clinician's integrity, a patient likely *feels* that something is wrong even though she has an extremely hard time *seeing* what exactly that might be. This dissonance creates a sense of being "crazy" and/or "just a bad patient" with a negative transference. If a clinician herself, she can easily make use of what she knows about developmental theory and personality disorders to pathologize her position. This perspective continuously oscillates with the use of her training, mentioned above, to critically assess the analyst. The result is a tortured perseveration between one "educated guess" and the other.

Much confusion over who is responsible for an impasse can extend over a considerable period of time, even indefinitely, both within and beyond the treatment, without such a patient receiving significant assistance. Yet that involvement from a third usually requires seeing a new analyst right at the time when faith in a therapeutic process is the most undermined and when the patient is also "paranoid" about being pathologized and blamed by the new analyst. After leaving the damaged treatment, she is likely to try to struggle forward on her own, as did Dimen, with no one to witness the degree of her loss—that a person is indeed *missing*.

In this chapter, I describe the loss of an analyst, experienced as a good object, when a felt sense of deception and betrayal intrudes on the analytic relationship and dismantles what has gone before. As is the case with infidelity, betrayal by a trusted other sends shockwaves reverberating not only forward into one's future but *backwards* into one's past. One's personal history is retroactively reconfigured (*Nachträglichkeit/après coup*): What has been becomes undone. Such unraveling of goodness is extremely painful in both the loss of the trusted relationship and in the assault on one's confidence in one's own mind, one's ability to detect deceit and bad faith. Without a viable termination, post-termination life is then undermined by a pernicious disintegration of the good internal object, along with a registering of the analysis as degraded. The patient is deprived of the treatment in the immediate present, *and* it is retroactively whisked away as well with little use to be made of it for the future. A loss of goodness infiltrates the representation of the object, the self, and the relationship of the two.

How does a patient cope with such an assault on her sense of reality, her ability to discern falseness in others? How does healing occur, and what is the role of a next analyst in helping a betrayed and despairing analysand to regain a sense of trust not only in the object world and in the analytic community, but in her own mind? What is needed in the analytic field of the new clinical setting that would be capable of transforming this particular source of mental pain? When the analysand is herself a clinician, what is the impact on her professional identity and how can a new analytic dyad repair such a multi-layered rupture and provide a time for grieving and integration?

A tear in the fabric of time

When confronted by the actual death of one's analyst (Deutsch, 2011, 2014; Elise, 2011, 2014), the sorrowful task of grieving is certainly demanding. Unfortunately, mourning becomes infinitely more difficult when the analyst has "died" as a good object. However sturdy one might be, mourning is initially overtaken by melancholia.

The absence of a hoped-for termination phase, though a somewhat obscured outcome of an ethical violation or a treatment broken off due to an impasse, is nonetheless quite malignant in its impact and reverberations. In these ruptured treatments, usually some, even many sessions were focused on the need to end prematurely but that discussion was definitely not a *good*, goodbye. Patients are then forced to construct their own termination not from a deceased good object but from an alive, bad object—a haunting, persecutory presence. The "sudden death" of the former good object must be mourned while contending with the intrusiveness of a "new" bad object that not only has taken over and destroyed the treatment trajectory but that gets in the way of a symbolic goodbye to the lost good analyst. The integrity of the analytic setting cracks and both participants fall through the fissures.

The egregious outcome of these damaged treatments results in the former analyst becoming a ghost—not at rest, or in peace—in the mind of the analysand. The clinician-analysand is robbed of a crucial ancestor (Loewald, 1960), and may come to feel that *only* ghosts haunt her professional identity. The parental generation collapses; along with it goes the foundation of the analysand's professional, as well as personal, well-being. Here we observe an attack on what should be positive manifestations of the oedipal complex; incest/perversion prevails instead of a generationally boundaried inheritance of maternal and paternal eroticism.

When one registers the import of a full termination to an analysis, one can more deeply understand how its absence contributes to the fallout of a breach of clinical integrity (see Burka, 2008). The actual breach understandably draws the focus, shadowing the reality that a true termination is foreclosed (Elise, 2014). One sees complicated bereavement rather than a productive process of mourning—something that *may* hopefully be fashioned by the patient at some *much later* point. In betrayal, mourning may be delayed in time far into the future—a crucial difference when confronted with the symbolic death of a good object versus a literal death of a good analyst. But that delay is only one aspect of how time figures into betrayal and deception: The vicissitudes of time enter the picture in significant, and quite complex, ways.

Betrayal introduces a rent in time. A thread is pulled and the fabric of time's linearity starts to unstitch itself, slowly then ever more rapidly unraveling. Unweaving itself, a psychic garment woven together by the clinical couple—both for immediate use and long-term wear—is dismantled. In a progressive erosion, a beloved figure is "disappeared." Where did they go; who took them away; who is at fault; where is the corruption to be located? There is now only a chalk outline where the good analyst used to be. And where did the "me" I know as myself go?

Losing one's past

In considering experiences of clinical betrayal, I want to call attention once again, as I did with the subject of sexual infidelity, to the sense of mental confusion that can result from the recognition of a deception regarding events that have been taking place over time, whether internal or external to one's own treatment. Here I will make use of my conceptualization of the dynamics of betrayal (Chapter 10) to examine clinical "infidelities." When a treating clinician fails to acknowledge a clinical lapse, the patient, upon discovery or realization, registers that she has been deceived. The patient now realizes that her sense of trust was being maintained in a situation that, unbeknownst to her, was compromised. In being deceived for some time, the *lived* reality of her treatment turns out to *not* be true. One now resides in the realm of betrayal.

This dynamic is most clearly evident when a boundary violation becomes an acknowledged fact, yet it also inheres in undermined clinical situations where a patient eventually comes to believe that her analyst has actively worked to deceive her into thinking a proper treatment was in place. One may be finally told the fact of a violation; subtle is the moment when denial falls away in one's own mind that one's analyst has not been functioning as he or she should. Even with a slowly dawning realization, a patient's sense of shock involves a feeling of suddenness and totality—that *everything* is changed "overnight" as one discovers that one's past is no longer.

As with sexual infidelity, the fact that clinical lapses of ethics and integrity have usually been occurring undetected for some time leads, upon discovery, to a need to rewrite one's treatment history. As the realization "hits" that one has been betrayed, the rug is pulled out from under the relationship to the good object, and the analysis is retroactively undone. This assault on truth (Elise 2012) can be potentially even more disruptive than the actual violation: One does not solely lose trust in the analyst, but in one's own mind, in one's hold not only on the object, but on reality (see Ferenczi, 1949). This dynamic is all the more powerfully disturbing when it resonates with similar elements in a patient's childhood history.

As theorized in Chapter 10, betrayal leads to a subjective experience of temporality such that meaning travels backward, suffusing one's object relational past and creating a *new history* that is personally registered—though not "remembered"—as immensely painful. A complex analytic literature on the subjective sense of time underscores the non-linearity of time in psychic life. Time is bi-directional such that past meaning can be re-transcribed retrospectively.

With deception, *truth is the trauma*. Discovering the truth reconfigures one's personal history without necessarily referring back to any prior event(s) registered as upsetting at the time they occurred. As mentioned above, a patient may have experienced her analysis, when it was in progress, as beneficial—a basically, good relationship. This earlier life, innocent of the knowledge that any distressing "event" is taking place, now needs to be completely restructured.

Deliberations over how to respond to a suspected betrayal generate intense feelings of anxiety and self-doubt. A long-standing stalemate is continually approached by the analyst as evidence of the patient's personal difficulties that brought her into treatment. Such a stance—reflecting a technical regression to a one-person focus that loses hold of an understanding of the co-created nature of the analytic field—is difficult to combat. Or a clinician–patient hears rumors about her analyst being involved in some wrong doing that leave her unsettled and unsure about how to proceed. In either situation, a patient wonders if she should try to confront her analyst; how should she go about it? What if her analyst denies any culpability or even responsibility?

Patients going through an experience of betrayal by their analyst can feel severely disrupted for extended periods; registering such betrayal can feel catastrophic. A patient may feel that she is truly losing her mind, her psychic stability, and may fear that she no longer knows "which way is up." This experience can be quite destabilizing. The analytic field, becoming psychotic, sado-masochistic, or both, is completely undermined in its function as a generative container.

One is then faced with the painful task of reconstructing *past* reality. As Dimen (2011) stated, one must "recast the past" (p. 39) in order to "restore depth and time" (p. 38) to one's experience. Efforts to go back in time often focus on intensive, "fact-finding" searches that are excruciatingly painful, yet urgent. A patient finds herself absorbed in researching the evolution of an acknowledged boundary violation by her analyst against another patient as she tries to line up the transgression with what was happening in her own treatment at that approximate time period. Another tries to put together her eventual understanding of her analyst's compromised clinical stance in her own treatment with what her experience had been as the treatment was unfolding.

In each situation, a patient cannot begin to heal until the treatment past is revisited and re-aligned with the reality of what has occurred rather than what had been believed at the time. While immersed in this excruciatingly painful process, the patient can suffer great anxiety and mistrust in all object relationships, *including and most especially in that with a new analyst*. As is the case for patients contending with sexual infidelity, restoration of psychic balance is typically preceded by a period of intrapsychic and interpersonal upheaval. In order to regain a grasp on the past, one must look back, so as to restore confidence in a personal sense of reality testing and thus to have any hope for the future.

Understandably, these patients fear being betrayed again. This fear of the future, based on a past betrayal, darkens the present. Since a betrayed analysand had never imagined being unable to rely on her analyst's integrity, how would she know if anything similar was occurring in a subsequent treatment? As identified in Chapter 10, undermined trust in one's mind in relationship to one's objects has far-reaching consequences and requires the exceedingly difficult, complex effort at rebuilding *trust in the self*— specifically, trust in one's mind, one's capacity to differentiate truth from fiction, to detect deceit. Each patient's unique personal history regarding the issue of trusting her own mind will add to the mix and to the need for further analysis. Can a betrayed analysand risk accepting a new analyst's help in this task of internal restoration and further growth?

Complicated beginnings

Dimen (2011) asked, "under what circumstances can the damage inflicted by such an ethical lapse be transformed?"(p. 35). She identified that:

> It is only after the fact, upon reflection—usually with someone else—that we can begin to name, with varying degrees of success, that which refuses symbolization" (Dimen, 2011, p. 53): "In helping you to re-represent your experience, the [next] analyst offers the means to reclaim and regenerate your own life.
>
> (Dimen, 2011, p. 45)

This outcome is certainly what we hope for in a subsequent treatment, yet we must also be aware that this endeavor is quite fraught. A next treatment is ideally an erotic project that helps a patient to re-invest in libidinal life through reconnecting with erotically based energies; yet, this effort must begin in a place where erotic vitality has been corrupted.

As when complicated bereavement leads to melancholy rather than grieving, a "complicated termination" leads to a complicated beginning phase of a next analytic effort with extensive challenges for both parties of the new dyad. The patient is usually in a state of agitation and deep depression, her equilibrium lost. Personal and professional angst are interwoven in clinician-patients: They lament, "What if I can't *be analyzed*?" This question leads directly to the next for candidates: "What if I can't *be* an analyst; would I be an analyst my patients could trust?" As Levin wrote (2014), "How does one go on being an analyst, or becoming one, after the traumatic rupture of one's faith in the profession?" (p. 193). What if being an analyst is *not worth being*? All this is at stake as a patient tries to begin again. It is a daunting task for the next analyst, as well, to cope with this particular "presenting problem"—one that presents such a challenge to analytic eroticism: The patient fears re-traumatization to the libidinally attached self and thus is wary of an embodied affective connection. What shape does the analytic field take when a patient comes to a new analyst after a devastating experience with a former clinician?

In working with a number of patients, often clinicians themselves, who have come from variously compromised treatments, I have been struck by the profoundly different cast this past places on a new analysis. I believe that it is crucial for clinicians to think about what is involved before actually starting such a treatment, as the situation requires an analyst to provide a very particular type of container—one that focuses centrally on an intricate, three person relation that includes the prior clinician for an extended period of time (often years). Unlike more typical clinical understandings of what will unfold in the "beginning phase" of an analysis, this treatment, if it does unfold, will be an embroiled *ménage à trois*. This therapeutic context is quite different from one with a focus on the new analytic dyad that might be more familiar in beginning analytic work. Any potential enthusiasm for the new analytic couple is foreclosed.

The new analyst must be prepared for a tormented triangle, without expectations of moving into any "cozy," or erotic, dyadic intimacy as she or he takes on the role of offering herself to a patient who is in the midst of a painful "break-up" with another analyst. Not only is this "other" a clinician like oneself, the individual's identity, if revealed by the patient as it frequently will be, may be a known colleague, and that reality is often recognized by a clinician–patient. Then both patient and new analyst will have the very difficult task of initiating their relationship by discussing a third person, known to them each, but with the exact nature of the "knowing" between the new analyst and the former one unclear to the patient. Although certainly a real person in external life, the former analyst also becomes a character in the newly forming analytic field, a character that can change shape in a dizzying sequence.

Decisions over whether or not to reveal the former clinician's actual identity are very conflicted for a patient and complicated for the next treatment. With an ethical violation widely known within the community, the patient may assume you already know of the problem. This situation explicitly illustrates the influence of the larger professional community on the setting within the consulting room; the analytic field of the treatment is porous and is permeated by external factors. In contrast, when the difficulty concerns impasse and more ambiguous clinical lapses within the patient's treatment, she may feel she is "telling on" the clinician and be anxious that she alone is potentially ruining your view of this colleague. She may both fear this outcome and wish for it. If guilt is a strong element, having revealed a name may reduce freedom to speak. Caution and care need to be taken regarding this one aspect alone. It is a challenge to hold open the virtual reality (Civitarese, 2012) of the analytic field, intersecting as it does with external reality.

When the identity of the former clinician *is* revealed by a patient, a torrent of questions about the possible real life relationship between the two analysts leads to further anxiety for the patient: "*How well* do you know each other? Are you friends, respected colleagues, supervisee/supervisor? Do you like my former analyst, or do you see something in him or her that correlates with my feeling betrayed?" If the new analyst is imagined to think well of the former, the patient quickly concludes in her mind that her tale of woe will not be taken as reasonable lament; instead, she will be blamed and the former analyst exonerated. On the other hand, if you are envisioned as knowing, but having doubts about the competence of the prior analyst, this view then seems to confirm that analyst's badness in the patient's mind and to deepen the sense of loss and of being the victim of therapeutic misdoing. This question is a looming presence in the analytic field: Who is "bad": the former clinician, the patient, *you as well*?

It is most apparent that a patient coming from a traumatic goodbye definitely does *not* want to say hello to a new analyst, though she or he is desperately in need of one. The patient is in a heightened state of mistrust about seeking help *from a clinician in a therapy context*. Faith in a "good analyst" is at its lowest; the analytic setting is tainted. The source of the pain is the former clinician, and a new analyst is another such person (see Celenza, 2007, 2014). The degree of ambivalence about entering a new treatment is rarely higher. Further treatment feels hopeless, futile, a painful and dangerous liaison with no good outcome; Eros is absent. To begin such a clinical venture feels completely daunting when one is already so traumatized and depleted. These patients seriously doubt that there is any therapeutic ground upon which to rebuild, re-establish, their own personal well-being and, if clinicians themselves, professional identity and sense of integrity.

Approach-avoidant impulses oscillate with stunning frequency and intensity. Some part of the patient recalls having had at one time a faith in therapists, but to be helped by you, she or he must trust you, and that feels like setting oneself up to be re-traumatized—a vital danger to be avoided at all cost. It is the force of their need that brings these patients to you, ever so ambivalently, and quite distraught. They are at their most vulnerable, immensely distressed, tearful, unable to sleep, regressed, agitated and aggravated, feeling tremendous conflict in their feelings about the former clinician and in angst over their confusion about how to understand their experience.

Often still quite attached to the analyst once trusted, even (erotically) loved, a patient is desperate to protect that experience—the image of the analyst, the relationship, and a sense of themselves as loving and good. Each patient is also suffused with grave misgivings: Was the former analyst ever *truly* good; was that belief a fantasy, self-deception? Is that analyst actually now "bad," or is it oneself—a "bad" patient—who has spoiled the analyst with the inability to still see him or her in a good light? Was it she, the patient, who acted destructively and damaged her analyst? All this torment is brought to the initial encounters with the new analyst, and will be the focus for many months, even years, as the new analysis "begins" and a new analytic field emerges.

The new analyst needs to be prepared for this intricate endeavor, to be sensitively attuned to the patient's competing anxieties, to contain complex pressures from within the analytic field, and to hold out hope for a transformative process, no matter how complicated and protracted. The new analyst, drawing on analytic eroticism, must be fully, libidinally available for an unfolding treatment, but not eager for it in a manner that overrides the patient's deep ambivalence about such a prospect. In this context, analytic eroticism refers to a capacity to be passionately patient. Even proving yourself trustworthy—as we typically hope to do with new patients—is a mixed blessing: You could betray her if she trusts you, and she knows she cannot sustain any more damage. If a clinician herself, a second analytic disaster would confirm that she is "crazy" and too disturbed to partake of, let alone practice, her own profession.

Mistrust is not limited to despair in her personal life but can seep deeply into the patient's own professional identity as a clinician. To lose one's faith in one's chosen profession is a very profound loss—a libidinal loss with many layers of investment now devitalized. Confidence built over years of training and clinical practice becomes undermined, as does any sense of promise for an analytic future as a member of professional community. This devastating sense of professional disillusionment eats away at work life right when absorption in work might be an adaptive effort. Each session in her practice is an hour in confrontation with her own former treatment, as well as with her current situation. Where to go? This new treatment is no escape, but a stepping right back into the den of the lion.

As the former treatment and image of the good analyst unravels with increasing momentum, the patient needs to be emotionally held in the onslaught of this disequilibrium. Yet the *"holding" of the new treatment will itself be threatening*, contributing as it does by contrast to further crumbling of the idealization of the prior clinician. The concept of therapeutic alliance takes on an entirely new set of meanings; the relationship is paradoxical from the beginning, "going downhill" even when the work is going well. "Going well" means being in a sharp descent into deepening realization of the prior treatment as having gone wrong somewhere, somehow, all of which is completely unclear and shrouded in confusion. There is a felt sense of being on a bicycle that is going too fast, and is now headed down a steep hill, careening wildly out of control.

Dismay in the countertransference

For the current analyst, especially when struggling with this predicament for the first time, an array of dismaying affects presents in quick succession. Any expectations and excitement regarding a promising new analysis unfolding in a relatively steady, potentially gratifying manner with a prospective patient quickly yield to the recognition that one is witness to a disaster. This next analyst hears something she or he does not want to be true: A treatment has left a patient feeling seriously damaged.

Clinicians have each gone into the "helping profession;" we want to help; we are identified as individuals who help, not hurt. We are deeply disturbed to hear of this reversal; it is an assault on our own professional ideals and pride in our efforts over many decades, encompassing years of education and training, and clinical practice. Now, up close and personal, we are hearing excruciating details of a treatment gone wrong, badly wrong. One's own analytic spirit may dive.

Typically, the patient had respected and trusted the former clinician for many years; idealization, with conscious or unconscious erotic elements, often had been high and sustained, and now hate is likely predominating, but both feeling states alternate in the wake of a crushing de-idealization. When patients speak to one side, they fear they have "seduced" you into a biased view, whether that be to the good or to the bad in "assessing" the former clinician. When they speak of their love, and thus their doubt about the clinician's culpability, they fear you will join with them in whitewashing the actions/role of the former clinician. When they speak of their hate, they fear they will have tainted your view of that clinician, and that in siding with the patient, you will have lost any objective balance that could eventually lead to a genuine working through. Varying erotic investments oscillate throughout the analytic field that is being newly, precariously generated.

Such anxieties in the patient create immense pressure in the clinician's experience within the analytic field. Integration of good and bad regarding the image of the former analyst is difficult for the next analyst, as well as for the patient. Yet, this analyst must try to create space for psychic reality in the face of these complex external circumstances. A certain form of balanced positioning is necessary, but can be perceived as suspicion of the patient. We like to be cautious about reaching for conclusions, but hesitation can be taken as disbelief and may sever any delicate bond that might be forming in the new treatment relation. Empathy is greatly needed, yet can seem like collusion with the patient.

Analysts hope to be empathic, especially with new patients in distress, but empathy can be taken as indictment of the former analyst. If you empathize with the patient's feeling of being betrayed, deceived, wounded, you are further "killing off" the good object. However, if you empathize with the patient's love for the lost good object, you can seem to be saying that the patient "made all this up" and that the problems are all of their own doing. Either way, your slightest expression, tone, comment, can be taken as a verdict; you are "the judge." Potential space is collapsed; clinical creativity is crushed. In a Catch 22, you are likely, *repeatedly*, to either confirm the loss of goodness in the former analyst or in the patient's sense of self. This analytic situation can feel like something of a bad dream repeating/seesawing in sessions for months. It takes significant time and therapeutic skill just to establish an analytic context that encompasses recognition of *all* that the patient feels toward their prior analyst, rather than falling to one side or the other.

One might say that the initial transference in this new treatment is an acute form of disordered attachment, a situation not unlike fostering an adolescent who has come from a disrupted home. This new relationship is going to start as a tenuous tie at best, threatening to come apart on a regular basis. For both you and your patient, the former clinician will be in your life, in this new treatment, for a long time. The path forward will be rocky, unstable, and this "other" love will shadow your every moment together. The atmosphere is dispiriting. Patience will be imperative.

Even when a positive connection starts building with this new patient, a new anxiety is generated for the clinician: Transitory transference idealization that could be developmentally appropriate in an initial phase with another patient, here can feel indistinguishable from "trashing" the prior clinician—a triangulation that would cement one side of the patient's feelings and prevent healing.

As time passes, often two or three years, hopefully a trusting and productive analysis is unfolding with wounds starting to heal and the patient feeling re-stabilized. Yet the lingering shadow of the former clinician can still seep in like a fog, chilling the climate of the analytic field. It may take the entirety of the second treatment before the first is *fully* worked through. The new analyst must never think that the former clinician is gone "for good;" she or he will return again and again and again. You are not choreographing a *pas de deux*; that "other" will have to be let on (often center) stage as a prominent character in the field. It will never be "just the two of you." One's own disappointment, disillusionment, narcissistic wounding, erotic jealousy—not feeling "important," trusted, even liked—must all be able to be contained while offering a vitalizing context for this patient to heal, with you a seeming bystander, though working hard in efforts crucial to the future of the patient and the analysis.

We well know that patients in analysis (including ourselves) want to be the "only one" for their analyst and experience jealousy of their analyst's other patients, supervisees, friends and partners. Much of clinical practice has us working on this issue as it surfaces in the analytic field. But we can tend to take for granted much of the time that we are the "only one" for each of our patients. Often, no other relationship can seem to be able to compete with what we can potentially offer to each patient: *We* are *the special one*. So it is a jolt to the analyst to so regularly hear of just how wonderful this former analyst was before the patient felt betrayed. Now *you* are the one to come second to a "competitor."

Narcissistic deflation can lead an analyst to join too "empathically" in a patient's critical feelings about the former analyst or, instead, to withdraw her own libidinal investment from the analysis. Clinicians know the dangers of triangulating against a third person, but in these circumstances quite a bit of balance is required over considerable time in order not to fall into such an enactment. It may seem that we are far from the significance of analytic eroticism; however, I stress that analytic ardor takes many forms and, in circumstances such as these, manifests in the capacity to create and maintain a life-line to a patient who is in danger of drowning. This effort requires that a clinician remain in contact with the vitality of his or her own being and thus with the desire to forge a generative connection.

Professional community "disappearances"

Just as a betrayed clinician–patient cannot go to her own therapy practice without being deeply immersed in these issues, neither can the analyst of these patients escape regular confrontation with the experience of betrayal, deception, and of having to go back and reconfigure the past. Much of the time, one *does* know, or know of, the former analyst, who may even be a member of your own institute. You now may be getting a very different picture of that colleague, one that is certainly more disturbing to hear of the closer you feel to that clinician. You may have to rework your relationship to this person, and yet can say nothing to that individual or to anyone else. Even though surrounded by the circumstances of the larger professional field, staying located within the analytic field of the treatment constitutes a crucial guiding principle.

The reality of this isolation is especially palpable when no overt violation has occurred that is openly acknowledged. Many possible clinical lapses are ambiguous rather than identifiable facts. Your new patient's disclosures may be being made solely to you. If you have had cause to register some doubts about that clinician's capacities, character, or ethics, hearing what may feel to be confirming disclosures from your new patient is a disconcerting experience as well. Containment of personal countertransference to such revelations can be a quite demanding, ongoing effort that calls on clinician integrity in maintaining utmost confidentiality.

Your new patient is definitely expressing the feeling that quite possibly no analyst is a reliable, grounded individual, and you may start to join them in wondering if that might actually be true. There is an assault on one's confidence in and respect for the profession: Are we all disturbed individuals unknowingly inflicting further damage on our patients, one generation to the next in a contamination of the field at large? Has an erring clinician been the recipient of misdoing in his or her own treatment and then participated in a transgenerational transmission of trauma (Faimberg, 2005)? This registering of subterranean doubt is profoundly disquieting, especially right when one is trying to convey to a traumatized patient that hope and trust can be restored, in herself, in you as her analyst, and in the vitality of the analytic field, both in and outside of the consulting room.

With confirmed ethical violations, the clinical community as a whole must also contend with "disappearances" of individual analysts. Institutes grieve. Silence must give way to shared lament. Much is being written (see Deutsch, 2014; Demos, 2017; Slochower, 2018) about this group level reaction to losses of individual members and of the piece of the professional tapestry that was in place in that individual's contributions. It is so very painful when an admired, respected, highly contributing colleague is suddenly "disappeared" from institute life. The task of coming to terms with this loss spreads out to include most of the community. Everyone is reworking their relationship to that colleague at the same time, but typically with group level basic assumptions and splitting rendering people at odds with one another (often for lengthy periods of time) in how they are holding their relationship to the erring clinician. Group level shame, blame, guilt, moralism, regret, and responsibility all come into play when confronted with a loss of pride in a profession that should garner respect.

What I am identifying in this discussion is the way in which an individual analyst will have a unique experience of a community-wide loss in treating a patient who has suffered the loss of this clinician as her own analyst. This new treatment relationship becomes a daily confrontation with something very sad. With a clinician–patient who has suffered a compromised earlier analysis, the next analyst is likely to empathically identify with such a loss in a profound manner; these two form a unique pairing in a very troubled circumstance where a dove-tailing of external and intrapsychic events creates a powerful intersubjective matrix within the analytic field. Perhaps one of the rewards of working through the loss of a colleague due to an ethical violation in the context of a treatment with an injured patient is that *splitting is not a tenable stance*. As together you both look back, acknowledge a loss, re-find a sense of sequence in time, and re-establish a trust in the capacities of one's own mind, the shock of betrayal and deception softens into poignant recognition of something hopefully more tolerable—the frailty of humanity.

Conclusion

Analysts are familiar with certain patients coming to us in a very traumatized state, yet when the focus of that distress is another clinician and a former treatment, we find that the clinical picture changes drastically. My intent in this chapter has been to elaborate a patient's subjective experience of betrayal—the loss of her analyst as a good object—and the undermining of confidence in her own mind to discern truth. The exact nature of a betrayal is definitely of central significance in working with any given patient who has come for subsequent treatment. Certainly a pronounced difference exists between an acknowledged ethical violation—often known to an entire community and incontrovertible—and a potentially problematic clinical stance. Narcissistic violations tend to be insidious and often cannot be proven to be facts. The contribution of such character problems in a clinician will typically remain a murky area where a patient has to learn to rely on her own discernment. Although in some situations an analyst's character difficulties may become so well known that some external validation may be acquired, frequently there will be little or no corroborating "evidence" from others. The patient must eventually make her own determination.

For a patient coping with such losses, both symbolic and real, complexity mounts in a layering of demanding psychic tasks: mourning the lost good analyst, the past as she knew it, her former self, and a lost future; overcoming melancholic submission to a persecutory object; risking new relationships—to others and to the self—in order to contend with the anguish of betrayal and to reconcile with a truth. As Dimen (2011) identified, "My struggle in writing this account has been to balance my loss, grief, and fear of shame with the capacity to think ... and to grieve while speaking" (p. 39). For a next analysis to be reparative, time must be fashioned into a web that can hold these intricate psychic maneuvers.

A grave disservice is done to the full potential of this new treatment to consider it as a "rebound relationship." In its confrontation with pain and loss, this endeavor is far from any attempt at escape and manic defense. This next clinical situation might be viewed as an extended consultation and/or as a bridge to a possible future analysis with another clinician. I believe, however, that an unfolding of a full analysis in the present context is a genuine possibility that this next analyst, through analytic eroticism, must hold "in trust" for this patient. In so doing, we envision a future, seeded in the present that will afford a space to look back. Later, *much later*, we two will also say goodbye—hopefully a *good* goodbye.

Notes

1 I will be using "ethical violations" as an inclusive term covering a spectrum of professional misconduct.
2 Of course, narcissism plays a significant role in sexual boundary violations as well.

References

Botella, C. and Botella, S. (2005). *The work of psychic figurability: Mental states without representation.* Hove, England: Brunner-Routledge.

Burka, J. B. (2008). Psychic fallout from breach of confidentiality: A patient/analyst's perspective. *Contemporary Psychoanalysis,* 44: 177–198.

Celenza, A. (2007). *Sexual boundary violations: Therapeutic, supervisory, and academic contexts.* New York: Jason Aronson.

—— (2014). *Erotic revelations: Clinical applications and perverse Scenarios.* New York: Routledge.

Civitarese, G. (2012). *The violence of emotions: Bionian and post-Bionian psychoanalysis.* London: Routledge.

—— (2016). *Truth and the unconscious in psychoanalysis.* London: Routledge.

Demos, V. C. (2017). When the frame breaks: Ripple effects of sexual boundary violations. *Psychoanalytic Psychology,* 34: 201–207.

Deutsch, R. (2011). A voice lost, a voice found: After the death of the analyst. *Psychoanalytic Inquiry,* 31: 526–535.

—— (2014). *Traumatic ruptures: Abandonment and betrayal in the analytic relationship.* London: Routledge.

Dimen, M. (2011). *Lapsus linguae,* or a slip of the tongue? A sexual violation in an analytic treatment and its personal and theoretical aftermath. *Contemporary Psychoanalysis,* 47: 35–79.

Elise, D. (2011). Time to say goodbye: On time, trauma, and termination. *Psychoanalytic Inquiry,* 31: 591–600.

—— The danger in deception: Oedipal betrayal and the assault on truth. *Journal of the American Psychoanalytic Association,* 6: 679–705.

—— Saying goodbye: Traumatic reverberations in the subjective sense of time. In Deutsch, R. (Ed.), *Traumatic ruptures: Abandonment and betrayal in the analytic relationship.* London: Routledge, pp. 199–215.

Elkind, S.N. (1994). The consultant's role in resolving impasses in therapeutic relationships. *American Journal of Psychoanalysis,* 54: 3–13.

Faimberg, H. (2005). *The telescoping of generations: Listening to the narcissistic links between generations.* London: Routledge.

Ferenczi, S. (1949). Confusion of the tongues between the adults and the child—(The language of tenderness and of passion). *International Journal of Psychoanalysis,* 30: 225–230.

Ferro, A. and Civitarese, G. (2015). *The analytic field and its transformations.* London: Karnac.

Hampton, C. (2003). *Imagining Argentina*. USA: Arenas Entertainment.
Harris, A. (2009). "You must remember this." *Psychoanalytic Dialogues*, 19: 2–21.
Kantrowitz, J. L. (1992). The analyst's style and its impact on the analytic process: Overcoming a patient-analyst stalemate. *Journal of the American Psychoanalytic Association*, 40: 169–194.
Levin, C. (2014). Trauma as a way of life in a psychoanalytic institute. In Deutsch, R. (Ed.), *Traumatic ruptures: Abandonment and betrayal in the analytic relationship*. London: Routledge, pp. 176–196.
Levine, H. B. (2010). The sins of the fathers: Freud, narcissistic boundary violations, and their effects on the politics of psychoanalysis. *International Forum of Psychoanalysis*, 19: 43–50.
Loewald, H. W. (1960). On the therapeutic action of psychoanalysis. *International Journal of Psychoanalysis*, 41: 16–33.
Ogden, T. H. (2000). Borges and the art of mourning. *Psychoanalytic Dialogues*, 10: 65–88.
— (2004). The analytic third: Implications for psychoanalytic theory and technique. *Psychoanalytic Quarterly*, 73: 167–195.
— (2005). *This art of psychoanalysis*. New York: Routledge.
— (2017). Dreaming the analytic session: A clinical essay. *The Psychoanalytic Quarterly*, 86: 1–20.
Slochower, J. (2018). Introduction to panel: Ghosts that haunt—sexual boundary violations in our communities. *Psychoanalytic Dialogues*, 27: 61–66.

Chapter 12

Narcissistic seductions and the collapse of the creative

In this final chapter of the book, I consider the broader professional context in which we train and practice—our larger analytic field—and address a tendency toward overconfident knowing on the part of a clinician that is reflective of narcissistic dynamics. I will be paying particular attention to the pressure placed on clinicians, especially in training, to perform a role as a knowledgeable and knowing authority. Such a stance interferes with the capacity I refer to as analytic eroticism—a capacity that flows from playful spontaneity, mutual inquiry, and creative interchange.

In Chapter 11, I discussed the impact of the subjective experience of betrayal by a clinician not solely upon the patient, but on the next analysis and analyst and on the community. Now we can enlarge our vantage point to include perspectives from the reverse direction: The impact of the professional community on the individual clinician and, thus, on each treatment pair and their particular analytic field. I want to identify another type of troubled dialectic between knowing and not knowing—not the anxious uncertainty of a betrayed patient described in the previous chapter, but a pressure toward interpretative certainty in an analyst that can overshoot the mark, where conviction turns to arrogance.

A complicated relationship exists to narcissistic gratification and deprivation within our field, in our professional training and life, and in our actual practice of psychoanalysis (see Levine, 2010; Wilson, 2003). Questions arise regarding the extent of narcissistic injuries that may be incurred by clinicians: What is it in our community life that may inadvertently foster ethical violations—that accentuates rather than ameliorates narcissistic difficulties and acting out in generations of clinicians? How might clinicians feel shamed in training, a re-wounding in areas of narcissistic vulnerability? To what extent are clinicians engaged in a struggle throughout professional life to subdue shame and achieve narcissistic balance by approval seeking? How does this effort play out in institute life and how might it then wreak havoc in treatments? What is the relationship between narcissistic injury/deprivation and undermined libidinal life? These questions are, of course, disturbing to contemplate.

It is evident that narcissistic difficulties in a clinician are an intrinsic part of sexual boundary violations (Dimen, 2015; Gabbard, 2015); narcissistic dynamics also contribute to impasses, stalemates, and ruptured terminations. Narcissistic fragility in the clinician is at the crux of these situations, whether this difficulty shows up as arrogant superiority—a sense of being special, "above it all," a need to be idealized—or as brittle defensiveness or as a pull toward erotic enthrallment. A sense of narcissistic deprivation can intensify hunger for forms of gratification that may undermine the integrity of an analysis and harm a patient. Narcissistic currents exert their force within the analytic field of a treatment until a vulnerable clinician succumbs to an ethical lapse, whether overt or undetected.

As narcissistic inducements would appear to underlie most clinician lapses, including a perverting of the erotic into sexualized assaults on the frame, then we must look to what it is about our professional life—"to institutional as well as human failure" (Dimen, 2015, p. 577)—that does not provide better holding and containment in this area to its practitioners. Training itself places inordinate pressure on this vulnerable area of the psyche—stimulating narcissistic wishes that may be gratified or dashed. It may be necessary to heighten significantly our attention to dynamics of narcissistic vulnerability that 1) lead individuals into the field, 2) become reinforced, even exacerbated, in training rather than worked through and attenuated, and then 3) result in various collapses of clinical functioning in unfortunate circumstances that are far too frequent.

Gabbard (2015) spoke of narcissistic blind spots in analysts, a narcissistic aggrandizement such that stature in the field comes to carry with it a belief that the "rules don't apply" (p. 580). As one patient expressed: "He is simply special. He knows what he is doing" (Gabbard and Lester, 1995, p. 135)—a belief thoroughly endorsed by such an analyst who likely has achieved a high level of professional success. However, Gabbard (2015) also noted that:

> analysts who become sexually involved with a patient have often become disillusioned, bitter, and resentful about their analytic training, their analytic organization, or the analytic field in general. There also

may be a deep narcissistic wound in such analysts who think that they have not been treated in the way that they deserve to be treated

(p. 583)

An explicit link is made here between narcissistic deprivation experienced in professional life and violations of a sexual boundary that constitute an erosion of the *aesthetic*, ethical use of analytic eroticism in the service of productive analytic work.

Gabbard (2015) mentioned examples of denied promotions to training analyst or to administrative positions; one can think of many other professional disappointments. Within the professional community, a clinician may feel special *or* may feel especially devalued. For the latter group, a deep feeling of narcissistic injury or insult and the resultant sense of shameful deficiency can intensify a vulnerability to libidinally gratifying temptations within the treatment relationship. As example, Dimen (2015) described the analyst who is "riding high on the pride and pleasure" (p. 575) of "an idealizing transference in which the analyst embodies all truth, authority, and perfection" (p. 573). Within such an analytic field, inappropriate libidinal gratifications persist as basic assumptions with no "second look" (Baranger and Baranger, 2008; Ferro and Civitarese, 2015) correcting the clinical course. The analyst does not reflect on his reveries (Ogden, 1997) of narcissistic pleasure. Things are as they are.

I want to draw attention to ongoing subtle practices with regard to the acquiring of knowledge and prestige—a "culture of narcissism" (Lasch, 1991) within our professional field—that can pervade even the best of programs/institutes/communities and that can negatively affect most any clinician. I suggest that such a narcissistic culture lends itself to boundary violations that are then a violation of analytic eroticism just as child abuse is a violation of maternal/paternal eroticism. Lack of professional attention to the *clinician's libidinal life* sets up a situation where analytic integrity can be undermined.

Harris (2015) described the effect on the treatment frame of "the setting, the surrounding ideologies, the prevailing theoretical frameworks and the institutional practices and experiences from which the analyst is functioning" (p. 588). She underscored that "we need to know much more about what is carried in an organization's history and practices" (Harris, 2015, p. 590) and about what can "befall treatments when the setting becomes the repository of disturbed and disturbing material" (Harris, 2015, p. 588).

Dimen (2015) referred to a hierarchical system of distributing power within psychoanalysis that establishes attitudes and practices that perpetuate these asymmetries. These dynamics then may be replicated in the analytic field of any given treatment. Discussing the emotionally powerful and deeply disturbing subject of patients who are left feeling harmed by their treatments, Dimen, Gabbard, and Harris have each emphasized fault-lines in the clinician's character posed by narcissism, shame, and identification with the aggressor, as well as the transmission of problematic institutional dynamics that are reiterated generationally in a "trickle down" effect.

I find it compelling to reflect on this issue of how the psychoanalytic community might be adversely affecting its practitioners. This inquiry seems to be a crucial project if we are to ever see a diminished incidence of damaging treatments. We need to know what it is about our professional community that fails to support individual clinicians in a manner that might reduce the potential for narcissistically motivated violations, overt and covert. As identified by Morrison (1989) in the title of his book, the underside of narcissism is shame. Shame—a shrinking in the face of undermined self-esteem—would be the antithesis of a robust libidinal vitality that could be employed productively, ethically, in clinical practice.

Unfortunately, a potential for shame reverberates in an unseen force field that is our professional life. Harris (2015) conveyed shame's power as a "truly terrible affect" which can be "transformed into various forms of action and erotic force, but at base it is a catastrophic system crash, where the person, from childhood on, feels the collapse of self" (p. 589). We need to appreciate the toxic effect of shame in the lives of clinicians, including in our childhood histories and in the repetitions within our professional life—the intricate relationship of narcissistic seductions and shame-filled collapses of narcissistic equilibrium. We must better understand how the specter of shame can haunt our professional training and community life, leading to various accumulated injuries and resentments that predispose to narcissistic enactments on the part of a clinician.

Knowing all/all knowing

It is said that we each use our self as our "instrument." This is a tall order: our instrument is human and flawed, fallible. To swim in tricky clinical waters, one must use something other than brute force (of intellect); one must use the self in a larger way within the intersubjective engagement of the analytic field. But what is the narcissistic balance in this self? Does training further, even reward, a libidinal imbalance where perfectionistic strivings persist, shadowed by the anxious apprehension of shame-filled "failures?" In what ways does our professional life perch on narcissistic tensions in the psyches of its practitioners, leaving a residue of injury to self-esteem and a depletion of healthy narcissistic supplies that ideally would support the aesthetic capacity for analytic eroticism? How can we support humility rather than inflict humiliation?

Gabbard (2015) warned that "analysts themselves cannot be sure when they are making narcissistic use of a patient and departing from what is optimally analytic or therapeutic for the patient" (p. 581). Reflecting on one's unconscious motivations is challenging and unlikely to happen without a theoretical model that supports this technical goal. Complex boundary dynamics are implicated, not solely where a boundary is crossed, but additionally in those situations where a boundary is held too rigidly, often in the service of the analyst's narcissistic investment in a theory, a technique, a representation of self as the one who knows. This pressure to be knowledgeable may intensify narcissistic resistances to ongoing *learning* that can infiltrate the entire training experience and then seep into treatment relationships such that the clinician forgets to learn *from, and with, the patient*.

Our training capitalizes on our investment in being willing to go to school longer than anyone else, a charged libidinal cathexis to a hierarchical mode of relating to knowledge. The very depth and complexity of psychoanalytic theory and technique, while compelling, can itself impose a subtle strain—a pressured quest to know, to keep acquiring *more* knowledge. Competitive strivings for status, and to impress, result in a narcissistic environment where the value is on performance with anticipated humiliation an associated threat. Clinicians can experience significant pressure to demonstrate intellectual prowess. Much emphasis is placed on intellectual mastery of an ever-increasing body of knowledge; knowing is privileged, with insufficient attention to *being*, and to being emotionally present with our patients. The fear of *not* knowing can generate anxiety about the anticipated shame of being identified as "stupid." An undermining atmosphere can infiltrate classes, case conferences, supervision, professional presentations, institutional politics, where anxious striving may leave individuals teetering on that edge between narcissistic triumph and collapse—a "narcissistic cliff" that may underlie professional life and clinical practice.

I want to call further attention to the "Father Knows Best" phallic-narcissistic dimension of the field as it can be occupied by both men and women and then transformed into an "Analyst Knows Best" identification that is deeply internalized over decades of training and post-training development. We witness the wish for idealized models of perfect knowledge to emulate. Emphasis on correct dynamic formulations and employment of "the best" theoretical model, with a proposed technical stance and interpretative strategy, can entrench a need to be right, to know best—a defensive rigidity rather than the humble flexibility needed in approaching impasses, stalemates, and disrupted terminations. If training is understood as aimed at being unassailable in our knowledge of psychoanalytic theory and technique—knowing more, more, and more at the level of intellect—is it any wonder that clinicians can get stuck in this mode, valorized as part of the "analytic conviction" that one has striven so long to acquire?

Most clinicians are in private practice; we don't actually *have* a job; we have to be rehired every week. Professional stature influences reputation, referrals, income—all part of a narcissistic economy to be attained, maintained or lost. With its promise of enhancements to self-esteem, professional life may instead reinforce narcissistic pathologies, resulting in a narcissistic brittleness so embedded that the entire surround is invisibly contaminated. We are shocked and dismayed when a clinician succumbs to the temptation of gratifications that turn out to be a riptide of destruction, integrity sacrificed to narcissistic seductions. Yet, should we be surprised that narcissistic difficulties underlie the negative contributions of clinicians (not solely of patients) to boundary crossing, impasses, and disrupted treatments?

Our classes on narcissism (with their very long reading lists) focus entirely on these difficulties in patients, not in clinicians. We would surely benefit from exploration of the narcissistic vulnerability inherent in becoming and being a clinician, with attention to our own histories in relation to the narcissistic features of our parents and how these factors have shaped us, even been foundational to our wish to be a clinician. Decades ago, Alice Miller (1979) wrote eloquently about the personal history of many psychoanalysts as children of narcissistic parents whose approval masqueraded as love, with the emphasis on achievement and successful performances. I would underscore that a narcissistic parental environment is one of diminished maternal/paternal eroticism that, if in place, would vitalize true self-experience. Instead, false self efforts aimed at pressured achievements overtake creative living (Winnicott, 1971).

Trying to repair and reverse a lack of empathy and respect for selfhood received as a child, clinicians hope to offer these qualities to patients, yet may be thwarted by blind spots in this very area—a perplexing cycle. Training that repeats an experience of narcissistic evaluation/devaluation intensifies the pathological dimensions. Miller (1979) noted the prevalence of intellectualization as narcissistic defense. Intellectualization poses an obstacle to analytic eroticism; arid erudition, disembodied and isolated from affect, crushes the life out of the desirable spontaneity, surprise, and vitality of analytic communication.

As Kurtz (1989) poignantly stated: "Transitional experience has its own integrative movement and must not be probed unnecessarily with the scalpel of interpretation" (p. 138). He argued, "When it does not try to be a science and, abandoning an impossible objectivity, embraces the poetic non-sense of unknowing, psychoanalysis realizes its true nature... and its goodness" (Kurtz, 1989, p. 15). Kurtz emphasized the addictive nature of a sense of power derived from knowledge achieved rationally, contrasting this aim with "the art of unknowing." He was building on Winnicott's (1971) caution that the "patient's creativity can be only too easily stolen by a therapist who knows too much" (p. 57).

The complexity and utility of psychoanalytic theory is fascinating—a profession where one need never be bored. Yet with so much energy invested in acquiring intellectual knowledge, to then embody a position of humility, especially within the clinical hour, may seem to be an "about face." In the struggle to develop an analytic identity, how does the establishment of analytic conviction not balloon into an aura of omniscience? It can be difficult in the clinical setting to step back from this knowing mode to a more humble appreciation of one's limits as a human being.

In working with patients who had come from a former treatment where an impasse or stalemate ended in a felt sense of betrayal, what I could glean retrospectively, about a situation I could only partially and imperfectly glimpse, suggested to me that the clinician may have become too wedded to his or her interpretive focus and/or technical stance. Caught in a defensively rigid reaction that loses sight of the co-created nature of the analytic field, the clinician may have stopped truly listening to the patient's experience. Blame for the impasse is externalized—flinging the "hot potato"—by persistent focus on patient pathology and by denial of any clinician contribution to the difficulty. The patient may also be caught in a blaming stance as each member of the dyad tries to ward off the sense of shame at being "in the wrong." A narcissistic riptide pulls the pair farther and farther out to sea until eventually the treatment drowns.

The lesson I could catch hold of in anticipating some form of repetition in the newly beginning treatment was to attempt to retain my bearings while also trying to remain flexible in the force of this threatening current. One cannot fight a riptide; one needs to go with it when its power is strongest, only eventually to swim sideways, not in opposition, to its direction. Indeed, it is frightening to let oneself be pulled along, *not* using one's well practiced swimming strokes, struggling to keep one's head above water along with a sense of direction and timing.

Swimming sideways

My use of the metaphor of a riptide in Chapter 6 to describe the pull of erotic transference and countertransference focused attention on oedipal erotic longings between two people. I am now looking beyond the specifically erotic to a more general consideration of narcissistic elements within the personality of a clinician that likely underlie most betrayals along a continuum of difficulties. Certainly narcissistic enhancement is a core aspect of erotic transference and countertransference; sexual desires are infused with narcissistic wishes and fantasies. When these prove too powerful, they pull toward boundary loss. But many narcissistic violations do not involve sexuality per se. I want to extend the riptide metaphor to include not solely the strong currents of the explicitly erotic, but additionally the significant undertow of narcissistic investments that can sink a treatment—an inexorable pull within the psyche, an internal force of danger—a psychic riptide.

I believe that this metaphor of a riptide has some advantages over the "slippery slope" metaphor that has come to be so commonly associated with erotic transference/ countertransference situations that lead to boundary violations. One can *see* a slope and usually identify (wet/icy) that it is likely to be slippery, dangerous, leading to a fall. The slippery slope metaphor can lend itself to a certain moralistic tone—"you should have been looking, should have known"—that is regrettable. An assumption is set up that if one is careful and doing the "right things," one will not "stray" from the path where one's footing is relatively stable (supposedly).

Whereas imagery of the ocean much more captures what our work is truly about: a swim in the unconscious, where little can be seen, only felt, and where dangers are not very predictable, nor easy to avoid. One can not do analysis from "the shore," yet getting in the water means submitting oneself to all sorts of currents; even a strong, careful swimmer is potentially challenged to the maximum of ability in encountering a truly threatening situation. One must contend with the experience of being out of control, in danger of drowning. This metaphor emphasizes the importance of advance awareness of the potential for being swept away in order to resist panic and to know what will likely be required. This is of course where our theory can "hold us" (a life jacket)—something that a moralistic approach will not accomplish. In this context I am shifting the metaphor of the analytic field to that of an analytic sea; "field" seems a bit too "dry" for what I want to capture here.

Gabbard (2015) decried the tendency within the profession to moralize about boundary violations: "A group of intelligent individuals who have chosen to spend their lives trying to understand the complexities of the human mind suddenly eschew complexity and devolve into finger-pointing" (p. 581). Moralizing—an "othering" of an erring clinician—is an attempt to distance from and buffer the pain of these situations. We need instead to appreciate the multi-faceted complexity of motives in boundary violations: As Gabbard (2015) warned, "We cannot know *a priori* what combination of analyst and analysand will trigger the road to self-deception that makes it somehow acceptable to transgress boundaries" (p. 582; see also Alpert and Steinberg, 2017) .

Why, *why*, we ask, in a profession aiming to help people, and with its practitioners sincerely wishing to do so, are there so many seriously failed treatments? How do clinicians who devote their lives to helping end up betraying their patients, themselves, their integrity, and that of the profession? Harris (2015) underscored that we need to keep searching for answers to these questions, to think about the institutional contexts within which these events transpire. The profession as a whole is challenged to resist thinking characterized by a splitting into "good" and "bad" categories of clinicians. The danger is hubris; the fear is humiliation; the lesson is humility.

Practitioners in our field are so easily dismissed, not solely from the community in reaction to overt ethical violations, but from the respect of others in a multitude of professional settings and endeavors. How does such an attitude cohere with the clinical goal of respect for each patient founded on care and concern for a person as an individual and imperfect human being? It behooves us to examine these complexities from many possible angles and to continue to direct our attention to these issues in the hope of effecting change. Toward that end, I am proffering my conceptualization of analytic eroticism as a theory of technique that centers on the analyst as a libidinal being who has the potential to use erotic energies aesthetically, with clinical integrity. Attention to, rather than avoidance of, the erotic might further develop our clinical ability to engage, manage, and creatively channel these potent forces and to help our patients to do the same. This creative engagement with the erotic can provide to the clinician narcissistic rewards appropriate to the endeavor, thus mitigating exploitation.

Creative expansions of the erotic

Kristeva (2014) explicitly stated her intent to offer provocation to conventional thinking in her linking of maternal and eroticism as a unified formulation. To conceptualize maternal eroticism is transgressive *in thought*, placing as it does two images together that are not typically linked, in fact, the opposite—kept apart. Whereas, sexual boundary violations are transgressions *in action* against what is ethically and legally binding. I am proposing that the transgressive thought inhering in the concept of analytic eroticism might work to contain transgressing, sexual(ized) actions.

To "contain" must be understood in its fullest Bionian meaning: to develop an emotional capacity that can bring into awareness and encompass all manner of embodied feelings, including in the realm of the erotic, without acting out or defensive maneuvers. Such a container—both spacious and sturdy—supports psychoanalytic use of these libidinal energies intrinsic to our humanity. It is unfortunate for psychoanalytic theorizing of technique that in general parlance "contain" typically implies suppression, as in "the fire is contained; we're hoping soon to have it completely extinguished." Clinicians can themselves be confused about what containing the erotic truly means.

We cannot "put out" the fires of erotic life, nor should we want to eliminate this powerful fuel to creative living, in spite of its combustible nature. Our species survival has depended on sexual procreativity; our psychic survival as unique individuals relies on personal creativity that draws upon the energies of our erotic/libidinal natures. The clinical aim should be to enlarge our capacity to hold a creative space for erotic elements that historically, both within our profession and in life more generally, have been under-contained and, unmanageable, have overflowed into boundary violations.

A repeating bad dream does not go away by avoidance, but only by paying *more* attention to its content and communication. Sexual boundary violations are bad dreams that repeat. We have not paid *enough* attention to eroticism in the analytic field. As a consequence, individual clinicians do not have a theoretical container to rely on in working with this realm of embodied energy and emotion. One then enters an area in the analytic field of a treatment that is not sufficiently "mapped" by our training. Our facility for handling aggression, a patient's and our own, often far exceeds our abilities with erotic material. When eroticism devolves into concrete gratifications, the play/potential space of analytic work collapses, and the "as if" or virtual reality (Civitarese, 2012) of the analytic field is lost. Instead of offering libidinal vitality in the service of the patient's growth, a clinician sacrifices the treatment to inappropriate gratifications. Although the concept of analytic eroticism evokes anxieties about sexual boundary violations, I believe that it is the *absence* of a conceptualization of analytic eroticism that contributes to such violations. I suggest that analytic eroticism is a concept that can be utilized to contain erotic engagement in the analytic field within a creative aesthetic.

Many patients need help from the clinician in locating their creative spontaneity and their erotic vitality. The analyst has to actively generate an atmosphere that facilitates, even brings to life, a patient's own libidinal energies. This task requires the clinician's libidinal investment, an investing that needs to be palpable to the patient as an alive aspect of the analytic field where the analysis becomes "a joint creation of two intercommunicating worlds. It's like sharing a space of virtual reality or a dream space, or entering into a kind of dance" (Civitarese, 2012, p. 172). A "blank screen" analyst may well be experienced as an anti-libidinal figure, possibly aligning with an absence of maternal eroticism in a patient's internal world. In contrast, an intertwining of the erotic and the creative in the embodied, affective interaction of the dyad supports an ongoing oscillation between forms of experiencing toward increasingly higher levels of integration and un-integration that allow for deepening contact with an authentic sense of being. In the Introduction to this book, I symbolized this evolution thus: erotic ←→ creative ←→ expansion of the personality.

As an example of what I have in mind clinically, I want to quote at length the following published vignette about a very inhibited, obsessive man who was now opening up to the experience of love:

> On his return, he described an experience he had when visiting the Louvre and seeing there for the first time Mesopotamian miniature sculptures from the third millennium before our era. At one point, he had the uncanny experience that one of these tiny sculptures, the body of a woman whose nipples and navel were marked by tiny precious stones, resembled the body of the woman he loved. He had been thinking about her, longing for her as he walked through the practically deserted halls, and while he was looking at the sculpture, a wave of erotic stimulation seized him, together with an intense feeling of closeness with her. He also was very moved by what he considered the extreme simplicity and beauty of the sculpture, and he felt that he could empathize with the unknown artist who had died over four thousand years ago. He had a sense of humility and yet of reassuring communication with the past, and felt as if he had been allowed to share the understanding of the eternal mystery of love as expressed silently in that work of art. The sense of sexual excitement had become fused with the sense of oneness, of longing and yet closeness with the woman he loved, and through that oneness and love he had been permitted entrance into the transcendent world of beauty. At the same time, he had a strong sense of his own individuality, together with a combination of gratitude for being permitted to share the experience of this work of art, and of humility in being faced with it.
>
> (Kernberg, 1977, pp. 96–97)

That a patient previously so constricted could bring to the analyst his experience—still imbued with its erotic vitality—of being profoundly moved, provides illustration of a transformation hoped for in analytic work. Although the reader is not given the clinical specifics, it is evident that the analysis not only helped the patient to open to passionate feeling in himself and toward the woman he loved—conjoining sexuality and art—but with the analyst as well. The patient's experience was communicated in a way that surely captured the analyst's erotic imagination and that is then evocatively transmitted to the reader as well. This material presents two men in the clinical dyad as deeply, mutually engaged in an erotic, aesthetic encounter. As far as the reader knows, this encounter was not experienced as desire *for* one another, though erotic transference/countertransference wishes could certainly be included as an additional layer.

This poignant vignette reflects analytic eroticism at play, and brings to mind Meltzer's (1988) statement that "meaning is in the first instance the fundamental manifestation of the passions of intimate relationship with the beauty of the world" (p. 14) which is first experienced in apprehending the beauty of the mother. The female statues in the Louvre, "nipples and navel . . . marked by tiny precious stones" surely evoke maternal eroticism. For adults, contacting the permeating passions of maternal eroticism has the power to destabilize the individuated sense of self, yet, we hope for an opening to a richness of experience and meaning. Such an opening of self, when shared in the resonances of the analytic field, may feel destabilizing to a clinician as well; something might be stirred that feels deeply personal, vulnerable, exposing, and not consonant with one's professional identity or persona. How fully can we allow *ourselves* to participate?

Conclusion

We recognize that the practice of psychoanalysis is creative in nature for the analyst. Untold hours of contemplative attention, reverie, inquiry, curiosity, and compassion, foster the potential space in which to focus on the human struggle to find meaning in life and in mortality, to deal with difficult situations both internally and interpersonally, and to locate an authentic sense of being. Hopefully the erotic nature of this effort can also be recognized and utilized.

Even though the erotic transference/countertransference literature has been growing at an impressive rate, the erotic is still little addressed (if at all) within training. This suggests that we need to find ways to facilitate discussion of this topic, both in theory courses and in case conferences. Hopefully clinicians will feel less inhibited in bringing up concerns related to erotic transference and countertransference, and to erotic life more generally, such that sexuality—the original cornerstone of psychoanalysis—will no longer be a silent taboo in our professional lives.

I want to conclude by underscoring that even within a treatment of analytic depth, the possibility of contacting, revealing, expressing true self-experience, while deeply meaningful work, may be more challenging to both patient and clinician than the exposure of the guilty, shamed, damaged self that is traditionally the focus of clinical work. Patients come to treatment with some recognition that they need to reveal their "bad" self; both patient and clinician are steeling themselves for this encounter with the wounded self, the "what's wrong with me" self. But attention to the "what's right with me" self may feel even more vulnerable and may lead to collusive avoidance in both patient and clinician. There is much value in exploring what is right with a person, who they rightfully are, an exploration that needs not primarily interpretation, but invitation. In my conceptualization of analytic eroticism, I emphasize "invitalization" as stimulus to transformative engagement. I invite you, the reader, to consider the fullness of being—including the vitality of the erotic—that can be brought to the practice of psychoanalysis.

References

Alpert, J. L. and Steinberg, A. (2017). Introduction: Sexual boundary violations: A century of violations and a time to analyze. *Psychoanalytic Psychology*, 34: 144–150.

Baranger, M. and Baranger, W. (2008). The analytic situation as a dynamic field. *International Journal of Psychoanalysis*, 89: 795–826.

Civitarese, G. (2012). *The violence of emotions: Bionian and post-Bionian psychoanalysis*. London: Routledge.

Dimen, M. (2015). Too much goodness: Another hazard on the road to sexual boundary violations in psychoanalysis. *Psychoanalytic Dialogues*, 25: 572–578.

Elise, D. (2015). Reclaiming Lost Loves: Transcending Unrequited Desires. Discussion of Davies' "Oedipal Complexity". *Psychoanalytic Dialogues*, 25: 284–294.

Ferro, A. and Civitarese, G. (2015). *The analytic field and its transformations.* London: Karnac.

Gabbard, G. O. (2015). On knowing but not knowing in the aftermath of traumatic betrayal. *Psychoanalytic Dialogues*, 25: 579–585.

Gabbard, G. O. and Lester, E. P. (1995). *Boundaries and boundary violations in psychoanalysis.* New York: Basic Books.

Harris, A. (2015). Discussion of Dianne Elise's paper "Unraveling: Betrayal and the loss of goodness in the analytic relationship. *Psychoanalytic Dialogues*, 25: 586–592.

Kernberg, O. F. (1977). Boundaries and Structure in Love Relations. *Journal of the American Psychoanalytic Association*, 25: 81–114.

Kristeva, J. (2014). Reliance, or maternal eroticism. *Journal of the American Psychoanalytic Association*, 62: 69–85.

Kurtz, S. (1989). *The art of unknowing: Dimensions of openness in analytic therapy.* Northvale, New Jersey: Jason Aronson.

Lasch, C. (1991). *The culture of narcissism: American life in an age of diminishing expectations.* New York: Norton Press.

Levine, H. B. (2010). The sins of the fathers: Freud, narcissistic boundary violations, and their effects on the politics of psychoanalysis. *International Forum of Psychoanalysis*, 19: 43–50.

Meltzer, D. and Harris Williams, M. (1988). *The apprehension of beauty.* Strath Tay, Scotland: Clunie Press.

Miller, A. (1979). The drama of the gifted child and the psychoanalyst's narcissistic disturbance. *International Journal of Psychoanalysis*, 60: 47–58.

Morrison, A. (1989). *Shame: The underside of narcissism.* Hillsdale, New Jersey: Analytic Press.

Ogden, T. H. (1997). Reverie and metaphor: How I work as a psychoanalyst. *International Journal of Psychoanalysis*, 78: 719–732.

Wilson, M. (2003). The analyst's desire and the problem of narcissistic resistances. *Journal of the American Psychoanalytic Association*, 51: 71–79.

Winnicott, D. W. (1971). *Playing and reality.* London: Tavistock Publications.

Index

agency 10–11, 60, 63–67, 72, 86–87, 108–109, 177–179, 183–184, 192–194, 204–209, 214–232
aggression 70, 78, 86, 95–98, 183–184, 193–194, 294–295
Altman, L. 240, 254–255
analyst–patient relationships, admissions of sexual desires 96–97; definitions 17–18, 262–263, 296–297; terminations 266–282, 285, 289–297; *see also individual topics*
analyst's sexuality 58, 64–66, 82–83, 96–98, 140–141, 285–287
analytic eroticism 1–6, 15–17, 25–49, 53–73, 75–98, 118–119, 137–142, 150–157, 179–186, 208, 222, 262–282, 293–297; ethics 16–17, 38–49, 53–54, 85, 261–282, 284–297; maternal eroticism 39–40, 47–48, 64–65, 67, 208; *see also individual topics*
analytic field theory 7–12, 18, 31–32, 45, 64–67, 69–73, 75–98, 118–122, 137–142, 172–186, 192–209, 225–232, 262–282, 294–297
Andersen, Hans Christian 154–155
anger 3, 8–9, 86, 127–128, 237–258, 263–264, 272–282
anxieties 15, 16, 29–30, 60–61, 76–77, 86–88, 91–92, 94–95, 125–142, 175–186, 197, 200–209, 222–232, 246–258, 270–282; male fears of psychic penetration 16, 125, 129–142, 177, 193; *see also* psychic pain; trauma
après-coup 248–251, 267–268
ardor 1–2, 38–49, 278–279; *see also* analytic eroticism; eroticism
Aron, L. 112, 113–115, 121, 140, 146, 182

arts 6, 9, 30–32, 39–40, 46, 47–49, 65–66, 84–85, 90–91, 154–157, 179–186, 295–296; erotic nudes 39–40, 265; persecution territory 89–90; psychoanalysis 30–32, 46, 47–49, 295–296; rejections 90–91, 93–94; *see also* creativity; dance; music; myths; paintings; poetry; sculpture; symbols; writing
asexuality 32–33, 34
attachment 3, 4–6, 14, 15, 16, 34–35, 36–39, 48, 55, 82–83, 118–122, 133–142, 145–157, 275–282; Harlow monkey study 34–35, 36–38; *see also* object relations; oedipal attachments
authenticity 18, 295
auto-erotic activities 208
avoidance 86, 94–95, 97–98, 172–173, 219–220, 274–282, 294; *see also* denial
awakenings 8–9

Bader, M. 171–172
ballet 154–157
Balsam, Rosemary 1, 19, 40, 49, 169, 177–179, 182, 186
Barnett, M. 197–198
Bassin, D. 106–107, 117, 164–165, 194
beauty 6–7, 27–28, 62, 71–72, 171–172, 295–296; objectification considerations 71–72
Benjamin, J. 58, 60–61, 95, 106–107, 115, 117, 121, 132, 134, 146, 163, 192, 213, 232
Bernstein, D. 164, 195, 197, 204
betrayal 16–17, 235–298; analyst–patient relationships 16–17, 261–282, 285–297; arrogance 47, 219–222,

227–228, 266, 284–297; de-idealization 276–277; empathy 277–279, 290; oedipal attachments 237–258, 267–268; self-esteem 251–258, 265–268, 287–288, 290; *see also* infidelity
Bion, W. R. 5, 10–12, 14, 18, 67, 69, 87–88, 98, 157, 256, 293–294; *see also* analytic field theory
bisexual matrix 106–107, 121
bisexuality 14, 15–16, 56–57, 88–89, 105–122, 128–129, 130–131, 148–149, 154–155, 179–186, 207, 243–258; literature 105–107, 154–155
blocked creativity 15, 75–98, 110
bodily imagery 56–58, 65–67, 71–72, 90–91, 96–97, 108–109, 163–186, 190–191, 195–209, 218–226, 295–296; *see also* clothing; shame
body ego 164–169
Bollas, C. 2, 55, 83, 131, 146, 149, 168, 178
Bram Stoker's Dracula (film) 59–60, 62, 227
Braunschweig, D. 118, 119–120, 194
breast-feeding 3–4, 5–6, 18, 27–30, 34–35, 55, 61, 112–115, 117–118, 119–120, 128–129, 130–132, 149–150, 178–179, 198–199; dreams 29–30; "weaning" 199–202; *see also* nursing couples
Breen, D. 118
broken relationships 190–191, 261–282; *see also* infidelity; marital dynamics
Butler, J. 115–116, 201

Call, J. D. 30, 42
castration 62–63, 80–81, 82–83, 89, 91, 94, 134–135, 167, 177, 182–183, 193–194, 200, 204–206; defense mechanisms 204–205
Celenza, A. 274
Chasseguet-Smirgel, J. 61, 73, 113, 115, 118, 119, 120, 130, 150, 168, 197, 205, 232
Chodorow Nancy J. 1, 117, 121, 130, 132, 146, 150, 154, 163, 175, 207
chora 28–29, 39–40, 43–49, 131; holding and containing environments 43–49; *see also* potential space; semiotics
Christiansen, A. 132
"citadel complex" 129, 134–142

Civitarese, G. 7, 10–11, 18, 27, 31–32, 36, 41, 44, 49, 69, 79, 262, 266, 274, 286, 294–295
clitoris 113, 168–169, 183, 190–191, 195–198, 205; literature 195, 196; roles 195, 196; *see also* genitals; vagina
clothing, women 56–58, 65–66, 71, 85, 110–111, 130–131, 220–222; *see also* bodily imagery
collapse of the creative 284–296
communications 7–9, 30–32, 42, 139–140, 201–202; creative living 7–9; men 139–140
Corbett, K. 169, 176–177
"couch relations" 76–77, 82–98, 265–282
countertransference 14–15, 25–26, 34–49, 53–73, 75–98, 151–152, 261, 264, 266, 276–282, 291–292, 297; dismay 261, 264, 266, 276–282
creative living 7–9, 13–14, 37–38, 39–43, 48, 150–157, 293–297 *see also* spontaneity
creativity 7–18, 37–38, 39–49, 54–73, 75–98, 105–122, 150–157, 179–186, 284–297; analytic exploration 87–94, 179–186, 290, 297; blocked 15, 75–98, 110; healing effects 11–12, 47; inhibitions 15, 16, 75–98
cross-sex identifications 106–107
cultural experiences 8–9, 65, 71–72, 83, 86–87, 95–96, 106, 116–118, 139–140, 146, 186, 193–209, 231–232, 237–240, 253–258, 286–287

"Daddy's girl" state 61, 63, 169, 202–204, 240–241, 254
dance 15, 25–49, 154–157, 295; analytic eroticism 15, 25–49, 295; artistic expression 30–32, 46–49; ballet 154–157; choreography of 15, 25–49, 295; clinician uses 28–32, 42–43, 46–49, 295; maternal eroticism concepts 27–30; metaphors 30–32, 42–43, 295; *see also* arts; creativity; symbols
danger situations, betrayal 250–258
daughters 58–61, 63, 68–69, 76, 117, 148–149, 175–186, 196–209, 213–232, 237–258; "Daddy's girl" state 61, 63, 169, 202–204, 240–241, 254; maternal sexuality 60, 148–149, 198–209;

oedipal desires 58–61, 68–69, 76, 148–149, 196–197, 237–258; *see also* infant; mother; women
Davies, J. 83, 86–87, 89, 94–95, 97, 145–147, 149–154, 157, 166–167, 185
de Beauvoir, S. 229
de Cortinas, L. P. 10, 42–44
de-idealization, betrayal in the analyst–patient relationship 276–277
"dead mother" concept 18, 41, 58
deadness 34–38, 43, 90–91
death 18, 34, 59–60, 62, 127, 179–180, 227, 248, 268–269, 281; analysts 268–269, 281; mourning capacities 98, 262, 268, 281; sexuality 59–60, 227
deceptions 235–298; *see also* betrayal; infidelity
"defects" focus, shame 167–168, 171–175, 184, 218–222, 291
defense mechanisms 15–18, 75–76, 86, 91–92, 115–116, 132–133, 137–142, 169–170, 172–173, 177, 191–192, 197, 204–209, 237–258, 262–282, 290–297; betrayal in the analyst–patient relationship 262–282; castration 204–205; narcissistic injury 255; phallus 129, 134–142, 169–170, 177, 197, 204–205; splitting 107, 120, 237, 262–263, 280–281, 293; *see also* avoidance; denial; repression
deficit problems, maternal eroticism 3–4
deflated sexual body 168–175, 176–177, 182–186, 193–194, 198–202, 203–209, 239–240, 278–279; *see also* erasure of the female erotic; shame
dehumanization 34–38
Demeter myth 58, 61, 62–63
denial 62, 69, 94–98, 112, 117, 133, 152, 172–173, 176, 238, 246, 247–253, 264, 269, 274–282, 291; *see also* avoidance
dependency concepts 70–71, 82–98, 150–157, 176–177, 209, 230–232, 247–258
depressed mothers 80–81, 128
depression 33–34, 47, 66, 80, 89, 126–128, 177, 190, 200, 256, 272; symptoms 33–34, 47; *see also* worthlessness
depression in analysts 33–34
derailment of female erotic agency 214–217
desexualization of the maternal 15, 38–39, 53–73, 81, 83–84, 118–119, 120–121, 152, 203–209; *see also* erasure of the female erotic
desire and disruption in the analytic relationship 15, 16–17, 53–73, 75–98, 261–282, 284–297
desires 15–17, 27–28, 36–37, 53–98, 111–112, 118, 130–131, 135–136, 145–157, 163–186, 191–209, 213–232, 235–298; clothing 56–58, 65–66, 71, 85; erasure of the female erotic 16, 76, 81, 174–175, 190–209, 213–232; masochistic submission 16, 213–232; men's wants 193–194, 206–209, 217–222; poisoned desires 16–17, 235–298; repulsion 217–222, 226; unrequited desires 92, 145–157, 163–164, 166–186, 197–209, 238–258; *see also* eroticism; *individual topics*; passion
destructive dynamics 3–4, 16–17, 40, 53–54, 82–83, 90, 128–129, 131, 206–207, 227–228, 237–258, 261–282, 284–297; analytic eroticism 4, 16–17, 40, 53–54, 82–83, 90, 227–228, 261–282, 284–297; maternal eroticism 3–4, 16–17, 40, 128–129, 131, 206–207, 227–228, 237–258; *see also* betrayal
Deutsch, R. 268, 280
developmental psychology 3–5, 8–9, 13–15, 25–28, 38–40, 45, 54, 70–72, 111–113, 131–135, 138–139, 145–157, 163–186, 213–232, 237–258; learning essentials about developmental surprises 248–251; *see also individual topics*; oedipal attachments
Dimen, M. 121, 193, 263–265, 267, 271–272, 281, 285–287
Dinnerstein, D. 121, 184, 205, 206–207
Dio Bleichmar, E. 201
disappearances, betrayal in the analyst–patient relationship 279–281, 292–293
disruption 15, 16–17, 53–73, 75–98, 261–282
Dracula 59–60, 62, 225–227
dread 256–257; *see also* anxieties
dreams 7–9, 13, 29, 54–55, 69–70, 77, 82–83, 151–152, 261–262, 294–295; breast-feeding 29–30; Carlos in *Imagining Argentina* (film) 261–262; lesbians 82–83; reality 69–70; waking

dreaming roles 262; *see also* fantasies; imagination
Ducat, S. 141, 177
dysphorias 16, 161–234; *see also* erasure of the female erotic; shame

earthquake metaphor, infidelity 258
ego 106–107, 112, 133–134, 151, 164–168, 250; phallus 164–165; *see also* self concepts; shame
Eissler, K. 129
embarrassment 167, 224–226; *see also* shame
emotions, dance 30–32, 44–45
empathy, betrayal in the analyst–patient relationship 277–279, 290
enigmatic messages, maternal eroticism 2–3, 6–7, 28, 38–39
envy 56–57, 61, 111–112, 115, 133, 164, 176, 180–184, 204–205; *see also* jealousy; penis envy
erasure of the female erotic 16, 76, 81, 174–175, 190–209, 213–232, 239–240; object relations 190–209, 213–232; *see also* deflated sexual body; desexualization of the maternal; dysphorias; loss
erections 113, 164–165, 168–169, 171–172, 177–179, 190, 205, 221–222; *see also* phallus
Erikson, E. 164–165, 194
Eros 1–2, 9–10, 25–26, 44, 128, 150–151, 154, 274; *see also* eroticism; libido
erotic betrayal 16–17, 235–298; *see also* betrayal
erotic dysphorias 16, 161–234
erotic hunger 193–194, 198–202
erotic masochism, definition 229
erotic nudes, arts 39–40, 265
erotic transference 14–15, 25–26, 34–49, 53–73, 75–98, 150–157, 172–173, 181–186, 192, 226–228, 242–258, 261–282, 293–297; betrayal in the analyst–patient relationship 261–282, 285–297; a blind eye 81–82; cautions 41; "couch relations" 76–77, 82–98, 265–282; creativity 15, 37–38, 41, 45, 75–98, 179–186, 293–297; inhibitions 15, 75–98, 150–151; Jan's case 78–83, 91–93; riptide metaphor 151–152, 291–292
erotic vitality 4, 13–15, 23–101, 128–142, 222, 262–263, 278–279, 287–288, 294–297; Sue's case 35–39, 47; *see also* analytic eroticism; libido; stimulation
eroticism 1–18, 26–49, 53–73, 75–98, 179–186, 190–209, 213–232, 278–282, 293–297; analytic field 12–14, 45, 64–65, 66–67, 69–73, 75–98, 120–121, 179–186, 294–297; derailment of female erotic agency 214–217; destructive dynamics 3–4, 16–17, 40, 53–54, 82–83, 90, 128–129, 131, 206–207, 227–228, 237–258, 261–282, 284–297; erasure of the female erotic 16, 76, 81, 174–175, 190–209, 213–232, 239–240; orientations 103–160; play 12–14; "thrill" 13–14; *see also* analytic eroticism; ardor; desires; Eros; libido; maternal eroticism; sexuality; tempestuous passions; unruly urges; vibrant frame of mind; vigor
eruption/disruption discussion, oedipal attachments 67–73
ethics 2, 16–17, 26–27, 38–49, 53–54, 85, 261–282, 284–297; analytic eroticism 16–17, 38–49, 53–54, 85, 261–282, 284–297; betrayal in the analyst–patient relationship 261–282; heretical ethics 38–49; maternal care ethics 39–40; violations 261–282, 284–297
excitement 1–18, 27–49, 54–55, 59–60, 71, 89–92, 95–96, 112–113, 114–122, 131–142, 181–182, 202–209, 221–222, 227, 295; cultural regulations 71; primitive excitements 114–122; *see also* libido
exclusions from parent's sexual relationships 67–68, 120, 153–154, 247–248
exhibitionism 169–175, 181–182, 205–206, 217, 221; *see also* grandiosity; narcissism
expansions of the erotic, creativity 293–297
exploitation issues, analyst–patient relationships 77–79
eye contact 85–86

"failure to thrive" 213, 231–232; *see also* masochistic submission
failures 37–38, 41, 80, 90–93, 153–154, 167–168, 197–198, 213–232, 292–297; *see also* shame; unrequited desires
Fain, M. 118, 119–120, 194

"fair fighting", families 95–96
false self, definition 8–9, 90–91, 121; *see also* self concepts
fantasies 15, 54–55, 58–60, 63–64, 68–69, 79–80, 86–87, 93, 95, 106–107, 112–113, 121, 171–172, 183–184, 200, 208, 217–222, 275, 291–292; strangling fantasies 95; *see also* dreams; imagination
Fast, I. 106–107, 142
fathers 3, 15, 18, 26, 29, 48, 53–54, 58–73, 114, 115–116, 120–121, 126–128, 132–142, 148–149, 169–186, 190–192, 196–209, 238–240, 243, 247–258; "Daddy's girl" state 61, 63, 169, 202–204, 240–241, 254; dominance in bed 120; "impenetrable penetrator" 115–117; law 73; maternal eroticism 3, 18, 26, 48, 148–149, 197–198, 201–203, 238–239, 243, 256–257; paternalistic structuring of sexuality 15, 53–54, 58–73, 114, 116, 120–121, 138–142, 146–157, 184, 190–192, 196–209, 238–240; phantom father figures 58–60; sons 62–63, 116, 126–128, 132–142, 148–149, 176–177, 215–217, 238–240; *see also* men; oedipal attachments; phallus
female passivity and male activity theories 108–112, 115–117, 129–131, 132–142, 154, 169–170, 174–186, 191–192, 193–194, 204–209, 215–232, 239–258; *see also* men; women
female-dominated profession, psychoanalysis 71
feminine masochism in females 228–232; *see also* masochistic submission
feminine masochism in males 229–230
feminization concerns, men 72
Ferro, A. 10–11, 18, 31, 36–37, 41, 44, 69, 79, 266, 286
fiction, reality 68–70, 132
films 35–36, 37, 59–60, 227, 261–262; lesbians 35–36, 37; *see also individual films*
Fisher, S. 209
flexibility 17–18, 47–48, 206–207, 290–297; good psychoanalysis 17–18, 47–48, 290–297
Fogel, G. 129, 139, 182
Fonagy, P. 165, 185
Freud, Sigmund 1–5, 9, 12, 28, 38–39, 41, 45, 48, 61, 87–88, 90, 94, 105, 108, 112–113, 119, 129, 140, 146–148, 150, 153–157, 164–170, 175, 179–180, 183–185, 192–204, 207, 215–216, 219, 222, 229, 238–240, 248–256
Friedman, R. 132
"frigidity" problems, women 136, 171–172, 195–196, 209
frustrations 3, 45, 93, 136–137, 192–193

Gabbard, G. 83, 89, 94–95, 285–288, 292
gay couples, "flagrant/flaunting" perceptions 73; *see also* homosexuality
gaze of the (m)other, masochistic submission 217–222
gaze of the other 174–175, 201, 206–207, 217–222
gender identities 14, 15–16, 59–60, 76–98, 105–122, 130–142, 148–149, 163–164, 179–186, 215, 227, 239, 295; background 105–122, 130–142, 148–149, 163–164, 179–186, 215, 239; psychic vulnerability in males 130–142; reality 107–108; renunciation 112, 121–122, 132, 254–255; truth 148–152; *see also* psychic bisexuality; sexuality
gender repertoires 16, 105–122, 128–129; *see also* psychic bisexuality; sexuality
"genital deficiency" 167–168; *see also* shame
genitals 15, 16, 53–73, 109–110, 112–115, 163–186, 190–206; "defects" focus 167–168, 171–175, 184; "hot" turned on state 64–65, 67–68, 168–169, 221–222; inadequacy and inferiority sense 15, 16, 53–73, 91–93, 163–186, 200–209, 213–232, 239–258; legs parted 57, 61–62, 115; meaning-making 186, 190–209; moist realms 55, 113, 221–222; smallness issues 168–169, 171–175, 184–186, 193–194, 217–222, 232; "swelling" 168–175, 178, 182, 198–202, 204–205; *see also* clitoris; phallus; vagina; vulva
"girls don't have what it takes" 181–185, 194–196
Goldberg, P. 43
Goldberger, M. 85–86, 165, 177–178
Goldner, V. 121
"good enough" mothers 201–202
good psychoanalysis qualities 17–18, 26, 36–38, 42–44, 45–49, 54–55, 63–64, 67, 69–72, 76–82, 97–98, 120–121,

140–142, 152–153, 157, 172–175, 180–186, 192–209, 222–232, 255–258, 262–263, 267–282, 285–297; see also psychoanalysis
grandiosity 114, 168, 170–175, 217, 266–267, 285–297; see also exhibitionism; narcissism
Green, A. 70, 82–83, 94, 118–120, 247
grief 237–258, 262–282
group mental functioning 10–11
guilt 89, 93–94, 167–168, 248–251, 273–274

Hades 58, 62–63
Hanly, C. 257
Hansbury, G. 129–130, 132
harem mentality 241; see also female passivity and male activity theories
Harlow monkey study 34–35, 36–38
Harris, A. 16, 42, 286–288, 292–293
Harris Williams, M. 6–7, 27, 62, 72, 179
healing effects, creativity 11–12, 47
"hello" and good "goodbye" requirements, psychoanalysis 18, 261–262, 268, 281
heresy 38–49
"heroic model of manhood" 139, 248–249
heteronormativity 16, 71, 89, 105–109, 114, 121, 131–132, 145–157, 200–209
heterosexuality 56–57, 60, 71, 82, 84–85, 89, 98, 105–109, 114, 116–117, 121, 135, 141, 145–146, 148–157, 163–164, 172–175, 199–209, 213–214, 237–258; challenges to the notion 201–204, 207; "frigidity" problems 136, 171–172, 195–196, 209; truth 148–152, 200–201; see also sexual intercourse
Hirsch, I. 141
holding and containing environments 5, 9–10, 11–12, 14, 17–18, 26–27, 43–49, 94–95, 172–175, 257–258, 279–280, 293–297; chora 43–49; parents 4–5, 9–10, 26–27, 29–30; psychoanalysis metaphors 5, 9–10, 11–12, 14, 17–18, 26–27, 43–49, 94–95, 172–175, 257–258, 279–280, 293–297
Holtzman, D. 58, 146, 214, 215, 222
homosexual "panic" 141, 151
homosexuality 53–54, 55, 56–58, 75–82, 105–122, 125, 140–142, 145–147, 149–157, 174, 202–203, 207–208, 226;

levels 55, 57; truth 148–152; women 35–36, 37, 53–54, 55, 56–57, 75–83, 91–93, 105–122, 130–131, 148–152, 202–203, 207–208; see also bisexuality; gay; lesbians; sexuality
hope 1, 12, 14, 17–18, 90–91, 203–204, 262, 268–269, 271–281, 290, 293–297
Horney, K. 196
"hot" turned on state, genitals 64–65, 67–68, 168–169, 221–222
humiliation 91–94, 166–186, 251–258; see also betrayal; shame

"ideal self-representation" 168–169, 171–172, 182–183, 184–186, 193–194
"idealized others" 166–169, 176–177, 184–186, 263–264, 276–278; de-idealization of betrayal 276–277; see also unrequited desires
identification considerations, betrayal 273–274
images, choreography of dance 25–49
imagination 7–9, 10–12, 14, 17–18, 41–43, 47–48, 93, 261–262, 291–292; creative living 8–9, 41–43, 47–48; true self 8–9; see also creativity; dreams; fantasies
Imagining Argentina (film) 261–262
"impenetrable penetrator", fathers 115–116
impotence 80, 89, 90, 94, 135, 171–172, 175, 176–178, 183, 207, 230, 255
improvisation uses 30–32, 44–45
in-dwelling experiences 13
inadequacy and inferiority sense 15, 16, 53–73, 91–93, 163–186, 200–209, 213–232, 239–258; see also shame
incest 58, 62, 89, 92, 95–96, 116, 197, 198, 200, 248–251, 268
"ineluctable monosexuality" 116, 148–149
infantile sexuality 3, 5, 25–26, 40, 48, 67–68, 70–71, 119–122, 131–132, 147–157, 168–169, 193–194, 198–202, 247–248; see also mother–infant erotic matrix
infants, adopted children 258; dead babies 34, 36; dependency concepts 70–71, 150–157, 176–177, 247–258; developmental psychology 3–5, 8–9, 13–14, 15, 25–26, 27–28, 39–40, 45, 54, 70–72, 111–115, 131–132,

134–135, 138–139, 145–157, 163–186, 213–232, 237–258; exclusions from parent's sexual relationships 67–68, 120, 153–154, 247–248; maternal eroticism 2–3, 25–49, 111–115; new siblings 253–254; penetration/penetrated dialectic 114–116; "wire mother monkey" 34–35, 36–38; *see also* daughters; oedipal attachments; sons
infidelity 6, 16–17, 237–258, 265–268, 269–282; background 237–258, 269–276; dynamics 237–242, 247–249, 253, 256–258, 269–272; Eva's case 242–258; metaphors 237, 258; passion 246, 250, 256–258; psychic pain 237–258, 265–268, 269–282; self-esteem 251–258, 265–268, 269–282; sexuality 247–253; statistics 237–238; treatment conclusions 255–258, 267–268, 269–276; triangularity 247–253, 257–258, 273–276; trust 238–240, 245, 251–258, 265–272; *see also* betrayal
inflated sexual body 168–175, 176–177, 182–186, 193–194, 198–202, 204–209, 239–240
inhibitions 15, 16, 75–98, 110, 121, 125–142, 148–157, 163–186, 198–209, 213–232; analysts 94–98; a blind eye 81–82; creativity 15, 16, 75–98; erotic transference 15, 75–98, 150–151; Jan's case 78–83, 91–93; men 16, 84–85, 110, 125–142
intellectuality 33, 39, 44–45, 63–64, 290; "victory of intellectuality over sensuality" 33, 44, 63–64, 290; *see also* rationality
intensity 54–55, 90–91, 93–94, 150, 186, 195–196
interpretation uses 17, 46, 284–297
intersubjectivity 2–3, 8–10, 31–32, 40–42, 66–70, 72, 147–148, 164, 183–185, 257, 266, 280, 288
intuition 44–45, 79, 94–95, 115, 252–253
invitation to vital exchanges, psychoanalysis 17–18, 36–38, 297
Irigaray, L. 55, 194, 205–206

jealousy 56–57, 119, 237–258; *see also* envy
Josephs, L. 237–238, 240, 251, 253–255
joy 18, 47, 90

Kaftal, E. 139, 140
Kernberg, O. 15, 111, 113, 119, 135, 175–176, 201, 203, 239–241, 295
Klein, M. 18, 68, 72, 88, 112–115, 133, 146, 149, 153, 178–179, 204, 247, 258
"knowing all/all knowing" critique, psychoanalysis 287–291
Kristeva, J. 1–5, 18, 25–45, 55, 58, 61–62, 72, 119–120, 131, 149, 168, 178, 198, 201, 232, 293; *see also* maternal eroticism
Kulish, N. 58, 146, 214, 215, 222
Kurtz, S. 290

Lacanian-influenced thinking 73, 205
Lamply de Groot, J. 111–112, 117, 176
language 30, 42, 165–166; childhood acquisition 42; symbols 30, 42
Laplanche, J. 2–3, 4, 28, 38–39, 55, 119, 131–132, 168, 178
Laqueur, T. 116
Lasch, C. 286
latency capacities 34–35, 151, 195–196
Laufer, M. E. 199–200
law, fathers 73
Lax, R. 200
Lerner, H. 177
lesbians 35–36, 37, 56–57, 75–83, 91–93, 108–122, 130–131, 149, 152, 207–208, 226; anticipation factors 109–110; dreams 82–83; films 35–36, 37; Jan's case 78–83, 91–93; Keri's case 108–111, 121, 130–131; orgasms 82–83; penetration/penetrated dialectic 109–122; seduction 77–79, 82–83, 85–86, 151; sexual activities 36, 37, 82–83, 108–111; *see also* bisexuality; homosexuality
Levin, C. 272
Levine, H. 41–42, 266, 284
libido 1–4, 5, 9–10, 12–15, 25–49, 62–73, 86, 128–142, 167–186, 222–223, 231–232, 256–258, 272–282, 285–297; anti-libidinal self 5, 33–34, 295; creativity links 12–14; negative aspects 3; shame 167–186, 287; *see also* analytic eroticism; Eros; erotic vitality; eroticism; excitement
listening qualities, psychoanalysis 17–18, 30–32
literature 31–32, 105–107, 154–155, 194–209, 297; clitoris 195;

masturbation 195–196; vagina 194–202; *see also individual authors*
"The Little Mermaid" (ballet) 154–157
"little tassel" 112, 176
Loewald, H. 214–216, 227, 231–232, 268
loss 9, 16, 66, 129–130, 157, 175–186, 190–209, 214–232, 238–258, 262–282, *see also* betrayal; erasure of the female erotic; object relations
lovers, "known" feelings between 79–80
lust 6, 60, 131, 171, 221–222; *see also* desires

McAfee, N. 42
McDougall, J. 116, 121, 148, 248
"maladies of the soul" 32
male *see* men
"manic penis" 133, 176–177
Manninen, V. 134, 139
marital dynamics 217–222, 223–228, 230–232, 242–258; *see also* betrayal; infidelity
masculinity 16, 117–118, 125–142, 176–177; "citadel complex" 129, 134–142; *see also* men
masochistic submission 16, 213–232, 241; derailment of the female erotic agency 214–217; feminine masochism in females 228–232; forms 229–230; gaze of the (m)other 217–222; Kate's case 223–228, 230; marital dynamics 217–222, 223–228, 230–232; Sara's case 217–222, 230; "trophy husband" case 223–228; *see also* shame
masturbation 12–13, 15, 64, 128, 166, 190, 195–196, 208, 217–222, 230; creativity 64; literature 195–196; play 12–13; Sara's case 217–222, 230
matching 35–38, 148–149
maternal care ethics, heresy 39–40; *see also* ethics
maternal deprivation 32–38; *see also* mother
maternal eroticism 2–18, 25–49, 55, 58, 60–62, 105–122, 128–142, 175–186, 197–209, 213–232, 237–258, 293–297; analytic eroticism introduction 39–40, 47–48, 64–65, 67, 208; critique 3–4, 16–17, 40, 61–62, 119–120, 128–129, 131, 206–207, 227–228, 237–258; deficit problems 3–4; destructive dynamics 3–4, 16–17, 40, 128–129, 131, 206–207, 227–228, 237–258; enigmatic messages 2–3, 6–7, 28, 38–39; fathers 3, 18, 26, 48, 148–149, 197–198, 201–203, 238–239, 243, 256–257; neurophysiology 4, 6–7, 27–28; over-stimulation problems 4–5; perverse manifestations 4, 226; repression 71, 203–204, 216–217; Sue's case 35–39, 47; *see also* dance; eroticism; mother–infant erotic matrix
maternal sexuality, daughters 60, 148–149, 198–209
matrisexual orientation, definition 149
meaning-making 30–32, 35–38, 70–71, 186, 190–209, 246–247, 248–253, 296–297; genitals 186, 190–209
meaninglessness 47; *see also* depression
Meltzer, D. 6–7, 27, 62, 72, 87, 179, 296
men 3, 15–18, 26, 29, 48, 53–73, 76, 81–82, 84–85, 88, 96, 106–107, 110–112, 115–120, 125–142, 145–157, 163–165, 176–177, 193–194, 196–209, 215–232, 237–258; Ben's case 125–128, 140; betrayal 237–258; "biological mission" 129; black man story 55–60, 63, 66–67; communications 139–140; "couch relations" 84–86, 96; dark good looks 59–60, 63–64, 66, 67; desires 193–194, 206–209, 217–222; fears of psychic penetration 16, 125, 129–142, 193; female passivity and male activity theories 108–112, 115–117, 129–131, 132–142, 154, 169–170, 174–186, 191–192, 193–194, 204–209, 215–232, 239–258; feminine masochism in males 229–230; feminization concerns 72; "heroic model of manhood" 139, 248–249; homosexual "panic" 141, 151; homosexuality 73, 76–77, 111–112, 122, 125, 140–142, 149–152, 154–157; impotence 80, 89, 90, 94, 135, 171–172, 175, 176–178, 183, 207, 230, 255; infidelity 237–258; inhibitions 16, 84–85, 110, 125–142; loss of the mother 139; marital dynamics 217–222, 223–228, 230–232, 242–258; paternalistic structuring of sexuality 15, 53–54, 58–73, 114, 116, 120–121, 138–142, 146–157, 184, 190–192, 196–209, 238–240; penetration/penetrated dialectic

105–106, 109–122, 125, 129–142, 169–170, 174–186, 191–192, 193–194, 204–209; Rob's case 136–139; self-sufficiency 16, 112, 125, 129–142; sex therapy 135–136; shame 166, 167, 175, 217; "trophy husband" case 223–228; undressing 110–111, 130–131; wants 193–194, 206–209, 217–222; "war between the sexes" 107–108; work focus 129–130; *see also* fathers; phallus; sons
mentalization development 4–5; *see also* ethics
mermaids, desire and disruption in the analytic relationship 54–55, 57, 61–62, 64; "The Little Mermaid" (ballet) 154–157; *The Mermaid and the Minotaur* (Dinnerstein) 184
Mesopotamian sculptures 295–296
metaphors, dance 30–32, 42–43, 295; infidelity 237, 258; nursing couples 113–114, 117, 130–132; penetration/penetrated dialectic 105–106, 109–122; phallus 182–184; psychoanalysis 5–6, 11–12, 17–18, 30–32, 41, 42–43, 79–80, 105–122, 151–152, 192–194, 227, 257–258, 291–297; uses 11–12, 17–18, 42–43
Miller, A. 289–290
Milner, M. 9, 43, 98
mind concepts 6–7, 17–18, 41, 48, 61, 63–68, 108–122, 208, 246–248; penetration/penetrated dialectic 108–122; sexuality 63–68, 108–122, 208, 246–248; sexy minds 63–67; *see also* psychic bisexuality
Mitchell, J. 131–132
Mitchell, S. 94, 119
monosexuality 116, 148–149; *see also* ineluctable; sexuality
moralizing stances 292–293
Morrison, A. 167–168, 216–217, 287
mortification 167; *see also* shame
mother hunger 193–194, 198–202
mother–infant erotic matrix 1–4, 5–7, 14–15, 27–49, 55, 61, 80–81, 113–115, 119–120, 130–132, 149–150, 152, 174–175, 182–186, 198–202, 217–222; dance of development 28–30, 38–39; *see also* infantile sexuality; maternal eroticism

mothers 1–7, 14–15, 25–49, 55, 58–73, 80–81, 113–115, 119–120, 126–128, 130–132, 149–150, 152, 163–186, 198–202, 217–222, 237–258; beauty 6–7, 27–28, 62, 71–72, 171–172, 295–296; "dead mother" concept 18, 41, 58; depressed 80–81, 128; desires 27–28, 149–151; "good enough" 201–202; maternal deprivation 32–38; myths 58, 61–62; perceptions 6–7, 15, 53–73, 178–179; role perceptions 15, 53–73, 201–202, 205–207; separation–individuation theory 163–164, 166–168, 179–186, 214–217, 227–228, 230, 248–251; "sexy mom" rarity 58, 67; vanquished/vanished erotic 60–63, 67–69; "wire mother monkey" 34–35, 36–38; *see also individual topics*; maternal eroticism; oedipal attachments; women
mourning capacities 98, 262, 268, 281
moving from within the maternal, choreography of dance 25–49; *see also* mother
music 30–32, 42–43, 46, 49; *see also* dance
myths 32, 58, 59–60, 61–63, 176–177, 205–206, 225–227; arts 32; Dracula 59–60, 62, 225–227; Persephone and Demeter myth 58, 61, 62–63, 227; positive maternal figures 58, 59, 61–62

Nachtraglichkeit 249, 267–268
narcissism 16–17, 60, 89, 92–93, 118–119, 128, 133–142, 163–186, 204–205, 206–207, 208, 213–232, 239, 265–282, 284–297; arrogance 47, 219–222, 227–228, 266, 284–297; "culture of narcissism" 286–287; exhibitionism 169–175, 181–182, 217; phallic narcissism "domain of omnipotence" 118–119, 133–134, 163, 176–178, 182, 206–207, 227, 230–231, 239, 289; *see also* grandiosity; shame
narcissistic injury 16, 60, 89, 92–93, 128, 134–142, 163–186, 204–205, 208, 213, 218–232, 251–258, 266–282, 284–297; defense mechanisms 255; *see also* betrayal; self-esteem
narcissistic parents of analysts 289–290
narcissistic personality disorder 167

narcissistic seductions 16–17, 219–222, 227–228, 266, 284–297
"narcissistic valorization of the penis" 118
narratives 30–38, 39–40, 41–42, 44–45, 79–80, 87, 256–258; dance 30–32, 36–38, 39–40, 41–42, 44–45
"negative oedipal situation" 55, 81–82, 92–93, 115, 116–117, 145–147, 150–157, 175–176, 238–239
Neumeier, John 154–156
neurophysiology, maternal eroticism 4, 6–7, 27–28
neutrality stance, psychoanalysis 5, 41–44, 65–66, 192
nipple/mouth connections 88–89, 114–115, 117–118, 178–179, 199–200; sexual intercourse 88–89
nipples 6, 88–89, 114–115, 117–118, 178–179, 199–200, 295–296
"non-gratifying" anti-libidinal analysts 5, 295
nursing couples 4–6, 27–30, 34, 55, 105–106, 108–110, 112–122, 128–129, 130–132, 149–150, 178–179, 198–199; critique 119–120; metaphors 113–114, 117, 130–132; *see also* breast-feeding; maternal eroticism

object relations 3–4, 8–9, 14–15, 38–39, 48, 60–63, 67–73, 92–93, 94–98, 118–122, 145–157, 163–164, 170–186, 190–209, 213–232, 237–258, 267–282; critique 94–95, 118–122, 145–157, 185; erasure of the female erotic 190–209, 213–232, 239–240; psychoanalysis potentials 8–9, 14, 15, 26–27, 60–63, 185; sexuality influences 118–122; *see also* attachment; loss
objectification considerations, beauty of women 71–72
obsessional preoccupations 125–128, 255–258, 295–296
oedipal attachments 3–5, 14–16, 28, 38–39, 53–73, 76–82, 87–98, 106–107, 114–117, 132, 145–157, 163–186, 196–197, 201–202, 207–208, 213–232, 237–238, 247–258, 265, 267–268, 270; danger situations 250–258; dark good looking men 59–60, 63–64, 66, 67; eruption/disruption discussion 67–73;

infidelity 237–258, 267–268; "negative oedipal situation" 55, 81–82, 92–93, 115, 116–117, 145–147, 150–157, 175–176, 238–239; post-oedipal sexuality 97, 106–107; pre-oedipal attachments 4–5, 53–73, 80, 82–83, 98, 114–115, 163–164, 165–168, 175–176, 201–202, 207, 214–215, 226–227; primary maternal oedipal situation 14, 28, 55, 76–82, 87–94, 95–96, 114, 147–157, 238–239, 253; retroactive reconfigurations 131, 245–258, 267–268, 270–272; triangularity 60–62, 70, 150, 247–253, 257–258, 273–276, 278–282; unrequited desires 92, 145–157, 163–164, 197–198, 238–258; *see also* attachment; fathers; mothers
oedipal complex 145–157, 164–186, 196–197, 201–202, 207, 215–217, 237–238, 248–250; complexity issues 152–154, 203; definition 248–250; resolution 151–152
Oedipus Rex (Sophocles) 248–249
Ogden, T. 7, 10–11, 31, 49, 68–69, 114, 203, 228, 247, 262, 286
Olivier, C. 201
"on not being able to paint" reflection 43
oral sex 84, 112, 199–200
orality experiences in early life 199–202
orgasms 64, 82–83, 90, 164–165, 191, 209, 217–218; anxieties 209; sexual intercourse inabilities 191, 209, 217–218
orientations of the erotic 103–160; *see also individual orientations*
over-stimulation, maternal eroticism 4–5

paintings 39–40, 43, 46, 49, 84–85, 88–90; erotic nudes 39–40, 265; "on not being able to paint" reflection 43; persecution territory 89–90
pairings 8–9, 11–12, 18, 25–26, 34, 44–45, 47–48, 65–67, 82, 85
pansexuality continuum factors, psychic bisexuality 106–107, 112–113, 131, 149, 179, 184–185
paranoia 76–77, 89, 256, 267
parent-infant erotic life 4–5, 118, 149, 194; *see also* maternal eroticism
parents 2–4, 48, 87–88, 92–93, 112–113, 126–128, 153–157, 168–186, 190–191,

214–215, 223–228, 231–232, 237–238, 247–258, 289–290; holding and containing environments 4–5, 9–10, 26–27, 29–30; narcissistic parents of analysts 289–290; severed ties 231–232; "unfaithfulness" betrayal trauma 251–254; *see also* daughters; fathers; infant; mother; oedipal attachments; sons

passion 17–18, 26, 47, 54–55, 63–64, 67, 76–82, 97–98, 136–137, 152–157, 166–167, 246, 250, 256–258, 296; definitions 90; good psychoanalysis qualities 17–18, 26, 47, 76–82, 97–98, 152–153; infidelity 246, 250, 256–258; transgressive elements 54, 87–89, 90–91, 93–94; *see also* creativity; desire; romantic love

paternal eroticism 140

paternalistic structuring of sexuality 15, 53–54, 58–73, 114, 116, 120–121, 138–142, 146–157, 184, 190–192, 196–209, 238–240; *see also* fathers; men

patience qualities, good psychoanalysis 17–18, 277–282

patrisexual orientation, definition 149, 152

Paul, C. 4, 48, 199

penetration/penetrated dialectic 105–106, 109–122, 125, 129–142, 169–170, 174–186, 191–192, 193–194, 204–209

penis envy 111–112, 115, 133, 164, 176, 180–184, 195–196, 197–198, 204–205, 239–240; *see also* phallus

penis-seeking activities, vagina 191–192, 205

perceptions 6–7, 15, 32–33, 37, 53–73, 178–179, 192–209; analyst's sexuality 58, 64–66; mothers 6–7, 15, 53–73, 178–179

Perelberg, R. J. 250

persecution territory, arts 89–90

Persephone and Demeter myth 58, 61–63, 227

perseverance psychoanalysis 17–18, 267, 277–279

Person, E. 135, 150, 232

personal appearance decisions, women 56–58, 65

personality expansion, good psychoanalysis 14, 17–18, 63–64, 97–98, 295

personalization experiences 13

perverse manifestations 4, 226, 265–282, 286–287; maternal eroticism 4, 226; normal sexuality 111

phallic narcissism "domain of omnipotence" 118–119, 133–134, 163, 176–178, 182, 206–207, 227, 230–231, 239, 289

"phallic phase" 166–186

phallic-as-breast representation 117

phallicism 16, 112, 125, 129–142, 169–170, 176

phallus 16, 59–63, 70–71, 84–85, 88, 110–120, 128–142, 154, 163–165, 166–186, 190, 195–198, 201–202, 205–209, 221–222, 227, 230–231, 239, 289; "citadel complex" 129, 134–142; "defects" focus 171–172, 175, 184; defense mechanisms 129, 134–142, 169–170, 177, 197, 204–205; definition 183; ego 164–165; erections 113, 164–165, 168–169, 171–172, 177–179, 190, 205, 221–222; exhibitionism 169–175, 205–206, 217, 221; impotence 80, 89, 90, 94, 135, 171–172, 175, 176–178, 183, 207, 230, 255; "little tassel" 112, 176; love affair 61; "manic penis" 133, 176–177; metaphors 182–184; "narcissistic valorization of the penis" 118; oral sex 84; penis envy 111–112, 115, 133, 164, 176, 180–184, 195–196, 197–198, 204–205, 239–240; premature ejaculation 171; responsibilities for men 135–136; women 169–170, 183, 190–192, 196–209; *see also* fathers; genitals; men

phantom father figures 58–60; *see also* fathers

The Phantom of the Opera (film) 59–60, 62

photographs, erotic nudes 39–40

play, eroticism 12–14; masturbation 12–13; psychoanalysis 8–9, 12–14, 17–18

poetry 31, 42, 46, 49, 154–157

poisoned desires 16–17, 235–298

pornography 39–40

positions 56–57, 83–84, 118–122, 172–174, 218

positive maternal figures 58, 59, 61–62, 179, 183–184

post-oedipal sexuality 97, 106–107
potential space 9, 18, 27–28, 35–36, 45, 69, 87–88, 103–160, 277–278, 281, 296–297; definition 9, 18, 27–28, 35–36, 45, 69, 87–88, 112–113, 128; *see also* chora
pre-oedipal attachments 4–5, 53–73, 80, 82–83, 98, 114–115, 163–164, 165–168, 175–176, 201–202, 207, 214–215, 226–227; shame 167–168, 175–176, 214–215, 226–227
pregnancy 3, 5–6, 28–30, 178
primal scene, creativity 87–94, 111–118, 294; psychic bisexuality 111–118, 148–157, 201–202
primary maternal oedipal situation 14, 28, 55, 76–82, 87–94, 95–96, 114, 147–157, 238–239, 253; definition 76–82, 238–239
primary sense of femaleness 165–166; *see also* women
primitive excitements, penetration 114–122; *see also* excitement
primitive group mental functioning 10–11
professional community disappearances, betrayal in the analyst–patient relationship 279–281, 292–293
professional development 45–47, 96–97, 279–281, 288–297; *see also* training
projective identification, definitions 10–11, 12
psychesoma experiences 13, 27–28, 36, 131
psychic bisexuality 14, 15–16, 88–89, 105–122, 128–129, 130–131, 148–149, 154–155, 179–186, 201–209, 243–258; bedrock and shock 148–149; creativity 105–122; Eva's case 243–258; Keri's case 108–111, 121, 130–131; literature 105–107, 154–155; Lyn's case 180–182; pansexuality continuum factors 106–107, 112–113, 131, 149, 179, 184–185; penetration/penetrated dialectic 105–106, 109–122, 129–142, 204–209; primal scene 111–118, 148–157, 201–202; restrictions 148–149; vulnerabilities 109–111; *see also* sexuality
psychic impotence 89, 135, 171–172, 175
psychic pain 7–8, 11–12, 13–14, 17, 25, 31–32, 43, 134–135, 150, 155–157, 166–167, 237–258, 261–282;

infidelity 237–258, 265–268; *see also* trauma
psychoanalysis 1–18, 25–49, 98, 114, 118–122, 140–142, 147–157, 169–170, 184–186, 194–209, 219–222, 227–228, 261–282, 284–297; agency 10–11, 60, 86–87; analyst's sexuality 58, 64–66, 82–83, 96–98, 140–141, 285–287; analytic approaches 10–12; arrogance 47, 219–222, 227–228, 266, 284–297; arts 30–32, 46, 47–49, 295–296; betrayal in the analyst–patient relationship 16–17, 261–282, 285–297; celibacy 58; choreography of dance 15, 25–49, 295; as creative projects 7–9, 11–12, 37–38, 41–42, 45, 290–291, 293–297; critique 5, 10, 16–17, 41–44, 45–49, 65–66, 92, 140–142, 192–196, 261–282, 284–297; "culture of narcissism" 286–287; depression in analysts 33–34; disappearances 279–281, 292–293; "do as I say, not as I do" psychoanalysis model 47; female-dominated profession 71; good psychoanalytic qualities 17–18, 26, 36–38, 42–44, 45–49, 54–55, 63–64, 67, 69–72, 76–82, 97–98, 120–121, 140–142, 152–153, 157, 172–175, 180–186, 192–209, 222–232, 255–258, 262–263, 267–282, 285–297; "hello" and good "goodbye" requirements 18, 261–262, 268, 281; holding and containing metaphors 5, 9–10, 11–12, 14, 26–27, 43–49, 94–95, 172–175, 257–258, 279–280, 293–297; inhibitions 94–98; "knowing all/all knowing" critique 287–291; metaphors 5–6, 11–12, 17–18, 30–32, 41, 42–43, 79–80, 105–122, 151–152, 192–194, 227, 257–258, 291–297; narcissistic parents of analysts 289–290; narcissistic seductions 16–17, 284–297; neutrality stance 5, 41–44, 65–66, 192; "non-gratifying" anti-libidinal analysts 5, 295; object relations potentials 8–9, 14, 15, 26–27, 60–63, 185; play 8–9, 12–14, 17–18; professional development 45–47, 96–97, 279–281, 288–297; roles 4–12, 14–18, 25–49, 63–64, 67–69, 75–98, 114–122, 140–142, 151–153, 157, 169–170, 184–186, 192, 222–232,

261–282, 284–297; stance 5, 10, 41–44, 45–49, 65–66, 92, 140–142, 192–196, 230–232, 270–282, 284–297; swimming-sideways metaphor 291–293; training 16–17, 45–49, 97, 264, 267–282, 284–297; *see also individual topics*
psychosexual stages 166–167, 185–186
public speaking 179–186

queer theory 121–122
questioning psychoanalysis 17, 194–195, 290–291

racism 59–60, 66
rationality 33, 44, 63–64, 290; "victory of intellectuality over sensuality" 33, 44, 63–64, 290; *see also* intellectuality
Real, T. 130, 135, 139–140
reality 68–70, 107–108, 132, 245–258, 267–268, 271–282; dreams 69–70; fiction 68–70, 132; gender identities 107–108
reflective practices 10–11, 31–32, 40–41, 43, 56–57, 66–67, 88, 140–142, 224–226, 288–289
regression 66, 83–84, 116–117, 141, 150, 166, 173, 256–258, 270–282
rejection 80–81, 90–91, 93–94, 97–98, 154–157, 166–186, 200–209, 220–232, 238–258; *see also* shame
relationships, good and bad losses, betrayal in the analyst–patient relationships 262–282, 285–297
reliance, definitions 25–27, 38, 45, 134–136; *see also* maternal eroticism
relinquishment of the maternal erotic object 16, 166
Renik, O. 140–141
renunciation, gender identities 112, 121–122, 132, 254–255; sublimation 45, 49
repression 71, 82–83, 197–198, 203–209, 216–217, 257–258; maternal eroticism 71, 203–204, 216–217; vagina 203–204
repudiations 151–157
repulsion, desires 217–222, 226
resistance to erotic desires 15, 75–76, 150
respect 17–18, 231, 290
responsibilities for men, phallus 135–136
retaliation fears 91–94

retroactive reconfigurations 131, 245–258, 267–268, 270–272
reverie 14–15, 296–297; *see also* creativity
Rey, H. 133–134
riptide metaphor, transference 151–152, 291–292
romantic love 15, 55, 76–77, 79–80, 84–85, 90–94, 96, 98, 166–167, 184, 227, 254–255, 295; *see also* passion
Rusbridger, R. 67–70, 247–248

sado-masochistic considerations, analyst–patient relationships 219–222, 227–228; *see also* masochistic submission
Scarfone, D. 178
Schafer, R. 154, 168, 229, 240
Schalin, L. J. 169, 176
schizoid mechanisms 33, 256
sculpture 46, 295–296
Searles, H. 76–77
seduction 2, 5, 16–17, 60, 77–79, 82–83, 85–86, 139, 151, 168–169, 174, 221–222, 240, 284–297; lesbians 77–79, 82–83, 85–86, 151; narcissistic 16–17, 284–297
self concepts 1–3, 8–9, 12–18, 25–26, 27–30, 36–38, 40–41, 56–57, 65, 81–82, 90–91, 97–98, 106–108, 120–121, 130–142, 150–157, 164–186, 192, 213–232, 251–258, 265–282, 284–297; arrogance 47, 219–222, 227–228, 266, 284–297; "ideal self-representation" 168–169, 171–172, 182–183, 184–186, 193–194; "knowing all/all knowing" critique of analysts 287–291; male fears of psychic penetration 130–142, 177, 193; masochistic submission 16, 213–232; "soft assembly" 16; talent contrasts 8–9; true/false self contrasts 8–9, 13, 90–91, 121; *see also* ego
self-assertion 183, 214, 232
self-assured positions 56–57, 192
self-control, Ben's case 125–128, 140
self-esteem 62–63, 81–82, 92–93, 135–137, 152, 167, 171, 183–184, 192, 218–222, 225–232, 251–258, 265–268, 287–288, 290; betrayal 251–258, 265–268, 287–288, 290; infidelity 251–258, 265–268, 269–282; injury

312 Index

tenacity 92–93; strengthening 92–93, 152, 228; *see also* narcissistic injury
self-inquiry 40–41, 296
"self-responsibility" needs, sexuality 214–216, 221–222
self-sufficiency, phallicism 16, 112, 125, 129–142
semiotics 27–28, 38–39, 42–43, 45, 131; *see also chora*; symbols
sensuality 27–28, 34, 38, 47, 55, 60, 61–62, 98, 114, 120, 149–151, 206–207; "victory of intellectuality over sensuality" 33, 63–64, 290
separation–individuation theory 163–164, 166–168, 179–186, 214–217, 227–228, 230, 248–251
sexual anorexia 194
sexual boundary violations 16–17, 40, 85–86, 94–95, 134–136, 154, 263–282, 284–288, 291–297
sexual intercourse 33, 38, 53, 55, 57–60, 88–89, 112–114, 117, 135–142, 172–175, 190–191, 209, 217–222, 245–258; nipple/mouth connections 88–89; orgasm inabilities 191, 209, 217–218; positions 172–174, 218; Tess's case 172–174; *see also* heterosexuality; phallus
sexual "liberation" 207
sexuality, breasts as desire emblems 61–62, 85, 109–110, 113, 117, 128, 171–172, 178–183; clothing 56–58, 65–66, 71, 85, 110–111, 130–131; dark men 59–60, 63–64, 66, 67; death 59–60, 227; definitions 1–2, 4–5, 15, 45, 56–57, 61–62, 67–68, 105–122, 134–136, 204–209, 247–248; desexualization of the maternal 15, 38–39, 53–73, 81, 83–84, 118–119, 120–121, 152, 203–209; excitement regulations 71; female passivity and male activity theories 108–112, 115–117, 129–131, 132–142, 154, 169–170, 174–186, 191–192, 193–194, 204–209, 215–232, 239–258; "ineluctable monosexuality" 116, 148–149; infidelity 247–253; legs parted 57, 61–62, 115; Mind concepts 63–68, 108–122, 208, 246–248; object relations 118–122; pansexuality continuum 106–107, 112–113, 131, 149, 179, 184–185; paternalistic structuring of sexuality 15, 53–54, 58–73, 114, 116, 120–121, 138–142, 146–157, 184, 190–192, 196–209, 238–240; penetration/penetrated dialectic 105–106, 109–122, 125, 129–142, 169–170, 174–186, 191–192, 193–194, 204–209; perverse manifestations 4, 111, 226, 265–282, 286–287; "self-responsibility" needs 214–216, 221–222; shame 16, 56–57, 163–186, 192, 287; "slutty" behaviors 57, 73; triangularity 60–62, 70, 150, 247–253, 257–258, 273–276, 278–282; truth 148–152; *see also* bisexuality; eroticism; homosexuality; *individual topics*; lesbians
sexy minds 63–67
"sexy mom" rarity 58, 67
shame 16, 56–57, 163–186, 192–194, 200–209, 213–232, 239–258, 284–287; causes 163, 167–169, 170–186, 192, 200, 216–217, 239, 251, 287; "defects" focus 167–168, 171–175, 184, 218–222, 291; gaze of the other 174–175, 217–222; inflated/deflated sexual body 168–175, 176–177, 182–186, 193–194, 198–202, 203–209, 239–240; Kate's case 223–228, 230; Lyn's case 180–182; men 166, 167, 175, 217; pre-oedipal attachments 167–168, 175–176, 214–215, 226–227; Sara's case 217–222, 230; Tess's case 171–174; treatment conclusions 184–186, 227–232; women 16, 56–57, 163–186, 192, 213–232, 287; *see also* failures; humiliation; inadequacy and inferiority sense; masochistic submission; rejection; unrequited desires
silences, women 194–196, 205–208, 263–264
sleeping vagina 196–198
"slutty" behaviors 57, 73
smallness, genitals 168–169, 171–175, 184–186, 193–194, 217–222, 232
"soft assembly", self concepts 16
sons 62–63, 76, 116, 126–128, 132–142, 148–149, 175–186, 199–200, 215–217, 238–240, 253; betrayal 240, 253; *see also* infant; men
Sophocles 248–249
spaciotemporal knowing 8–9, 10–11, 14, 18, 27–28, 35–36

Spezzano, C. 4, 89, 95, 153
splitting, defense mechanisms 107, 120, 237, 262–263, 280–281, 293
spontaneity 8–9, 13–14, 17–18, 31–32, 41–43, 44–45, 47–49; creative living 7–9, 13–14, 37–38, 39–43, 48, 150–157, 293–297; true self 8–9
squiggle games 31–32
stance, psychoanalysis 5, 10, 41–44, 45–49, 65–66, 92, 140–142, 192–196, 230–232, 270–282, 284–297
Stein, R. 2, 55, 157, 168
Steyn, L. 229–230
stimulation 4–5, 6–7, 13–14, 17, 47–49, 131–132, 191–192, 202–209, 295; creativity 7, 14; over-stimulation problems 4–5; *see also* analytic eroticism; erotic vitality
Stoller, R. 105–107
strangling fantasies, analyst–patient relationships 95
subjectivity 9–11, 16, 58, 69–70, 79, 192–194, 200–209, 213–232, 261–282
subjects of beauty 72, 295–296
subjugation 64, 228; *see also* masochistic submission
sublimation 45, 49, 97–98; renunciation 45, 49
substitute objects 197–198
survival 89–90, 294
"swelling", genitals 168–175, 178, 182, 198–202, 204–205
swimming-sideways metaphor, psychoanalysis 291–293
symbols 9–10, 25–49, 64–65, 67–70, 75–76, 247–248, 268–269, 272; failures 37–38, 41, 80, 90–93; types 30, 42–44; *see also* dance; semiotics

talents, self concepts 8–9; training 46–47
Tan, Yuan Yuan 156
tempestuous passions 1–2; *see also* eroticism
tenderness 206, 231
terminations, analyst–patient relationships 18, 261, 266–282, 285, 289–297
Tessman, L. H. 98
Thanatos 128
Thomson-Salo, F. 4, 48, 199
"thrill", eroticism 13–14
tolerance 93–94, 97–98
Tooley, K. 135

Torsti, M. 29–30
training 16–17, 45–49, 97, 264, 267–282, 284–297; creativity shortfalls 46–47; talents 46–47; *see also* professional development
transference 14–15, 25–26, 34–49, 53–73, 75–98, 150–157, 172–173, 181–186, 192, 226–228, 242–258, 261–282, 293–297; betrayal in the analyst–patient relationship 261–282, 285–297; cautions 41; creativity 15, 37–38, 41, 45, 75–98, 179–186, 293–297; desire and disruption in the analytic relationship 15, 53–73, 75–98, 261–282, 291–292; inhibitions 15, 75–98, 150–151; riptide metaphor 151–152, 291–292; *see also* countertransference; erotic transference
transgressive elements, passion 54, 87–89, 90–91, 93–94
transitional phenomena areas, life experiences 9
trauma 2–3, 7–8, 11–12, 43, 70–71, 134–135, 237–258, 261–282; infidelity 237–258, 265–266, 270–272; *see also* anxieties; psychic pain
triangularity, infidelity 247–253, 257–258, 273–276; oedipal attachments 60–62, 70, 150, 247–253, 257–258, 273–276, 278–282; sexuality 60–62, 70, 150, 247–253, 257–258, 273–276, 278–282
"trophy husband" case, masochistic submission 223–228
true self 8–9, 13, 90–91, 116–117; *see also* imagination; self concepts; spontaneity; vitality
trust, betrayal in the analyst–patient relationship 16–17, 261–282; infidelity 238–240, 245, 251–258, 265–272
truth 7–9, 16–18, 54, 146, 148–152, 200–201, 237–258, 270–282, 295, 297; betrayal 16–17, 237–258, 270–282; heterosexuality 148–152, 200–201; homosexuality 148–152; sexuality 148–152
tsunami metaphor, infidelity 237, 258
Tyson, P. 106, 195

unconscious 2–3, 44, 55, 66–67, 69–71, 83, 88–89, 106–107, 108–109, 112–114, 147–157, 166–167, 175–176,

196–198, 240–241, 257–258, 276–277, 288–289, 292
"unfaithfulness" betrayal trauma, parents 251–254; see also betrayal
unrequited desires 92, 145–157, 163–164, 166–186, 197–209, 238–258; see also failures; "idealized others"; shame
unruly urges 1–2; see also eroticism
urgency of life 38, 134

vagina 113, 117, 172–173, 178, 182–183, 190–191, 194–202, 204–209; contractions 205; literature 194–202; lubrication 113; penis-seeking activities 191–192, 205; repression 203–204; roles 195–198, 205–206; sleeping vagina 196–198; see also clitoris; genitals
vaginal sucking 199–200
Van Patten, S. 156
vanquished/vanished erotic mothers 60–63, 67–69
vibrant frame of mind 1–2, 40, 44; see also eroticism
"victory of intellectuality over sensuality" 33, 44, 63–64, 290
vigor 1–2; see also eroticism
Virgin Mary 65
vitality 8–9, 13–15, 23–101, 128–142, 222, 262–263, 278–279, 287–288, 294–297; creative living 8–9, 13–14, 37–38, 39–43, 294–297; true self 8–9, 90–91; see also erotic vitality
Vivona, J. 183
vulnerabilities 5–6, 84, 87–88, 90–92, 109–111, 129–142, 166–186, 190–209, 218–232, 241–258, 274–282, 284–297; psychic bisexuality 109–111
vulva 169, 172–173, 194–196, 204–205; see also genitals

wanting-to-want, women 192–194, 206–208, 231–232
"war between the sexes" 107–108
"weaning" 199–202
well-being 14, 137, 184, 190–191
Welles, J. 98, 119, 131
Westen, D. 83, 89, 94–95
white men, racism 59–60

Wilkinson, S. 198
Wilson, M. 43–44, 284
Winnicott, D. W. 4–5, 7–9, 11–14, 27–28, 31–32, 45, 47, 55, 69, 87, 90–91, 105–106, 108, 109, 112–113, 121, 150, 153, 156, 201–202, 249–250, 290; see also analytic field theory; creative living; false self; true self
"wire mother monkey" 34–35, 36–38
Wolf, N. 196
"womb" 28–29, 55, 142
women, beauty 6–7, 27–28, 62, 71–72, 75–98, 171–172, 295–296; betrayal 16–17, 235–298; clothing 56–58, 65–66, 71, 85, 110–111, 130–131, 220–221; "couch relations" 76–77, 82–98, 265–282; erasure of the female erotic 16, 76, 81, 174–175, 190–209, 213–232, 239–240; exhibitionism 169–175, 181–182; female passivity and male activity theories 108–112, 115–117, 132, 154, 169–170, 174–186, 191–192, 193–194, 204–209, 215–232, 239–258; "frigidity" problems 136, 171–172, 195–196, 209; gaze of the other 174–175, 201, 206–207, 217–222; "girls don't have what it takes" 181–185, 194–196; homosexuality 35–36, 37, 53–54, 55, 56–57, 75–83, 91–93, 105–122, 130–131, 148–152, 202–203, 207–208; infidelity 6, 16–17, 237–258, 265–268; marital dynamics 217–222, 223–228, 230–232, 242–258; masochistic submission 16, 213–232; mating "calls" 72; penetration/penetrated dialectic 105–106, 109–122, 125, 129–142, 169–170, 174–186, 191–192, 193–194, 204–209; penis envy 180–184, 204–205; phallus 183, 196–209; shame 163–186, 213–232, 287; wanting-to-want considerations 192–194, 206–208; "war between the sexes" 107–108; see also daughters; lesbians; maternal eroticism; mother
work focus, men 129–130
Wrye, H. K. 98, 119, 131

Zak de Goldstein, R. 192–193, 201